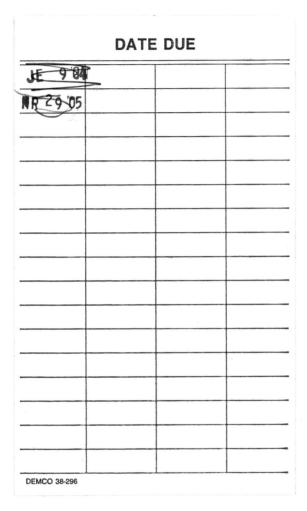

DATE DUE

JE 9 '04			
NR 29 '05			

DEMCO 38-296

The American City

The American City

A Social and Cultural History

Daniel J. Monti, Jr.

Boston University

BLACKWELL
Publishers

UK

Library of Congress Cataloging-in-Publication Data

Monti, Daniel J.
    The American city: a social and cultural history / Daniel J. Monti, Jr.
        p.   cm.
    Includes bibliographical references.
    ISBN 1–55786–917–0 (hardcover: alk. paper). — ISBN 1–55786–918–9 (pbk.: alk. paper)
    1. Cities and towns—United States—History.   2. City and town life—United States—History.   3. Community life—United States—History.   4. Sociology, Urban—United States.   I. Title.
    HT123.M635   1999
    307.76'0973—dc21
                                                                                99–22427
                                                                                CIP

British Library Cataloguing in Publication Data

A CIP catalogue record for this book is available from the British Library.

Typeset in 10½ on 12pt Sabon
by Grahame & Grahame Editorial, Brighton

Printed in Great Britain by MPG Books Ltd, Bodmin, Cornwall

This book is printed on acid-free paper.

Contents

Preface and Acknowledgments

The origins of this book are to be found in years of frustration, both as someone who writes about cities and as a teacher who had to convey the richness and vitality of a way of life that most persons dismiss as hopelessly corrupt or out of step with the rest of the world. My students declared their ignorance of what it meant to be part of a community. They did this even as they mouthed the rhetoric of older and wiser heads who declared with absolute certainty that our way of life was in deep trouble and that we had to find new ways of coming together, if we were to survive as a people.

A colleague from the History Department at Boston University, Saul Engelbourg, opened a big door for me when he suggested that I look at city newspapers to get a better picture about what persons living and working in different places actually did with themselves on a daily basis. I was a little embarrassed. I knew that New York and other big cities had newspaper records going back to the nineteenth century. Indeed, I had relied upon *The New York Times* for information about racial controversies in New York during the 1960s for my dissertation more than a quarter-century earlier. What I did not know was that the daily or weekly newspapers of all cities and a great many larger towns as well had been preserved on microfilm in various state archives and university libraries. In most cases, the material went back to the mid-nineteenth century.

That summer I embarked on a little odyssey with a band of students who were hanging around Boston and wanted something to do after they were finished with their jobs or courses every day. With the patient assistance of the staff from the Interlibrary Loan office of the university's main library, we began collecting and reading microfilm records of newspapers from different cities. We were trying to learn what was going on locally, and how persons reacted to events taking place outside of their city.

The undergraduate students that first summer – Ann Hackett, Barbara Govea, Michelle Jatkiewicz, Juliet Lee, Nikki Manning, Edwin Molina, and David Waxman – worked closely with me and one graduate student, Julie Plaut Mahoney. We read more newspapers than we probably realized at the time and met once or twice a week for extended discussions about what we were reading and learning. The work and discussions continued throughout the following academic year as the group worked on special projects and even taught some other students how to do this research. Everyone shared what they were learning, and sometimes we even coded each other's newspapers just to get a feel for what everyone in the group was seeing.

The small but growing archive of coded newspaper stories was used by students in several other graduate and undergraduate classes and contributed to by them as well. In the process of compiling these records, students have taught each other about the social customs and codes followed by persons who lived in specific cities at a given moment in history. They learned how similar their problems are to those experienced by persons who lived a long time ago, and they have seen that we have not made much progress in the way we deal with many of the problems we face. They also came to understand how men and women were attached to a place by more than their residence. Most important, perhaps, they experienced, albeit in a second-hand way, the humanity and hard work that went into making a world that made sense to the persons who had to live there. They learned what it meant to be part of a community from persons whose lives were at once different and startlingly similar to their own.

Our understanding at all times has been that if you give to the pot, you take from the pot. I have studied their work and borrowed pieces of it for this book. I gratefully acknowledge their contribution to my thinking, and here I will begin to share some of the lessons I have learned and continue to teach my students. I also owe a big debt to several colleagues who served as an advisory panel for me as I wrote this book. Stephan Thernstrom of Harvard University, Paul Boyer from the University of Wisconsin, and Roger Lotchin from the University of North Carolina offered their careful eyes in service to my sometimes sloppy thinking. My mother-in-law, Dr Katherine Nuckolls, read each page of the manuscript and caught more than a few of my literary lapses. I thank them all for their help.

In the future I hope to share these lessons with even more students. I have embarked on a similar study of Gloucester, Massachusetts, as part of a much larger project involving that town's civic culture. Gloucester is a famous fishing town of some 28,000 persons about an hour's drive north of Boston, and I am exploring the possibility of describing some of the changes which it is experiencing at the end of the twentieth century. In the meantime, I already have hooked up with a social studies and history teacher at Gloucester High School, Tim Kearns, and will be helping his students conduct a study of their community's social history by using their local newspaper and other sources of archival information.

Inspired in no small part by Mr Kearns's enthusiasm and keen insight into the workings of his town and students' lives, I also have begun contacting history and social studies teachers at high schools in each of the 50 cities featured in this book. To the extent that I am successful, we will build an archive of events drawn from the histories of communities from each state in the nation and share this information through the electronic wizardry afforded by the Internet. Inasmuch as this project grew out of my desire to be a better teacher, I see no reason why the lessons I have learned should not be shared with my colleagues and their students. When you get something, after all, you should give something back. History, it turns out, is a lot like life.

1

What Makes the Good Society?

Years ago I would bring a film to class that compressed into five minutes all the traffic and pedestrians pushing through Times Square, I think, during a 24-hour period. The demonstration in time-lapse photography was chock full of action. The film left one with the impression that the arteries of cities pulsed with life and sometimes clogged the same way human arteries do. It was amusing and a little disturbing. After viewing the movie, few of my students expressed any interest in living in such a place or being stuck in a world with lots of persons who would. It was all too hurried and seemed pointless.

That pretty much captures what many persons have thought about city life for a long time. Whoever those men and women in the film were, they surely were not us. Whatever it was they were doing, or thought they were accomplishing, had nothing to do with the life we led.

Cities were big places.[1] They reached out in all directions at the same time, grabbing pieces of land and throwing buildings into the sky without much thought being given to everyone left bumping into each other on the ground. Every day men and women lived and worked inside cities, but they were all but powerless to shape the most important things that went on there. That privilege belonged to a comparatively small number of persons, most of whom worked in the private arena and whose social position and authority was unassailable. We did not know much about these individuals except that few of them, if any, still lived in the cities where their influence was most keenly felt. At least that was what we had been led to believe.

There is more to what we have been led to think about the outfitting of cities, and it does not make them or the persons who live there look any better. Apparently, we are not powerful and do not have much in common any longer. Public spaces where many of us once found each other have been gobbled up in big chunks by businesses that want to substitute a sanitized notion of parallel play for animated public discourse. Public culture today is equated with shopping, commodities, and individual competition. Otherwise, we live in "closed social cells" and are surrounded by individuals we do not know well and may not like at all. Our only shared purpose, many persons believe, is to be left alone.[2]

Much of the supposed deterioration in our once vital civic culture is apparent to urban planners, social scientists, and everyday folk in the way we have carved up the spaces inside cities and taken to hiding in corners. The logic of their critiques is built on the back of a straightforward observation about the way cities are organized. To wit, human beings are not scattered about like so many dustlike spores. They clump together in identifiable masses or groups, and these clumps are more likely to be found in some parts of the city than others. Furthermore, there is a characteristic look and feel to the areas where certain types of human beings congregate and social activities take place.

Now it happens that some of these geographic areas inside cities are better looking than others and the persons and activities which take place there are deemed by somebody to be more or less desirable. Herein lies the basis of their scientific approach to the urban world and the shaky foundation of all their judgments about how to make it better. Specific areas inside cities not only look different but they also have distinctive social and moral profiles. If you want to make a better world, or at least make the part of the world you know a little less scary, you have to change something about the area in which these persons live or change something about the persons. Either way, the changes are going to show up in how the area looks and the kinds of activities that take place there.

Whether the persons in question were all that threatening to begin with is quite beside the point. Equally irrelevant is the fact that no amount of purposeful rearranging of what is built in these areas or who fills it can guarantee that the people will be redeemed or the place will look demonstrably better. Indeed, more than a century's worth of social and physical re-engineering inside cities has shown that what we do is as likely to end in big and little disasters as it is in an agreeable reshuffling of all the persons who live and work there. This, however, has not stopped generations of social scientists, planners, policy wonks, builders, and politicians from acting as if they were making a difference in the physical appearance and moral content of cities by pushing human pieces around a big-city chess board.

American historians have not had that much to say about the way cities are laid out and how the buildings inside them make life good or bad for most persons who live there. They have spoken more often and clearly on the newer spaces being carved out in suburbs and what this tells us about our urban way of life. While their ideas about tract housing and shopping malls are not as pointed as those of social scientists who write about these subjects, many of the words they use to describe these buildings have a sharp edge. They look at these artifacts as a sign that private-regarding ways continue to creep over the length and breadth of America and eat away at some of our public spaces and civic habits.[3]

Lynn Hollen Lees is not sure the situation is as desperate as many contemporary writers think, at least not yet. "The great urban spaces," as she refers to them, "remain alive." Persons still use them as sites for staging all manner of "public" acts. Protests and other acts of "celebration, commemoration and conversation" all find their "proper homes" in these spaces, though maybe not as often as they have in the past. Yet she concedes that urban public space seems to be under siege "as life in cities has ... become less civil and less open." She is particularly concerned about the way that many "commercial public spaces" like big-city "malls and urban atria" have come to lose at least some of their "wider civic functions."[4]

She might have reminded us that throughout the nineteenth century many private groups held meetings in theaters and commercial buildings of all types. It almost seemed at times that the buildings doubled as community centers after business hours. Those, we might think now, were the good old days of civic life in American cities.

Today the situation looks different to a great many persons. The few civic ceremonies and public rituals that leach into commercial buildings and malls appear to be patiently endured rather than solicited or welcomed warmly. Sometimes the sponsors of groups have to go to court just to gain access to these sites. Many critics of contemporary America cannot help but wonder just how long the erosion of usable public spaces and civic routines can go on before there is no place left to practice public habits and we lose an important part of who we once were as a people.[5]

Taking Our Bearing from Buildings

Historian David McCullough grappled with this problem in November of 1994 when he spoke to members of the National Trust for Historic Preservation from inside Boston's famous Trinity Church. McCullough wanted to know "What makes the good society?" "What makes civilization?"[6]

These certainly were not new questions, but they were good ones. Mr McCullough's answer did not just fill the church and take in the blocks surrounding the cathedral. It took in the whole city. Indeed, the city was his answer.

Clarendon, Dartmouth, Boylston, and St James are the streets that border Copley Square and surround the church where McCullough spoke that November evening. On the surface, there does not appear to be much that would distinguish these blocks from many other streets in the city. The grass, brick walkways, and fountains which dot the Copley Square also are not especially eye-catching. They are not what makes these streets or Copley Square important.

Standing in the middle of Copley Square you know that the Charles River and Atlantic Ocean are not far away, but you cannot see them. There are no broad vistas stretching out from the city to spy from Copley or any tall mountains to admire in the background. As a piece of urban real estate, Copley Square would seem to have no more going for it than most other places in the city where big streets intersect and lots of persons pass every day. It is no big deal.

The buildings surrounding Copley Square, on the other hand, certainly are a big deal. The Boston Public Library, a book-lined box of shiny granite and well-worn marble, anchors one end. At the other end is Trinity Church, a handsome stone-faced cathedral with a Victorian-era rocket ship pushing its way through the roof. The church's reflection is captured and returned to passersby in the latticed-glass face of the very modern-looking Hancock Tower. McCullough calls this I. M. Pei building a "vast sliver of ice," and it reaches heights that the earth-bound cathedral could only touch through prayer. The Old South Church and Copley Plaza Hotel are distinguished buildings in their own right, no less wonderful to view and pass through than their bigger neighbors in the area. Together they make Copley Square something more than a spot where four streets and many thousands of human beings cross every day. They bring a little piece of the earth closer to heaven and put the idea in our heads that we are seeing something important, something which is part of us and reaches way beyond us at the same time.

Impressive as these buildings are, they do not hold the secret to what makes a city great and a society good. The secret is found, as David McCullough sees quite clearly, in the warm remembrances of a walk down a celebrated street lined with statues of long-dead heroes and great buildings. It is locked up in stories about the way all of us fill those streets and buildings and the meaning we attribute to our actions.

McCullough believes that there is no better place in the world to tell these stories than cities, because no place made by people is so full of life and has so many good stories to tell. Fortunately for those of us who try to make sense of these stories, no one works especially hard at keeping the secrets of how cities are made hidden from the rest of us. They either leave a paper trail of their exploits which someone almost always trips over, or they talk quite openly about what happens in the city everyday and what they intend to do about it. "We are and must be storytellers," David McCullough believes. "We need stories. And in the loud, tawdry, throwaway culture of modern television, we need stories, a longer-lasting kind with character. And communities have stories."

Communities of believers leave the best and most complete stories behind. They tell us what they did to make a good city, and they show us that the action takes place on street corners and ball parks, in board rooms and stores, and everywhere else human beings congregate inside cities. The secret of great cities, quite simply, is found in what we do there and how we explain it to ourselves. It is in the routines and customs we follow, the ceremonies we attend, the rules we embrace, and in the beliefs to which we subscribe. These are the bedrock of our culture and the touchstones of our history as a people.

The secret of who we are as a people, why we mattered at all and the difference we made, is locked up in the civic diary we call newspapers and in the everyday routines that we left behind for others to follow or amend as they saw fit. It is not just the best and worst of who we were that we pass on, but the story of all our glorious near hits and misses as well, all the ways and occasions when we came together and how me made sense of those moments. This is the point that David McCullough had in mind to make, I think, when he spoke at Trinity Church in 1994. At least it is the way I have come to make sense of what he said.

I am hesitant to read much more into his words, because he is not speaking for himself on these pages. I am. My responsibility, and it is a big one, is to do the best job I can in relating what he meant with the words he chose at that time. This is harder than it looks, particularly when one is trying to make sense of something as big as a city or so important as the way of life being practiced by the people living there.

I do not doubt that the way we litter the landscape with big objects or carve up spaces inside cities tells us something about who we are as a people. McCullough draws a congenial, even uplifting, lesson from all these buildings and spaces. Many other commentators are far less kind. The fact that I happen to like what McCullough says is irrelevant. He could just as easily be blowing smoke, and I might not know it. The problem is that he is speaking for the artifacts he looked at and I am parroting what he says.

McCullough tells us that "we take our bearings from buildings" and suggests that we can learn a great deal about ourselves from them. This may be so, and I already have confessed to liking what some of the buildings in Boston tell him. Again, however, he also could have gotten the story wrong, just as I might play with his words and bend their intended meaning so they fit in boxes that I like to use. Whether he and I are correct in what we say about all the buildings and space inside cities is quite beside the point. Right or wrong, one has to be careful when composing a portrait with someone else's paints or telling a story using someone else's words.

Unfortunately, many persons who try to tell us about the meaning of life by touching a building's bones or ambling past a park do not seem as wracked by self-doubt or limited in imagination as I am. There may be times when they are troubled by the prospect of putting their words into some building's mouth, but they seem to get over it quickly or at least hide their discomfort a lot better than I can.

The long and short of it is this. Almost anything goes when dreamers and schemers describe how they would fill cities with architectural wonders and peaceful hideaways. Indeed, the only persons who take more liberties with history or the English language than would-be builders are their critics. They are bedmates, if not soulmates, and we are doomed to play the part of voyeur in their romps and to gag on all their fluffed-up pillow talk.

In searching for the right come-on or comeback about the wonderful world they will soon make for us, they often draw pictures with their words of things that cannot be found anywhere else on the planet. Sometimes they have to go a lot farther than that to drive their point home. When that does not work, they have been known to lie. The result in any case, they hope, will be the same. We will buy whatever buildings or piece of space they happen to be selling at the moment.

As in all matters related to the way human beings set about the hard work of making and selling the magic of cities, sometimes their inspiration is enough to carry the day. There are other occasions, of course, when even the best magician needs a little help from his friends. Such was the case for all the would-be wizards in Flagstaff back in 1896 when Arizona was still a territory and we were still earth-bound.

"Good Evening Mars!"

Flagstaff, Arizona was small in 1896; but some of its residents had big plans for their town. The construction of a new road between Flagstaff and the Upper Verde Valley already was being considered. Farmers in that area certainly wanted it, because they could then bring their produce to Flagstaff more easily. And, by all accounts, it looked like a good deal for the people of Flagstaff as well.[7]

Important as the road would have been for Flagstaff, there was something that the town needed even more. It was water. Having settled in a desert, the residents of Flagstaff knew that their town never would grow beyond its current size without more clean water. And the people of Flagstaff *really* wanted their town to grow.

The campaign to bring water to Flagstaff started innocently enough. Plans for a new water system were discussed first on June 11, 1896 during a public meeting which was "attended by nearly every taxpayer in the town."[8] The local newspaper carried big stories on the plans throughout the summer, and residents were able to follow every step of the process leading up to its construction.

Town leaders were enthusiastic about their plan and about the prospects for Flagstaff. The place could be made prettier and manufacturers might be enticed to bring their businesses to this part of Arizona, if only they had more water. Flagstaff's best citizens did the only thing they could think of doing at the time. They formed a stock company and bought large portions of the bonds that would have to be sold in order to carry out their plan. That was an important step. If local residents could not see the benefit of investing in their own future, it was unlikely that any outsider would ever do so.

A survey for the pipeline was carried out in July of that year. The first plans called for nearly 17 miles of pipe to be laid.[9] Residents became increasingly more excited about all the water they would soon have and what it would mean to their town. They hoped that Flagstaff would become an important place, and they worked hard to find a way to explain the future to themselves and anyone else who might want to jump on their fast train before it left the station.

It just so happened that Flagstaff had a visitor that year who was able to provide them with all the proof they would need of the town's bright future. The visitor was Dr T. J. See of Boston, who was on loan from the Lowell Observatory at the time and touring the southwest with a portable telescope. At every stop on his itinerary, the good doctor presented lectures about the solar system.

His arrival in Flagstaff could not have been timed better. He and his 24-inch telescope were the toasts of the town. Everyone, it seemed, wanted a peek at what Dr See saw. They were not disappointed. Indeed, their enthusiasm and confidence were simply out of this world. Their future good fortune was described to them, in part, this way.

GOOD EVENING MARS!
Flagstaff Has the Pleasure of Meeting a Neighbor
A Golden Opportunity to Make a Million and Get Prestige in Two Worlds
Flagstaff folks had an introduction to the inhabitants of Mars last Thursday evening.

The Martians are pleasant people ... and peculiarly congenial to us

Arizonans. Mars is almost one grand Arizona without the canyons or mountains – or Flagstaff.

They have deserts bigger than our North and South America, and ... they knew how to make the desert blossom as the rose, though the roses are blue instead of (red) like ours.

We of Arizona should feel distinctly friendly to those new acquaintances of ours, for they are liable to give us some valuable pointers in the way of irrigation. Already we have learned something.

The proper way to irrigate is to run canals, diverging from the poles to the equator, tapping the melting snows of the polar regions. This Arizona should do.

The territory should forthwith annul all corporation and farmers' canals, and go in on the Martian plan. Buckey O'Neill can furnish any little ideas that may be lacking on how to accomplish it, in the way of raising money from the government, and of condemning existing canals. All being in readiness, the Mars system could be introduced in Arizona.

Now, what is the matter with drawing on our San Francisco peaks for melting snows? They would assure plenty of gravity for the canals.

Arizona could make the desert blossom with roses. Again, such a move would make Flagstaff solid with the Martians. No doubt they are anxiously looking this way to detect some signs of intelligence in us. When they saw a system of canals like their own and all diverging from ... a handsome town among the pines, they would at once conclude that in that town were the only intelligent people on earth.

In the event of regular communication being established, all dispatches would be dated Mars, via Flagstaff, Arizona. That would give us prestige in their world, too. There would be a distinction – to be known all over the two worlds.[10]

Talk about high-tech industries and global villages, Flagstaff would have possessed the best of both, maybe for both worlds. Silly as all the talk about Martian neighbors and blue roses may have been, Flagstaff and other towns and cities across the southwest eventually got the water they needed from more mountainous areas. Furthermore, the federal government provided a great deal of money to further this and many other development projects in that part of the United States. The deserts bloomed. Millions of persons moved there. Thousands of big new businesses were opened, and many of them pushed space-age products.

The Martian plan for building canals to the polar ice caps probably was a bit too ambitious. On the other hand, we still hear talk from time to time about capturing migrating icebergs and tapping them for the fresh water they have locked up inside them. Maybe we had a thing or two to teach those Martians after all.

Any visiting Martians today might be disappointed that we had failed to create an elegant system of canals or perennially lush gardens in the desert like the ones they have. But they probably would feel a whole lot better once they visited a city that had managed to blossom in the desert and whose level of cultural sophistication probably exceeded that of any place on their home planet. That city, of course, would be Las Vegas.

Room to park a space ship or the family? No problem. If Martians dropped by for a visit in the year 2000, they should have no trouble finding a place to stay. By then, Las Vegas was slated to have 127,000 hotel rooms, a number that would surpass the number of comparable spaces in New York, Paris, or Los Angeles. Martians still could have lost their shirts, if they wore any, at the gambling tables. But there would be plenty else for them and their families to see and do after they declared bankruptcy at the First Inter-Stellar Savings and Loan of Flagstaff.[11]

With no earthly reason to visit the desert surrounding Las Vegas, the visiting Martians could turn all their attention to the 24-hour spectacle into which city leaders and outside investors have transformed Las Vegas. For many of them it probably would be enough just to tour the billion-dollar hotels and casinos, or to take in a few stage shows featuring many scantily-clad young Earth women and performers whose acts are as canned as store-bought hams. If the Martians still had time to kill, they could busy themselves with visits to the eight-acre replica of Italy's Lake Como, a twelve-acre South Seas beach, daily battles between a land-locked British frigate and dozens of pirates, surfing competitions, and mock-ups of Venetian canals complete with gondolas. Or, they could run by half-scaled replicas of the Eiffel Tower and Paris Opera House, the Great Pyramids and Sphinx, Manhattan landmarks such as the Statue of Liberty and Empire State Building (blessedly free of King Kong), or King Arthur's castle.

All of this may seem a bit out of place in a region otherwise inhabited by tumble weeds and critters that slither and crawl. But until someone turns off either the spigot or the money, the party will not stop. It is fine to huff at the opening of a brand-new hotel with over $300 million worth of modern art affixed to its walls, and to dismiss Las Vegas as "the Disney World of terminal public greed" where "every cultural citation is fake."[12] Somewhere along the line, however, all the dreams about Martian canals, endless supplies of fresh water, money, and the power to make cities and culture in places that had neither came startlingly alive.

The lesson for the earthlings called Americans seems clear enough. Nothing succeeds like excess. Of course, it helps if the excessive success is wrapped up in an elegantly appointed and orderly place where persons are allowed to play out their urban fantasies. Whether the dreamscape is found in a desert or in the comfy confines of a downtown shopping mall matters not one tiny bit.

It matters a little that buildings are often put in spaces no one really wanted. It matters more that having been rescued or captured by pirates with decidedly capitalist tastes these places now are generally out of the reach of persons who cannot afford the luxury of living out their own fantasies, much less someone else's. Important or not, there is nothing new in any of this.

The Palais Royal, Witold Rybczynski reminds us, was a five-story commercial and recreation arcade built in the middle of eighteenth-century Paris. The lower floors housed a variety of "cafes, eating places, social clubs, gambling rooms, music rooms, auction rooms, a puppet show, a silhouette show, a wax-works, several small hotels, a Turkish bath, and a theater." The upper floors contained apartments and rooms that were rented to persons of some means, including a good number of "high-priced prostitutes for which the Palais became famous." The central courtyard held a large garden as well as an amphitheater which was used for "public performances, concerts, and balls."

The Palais Royal was not a democratic place in the sense that all Parisians visited or shopped there. "Most of the establishments of the Palais were luxurious and could be afforded only by the rich – or by army officers on a spree – but arcades and the garden were open to all except the poorest classes." The latter were invited in on three "special days" each year. On the other hand, anticipating what we will learn about the civic culture of cities, it was not surprising that the "aristocrat and bourgeois mixed" openly in the garden and shops.[13]

There are architectural and social parallels between places like the Palais Royal or the enclosed galleries of nineteenth-century European cities and our latter-day malls and shopping plazas. Places like the Galleria in suburban Houston, the Mall of America outside of Minneapolis, and dozens of smaller shopping centers in rehabilitated train stations and along river or lakefronts and in glass-enclosed malls in cities across America are part of a grand commercial tradition. They bring commerce and recreation together in a pretty, safe, and unmistakably urbane environment.

These are not public spaces in the sense that everyone is welcomed or can enter them. Nor are they exactly private spaces where all less desirable persons and practices, whoever or whatever they may be, are always kept out. They are undeniably *shared* spaces, however, in which a variety of persons routinely meet and different tastes are accommodated.[14] The prosperity on display in these places is the ostensible excuse or vehicle for bringing them together, and the fact that they can get along as well as they do on those occasions has everything to do with their commitment to behaving in an orderly, if not always proper, way. Such are the hallmarks of an urban way of life.

Meanwhile, Back in the Hub of the Universe

When David McCullough came to Boston in 1994, the city was celebrating its 364th anniversary. His reflections on what makes a city great were part of an extended discussion that persons in Boston carried on that whole year and, indeed, one that kept going right to the end of the millennium. One year earlier, in 1993, a reporter had set the parameters for this public debate and anticipated its likely outcome in this way. Clearly captivated by the idea that Boston's best days always had been behind it, he asked "Is Boston still the Athens of America? Or is it Rome in decline? Or is it becoming something in between, say Topeka?"[15]

Given the way he presented the problem, Boston had at best one chance in three to come out looking all right. It did not do that well. To get answers to these questions the reporter talked to learned persons across the country about what they thought of Boston. He shared some of their observations with his readers. The results were not comforting or encouraging.

One observer from Atlanta noted that "as far as people here are concerned ... Boston is seen as a city that's had its day, a nice place to visit, but not a city to emulate." Except for having sampled parts of the state's rich literary heritage, for most persons "Massachusetts has no more meaning here than Minnesota." Trying to be a bit kinder, perhaps, a Californian said that it is not as if Massachusetts were actually "going downhill." Rather, the rest of America is "getting bigger and brighter."

Even local savants did not have much good to say about Boston and the state's future. Once you get past all the big brains hunkered down in local universities and high-tech industries, one said, "if you look logically, there never was a reason for Massachusetts to be important. It's got bad weather, bad soil, no steel, no coal." About the only other good thing that he could say about the place was that since it always had fared well in adversity, he "wouldn't bet against it."

Sounding way too much like a small-town booster trying to explain why it was all right that the town next door got the railroad, this writer looked to the city's past for its future just as dejected town leaders in America had been doing for generations. Maybe the universe Boston knew was falling apart, but it still had great traditions. There was the Marathon, carolers in Louisburg Square, Fenway Park and the hapless Red Sox, the Public Garden, the swan boats, and the Charles River. For its citizens, "Boston endures because for all its flaws, it remains a delightful place to live, one that arouses pride and, on a clear day, even affection."

David McCullough, for his part, was having none of it. Called upon once again by city leaders to find some silver lining in an otherwise dark cloud, he delivered a speech at the opening of the new Fleet Center, which stands on the hallowed ground of the famed Boston Garden. "We have troubles, but we always have had troubles and we have overcome. This great city ... is where the future will be decided as it will be decided in the cities of our country, everywhere." "Evenings like this," he added, "don't happen except in ... great cities ... all of us together in a great public event. And we were here. We can tell everybody: we were here."[16]

Sounding not at all like someone trying to put lipstick on a pig, McCullough's call to arms was uplifting and had the advantage of being historically sound as well. What face to put on one's city, after all, has been a great concern to town and city leaders since before the American Revolution. Particularly in trying economic times or moments of social unrest, leaders and everyday people alike have wondered aloud about what the future held and what their role in it would be. These were the concerns and feelings that McCullough and others were tapping into whenever they talked about the future of Boston, and every other American city for that matter, at the end of the twentieth century.

It is not surprising that we spend time worrying about how to show others that we were here and trying to convince ourselves that we left our mark on the world. Nor should we be surprised that the focus of our conversation often revolves around what we do with bigger pieces of real estate inside our cities. After all, large spaces and buildings have a bigger impact on our lives than do small ones.

What is surprising, perhaps, is that so much of what we read into these spaces, places, and decisions is taken to have great value for all of us. Indeed, it seems that the public significance of our deliberations is tied directly to the size of the parcel being disposed or the amount of money involved in putting something on it. It would not matter that most or even all of the land were held by private parties or that the money spent on it came largely from private sources. What we did with it would still have great public import.

However accurate a portrayal this is of the way we look at cities and build them today, it is even more true of the places and spaces inside cities which abut or belong to the governments which ostensibly represent us and are supposed to take our interests into account. Thus, the question of what to do with the plaza left in front of the concrete carbuncle which is Boston's city hall gets more attention than the makeover of historic downtown commercial districts in smaller industrial cities elsewhere in Massachusetts.[17] And putting a miniature version of the Palais Royal in the nine-to-ten acre plaza matters more than restoring a century-old shopping district to the way it might have looked when persons lived and worked in buildings from which one could jump and not leave much of a mess on the sidewalk.

No matter what is put in any of these places it will be viewed as making a public statement or saying something important about us and the life we lead. Aside from the way persons actually live with these buildings and use the space left for them, the most important lesson we may take from buildings and spaces in cities is that history matters. A reverence for time-honored conventions and the way things used to be counts for a lot whenever human beings sit around and try to figure out what they ought to do with the places in which they live and the persons with whom they share these places. For better and worse, these conventions and values come most to mind whenever we try to build something that is big and new.

Sometimes important beliefs about the responsibility of local governments to maintain sites as "public areas" have been challenged even when persons were trying just to repair older buildings or to keep the grounds around them looking good. Questions of this sort emerged during the 1990s with growing frequency as local business owners tried to figure out how to make the areas where they were located look better and feel safer. Local governments could not afford to pay for additional services or physical improvements to a few blocks in the city, so business owners taxed themselves and spent the extra money on things they thought would help bring in more customers. "Business improvement districts" have been around for several decades. Their popularity increased dramatically in the closing years of the twentieth century, however, and local officials in different cities have found themselves working with business owners in several areas at the same time.[18]

Persons who have dealt with these so-called "BIDs" or ventured forth to comment on what these areas bring to the city, or take from it, are not timid about expressing their opinion. Basically, you either love or hate the things. There does not appear to be a lot of middle ground in the debate over BIDs. Proponents view them as a necessary and desirable tool in their long-term campaign to solidify downtown and neighborhood commercial districts or bring them back to life. Critics see BIDs as only one of many attempts by city governments to "privatize" public services and by businessmen to keep certain "undesirable" individuals or activities away from their storefronts.[19]

What neither the defenders nor the detractors of BIDs seem to realize is that there is nothing new about businessmen dunning each other so that they can improve the areas where their shops are located. This has been going on for more than 200 years in the United States. Local store owners initiated subscription campaigns to add sidewalks, put in sewer lines, or to pave the roads in front of their places of business long before local officials began taxing citizens for the privilege of extending these improvements to many other parts of the city. These additions were seen as benefiting the whole town or city, even if they only went to a small part of the municipality at first.

Looked at in another way, all the physical improvements and additional services that went to business districts helped to fix the identity of these areas as places dedicated to order and, of course, prosperity. These expressions of bourgeois sensibility made the city more "progressive" and successful in the eyes of local folk and visitors alike. In much the same way as street lamps lit the night and extended not just the waking hours of cities but also persons' commitment to good habits, latter-day "business improvement districts" reassert the legitimacy of bourgeois values in parts of cities which seem to have forgotten them.

Everything New Is Old Again

What happens in "business improvement districts" is smaller and less ambitious than the rebuilding campaigns that we associate with urban renewal and redevelopment projects. Nevertheless, these BIDs remind us that whenever a corporation or institution like a university or museum expands its territorial horizons there is more at risk than money. These profit and not-for-profit makers are also recommitting their owners or managers to taking good care of the place where they work and to supporting bourgeois habits and values.

We are reminded also that history is a good teacher. Much of what we think is new or a radical departure from past practices is only a paler or sharper version of an idea that someone had before. More often than not, everything new turns out to be older than we thought.

Among the wretched excesses visited upon American cities after 1950, a period when so many of them were being rebuilt at a break-neck pace, was a nostalgic piece of re-engineering called the "new town-in town" movement. The idea behind it was to take part of the vacant ground left by bulldozers that leveled old slums and fill it with new buildings which could bring an old-town feel to big-city spaces. Smaller structures arranged in ways that helped residents interact with each other, ponds, more pedestrian-friendly streets, intimate little parks, and neighborhood shops were all part of the mix. Not a bad idea really, but it did not work as well in cities as some urban planners and public officials hoped it would.

The idea worked much better in the places for which it had originally been intended: new towns. Places like Reston, Virginia and Columbia,

Maryland certainly were conceived and built with this idea in mind. The communities in these places worked, after a fashion, and in ways that their designers would recognize. Residents created a history for themselves as their towns grew into small cities, and the marks they left were every bit as important as the footprints first laid down by each town's builder.

Some of the same ideas took on new life during the 1990s as something called the "new urbanism." Its notion of how to build good places to live and better communities was promoted by a group of planners, policy-makers, academic types, and developers who called themselves the Council on New Urbanism. Their most notable work was found in a place like Seaside, Florida which combined "traditional" architectural styles and brightly colored buildings with neighborhood shopping areas and nice vest pocket parks.[20] Elements of the "new urbanism" also were seen in Celebration, Florida which was developed by the Walt Disney Company.

Although criticized for creating something that looks more like "a kind of 'new suburbanism' because of its low density and rural location," the New Urbanists hoped "to reenergize our cities through planned neighborhoods linked to lively downtowns by pedestrian paths." They also wanted to end "our obsessive love affair with the car ... do away with strip malls ... [and] create places where people meet each other in informal ways as they do in small towns." As I said, these were not bad ideas.

We have heard this all before, however, and it did not work the first time we tried it in cities. We know that persons who live in small towns have adopted many practices found in bigger cities and that city dwellers have borrowed a great deal from their small-town neighbors. Unfortunately, no one has yet figured out how to graft one of those places onto the other. It just does not work.

What might work better is to take a brand-new place and give it a history that never happened, the kind of history ordinarily found in urban outcroppings like old mill towns and county seats. Instead of trying to find a robust town that never became a city but still enjoys the trappings of an urban way of life, build one from scratch. If that sounds crazy, stay clear of Riverside, Georgia which apparently can be found on the Chattahoochee River just outside of Atlanta.

Riverside, according to local observer Rafael Garcia, was founded as a settlement before the Civil War and had to be rebuilt in the years between Reconstruction and World War I. Its historic buildings have been "painstakingly renovated" and include offices and shops, several hundred apartments, and even the new corporate headquarters of Post Properties, Inc., "one of the South's largest apartment developers."[21]

The problem is that Riverside is not old, never had a building fall down, a mill, ferry crossing, or anything like them. The idea to build Riverside "was hatched" in the mid-1990s. That was when Post "embraced" the principles of "new urbanism" which "holds that neighborhood design should allow people to live near their work, interact better with their neighbors and get around more on foot." The company took these ideas to a new level by "making up a detailed history for Riverside" and creating "overnight what has evolved over hundreds of years in many other cities: a past." Post employees visited places like Princeton, New Jersey and Manhattan's Upper West Side "to inspect streets that welcome pedestrians ... drove around Atlanta, snapping hundreds of pictures of buildings" then brought the best elements together in what became a new old town.

While some observers have expressed doubts about fabricating a history for this brand-new place, it is not a tactic that is likely to be copied by many developers. It was a clever marketing tool and funny, but nothing that would last. Inasmuch as the whole story was a fake the only persons who really could make it part of their corporate history worked for Post Properties. For most of the persons who eventually came to Riverside to live and work, it would become little more than a curious footnote to the history they made for themselves.

A history cannot be made up, and one that is cannot serve the persons who need it when they need it most. They will not be able to call upon it so they can remember something important about themselves. They cannot look back on it for some hint as to how to deal with any problems that come their way. It cannot provide them with the hope that they can face an uncertain future together nor give them the kind of confidence which grows only from having seen it all before. Such a history can only be found in places like cities where generations of men, women, and children have done the hard work of building a world for themselves and inventing traditions that matter to them.[22]

A great deal has been written about cities during the second half of this century. We know more today than we ever have about the way cities are built, how persons earn a living there, how they are governed and pay for what governments do, about who lives there and where they live, and about some of the things they do while they are there. As much as we have come to know, however, we still do not know much about the city itself, that is, about what makes these places the way they are. I take my cue from Blair A. Ruble who tells us that "we have a far easier time talking about the city in the abstract than in confronting the actual city in all its glory and shame. The result is that we barely know the city at all."[23] I think Ruble is right, and that is too bad.

If we are to know these places better and to understand not only how they came to be as they are but also what they can be in the future, then we shall have to come to know them not as a series of discrete pieces but in their totality. It is not that we have avoided these places or failed to explore some of the more interesting worlds tucked away in the corners of American cities. In fact, we have paid much attention to these separate worlds and can describe many of them in great detail.

Our problem, historian Thomas Bender correctly observes, is that we come to see these worlds as being autonomous. We get "no image of the whole," he says, and can make "no suggestions about how the parts might go together or even whether they are intended to go together."[24] What I take from Bender is that we need to step back from all the small worlds we have examined in great detail and consider how they already fit together before we declare them broken or irredeemably lost. This is a modest plea to take things as they are before we rush off to make them better. I think this is good advice.

City dwellers occupy a world filled with spontaneity and, yes, sometimes a lot of scurrying around. Yet there is a lot more order to all their bouncing about than meets the eye, more certainty in their daily comings and goings, and a greater understanding about what really matters in life and how persons are supposed to act than we have been led to believe. What they value and do every day ends up looking a lot like what most persons believe in or do.

We should be much more surprised to learn, perhaps, just how much of what city dwellers believe and do was conjured up in places a great deal smaller and quieter than many cities and a lot earlier than we ever imagined. Different ways of looking at the world and being with persons who were not like oneself were tested and refined once these towns became cities, but they never were lost to smaller places. Indeed, men and women who did not live in cities often adopted the cultural practices of city folk and worked on them a little more. All the experiments and shameless borrowing back and forth provided us with some shared understanding about what matters and how persons should be treated. Yet it did not stop persons who live in cities from creating ever more elaborate and novel ways of looking at the world and being in it together.

There really is something different about the way city folk live and make sense of their world. It is seen in their willingness to embrace some new ideas or neighbors even as they run away from strangers. It is apparent in the obedient way they follow some rules while willfully violating others. And it is found in their insistence to be whomever they like and still go to church, declare their fidelity to an ancestral people, buy the same items their neighbors do, and pay their taxes.

Not everyone who lives in cities has to act this way for cultural practices to work their special magic on us. Enough persons do, however, and they leave a lasting impression on the rest of us. Granted, some parts of the culture seem to hang together better than others. Yet no matter how much city folk try to confuse themselves with all the different ways they find to be in the world together, the liberal and conservative mix of their ways seems to work pretty well. We all own parts of this civic culture. City dwellers own them all.

My purpose in writing this book, then, is to discover something that might help us better understand American cities as a whole and the way of life practiced there. I also hope to be able to say something important to the rest of my countrymen about the contribution that cities make to the lives they lead. Given our concern about the future of our country and our ability or willingness to remain a united people, I believe this to be a worthwhile venture.

I come to this task with an open mind, but with my heart proudly displayed on my sleeve. After all, cities are the largest things human beings build that actually work. They are important to civilization, but not merely because they are places where some of humankind's bigger catastrophes and accomplishments are laid out for everyone to see. Cities are important because they are the actual wellsprings of civilization. They are the places where human beings create much of what passes for a way of life that matters.[25]

I love cities. I am drawn to their early waking, to ships that suddenly appear with the light and to trains stocked with people whose untold stories and steady steps take them to fill another day. I join them in the unbounded energy of those days, all the passing and being passed, our reflections on store windows and voices in each other's ears. Whether together or alone we bear witness to the sights and sounds of a world in the making. But it is at night that I find myself lingering most, viewing the city's lights and shadows in quiet communion, ushering in tomorrow as a promise and closing it like a prayer.

We who have the privilege of living among the men and women who make cities and sharing what they have learned are nothing less than attendants to a community of believers. If we take seriously the lessons of history, however, I believe we will find that many of us are more deeply committed to their community than we may have thought and are dedicated to spreading the bourgeois habits and values it fosters. Cities turn out to be very big places indeed.

NOTES

1   Architects who design buildings for cities, planners who help to decide
    where everything from sewers to skyscrapers should go, policy-makers and
    politicians who help make it all happen with their laws and regulations, and
    academic types who try to make sense of all the rearranging that human
    beings do inside cities – all have their fingers in this pot. The geography and
    ecology of urban space are crucial to what they do in their jobs and how
    everyone else moves around and through the buildings and spaces they leave
    for us. Most any good textbook dealing with urban sociology or urban plan-
    ning will provide whole chapters and dozens of references to published
    research dealing with these subjects. For a good overview of some of the
    basic ideas conveyed in these works, however, I suggest the following books:
    Amos Hawley, *Urban Society* (New York: Ronald Press, 1971); William H.
    Whyte, *City: Rediscovering the Center* (New York: Doubleday, 1988);
    Henri Lefebvre, *The Production of Space* (Oxford: Blackwell Publishers,
    1991); Spiro Kostof, *The City Assembled: The Elements of Urban Form
    Through History* (Boston: Little, Brown, 1992); Susan S. Fainstein, *The City
    Builders: Property, Politics, and Planning in London and New York*
    (Oxford: Blackwell Publishers, 1994); Sophie Watson and Katherine
    Gibson, *Postmodern Cities and Spaces* (Oxford: Blackwell Publishers,
    1995); Peter Hall, *Cities of Tomorrow* (Oxford: Blackwell Publishers,
    1996); and John Rennie Short, *The Urban Order* (Oxford: Blackwell
    Publishers, 1996). Social historians have had only a small hand in these
    discussions. Several have written about innovative housing reforms that
    were developed during the nineteenth and twentieth centuries, particularly
    those involving tenement construction and rent control. They also paid
    some attention to the way that highways and other public works projects
    helped to create slums or to replace them with buildings and tenants deemed
    more attractive by whoever was making public policy at the time. In general,
    however, historians have let social scientists and planners worry about how
    cities should be designed or how buildings can be used to make better
    communities. See Eugenie Ladner Birch and Deborah Gardner, "The Seven
    Percent Solution: A Review of Philanthropic Housing, 1870–1910," *Journal
    of Urban History*, Volume 7, Number 4, August 1981, pp. 403–38; Neil
    Lebowitz, "'Above Party, Class, or Creed': Rent Control in the United
    States, 1940–1947," *Journal of Urban History*, Volume 7, Number 4,
    August 1981, pp. 439–70; Robert Fairbanks, "From Better Dwellings to
    Better Community: Changing Approaches to the Low-cost Housing
    Problem, 1890–1925," *Journal of Urban History*, Volume 11, Number 3,
    May 1985, pp. 314–34; William Wilson, "The Billboard: Bane of the City
    Beautiful," *Journal of Urban History*, Volume 13, Number 4, August 1987,
    pp. 394–425; Michael Holleran, "Boston's 'Sacred Sky Line': From
    Prohibition to Sculpting Skyscrapers, 1891–1928," *Journal of Urban
    History*, Volume 22, Number 5, July 1996, pp. 552–85; Thomas Sugrue,
    "More Than Skin Deep: Redevelopment and the Urban Crisis," *Journal of*

Urban History, Volume 22, Number 6, September 1996, pp. 750–9.

2 Lyn H. Lofland, *A World Of Strangers: Order and Action in Urban Public Space* (Prospect Heights, IL: Waveland Press, 1973); David Hummon, *Commonplaces: Community Ideology and Identity in American Culture* (Albany, NY: State University of New York Press, 1990); Thomas Bender, "The Erosion of Public Culture: Cities, Discourses, and Professional Disciplines," in Thomas L. Haskell (ed.), *The Authority of Experts: Studies in History and Theory* (Bloomington: Indiana University Press, 1984), pp. 142–55; Sharon Zukin, *The Culture of Cities* (Oxford: Blackwell Publishers, 1995).

3 Kenneth Jackson, "All the World's A Mall: Reflections on the Social and Economic Consequences of the American Shopping Center," *American Historical Review*, Volume 101, Number 4, October 1996, pp. 1111–21; Carol O'Connor, "The Suburban Mosaic: Patterns of Land Use, Class, and Culture," in Howard Gillette and Zane Miller (eds), *American Urbanism: A Historiographical Review* (New York: Greenwood Press, 1987), pp. 243–56; Sam Bass Warner, Jr., "The Public Settings of Everyday Life," *Journal of Urban History*, Volume 20, Number 1, November 1993, pp. 133–41; Dolores Hayden, "The Power of Place: Claiming Urban Landscapes as People's History," *Journal of Urban History*, Volume 20, Number 4, August 1994, pp. 466–85; Joel Schwartz, "Postindustrial New York and the End of Urban History," *Journal of Urban History*, Volume 21, Number 2, January 1995, pp. 265–73.

4 Lynn Hollen Lees, "Urban Public Space and Imagined Communities in the 1980s and 1990s," *Journal of Urban History*, Volume 20, Number 4, August 1994, pp. 443, 445, 446, 448, and 452.

5 Bruce J. Schulman, *The Strange Death of American Public Life* (New York: Free Press, forthcoming).

6 *Boston Sunday Globe*, November 27, 1994.

7 *Coconino Weekly*, January 26, 1896.

8 *Coconino Weekly*, June 11, 1896.

9 *Coconino Weekly*, June 18, 1896; July 9, 1896; July 30, 1896.

10 *Coconino Weekly*, August 6, 1896.

11 Richard Wolkomir, "Las Vegas Meets La-La Land," *Smithsonian*, October 1995, pp. 51–9; Stephen Budiansky, "Community Instead of Kitsch," *US News & World Report*, April 21, 1997, p. 7; Robert Hughes, "Whyn Win?," *Time*, October 26, 1998, pp. 77–83; Cathy Booth, "In With the New," *Time*, October 26, 1998, pp. 84–6.

12 Hughes, "Whyn Win?," p. 79.

13 Witold Rybczynski, "The New Downtowns," *Atlantic Monthly*, May 1993, p. 104.

14 Ibid., p. 98.

15 *Sunday Boston Globe*, January 3, 1993.

16 *Boston Globe*, October 2, 1995.

17 *Boston Globe*, November 24, 1995; January 21, 1996; August 6, 1997; November 1, 1998. The term "concrete carbuncle" is an adaptation of a phrase used by Prince Charles, who described a planned modernist

extension to the National Gallery in London as a "monstrous carbuncle on the face of an old friend." I trust that he will not think less of me for borrowing his words.

18   *Boston Globe*, November 21, 1998.
19   Zukin, *The Culture of Cities*.
20   *Boston Sunday Globe*, June 15, 1997.
21   *Wall Street Journal*, February 10, 1998.
22   I should like to say that I came up with the idea that peoples and traditions are "invented," but recognition for that contribution must go to historians Edmund S. Morgan, John Bodnar, and Eric Hobsbawm. What I propose to do here is apply their rich insight to the production of community life inside American cities. The urban way of life found in cities provides the ceremonies, customs, and codes that bring order to the world we inhabit. It also conveys the meaning that we ascribe to our actions, even though we can only partly understand it ourselves and rarely bother to describe it to others. My aim is to explain that world more completely than has been done in the past. It also is to suggest that whoever we Americans turn out to be and whatever world we made for ourselves was created in the very cities that so many of us seem to hold in low regard these days. Even as I acknowledge my intellectual debt to them, however, I must distance myself a bit from the enterprises of Morgan, Bodnar, and Hobsbawm. In some ways they had a much grander vision in mind when they spoke about the invention of a people and traditions. None of the gentlemen really was interested in the more mundane and routine dealings that human beings have with each other or in the ways which these same persons try to make some sense of their small parts of the world. They were after bigger game. Morgan is surely right when he describes the rise of popular sovereignty as a big deal. Still, it depended upon the willing compliance of a great many small persons and the untold sacrifice that so many of them made when they gave up their lives to carry it off. Morgan wants us to understand that a grand fiction was required to make common persons feel that they were part of a united people and engaged in an enterprise which mattered to them and to their children. He is not so interested in the small ways in which bonds of fealty and responsibility were forged every day between common people and their betters. Yet it is those same bonds and the beliefs that lay behind and increasingly before them that pulled everyone forward. Bodnar and Hobsbawm are not worried about something quite so big as the rise of popular sovereignty, but they are concerned with the same general problem that Morgan was tackling. They want to describe, according to Hobsbawm, the "new public holidays, ceremonies, heroes or symbols" that human beings create in order to make better sense of their world whenever that world changes in big ways. These smaller fictions, or invented traditions, help "to ensure or express social cohesion and identity and to structure social relations" at times when social cohesion is problematic and social identities are less secure. Bodnar wants to connect these new traditions to the gradual triumph of the nation-state in the twentieth century over more vernacular cultures found in American towns and cities. Public acts of commemoration create

a "public memory" that enables otherwise unrelated persons and groups to fit into America's past in a "personal and manageable way." These creations are different from customs, which Hobsbawm says are too invariant to be useful in dealing with new conditions. Invented traditions also are different from conventions or routines, which he believes have no symbolic quality or ritualistic significance. Yet the invented tradition draws heavily on the ideas and precedents established in these more common actions. Indeed, it is unlikely that new public commemorations and symbols would be able to capture our attention or provide some "continuity with the past" were they not rooted in everyday practices or at least mindful of them. Bodnar and Hobsbawm invite us to draw this very conclusion when they talk about the United States and the problem it faces by trying to incorporate so many persons from different backgrounds into the same society. They observe social innovations like the spread of professional sports, the proliferation of organizations like the Daughters of the American Revolution, the Fourth of July, and Vietnam Memorial as invented traditions that make it easier to draw more persons into a changing cultural landscape. Yet these very new endeavors are tied to an older and healthy tradition of communal recreation and secret societies that was present in small cities and towns well before the onset of mass immigration after the Civil War. Their invented traditions were built on the back of more commonplace customs and routines. That is why they were so readily accepted and could spread so rapidly across the United States. I am interested in the kind of activities that Hobsbawm calls "invented traditions." I also am fully aware that the big fictions Morgan talks about draw us into a common fold every bit as much as he says they do. At the same time, I recognize that the foundation for both is laid in the routine dealings that persons have with each other and the shared under-standings that they create as a result of those meetings. These, too, are crucial to the story that I intend to tell about the life they made in cities and an integral part of the order and prosperity that are their legacy to us. See: Edmund S. Morgan, *Inventing the People: The Rise of Popular Sovereignty in England and America* (New York: W.W. Norton, 1988); John Bodnar, *Remaking America: Public Memory, Commemoration, and Patriotism in the Twentieth Century* (Princeton, NJ: Princeton University Press, 1992), pp. 3, 13, 96–100; Eric Hobsbawm, "Inventing Traditions," in Eric Hobsbawm and Terence Ranger (eds.), *The Invention of Tradition* (New York: Cambridge University Press, 1994), pp. 1–14; Eric Hobsbawm, "Mass Producing Traditions: Europe, 1870–1914," in Hobsbawm and Ranger, *The Invention of Tradition*, pp. 263, 288–93.

23   Blair A. Ruble, "Where's the City?," *Wilson Quarterly*, Autumn 1997, p. 15.

24   Thomas Bender, "Wholes and Parts: The Need for Synthesis in American History," *Journal of American History*, Volume 73, Number 1, June 1986, p. 127.

25   Sir Peter Hall, *Cities in Civilization* (New York: Pantheon Books, 1998). This book, written with the same ambition that drove Lewis Mumford to compose his own monumental works about the culture and history of cities,

covers a lot of ground and walks us through several millennia. With the notable exception of his discussion of Manchester, England and the "innovative milieu" which provided the social capital on which an industrial empire was built, however, Hall attends to the bigger artistic and technological breakthroughs that have been made in cities over the last few thousand years. While a refreshing and enlightening break from much of the literature about cities which focuses on how they fail us or fall apart, the accomplishments which Hall describes remain surprisingly aloof from the cultural context in which they unfolded.

2

We Are a Bourgeois People Who Made an Urban World

A people is known by the way of life its members follow and by the places where they practice that way of life most fully. The people called "Americans" often are portrayed as fiercely independent, or willfully self-absorbed, hard working and hard praying men and women who donate lots of money to charitable causes even as they kill each other off in alarmingly high numbers. Not as well known or maybe just not appreciated, I think, is the fact that they have created a bourgeois culture in which prosperity and order are valued more than anything else. Whether all of them recognize this or openly endorse these ideas is important. There are times, in fact, when being reminded about the principles by which we guide our lives is absolutely necessary. Today, I believe, is one of those times.

As an everyday concern, of course, it is not so important to be reminded of these guiding principles. It would have little practical effect on the routines of most persons. Frankly, it matters far more that Americans can be counted on to behave in prosperous and orderly ways much of the time. We do far better than that most of the time, however, and that is a good thing.

Elements of our bourgeois culture are practiced in all communal settings: in villages, towns, or cities. Nevertheless, one is likely to find this culture put to its best and fullest use in cities. This is because cities are big enough places and have populations of sufficient size and diversity to support an urban way of life in all its complexity and richness.

Many persons in cities do not look and act the way we do, and this has prompted city dwellers for countless generations to wonder about these other persons and the way they live.[1] Unfortunately, the fact that cities are big places filled with persons different from ourselves tells us little about the way they live or what they value.[2] We have to look elsewhere to understand who they are and how they make an urban way of life that suits them most of the time.

I read a book years ago whose author maintained that we would have no culture without leisure time. If persons were too busy hunting or gathering food or sacking someone else's village to get more of whatever they needed to live, then it stood to reason that they could not be off producing art, creating novel tools, or developing new institutions. Leisure was the basis for all cultural production.

Cities are palaces of leisure. Their inhabitants have managed to capture sufficient resources long enough to support the creation of more full-time culture makers than can be found in any other kind of place. Furthermore, this has been going on for a long time, maybe as long as 5,000 years.

Human beings in cities take on more roles, assume a more varied set of obligations, generate more ideas, and simply have more stuff to play with than do persons who are not immersed in an urban way of life. They also find many more ways to work together and at cross-purposes than do individuals who do not live in cities. The city turns out to be a place where human beings do more of what they do best: invent better ways to organize themselves and create new ideas about why and how this should be done. A city thus imagined becomes a theater dedicated to a particular kind of religious production, a round-the-clock morality play put on by the best artists who ever slopped paint on a canvas or on themselves as a way to fix their place in the world and to learn about themselves at the same time. It is a place, to paraphrase Peter Hawkins, where heaven marries earth and human beings experience the mystery of their own part in the cosmic drama.[3]

It is easy to imagine cities in this way and to think about what persons do there in big terms. We certainly are accustomed to talking about cities as hives of activity where important events occur. What all the persons moving in and around cities every day do can be hard to figure out. Furthermore, the rules that persons use to guide their dealings with each other may be only slightly less indecipherable to them than they are to outsiders. It all makes for grand theater.

Still, an urban way of life is not the exclusive property of persons who live in cities. Elements of this kind of life, as we shall see, are easily observed in places that are much smaller than cities and even quite rural in character. It is just that more parts of this way of life are routinely played out in cities than in places that are not cities.

There are many reasons why this might be the case. The most important one may be that persons in cities are accustomed to expressing themselves more openly about what distinguishes them *and* to working harder at ignoring these differences because they are so readily apparent. Either of these stratagems would require a great deal of work to carry off well, and city dwellers may succeed more often and openly than persons in other kinds of places because they have created more ways to carry on a dialogue with each other.[4] Persons in cities simply may fret and fight more often about the real and imagined consequences of being different than do persons who live in other kinds of places. At the same time, they also might have more ways to manage, massage, and reconcile whatever disagreements they may have with persons different from themselves. This may help city dwellers deal with each other in the short run, but it also may make it harder for city residents to look beyond what divides them and to fashion completely new understandings about their obligations to each other.

This in a real sense is the most important work accomplished by persons who carry on an urban way of life. The creation of such understandings and civic rituals helps to organize the way persons treat each other in public. They make it possible for us to talk, fret, and fight about our differences most of the time without doing much damage to each other or to the places where we live and work. These rituals are the most important social tools that city dwellers have to work through their disagreements or to map out a plausible response to the problems they face.

Places that are not cities have every bit as much need for rituals of this sort. It is likely that their residents do not create as many of them, however, or that the ones they do create follow more predictable scripts. It is the idiosyncratic character of these customs and the lessons they teach us about how we should treat each other that help us distinguish our community from others that we know or have occasion to visit. They also are the cultural "stuff" that makes us into a more united people, or keeps us from becoming so.

The central problem, I think, is that Americans had come to see excess resources and leisure as the most important signs of their city's success. Progress was equated with prosperity. Nothing else seemed to matter. We forgot that to make a successful bourgeois people it was necessary to cultivate order every bit as much as it was to create more wealth.

Even if I make this point too strongly, there have been many moments in the recent history of United States cities when we could have reminded ourselves of the benefits that come from doing the right thing. This might seem a toothless gesture in an age when the problems we face are bigger than those we have met in the past or decidedly different from anything we have seen before. It may not appear useful or even appropriate to remind ourselves today of the good times we once knew or how we worked our way through the problems we had then. Yet it may be precisely at such moments that the members of a community most need to take a close look at how they came to be the people they are, if only to better assess who they can be in the future. As the people of Dayton, Ohio discovered during the 1990s, however, it is easier to talk about good communities than it is to keep one in good running order.

Did You Ever Read de Tocqueville?

The residents of Dayton were going through some bad times during the closing years of the twentieth century. Dayton was one of those older American cities that had been built on industrial muscle and now was hurting as parts of that muscle were being torn away. As the reporter from *The New York Times* who visited Dayton early in 1996 told the story, the loss of the city's major employer and corporate patron was a big blow to local residents. It may have been the National Cash Register Company or NCR to Wall Street and the rest of the world, but to Dayton "it was always just 'the Cash.'"

> The Cash got rich selling its cash registers to the world, and it rewarded its workers with good livings and unrivaled benefits, and its hometown with a firm hand of civic guidance and millions of dollars of good works. They were all bound together – the company, the workers and the town. To a lot of people here, Dayton was the Cash, and the Cash was Dayton.
>
> Nearly all of it has vanished in the steep decline and takeover of NCR: the buildings, 20,000 jobs, even the NCR name; the security, the middle-class aspirations, the way of life. And today, as its faraway corporate parent, AT&T, prepares to break into three pieces, the future of Dayton's hometown company is profoundly unsure.[5]

The changes brought on by NCR's reorganization, including the closing of other companies and jobs that complemented the work of NCR, left a lot of discouraged workers and some serious questions about the city's future. It was not so much that everyone in Dayton had lost their job. New jobs had become available for many displaced workers in service, wholesale, and retail companies or through the expansion of government agencies in the area. These jobs may not have been as lucrative as the lost manufacturing jobs, but many persons could still find work.

Something else was troubling Dayton's residents. The reporter observed that the disappearance of many jobs and local companies from Dayton had disrupted the social fabric of the city. "Now that there are only a few big hometown companies left," said the publisher of the

Dayton Daily News, "it creates tremendous uncertainty in people's lives. The tie between individuals and the community is ... more fragile. It's scary for everybody."

Persons were having to work harder to match their previous style of life. There was less time to spend with one's family and friends or to volunteer for chores that helped the community. Leaders of some organizations had left town to find new jobs. Other individuals were not stepping forward to assume those tasks or were unable to fill all the big social spaces left in their neighborhood or the city as a whole.

One of the persons interviewed by the reporter was a middle-aged banker named George Bayless. At one point during their drive through Dayton, Mr Bayless asked the reporter a question. "Did you ever read de Tocqueville?" he inquired. The reporter did not say how she responded to his query, but she did convey how Bayless answered his own question. "One of his points was that Americans in 1831 ... associated together. There were all these associations. It was one of the things that made America work, that made it unique. The safety net was not just government. It was us."[6]

In the mind of George Bayless and more than a few of his fellow Dayton residents that safety net was coming undone in 1996, and the hard work of keeping their community together was being ignored. As the reporter put it in her story,

> All workers may be replaceable. Not so volunteers. When one man, Vinnie Russo, left NCR in the turmoil after the takeover ... and found a new job in Louisville, the 85 boys of Pack 530 lost their Cubmaster; a new one has yet to sign on. It is harder to find people to help in the schools and libraries. Churches are losing members. So are service organizations; people say they cannot leave work for meetings, even if they last only an hour. In a town with a tradition of charity, the United Way has missed its $20 million goal by $1 million in each of the last two years.[7]

If their hometown really did feel less like home, which was the idea conveyed to the reporter, then it was because the people of Dayton had forgotten half of what had made their community a good place to live. They fretted about the loss of jobs and money; and they apparently had to work harder and longer just to maintain the standard of living they had known in the past. If not exactly prosperous, or as well off as they had been, they seemed to be doing all right on that score. Where they were doing less than all right was with the hard work of maintaining the sense of community they had once known and all the social and organizational ties that give substance to the claim that their community was whole and vital.

At the end of the twentieth century many Americans expressed sentiments about their lives and communities that were similar to those
uttered by residents from Dayton, Ohio. Not many may have believed
that the whole of America was in a state of absolute decline. Fewer yet
may have thought it impossible for all the different peoples lumped
together as "Americans" to have a common view of the world or a set of
beliefs and customs that united them in anything but a superficial way.[8]
Yet many thoughtful persons suspected that America's moral and social
center had been stretched thin under the pressure of an increasingly
diverse and divided population.[9] To them we no longer were the people
we used to be. Maybe we never had been.

Blame for the supposed raveling of America, and perhaps of western
societies generally, might be traced to a number of causes. If one follows
the separate paths left by whatever was dropping one problem after
another at our feet, however, the search always leads us to the same two
sources: industrial capitalism and cities. Industrial capitalism, far and
away the central villain in this piece, is said to have transformed America
into a modern bourgeois society riven by "dislocation, alienation, and
mediocrity."[10] Cities, for their part, are the foremost stage on which the
effects of industrial capitalism have been played out. Persons who live in
cities express all the pressure that builds up in the divided and antagonistic world created by industrial capitalists, and they let it out in great
gulps of pain and anger.[11] All the problems that we see in America are
problems we see first and worst in American cities, places like Dayton,
Ohio.

What Went Wrong: Too Much Prosperity, Not Enough Order

The short explanation about what went wrong is that Americans concentrated too much on being prosperous and not enough on being orderly.
I had a colleague, the late political scientist Norton Long, who used to
take grim satisfaction in attributing the sorry state of urban civic life to
the work of "laissez fairies." Those of us who heard about the laissez
fairies were treated to images of unbridled profit-making and grinding
poverty, hard working but prejudiced laborers stuck in dingy ghettos,
and wealthy businessmen who found refuge in exclusive suburban
enclaves. The only thing of any note they left behind was a legacy of
mistrust, mismanagement, and decidedly uncivil conduct for city folk to
copy. It was not a picture that inspired much confidence or a sense of
well-being.

Other popular and academic writers who shared their impressions
about city life with us over the last 200 years have evoked similar feelings

and conjured up images that play to the same set of contradictory themes alluded to by Norton Long. Some scholars like Lewis Mumford offered a more systematic critique of urban life, but there was a common theme in all their work. The modern city, that is to say the city of industry and unrestrained capitalist appetites, brought out what was the best and worst, but more of the worst, that is in human beings to give. Cities had become pretty dreadful places.

> For many, life was indeed nasty, brutish, and short. High levels of density produced not only high levels of illness and mortality but also profound changes in the ways men interacted (or failed to interact) with their neighbors and other citizens. Individuals felt a sense of liberation from traditional agencies of social control, such as the Church and the family. Moreover,... there was growing social as well as spatial separation between classes. The members of these groups became increasingly aware that although they shared residency and some of the rights of citizenship in the same municipality they did not belong to a moral or cultural community.[12]

The influence of these new ideas and ways of behaving were spread across whole cities and, in the age of mass media, to persons who lived in places far away from cities. "At the same time," historian Andrew Lees has said, "all of these problems and possibilities powerfully stimulated the anxieties and the hopes, the emotions and the intellects, of thoughtful and articulate observers of the social scene."[13] It was around this powerful set of images that thinkers like Long, Mumford, and many others spawned a whole intellectual tradition predicated on the idea that urban life was inherently disorganized or had been left unattended for so long that it could not be put back together in any satisfactory way.[14]

Edward Winslow Martin was one of many Americans who made an effort to capture what was going on in cities at this time. Writing of New York in 1868, Martin chose his words carefully and with a seriousness of mind that befit his subject. "Our purpose has been two-fold, to satisfy a reasonable curiosity on the part of those who never have seen ... New York, and to warn those who design visiting the city, of the dangers and temptations which await them there." He beseeched his readers "to confine their visits to the numerous harmless and innocent attractions of the Metropolis, and to shun those other, darker quarters of the city, which are but so many gateways to the paths that lead to ruin and death."[15]

As if to convince them of his intent and to demonstrate the range and depth of his knowledge, Martin filled 552 pages with a curious mix of sightseeing tips, commentary on New Yorkers' customs, and woeful stories about heinous criminals, innocent farm girls come to the big city, and the dastardly fellows who did them wrong. His book, *Secrets of the Great City*, apparently was not one of the more notable pieces of literature about cities to emerge in the years immediately before or after the Civil War.[16] No other work with which I am familiar, however, draws on so many of the themes that writers of the period invoked when they turned their attention to city people and city ways.

Whatever else one might say about Edward Winslow Martin, he most certainly was earnest and thorough. He described the various means the traveler could use to move through the city, and he introduced the reader to some of the businesses that drove New York's economy. He liked the city's public buildings, calling them "handsome." He spoke fondly of the public schools, stating that "New York stands at the head of all American cities in the excellence and extent of its system of public education." He even admired the city's modern boulevards, declaring Broadway to be "the most wonderful street in the world."[17]

Martin also wrote about several of the city's more stylish customs and popular holidays. He told his readers where to go shopping for the finest products. He instructed them about New Yorkers' habit of going on lovely Sunday afternoon strolls through Central Park, but only after attending services at one of the city's grander churches, of course. Finally, he turned his attention to the public's fascination with visits on New Year's Day, Thanksgiving, and Christmas. He was somewhat less enthusiastic about Independence Day, which he dismissed as a "nuisance" largely "devoted to drinking and acts of lawlessness."[18]

Much of his book, however, was reserved for rather lurid stories about less attractive aspects of life in New York and morality tales dealing with the poor souls who were caught up in the gay and immoral adventures that New York offered unsuspecting visitors. He spoke of the hardships faced by sewing girls, newsboys, bootblacks, beggars, "emigrants," and "bummers."[19] He railed against "the social evil" of prostitution, and he felt great pity for the "soiled doves" who were caught up in this cruel trade. He described in detail the character of dance houses, blackmailers, thieves, pickpockets, gambling dens, "baby farming," fortune tellers, quack doctors, lawyers, and pits where rats and dogs were set against each other for the amusement of betting customers.[20]

The fancy stores and vice dens, fine public buildings and brothels, elegant boulevards and crowded alleys, and the wealthy strollers and streetwalkers were different parts of the same big world. None alone could have conveyed all the energy and drama of the lives that filled the city every day and evening. Nor could a description of any one of the places and activities have captured the clumsy and sometimes tortured symmetry of their presence in the city together. All had a place and played a part in the thriving bundle of contradictions that was New York City shortly after the Civil War.

The city's permanent population, which Martin estimated to be over one million, was augmented by the "immense throng of visitors for business and pleasure [who] arrive and depart daily." He put this number at 40,000. To these one would have added persons who came for special occasions such as the recently concluded Democratic National Convention, which Martin said temporarily ballooned the population by another 200,000.[21] However inflated these figures may have been, Martin needed them every bit as much as he needed all the denizens of the city's darker corners to paint his picture of New York City as a place that pulsed with the lives of persons drawn from every walk of life.

The population of New York, he stated, "is made up from every nation under Heaven. The natives are in the minority. The foreign element predominates. Irishmen, Germans, Jews, Turks, Greeks, Russians, Italians, Spaniards, Mexicans, Portuguese, Scotch, French, Chinese ... abound. These frequently herd together, each class by itself, in distinct parts of the city, which they seem to regard as their own." Though a cosmopolitan city, New York remained "eminently American." The native element had retained much of its influence over affairs in the city. Furthermore, its modest size was enhanced by migrants from other states in the Union, and "this constant influx of fresh American vitality does much to keep the city true to the general character of the country." One might add that these "American" migrants also helped to keep New York a good place to live and work.

Martin was one of those writers who was optimistic about what he saw on that count. "In point of morality," he suggested, "the people of New York, in spite of all that has been said of them, compare favorably with those of any other city. If the darkest side of life is to be seen here, one may also witness the best. The greatest scoundrels and the purest Christians are to be found here." The charities, churches, and municipal government spend millions of dollars each year to help less privileged persons. The people of New York, he added, "are the most liberal of any in America in matters of opinion." All religious faiths, "every shade of political opinion, is tolerated and protected."

However promising these signs were, one also had to acknowledge that city life had a tendency to drive persons apart. Martin observed that "men concern themselves with their own affairs only. Indeed, this feeling is carried to such an extreme that it has engendered a decided indifference between man and man. People live for years as next door neighbors, without ever knowing each other by sight." Furthermore, it is clear "that there are but two classes in the city – the poor and the rich. The middle class, which is so numerous in other cities hardly exists at all here."

Persons "of moderate means" are required to "reside in the suburbs, some of them as far as forty miles in the country. They come into the city ... in the morning, and literally pour out of it ... in the evening."[22] There were substantial divisions built into the society that was New York, and persons were well aware of them.

Captured in Martin's vivid portrayal of New York immediately after the Civil War, then, are all the contradictions that twentieth-century social scientists saw splitting and aggravating city residents in their time, and ours. He saw the highest and lowest of society filling city streets. There were fine buildings and hovels, culture and depravity, hard work and sloth. It was all there. All that twentieth-century social scientists did in many instances was to render these observations into a more systematic theory about how the urban world worked and to provide many numbers to back up their claims about the magnificent and sordid conditions of life in cities.

Are We a Liberal or a Conservative People?

The many persons who worried about America and its future may have been of one mind when they identified industrial capitalism and cities as the sources of their discomfort. They were decidedly split, however, on which problems should be worked on first and how persons should fashion solutions that would last. Fortunately for us, the persons who worried about such matters then, as now, divided themselves into readily identifiable camps. Those individuals who were left of center in their politics tended to be "more concerned with the rise of mass poverty and inequality." Back then, no less than today, they were critical of capitalism "not for creating wealth but rather for not creating enough of it, and distributing it inequitably." Those persons whose politics were more right of center saw the central problem as having more to do with "the waning of patrician society and its standards." They were "cultural conservatives" back then, and they remain so today.[23]

These different ways of defining what is wrong and how to fix America each have strong and persuasive champions. Were one inclined to view this as a contest, though, it would have a very lopsided score. This is because there seem to be many more voices speaking against poverty and in behalf of efforts to redistribute some portion of our wealth in cities than there are speaking against the erosion of patrician rule and standards for good conduct. Both persons from the left and right ends of our political spectrum, however, see America as breaking apart or in imminent danger of doing so.

The view that modern societies are seriously fractured has strong intellectual roots. We only traced it as far back as the eighteenth century when persons began to worry about the onset of the industrial revolution, the rise of nations and nationalism, and the growth of large cities. These changes were unprecedented in human history, and they compelled human beings to alter the way they thought about themselves and dealt with each other.

Societies, it was imagined, had once been filled with persons who were more or less alike. They had familiar jobs with predictable routines. Men and women conducted themselves in time-honored, if not always congenial, ways. Their beliefs may have been primitive by our standards, but they were filled with a sacred quality that gave purpose to the persons who held them and meaning to the lives that these persons led. It was a quite conservative way of life. Nothing much changed, and persons did not stray far or often from the well-marked paths left by their ancestors who probably were watching them from on high in any case.

Modern society was different. Indeed, modern society was organized around differences. Persons were not similar to each other. No longer did their jobs and work lives conform to traditional methods and revolve around seasonal rhythms. They had more options in how to dress, talk, and relate to friends and family members. Their minds were filled with new ideas. Men, and sometimes women, became more involved in political matters, if not in electoral politics as we think of it. They made their opinions known in new ways, and sometimes these new ways were quite rowdy. This was a decidedly more open and liberal world. It catered to the whims and wants of individuals who no longer were constrained by rules infused with sacredness and rulers to whom they were bound by any notion of fealty, divinely inspired or otherwise.

These changes were exciting, but they also were disruptive. Social relations, it was supposed, had a fluid quality to them that had not been there before. Persons were free to imagine themselves in new and different ways. It may not have been the case that modern societies had any more divisions built into them than premodern societies had riddling them. However, persons and groups certainly were able to identify, talk about, and act on these differences more than they had been able to in the past.

Applied to a country like the United States, the points of tension would fall along predictable lines. They corresponded to differences between social classes or ethnic and racial groups or to the social barriers separating men from women or younger and older persons. The gaps between persons on one side of these fault lines and those on the other side were real and considered serious. Many social and political commentators worried about how these changes would be played out and whether life as we had come to know it could be carried on in the future.

We often succeed in ignoring the fact that we built a world on top of these pressure points. Persons from one side or the other of the lines in question may not like each other or get along especially well, but we take some comfort in the fact that they manage to go on with their lives much of the time. There are moments, though, when the differences between them are openly expressed. It is hard to know how long and nasty these conflicts will be. For that reason alone, perhaps, but also because we never know how much larger the rifts between us might grow as a result of our open disagreements and fights, we spend a great deal of time trying to patch little problems before they become too large to handle. Rarely, if ever, do we address straight on the underlying problems that divide us. Sometimes this strategy works satisfactorily. Sometimes it does not.

There have been social philosophers and theorists who believe that these unresolved tensions cannot be avoided forever. Eventually, the argument goes, there will be a serious rupture in our social world. Violence of a revolutionary sort will break out, and even bigger and more unpredictable changes will inevitably occur.

This does not happen all that often, of course. When rifts do open we usually wait until the pressure dies down and then try to rebuild the world as best we can. There are many more times when we see persons trying to warn us of impending ruptures or suggesting that they have a patch that can be applied to the hole which has opened up between groups with serious disagreements. That is the job which social and political commentators have taken on as their special duty. Evidence of their dutifulness is all around us, particularly when the problems of cities are discussed and we are asked to consider how to deal with all the different persons who live there. What happens there will be felt across the rest of society.

Both liberals and conservatives will talk about what groups and communities can do to make life better for city residents. However, not all of them take seriously the work that city-based corporations and government institutions can do. Nor do they expect that voluntary organizations and informal groups can make a great difference in the lives of city residents. These more parochial groups usually are seen as being less important to the city's future than the much larger government agencies that are found in Washington, DC and the multinational corporations that work in the "global economy."

There are two good reasons why many liberal and conservative persons say these things. The first reason is that they both believe that the power and cultural significance of cities has diminished greatly. The real seats of power today have shifted to the national government and to multinational corporations. Unfortunately for cities, the federal government has many groups and pieces of territory to watch over, and it is not likely to spend as much time worrying about the problems of a single city, or even a number of cities. Multinational corporations, for their part, also have interests spanning many borders. Their first loyalty is not to the city where their headquarters may be located or to the towns where their manufacturing plants are found, if they build anything at all. As the people of Dayton, Ohio learned, capital is mobile and a good dose of tradition today does not take you as far as it once did.

The second reason why many liberal and conservative commentators have little expectation or faith that cities will do better in the future also revolves around the large government agencies and corporations that are supposed to be running our lives today. They do not believe large organizations and their caretakers work in ways that can do much directly to help local municipalities and groups. The work accomplished by governments and in the marketplace is directed, even dedicated, to what individual persons do and want as citizens, shoppers, and investors.

This is not at all an odd or new idea. We are children of the Enlightenment and bound to take what happens to individuals as the principal yardstick against which we measure progress or assess what is good and right. It is the individual that is most responsible for making good things happen, who transforms the world, and who must keep it whole. It is not groups, or at least not the groups that George Bayless and his neighbors in Dayton seem to be worried about losing, that make a big difference in our lives. Government and the marketplace have become the primary spheres of moral obligation in the modern world in the minds of many observers, and their agents are primarily concerned with the condition of citizens and shoppers.

Classical theorists anticipated the rise of the market and the state. They thought the market would cater to a growing cult of individualism by supplying ever more goods and services to persons with increasingly more money at their disposal. It would help persons define and carry out codes for proper conduct. They also believed that government would wield increasing influence by offering authority and protection to individual citizens against the excesses of the market. These same theorists may have underestimated the extent to which government would absorb or redirect the work of voluntary groups and local attachments, but they did not misjudge the coercive power of the state or underestimate its influence as an arena for defining how persons should treat each other.[24]

The problem with this view of the world, Alan Wolfe correctly notes, is that "neither the liberal market nor the democratic state is comfortable with explicit discussions of the obligations such codes ought to impose." Both view social obligation as a by-product of individual action and prefer present benefits to sacrifices for future generations. Rights rather than obligations are emphasized in the market and state, and both value procedures over purpose.[25] Therein lies the rub for many contemporary liberals and conservatives who express an interest in helping cities and speak about creating a sense of "community" in the modern world. These same persons look to governments and the marketplace to show us what the right thing to do is and to bring us together so that we might do good; but the agents of the state and market make it devilishly hard to define what that good might be and how to apprehend it.

Many persons who claim they are liberals have an abiding faith in the idea that a "public interest" can be identified, but they usually turn to trained professionals and politically untainted bureaucrats to find it. At the same time, they are hard put to say ahead of time what values such a public interest would serve or what principles should inform our pursuit of more limited and personal ends. The experts embraced by liberal partisans devise and implement plans that are intended to make the world a better place, as long as it can be done with a modicum of efficiency and without spilling too much blood.

Liberals tend to have a mean managerial streak, though it sometimes does not extend to questions involving financial costs. They embrace a kind of middle-class populism that would restore "responsibility and competence (and) power once and for all to those members of society most able to exercise it." Those persons would be "planners."[26] In their programs for action liberals often try to change the way that government is organized, and one imagines that professional managers and planners would help out here as well. In fact, the notion of the "public good" that liberals embrace usually ends up being wedded to procedural reforms at least as much as it is to changing what governments do.[27]

Persons who are critical of the idea of using government to make our society and ourselves better often point out that even when governments do a great deal not much appears to change. Despite all of the programs launched by the federal government in this century, for instance, it does not seem that our society's wealth is distributed much differently today than it was a hundred years ago. Rich persons usually remain that way. So do the poor. The rest of us end up muddling around somewhere in the middle and hope that the value of our homes increases and younger persons will want to buy the stocks we own when we retire. To the extent that many persons believe that such a redistribution of wealth is absolutely necessary for the smooth and effective working of our society in the future, it would seem that we have not made much progress in righting old wrongs and in keeping faith with whatever we think the "promise of America" is supposed to be. In other words, it may be terribly difficult to identify what is in our greater "public interest" or to assert that there is a transcendent good that government can serve and we can articulate within some well-marked borders of principled discourse and action.

There also are other more conservative persons who worry a great deal about such matters and who believe that it is possible for human beings to create ways of being in the world together and to take stock of their behavior in a principled way. Many of these same persons tend to think that government cannot help us much to accomplish such ends and actually may do more harm than good. Whatever progress we see in our lives or in society generally, conservatives believe, is much more likely to be the result of "the unplanned and unintended consequences of normal human endeavor, rather than the result of purposive, governmental action."[28]

Conservatives believe that the marketplace, not government, is the most important arena in which good things will happen for more persons. Here too, though, it may prove harder to define what is good and how to do what is right than many of us think. In a given place there may be a number of persons who have similar views of the world and act toward the world in complementary ways. Some conservative persons believe, however, that it is foolish to speak of such an aggregation of needs and desires as a "public interest." To them there is no good "that pertains to the community as a whole, that transcends and even undermines the particular interests and passions of private individuals" working together or at cross-purposes within the marketplace.[29] Talk about a common good is little more than that, talk. It may be used by clever persons to justify their own preferred positions on an issue, but it has no life within a group or community. Moral discourse in the marketplace may be nothing more than the assurance that someone will pay for goods or services provided by another person.

In sum, the decidedly atomistic view of humankind that is embraced by citizens, investors, and shoppers may tell us something about liberty and the pursuit of happiness, but it cannot show us how to come together and accomplish something worthwhile. Nor does it suggest any reason why we should try. In principle, no one may be turned away or denied a chance to pursue his own talents and dreams. On the other hand, we are selfish beings and not likely to give up willingly all that we schemed so hard to get. A world so constructed will be open to all manner of ideas and practices, which will make it a more interesting place to be. It may not provide many standards by which to judge the relative value of those thoughts and actions in anything but monetary terms, unfortunately, and to the extent that this is so our life together is impoverished.

That realm of human action we call "community" is not well known or easy to apprehend in such wide-open moral spaces, except perhaps in a vaguely philosophical or abstract way. Yet it seems to be something that an increasing number of persons think they want. They see a need for "community" and something that can help them to remember who they are as a people and what they should be doing with themselves and for each other.

It is not that we can deny the importance of governments and the marketplace in our lives. We simply may have come to a point in our history when we no longer think that we can afford the luxury of relying on the "distant obligations" imposed upon us by the marketplace and the state to make us whole or better.[30] The self-interested individual, long admired for his love of freedom and acquisitive nature, may prove to be less attractive in an age when unlimited appetites have to deal with more limited resources. We may find renewed interest and relief in the moral certainty and intimate obligations found in our families and neighborhoods, at the workplace, and in a host of voluntary organizations. These groups provide individuals with the opportunity and means to practice citizenship in its broadest sense.[31] They teach us about self-denial and help us to practice responsibility in the places where we live and with the persons we know best.

I think that we may have exaggerated the extent to which our lives are dominated by unseen forces and unapproachable institutions, but I am prepared to acknowledge that mine is a minority opinion. After all, entire schools of thought have developed around the ideas that the world is coming apart and we are losing sight of what is important to us as a people.[32] Many social scientists and social philosophers see the world as a pretty problematic and unsteady creation. They expect a host of bad things to happen because the bonds that keep persons behaving in more conventional ways have been abandoned or repudiated by too many persons. The institutions that are thought to provide most of the structure and rationale we need to deal with the modern world – government and the marketplace – are either too distant to stop bad things from happening or they subvert the work of more intimate and local associations that stopped bad things in the past.

I am not yet prepared to believe that the situation we face today is as desperate as many persons seem to think it is or that we have forgotten how to get along and do important things together. I am quite certain, on the other hand, that much of the evidence adduced by social scientists and historians in the last half century which speaks to our coming apart and shallow values is overstated and takes for granted the very ideas about America's fractured state that it should hold up to a critical light. They look for disorder and discord, and they find it.

It is time to move beyond the simple picture of ourselves as a people tumbling through the world without much of anything to keep us standing upright and moving forward. There may be more right with us than we have been told, and we may be more united and whole than we think.

In short, the world left to us by our ancestors may have held up better than anyone imagines. It may not be paradise, and we may not always be on good terms with each other. From time to time, groups may even take violent steps to bring about changes they want. Nevertheless, society as we know it has not crashed and burned. In fact, when you consider all the potential sources of discomfort and discord, our society usually remains pretty calm.

We are a Bourgeois People

When George Bayless, the banker from Dayton, asked the reporter from *The New York Times* whether she had ever read de Tocqueville, he may have posed it as a rhetorical question. Yet he seemed to be touching an important idea with his query, and the reporter knew it. There were no deep ideological divisions among Dayton's residents so far as anyone had been able to see. Nor had any substantial fissures been revealed among its several social classes as a result of the unsettling economic changes they had witnessed. Nevertheless, something was wrong. The banker put his finger on it with his question about de Tocqueville and his assertion that the people of Dayton had forgotten that they had once been their own best "safety net."

Being well off is only half of what had made Dayton a good place to be. The doing of things together, for oneself and for each other, is the other feature that had made it a good place to be and made Dayton's residents into a viable and vital people. It may have marked their democratic society "with an undeniable mediocrity of culture," but it also blessed it "with widespread affluence and orderly ways."[33] It was the promise of *prosperity* and the accomplishment of *order* that had kept their community together in good times and bad. It is what had made them a bourgeois people.

The failure of less well-to-do persons from Dayton to give fuller expression to whatever animosity they may have felt for having lost a measure of security and some portion of their wealth, one supposes, may have had something to do with their search for more and better work. Being "preoccupied with individualistic opportunity and advancement, not with class solidarity and class struggle," they may have willingly abandoned any "dreams of socialism" their social position should have dictated they hold.[34] There could also have been something more important and basic at work.

Richard Hofstadter, writing in 1969, suggested that Americans were united by "a subtler, more intangible, but vital kind of moral consensus" that had nothing to do with their wealth or social position. Americans, he maintained, had created a "covenant of comity" in which even bickering groups had "a basic minimal regard for each other."

> The basic humanity of the opposition is not forgotten; civility is not abandoned; the sense that a community life must be carried on after the acerbic issues of the moment have been fought over and won is seldom very far out of mind.

As Hofstadter had come to see it, the voluntary recognition and courtesy extended to these other groups could not be taken for granted. There were periods in which Americans expressed more or less of it, and not all groups were granted the protection of the covenant quickly. Catholics, for instance, had "won acceptance only very slowly and by degrees." Immigrants who came after the Civil War were in the same poor position. They were incorporated into the system of comity only in this century. Black Americans never had been given a real part in this covenant, he believed, and their inability "to fight or bargain their way in" was at the root of many problems on the contemporary American scene.[35]

My point is simply that the covenant of comity persists today. Those groups accepted into it constitute a community of believers dedicated to the ideas of prosperity and order. Recognition as a member of this community still carries special obligations and privileges. That same recognition, however, does not guarantee that a group will be warmly embraced by all the other parties to whom recognition has been extended. It means only that their presence is accepted and their contribution to the hard work of sustaining a prosperous and orderly way of life is valued.

This view of the world is different from what most classical observers of modern urban and industrial societies long ago embraced. The world is not necessarily falling apart. It is not populated exclusively by especially liberal persons, as most conservatives feared. Nor is it inhabited by a backward looking or even reactionary collection of persons, as many liberals have asserted on one occasion or another. It is, in fact, an interesting hybrid of persons who embrace both liberal and conservative ways of thinking about what is good and right and of being in that world together.

Membership in the community of believers is not extended to every group or to every person that is present in the larger society. It has to be earned by those who want to share in the covenant of comity, and membership must be granted by those who already are part of it. The important point is that it usually is possible for new groups to "fight or bargain their way in" just as Hofstadter asserted.[36]

There are rules to be followed and standards that must be accepted as legitimate by those who gain entrance to this special confederation or who wish to maintain their affiliation with its members. Still, should a group fail to embrace all these rules or to follow them strictly all the time, it does not mean that its members will be immediately censured. Nor does it imply that they will be permanently banished from the community.

Groups are expected to attend to the interests and needs of other parties that have been accepted into this community of believers. They cannot take into account only the wishes of the persons in their own group. At the same time, they are able to express preferences. They are granted some latitude in the beliefs they cherish and the customs they follow.

The covenant of comity imagined by Hofstadter provides a set of principles and a code of behavior for all the groups that have been admitted into the community of believers. The rights and duties implied in that special covenant do not preclude the eventual incorporation of other ideas and ways of behaving. Nor is membership into the community of believers limited to a fixed number of groups. New groups can petition for membership. Even if they voluntarily adopt the codes, ceremonies, and customs used by groups that subscribe to the covenant of comity, however, it does not guarantee them admittance into the community of believers any time soon. On the other hand, it couldn't hurt.

A central theme in this book is that much of what passes for everyday life in American cities today reflects the covenant of comity that Hofstadter described. Indeed, prosperity and orderliness have been an integral part of life in cities since they were founded as small towns, military garrisons, and trading posts in some cases over three hundred years ago. Not only are prosperity and order the central features of our urban way of life, they also are the twin pillars upon which our whole culture is built. They are what make it a bourgeois culture.

The notion that Americans embrace a bourgeois existence is not new. Yet the term "bourgeois" as it is used today does not have the muscular quality that Richard Hofstadter had attributed to it. When he wrote about Americans as a bourgeois people Hofstadter intended to use the word in the very way we do here. To him and to us it is a collective accomplishment, a state of being or a set of ideas that embraced the principles of prosperity and order. Within five years after Hofstadter had offered his interpretation of that term, his biographers advanced a more popular but watered-down understanding of "bourgeois" as being something more like "middle class." They described Americans as possessing "a bourgeois culture informed by bourgeois assumptions – the rights of property and the values of opportunity, self-interest, and self-assertion 'within broad legal limits.'"[37] Presented in this way, Americans look much more like the acquisitive, self-seeking bunch of hungry hippos that classical theorists imagined that human beings would become and only a powerful central government could restrain. Being reminded of the richer meaning that Hofstadter brought to his understanding of Americans as a bourgeois people should make us think harder about who we are and what kind of communities we ought to create, but it probably will not.

Many of the divisions and problems we see in American society generally were said to have been observed first in cities or felt more strongly among the people living there. American society allegedly became less solid and more broken down when these same persons or their ways of thinking and behaving began to spread into the general population. The fact that many cities are not as prosperous as they once were only makes them more vulnerable, the dissolution of social order more likely, and the potential damage they can do to the rest of us more severe. With the decline of both prosperity and order in cities, the twin pillars of the bourgeois culture upon which American society is built will become increasingly suspect.

While I share the view that finds cities to be places where crucial elements of our culture originate and are refined, I do not believe that cities are places where only the less esteemed parts of our way of life are produced. Persons who live in cities, prosperous or otherwise, are capable of maintaining a way of life that is full, orderly, and rich with meaning. These elements of our culture, no less than the sordid parts, are shared with the rest of us who do not live in cities.

We Made an Urban World

If Americans are a bourgeois people who practice an urban way of life, then the world they make for themselves should reflect their essential urbanity and bourgeois character. They should be seen as a people who are not just liberal or conservative, but a little bit of both. Their covenant of comity should reveal both liberal and conservative themes, and the community of believers which embraces that covenant should consist of groups which act in both liberal and conservative ways.

Most persons who worry about such matters would not agree with me. These social philosophers and scientists are called "communalists." They see the world in pretty clear-cut ways; and we should not be surprised that these ways have a distinctly leftward and rightward slant to them. Liberal and conservative communalists do agree on some issues, and these points have been identified nicely by Peter J. Steinberger. First, like de Tocqueville they all are great believers in persons going out and doing things together. Second, whatever these persons do together will be done better and achieve more good when it is accomplished in "smaller, geographically distinct social entities."[38]

On most everything else that goes into making a good community, liberal and conservative communalists disagree.

> What distinguishes the more conservative variant is its veneration of community traditions and its willingness to tolerate and even encourage class-based forms of political organization internal to the community. Whereas the left vision sees community action as a liberating process in which neighborhood members can participate on an equal footing to develop fresh solutions to old problems, the conservative vision sees it as a process of rediscovery in which traditional approaches and ties are uncovered and nurtured under the leadership of a steward class.[39]

The disagreement between liberals and conservatives over the best way to create good communities may have emerged in the eighteenth and nineteenth centuries. This was when philosophers were trying to imagine how new citizens would fit into an entirely new political world organized around individual liberties and national governments. However, the earliest communalists trace their intellectual origins to the ancient Greeks, and especially to Plato whose discourse on the *Laws* is our first treatise on urban planning.

Plato drew his ideas for what a good city would look like from observations he made of life in Sparta and Athens. It is clear that he preferred a well-organized and orderly society which was not influenced too much by outside forces. He offered extended discussions on the place of property and family in this city. He talked about the several arms of local government and what they did. He also paid a great deal of attention to the administration of justice, education, religion, and the work of a "nocturnal" council of elders who served as the city's memory and arbiters of taste and changing customs.

Plato was keen on customs, festivals, and ceremonies that everyone in the city could observe and embrace. Communal dances and meal taking were especially favored. These routine occasions for doing things together surely would have helped the natives remember who they were and how to get along. However, Plato apparently thought them just as important as devices for integrating non-natives into the life of the city and for keeping the distinctive peoples residing there from spinning out of the community's well-defined orbit.

Like the religion of the Greeks, the city itself "was always a complex of beliefs and practices only loosely related to one another and of diverse provenance – some local in origin, some imported from elsewhere under the influence of war, trade, or political alliances." To be sure, each city "had its patron deities whom it especially revered." Nevertheless, "within the city each tribe and clan had its own special deity or hero, with its separate rites and ceremonies of worship," and Plato thought it important to preserve "every available feeling of veneration in his citizens, no matter whence obtained."[40] Each group could find a place in Plato's city, as long as its members were willing to accept certain customs, rites, and beliefs that were supposed to belong to everyone and to follow them when the occasion called for it.

There is no doubt that some practices and ideas were to be given more attention in Plato's city than were others. Nor was everyone free to determine what his or her own path would be. There was a social hierarchy in the city. Decisions made by persons on its higher rungs had a great deal to do with how persons on the lower rungs went through each day. The influence of those higher persons and groups was put in practice every day and readily observed by those beneath them. If breaches in faith and practice were witnessed, there were institutions that could help put things right.

The world as it is imagined by communitarian thinkers whose politics are more liberal than Plato's is a much different place. Society has to be built from the bottom up, and equality rather than fealty would seem to be the cardinal principle underlying all their construction efforts. To the extent that the members of a community agree on anything, they will reach their accommodations on the basis of mutual respect and their adherence to principles of fair play. The institutions that human beings make to conduct their affairs are intended to teach them "how to participate peacefully in a competitive society of co-equal individuals." Their culture may be "animated by dreams of monetary success in the competitive marketplace but is softened by an ethic of generalized social trust and a pervasive interactive style that combines 'niceness' with moral minimalism."[41] Persons are generally left alone to do what they want to do, and they are not subjected to much public scrutiny. Nothing is handed down by one's betters. Everything important grows up from what we would call the "grassroots" level.

In a world imagined by liberal communalists, individuals have much more authority and responsibility to figure things out for themselves. Their sense of worth is not rooted in a system of fixed beliefs or learned through routines and relations that were set by others some time ago. No less a proponent of this view than Philip Selznick puts the individual, not the group, at the center of all social relations and discussions about the community. Indeed, he pays much more attention in his treatise *The Moral Commonwealth* to the development of individual talents, commitment, and personal feelings, self-regard, self-preservation, and personal

morality in the making of good communities than he does to the organization of roles and the existence of rules in these same places. Liberal
communities leave much more room for individual choice and varieties
of belief and practice than would be left in the kind of community that
a conservative would build.[42]

This does not mean that liberal communtarians hold nothing sacred.
It is just that they emphasize principles that are different from those advo-
cated by more conservative persons. Selznick, for instance, believes that
civility is the most important value that a community's members can
embrace. It is at the heart of their acceptance of themselves as a diverse
people. Civility also is at the center of their willingness and ability to
tolerate the introduction of new ideas and ways of behaving to their
world. Finally, it protects the autonomy of every person in the community by giving them the social space they need to develop their peculiar
interests and to express their unique views.[43] A world that conforms to
such principles may be a bit impersonal, but it would not turn many individuals away.

If liberals advocate civility as their guiding principle, this does not
mean that conservative thinkers would build a world around the idea of
being discourteous. The virtues that they would embrace are humility
and loyalty. These ideas fit better in a world that "expresses devotion
and demands integration," just as Selznick says.[44] It would be a world
that does not make as much room for new persons, ideas, or ways of behaving. In much the same way as Plato thought to keep the noise and
confusion down to an acceptable level in Greek cities, conservative
communalists would push persons to follow established rules in more
modern cities. Individuals either would have less personal freedom in
this version of the world or they would have to pay more attention to
the wishes and needs of the other persons around them whenever they
acted.

Liberal and conservative communtarians see the world differently. Yet
their disagreements over the best way to make viable and vital communities have helped us identify three problems that the members of any
community must address, if they are to build a social world that
works and lasts. The first involves the matter of how open or closed the
membership of the community is to be. A community with an exclusive
membership emphasizes the idea of *belonging*. One whose membership
is more open or inclusive embraces the idea of *sharing*.

Town leaders in colonial America exercised a great deal of control over
who was allowed to move into their community on a full-time basis. This
practice was consistent with their wish to maintain strict control over the
local economy, but it also played to their interest in keeping town society
orderly. There were other ways in which townsmen and city dwellers

tried to ensure that everyone knew who was a permanent resident and who was not. Well into the nineteenth century, for instance, the names of persons staying in the local hotels of some cities were published in the daily newspaper. Long after this practice was ended some newspapers still noted the leave-taking and return of some of the city's more prominent citizens. These are all examples of how city residents drew a line around themselves in order to show who belonged in their world and who did not.

City dwellers were not always interested in restricting who could live and work among them. Sometimes they would go in the opposite direction and show how welcoming they could be to strangers and newcomers. There are cities today, albeit smaller ones, and towns that still invite new residents to join older ones in regular meetings or some kind of communal feast once a year. Several towns outside of Boston, for instance, still have active "newcomers clubs" where more established residents introduce newer ones to the town and tell them "where to eat, who's available for babysitting, and all sorts of wonderful things like that." These clubs serve as "modern-day Welcome Wagons" which help to integrate persons into the life of their new town.[45] Some cities in the past also have sponsored trips that sent local businessmen to distant places in search of more workers or persons who were willing to relocate their company. In these and many other ways, the residents of cities demonstrated their willingness to be more inclusive and to share part of what they had with persons they did not yet know. Like many of the discussions about belonging and sharing in cities, these focused on the part that transients and migrants played in the creation of an urban way of life.

A second problem that all communities have to face is of how tightly their members want to regulate and monitor each other's behavior. A community that promotes *piety* expects persons to conduct themselves in accordance with a prescribed set of rules. One that practices *tolerance* is more accepting of novel types of behavior and has a looser set of standards by which the acceptability of any act is judged.

Discussions about piety and tolerance in cities usually are considered in relation to deviant or illegal activities. We are accustomed to thinking of cities as places where persons are allowed to do most anything they want, and there certainly are many illustrations of city residents being tolerant. Well into the nineteenth century, for instance, celebrations around holidays like Christmas and New Year's Eve were expected to turn rowdy, and this behavior was accepted up to a point. On the other hand, behavior such as prostitution and gambling which usually is deemed illegal has often been practiced openly and with the support of local officials and businessmen. The same can be said for violence that has been directed intermittently against certain despised classes such as slaves, sailors, and immigrants.

At the same time, it is not hard to find many examples of city residents acting piously or showing their displeasure with persons who do not conduct themselves properly. Local newspapers still publish the names of persons who have been arrested for committing some crimes. It was the case in many cities during the nineteenth century, however, that the names and addresses of all local miscreants were published in the daily newspaper along with a summary of their misdeeds.

Piety also could be demonstrated in other ways. Earlier in this century, for instance, young persons in Chicago and several other eastern cities formed something called "slow clubs" whose purpose, one report noted, was to "wrap a wet blanket around flaming youth." A story published in the *Idaho Falls Post* on March 2, 1925 declared that the Chicago youths planned "activities in dramatics and debate," but barred "petting and drinking." Smoking, on the other hand, was "left to individual choice." The practice of piety in this case, and in many others that we shall see, had nothing to do with illicit acts.

Alluded to in the third problem that all communities face is the classic distinction between *public* and *private behavior*. A community that extols the virtues of privacy will promote behavior that attends to one's own person or to a smaller, more homogeneous group. A community that pays more attention to the impact that actions have on more than one's own group or person is thought to promote public roles and behavior.

The idea that one could characterize a political or social ethos as being either *public regarding* or *private regarding* was first advanced by Richard Hofstadter in his book *The Age of Reform*. It was elaborated upon a few years later by Edward Banfield and James Q. Wilson in their own classic work entitled *City Politics*.[46] Their notion was that native Protestant and middle-class leaders practiced a brand of politics that played to broad city-wide audiences, while immigrant politicians paid more attention to the particular interests of their group and class. Although I think their view overstates the extent to which each of those groups played only one type of politics, I believe that the distinction between *public* and *private regarding behavior* is invaluable and something about which all communitarian thinkers worry.

Historians and social scientists who write about the changing role of women in urban life often frame their observations in terms of the distinction between private and public behavior. They usually consider what transpired at home, for example, as a strictly private affair. Once women moved out into the workforce, however, their behavior and roles often were tied to more public themes and associations. How early in the history of the United States women began to act in more public regarding ways and what they did once they moved beyond hearth and home is a good deal more complicated than social scientists have led us to believe, and the picture we get of their early civic activities tells a far more promising story about the vitality of civic customs in American towns and cities.

In more general terms, the kind of community one ends up with is determined in large part by the way its members apply each of these different themes in their dealings with each other and outsiders. Members of any community end up asking themselves three questions. Are we to be selective in whom we let into our community, or are we more welcoming? Will we adhere to a strict code of behavior, or are we willing to ignore and even accept behavior that violates our standards? Finally, is our behavior more heedful of particular individuals and groups, or does it play to a broader array of groups and interests?

A great deal of our current unease about the future can be traced to these different ways of addressing the three problems that all communities face. We may indeed live in a time when there is no clear answer to these questions. Indecisiveness and moral uncertainty might be the guiding principles of our age and in our communities. The sociologist Emile Durkheim referred to such a state as "anomie" or being without clear rules, and it points to a society whose members are having a difficult time making up their minds about where they are going and how to get there.[47] If we are living in such an age, and there are a lot of persons who think we are, then we may be suffering because we just have too many ways of thinking about who we want to be and how we are supposed to act.

Moments like this, the late political scientist Sam Sharp was fond of saying, are "hopeless, but not serious." We find a way to push through them, and that way usually turns out to work well enough. In our own time, there are thoughtful persons who are trying to find a way to break through all the dissonant noise and confusion around us. They speak with strong voices and offer the kind of clear and unambiguous vision for a world that we will need, if we are to be a whole people and have communities which are solid. Some of these persons we know are called "liberals." The others are called "conservatives."

We found that liberals and conservatives usually disagree with each other on how to build a good community. There is enough similarity among the representatives of each camp, however, to allow us to describe the essential features of *liberal* and *conservative communalism*. The easiest way to do this is to compare the two camps on the basis of the answers they would give to the three problems I posed earlier. Liberal communalists seem to favor a world in which *sharing, tolerance,* and *privacy* are the most important principles. Conservative communalists prefer a world organized around the ideas of *belonging, piety*, and *public regardfulness*.[48]

Individual liberals and conservatives may fudge and fiddle around the edges with respect to their views on such matters. However, as we shall see, their positions on how to build a better world are remarkably consistent. They also are remarkably at odds with each other. If we are living in an age of uncertain rules and standards, then liberal and conservative communalists provide us with no comfortable way to push ourselves through it. We have to do things one way or the other, and the champions of each camp say that the other's approach is bound to lead us to perdition. They do not make it easy to choose a path that will help us build better communities.

If the disagreements between liberal and conservative commentators can be likened to a contest, then one would have to say that the advantage thus far has gone to persons holding more liberal views. Their particular approach to the world – one that emphasizes *sharing, tolerance*, and *private regarding behavior* – has shaped the way that generations of scientists and moralists have looked at our urban world and tried to fix its broken parts. A more conservative approach to understanding and fixing that same world – one that would emphasize *belonging, piety*, and *public regarding behavior* – has been favored much less by academic and lay writers or contemporary reformers.

To find some common ground between these different ways of viewing the world I think we would be wise to follow Durkheim's lead again. After all, he was among the first social scientists to draw our attention to the persistence of traditions in our all-too modern world. It also is Durkheim who first raised the possibility that the fragmentation and apparent lack of solidarity we see in the world masks the work of a deeper and quite effective set of beliefs and customs that really hold us together. Indeed, it is these deeply embedded beliefs and customs that helps us to be a moral people. "Men," he observed, "cannot live together without … making mutual sacrifices, without tying themselves to one another with strong durable bonds. Every society is a moral society."[49] That would include our own.

If we take this idea seriously, then we should look for ways in which men and women might join more liberal and conservative approaches to making an urban way of life, or at least hold open the possibility that they do this during the course of their daily lives. Should we find that human beings actually bring liberal and conservative themes into their lives it would mean that they have found ways to reconcile views of the world that are not supposed to be blended or work well together in practice. It may be, of course, that much of the complexity and confusion associated with an urban way of life can be attributed to such a blending of liberal and conservative ways of putting a world together. Insofar as the primary contribution of cities is to provide a forum in which the past and future may be brought together in something approaching a fruitful dialogue, however, then the mixing of liberal and conservative ways of community building is not only predictable but also necessary for the smooth and effective working of our whole society.

The city thus is both a laboratory and a stage where the hardest work of putting a culture together and making a people takes place. "Every culture has its characteristic drama," Lewis Mumford told us more than a half-century ago. "It chooses from the sum total of human possibilities certain acts and interests, certain processes and values, and endows them with special significance; provides them with a setting; organizes rites and ceremonies; excludes from the circle of dramatic response a thousand of the daily acts which, while they remain part of the 'real' world, are not active agents in the drama itself. The stage on which this drama is enacted ... is the city."[50] Cities and the way of life created there really matter, to all of us. The remainder of this book is dedicated to discovering why that is the case and how we make an orderly and moral world for ourselves inside cities.

NOTES

1 Louis Wirth, "Urbanism as a Way of Life," *American Journal of Sociology*, Volume 44, 1938, pp. 1–24; R. N. Norris, *Urban Sociology* (New York: Praeger, 1968), pp. 15–38, 62–100.

2 David Karp, Gregory Stone, and William Yoels, *Being Urban: A Sociology of City Life* (New York: Praeger, 1991), pp. 20–44.

3 Peter S. Hawkins, "Introduction," in Peter S. Hawkins (ed.), *Civitas: Religious Interpretations of the City* (Atlanta, GA: Scholars Press, 1986), p. xi; John A. Agnew, John Mercer, and David E. Sopher (eds.), *The City in Cultural Context* (Boston: Allen & Unwin, 1984).

4 M. P. Baumgartner, *The Moral Order of a Suburb* (New York: Oxford University Press, 1988).

5 Sara Rimer, "A Hometown Feels Less Like Home," *The New York Times*, March 6, 1996.

6 Ibid.

7 Ibid.

8 Arthur Herman, *The Idea of Decline in Western History* (New York: Free Press, 1997).

9 Arthur Schlesinger, Jr., *The Disuniting of America* (New York: W.W. Norton, 1992); Michael J. Sandel, *Democracy's Discontent* (Cambridge, MA: Harvard University Press, 1996); Edward Countryman, *Americans: A Collision of Histories* (New York: Hill & Wang, 1997); Seymour Martin

Lipset, *American Exceptionalism: A Double-Edged Sword* (New York: W. W. Norton, 1997); Charles Lindholm and John A. Hall, "Is the United States Falling Apart?," *Deadalus*, Volume 126, Number 2, Spring 1997, pp. 183–209.

10 Fareed Zakaria, "An Optimist's Lament," *The New York Times Review of Books*, March 30, 1997.

11 No one expresses these ideas better among contemporary writers than Richard Sennett. See his books *The Fall of Public Man: On the Social Psychology of Capitalism* (New York: Random House, 1978) and *The Conscience of the Eye: The Design and Social Life of Cities* (New York: Alfred A. Knopf, 1990) for good examples of this line of reasoning and style of writing. The logic of this argument will be laid out in greater detail below as we explore precisely what it is about cities that is supposed to make them unlikely sites for creating viable and vital communities.

12 Andrew Lees, *Cities Perceived: Urban Society in European and American Thought, 1820-1940* (New York: Columbia University Press, 1985), pp. 5–6.

13 Ibid.

14 Wirth, "Urbanism as a Way of Life"; Robert E. Park, "The City: Suggestions for the Investigation of Human Behavior in the Urban Environment," in Robert E. Park, Ernest W. Burgess, and Roderick D. McKenzie, *The City* (Chicago: University of Chicago Press, 1925), pp. 1–46; Robert E. Park, "The Urban Community as a Spatial Pattern and a Moral Order," in Ernest W. Burgess, (ed.), *The Urban Community* (Chicago: University of Chicago Press, 1926), pp. 3–18; Gerald D. Suttles, *The Social Order of the Slum: Ethnicity and Territory in the Inner City* (Chicago: University of Chicago Press, 1968); Joseph T. Howell, *Hard Living on Clay Street: Portraits of Blue Collar Families* (Prospect Heights, IL: Waveland Press, 1973); William Kornblum, *Blue Collar Community* (Chicago: University of Chicago Press, 1974); Sally Engle Merry, *Urban Danger: Life in a Neighborhood of Strangers* (Philadelphia: Temple University Press, 1981); Scott Cummings, *Left Behind in Rosedale: Race Relations and the Collapse of Community Institutions* (Boulder, CO: Westview Press, 1998); John Schneider, "Urban Growth, Community Change: Studies in the Nineteenth-Century US City," *Journal of Urban History*, Volume 15, Number 1, November 1988, pp. 87–97.

15 Edward Winslow Martin, *Secrets of the Great City: A Work Descriptive of the Virtues and the Vices, the Mysteries, Miseries and Crimes of New York City* (Philadelphia: Jones, Brothers, 1868), p. 552.

16 Lees, *Cities Perceived*.

17 Martin, *Secrets of the Great City*, pp. 496, 241, 41.

18 Ibid., pp. 168–9, 176–9, 225–30, and 233–8.

19 Ibid., pp. 252–76.

20 Ibid., pp. 285–317, 373–99, 409, 431–7, 446, 453–4, 487.

21 Ibid., p. 35.

22 Ibid., pp. 35–8.

23 Zakaria, "An Optimist's Lament"; Christopher Lasch, *The Revolt of the*

Elites and the Betrayal of Democracy (New York: W.W. Norton, 1995), pp. 26, 64, 77–9, 99–101, 121, 127, 131, and 135.

24 The reader should consult three works within the larger volume entitled *Between States and Markets: The Voluntary Sector in Comparative Perspective* (Princeton, NJ: Princeton University Press, 1991) which was edited by Robert Wuthnow. Robert Wuthnow, "The Voluntary Sector: Legacy of the Past, Hope for the Future?" (pp. 3–29) and "Tocqueville's Question Reconsidered: Voluntarism and Public Discourse in Advanced Industrial Societies" (pp. 288–308); and David Harrington Watt, "United States: Cultural Challenges to the Voluntary Sector" (pp. 243–87).

25 Alan Wolfe, *Whose Keeper? Social Science and Moral Obligation* (Berkeley: University of California Press, 1989), p. 2.

26 Peter J. Steinberger, *Ideology and the Urban Crisis* (Albany, NY: State University of New York Press, 1985), p. 29.

27 Ibid., pp. 27–35.

28 Ibid., p. 103.

29 Ibid., p. 104.

30 Wolfe, *Whose Keeper?*

31 Ibid., p. 20.

32 Charles Tilly, *From Mobilization to Revolution* (Reading: Addison-Wesley, 1978); Charles Tilly, Louise Tilly, and Richard Tilly, *The Rebellious Century, 1830–1930* (Cambridge, MA: Harvard University Press, 1975). There are a variety of places one can go for a detailed description of these different schools of thought, and there is considerable variation in the views expressed by persons who are champions of one or the other of these schools of thought. Tilly's discussion of "breakdown" and "solidarity" theories in principle deals only with the likelihood that violence emerges from a society that is coming apart at the seams or rebuilding itself. It is suggestive, however, of a larger division among social scientists who view society generally as being comparatively whole and united or systematically riddled with conflict and subject to dramatic change. It is to this larger division among social philosophers and scientific thinkers that I am addressing my comments. Most of us subscribe to the view that our world is not put together well or holding its center.

33 Richard Hofstadter, *The Progressive Historians* (New York: Alfred A. Knopf, 1969), p. 440.

34 Ibid., p.446.

35 Ibid., pp. 454–5.

36 This view of how Americans have organized their urban way of life effectively splits the difference between those who see society as being comparatively united and those scholars who think society is riddled with conflict and subject to dramatic change. When we look at cities from different countries or periods of history, medieval towns and cities usually are portrayed as places whose social world was well defined and kept whole through a variety of overlapping institutional, ceremonial, and familial ties. There was no denying one's membership in different groups or the obligation to work in behalf of the larger community, no matter what one's rank.

One's fidelity to the community was demonstrated over the course of one's whole life by taking on a number of elected or appointed positions through which the hard and unpaid work of keeping the city up and running was actually accomplished. This arrangement broke down with the passing of the Middle Ages. See: Charles Phythian-Adams, *Desolation of a City: Coventry and the Urban Crisis of the Late Middle Ages* (Cambridge: Cambridge University Press, 1979); Diane Owen Hughes, "Kinsmen and Neighbors in Medieval Genoa," in Harry Miskimin, David Herlihy, and A. L. Udovitch (eds.), *The Medieval City* (New Haven, CN: Yale University Press, 1977), pp. 95–112; and Philip Benedict, "French Cities from the Sixteenth Century to the Revolution: An Overview," in Philip Benedict (ed.), *Cities and Social Change in Early Modern France* (London: Unwin Hyman, 1989), pp. 7–68.

Cities in the modern world are generally portrayed as places where such overlapping and mutually reinforcing ties do not exist or have lost their obligatory hold on us. According to Lewis Mumford in his book *The Culture Of Cities* (New York: Harcourt, Brace, 1938, p. 155), "this contempt for the civic business of the local community, this scorn for the old agents of the common weal, this childish belief in the industrialist ... prepared the way for the un-building of the city. The brakes of tradition and custom were lifted ... there was no limit to congestion ... no standard of order or decency ... only ... profit." "Old neighborhoods ... the social cells of the city, still maintaining some measure of the village pattern, become vestigial," Mumford went on to argue in *The City in History* (New York: Harcourt, Brace & World, 1961). However, the "congestion of the metropolis has tended to suppress or destroy the organic tissue of neighborhoods" leaving them unprotected from the wickedness of ravenous businessmen and powerful government agents (ibid., pp. 543 , 552). See also Donald Miller, "Lewis Mumford: Urban Historian, Urban Visionary," *Journal of Urban History*, Volume 18, Number 3, May 1992, pp. 280–307.

37   Stanley Elkins and Eric McKitrick, *The Hofstadter Aegis: A Memorial* (New York: Alfred A. Knopf, 1974), p. 310.

38   Steinberger, *Ideology and the Urban Crisis*, pp. 66–8.

39   Ibid., p. 78.

40   Glenn R. Morrow, *Plato's Cretan City: A Historical Interpretation of the Laws* (Princeton: Princeton University Press, 1993), pp. 402–3.

41   Lindholm and Hall, "Is the United States Falling Apart?," pp. 194–6.

42   Amitai Etzioni, *The Spirit of Community* (New York: Touchstone, 1994); Amitai Etzioni (ed.), *New Communitarian Thinking: Persons, Virtues, Institutions, and Communities* (Charlottesville, VA: University Press of Virginia, 1995); Stephen Mulhall and Adam Swift, *Liberals and Communtarians* (Cambridge, MA: Blackwell Publishers, 1992).

43   Philip Selznick, *The Moral Commonwealth: Social Theory and the Promise of Community* (Berkeley: University of California Press, 1992), pp. 390–1.

44   Ibid., p. 387.

45   Sacha Pfeiffer, "Many Clubs Not Just for Newcomers Anymore," *Boston Globe*, August 24, 1997.

46 Richard Hofstadter, *The Age of Reform* (New York: Alfred A. Knopf, 1955); Edward C. Banfield and James Q. Wilson, *City Politics* (New York: Vintage Books, 1963).

47 Emile Durkheim, *The Division of Labor in Society*, translated by George Simpson (Glencoe, IL: Free Press, 1947 [1893]).

48 In commenting on the distinction I make between liberals and conservatives, Stephan Thernstrom is certainly right when he observes that I am ignoring many of the fine distinctions that divide members of these respective camps *and* the ways in which their ideas have changed over time. Whether we are looking at the illiberalism of contemporary liberals or the advantages that would be conferred upon individuals under a libertarian brand of conservatism, the fact remains that it would be difficult today to find "pure" examples of liberal and conservative communalism of the sort that I am describing. Maybe the distinction would have held up well in 1790, but not 200 years later. Fair enough, perhaps, but contemporary social philosophers who want the world to be built with such "old fashioned" ideas in mind still make them the centerpiece of their arguments about how to build a better America. One of my major chores in this book is to show each of them just how much of the way they like to look at the world has actually managed to worm itself into the way we live every day.

49 Durkheim, *The Division of Labor in Society*, p. 228.

50 Mumford, *The Culture Of Cities*, p. 60.

3

On Small Towns and Their "Citified" Ways

Most places that become cities do not start out that way. They begin as towns. And no matter how urbane their founders may have been, townsmen do not think or act like city dwellers. At least that is what we have been taught to believe.

An urban way of life is supposed to be something practiced by city dwellers, not villagers. Persons who live in smaller places may not be immune to the influence of big-city customs and values, but their way of life is expected to look and feel different from anything experienced in cities. Inasmuch as cities usually grow from smaller places into much bigger places, however, it stands to reason that many elements of an urban way of life might have sprung from more modest towns and villages.[1]

How Like a City

Carl Bridenbaugh, the great chronicler of colonial American town life, showed how village society had already taken on many features of what he called an "urban existence" by the end of the seventeenth century. What he had to say about those small towns bears repeating.

> In the villages representatives of different Old World nationalities lived in close proximity, at New York in sufficient numbers to produce a varied and conflicting culture, and at Boston and Charles Town to encourage a sense of superiority in the dominant group. Distinctions between rich and poor ... had also appeared. Society in the villages was no longer in 1690 a simple democracy of small property holders, but a definite hierarchy of commercial, clerical or official aristocracy, tradesmen, artisans, common laborers and slaves.

Religious uniformity was giving way before the appearance of sectarianism or of complete unbelief, and the discipline exercised by an established or quasi-established church was having to meet the challenge of a more attractive secular life. The joys of the marketplace or tavern contested with the church for the soul of the town-dweller.

In general, the close associations and sociability of town life, and the contacts ... with the thought and manners of Europe made for an awareness of new ideas, a willingness to consider innovations, and an opportunity to indulge individual tastes, unfound elsewhere in the colonies at this time.[2]

The emergence of more clearly defined classes of workers reflected the array of jobs that needed to be done in towns as compared to more rural settings. It also spoke to the degree of wealth that was being generated in colonial towns and to the unequal way in which that wealth was distributed among the different classes of workers. The economies of colonial villages were beginning to take on features that later would be attached to the emergence of industrial cities, and they already were well tied into a worldwide system of trade that revolved around the great European colonial powers.

There were important differences, to be sure, between the economies of colonial villages and those of nineteenth-century cities. At the risk of stating the obvious, the economies of seventeenth-century towns were much smaller and less complex than those of industrial cities. Villages also had not yet thrown off the "system of rigid control of all trade, industry and labor within their bounds" they had inherited from their "mother towns." That would happen soon enough. Until then, however, colonial town leaders took great care in overseeing the growth and development of their local economy, monitoring closely who was allowed into the town to work, and helping to determine the price of different goods. Nevertheless, according to Bridenbaugh, colonial townsfolk already had learned some of the "formulae for modern wealth" that would emerge full-blown in nineteenth-century cities.[3]

There was sufficient wealth available in colonial towns and it was spread broadly enough to support the emergence of a service industry built around commerce and retail trading in more specialized goods, particularly those that came from foreign lands. Furthermore, such industry that existed was geared to satisfying the demands of traders and their customers, some of whom lived in more remote areas outside of town. Just as familiar to us today were other features of town economies that were germinating well before the American Revolution. These included being tied into the world market and the development of a rudimentary finance and investment system.[4]

The similarities between colonial towns and more contemporary cities did not end with their economies. There were other indications that village life was taking on a more urban character long before heavy industry came to American cities. Although the pull of traditional customs and of institutions like the church generally remained strong for the majority of townsfolk, there were many persons who did not follow strict rules or embrace biblical admonitions against bad behavior. Part of the reason may have been that some religious groups were more tolerant than others in what they allowed their members to do. Still, there was no doubt that certain vices like gambling, taking alcoholic beverages, and visiting "disorderly houses" for illicit sexual encounters were becoming more widely practiced by persons from each of the town's several classes.

Some types of disorderly behavior, on the other hand, were more likely to be engaged in by the town's less well-to-do residents and visitors. Assaults and robberies became more common in the years preceding the American Revolution, and mob activity was a frequent occurrence. Observers attribute these events to tensions generated by the social cleavages in colonial towns and the animosity against better-off townsfolk felt by persons whose position in colonial towns was not at all secure. On these occasions, Bridenbaugh says, the "inferior sort" acted out against the aristocrats "who now lived, economically, socially, morally, and in many cases religiously, apart from the rest of the community, while continuing to control it in their own interests."[5] The social and physical spaces that were supposed to separate persons in industrial cities and make relations between the city's several classes tense apparently existed inside colonial towns as well.

Whatever antagonism less well-to-do colonial townsfolk felt toward their betters, however, usually was not expressed openly. When these feelings were made public, they often took the form of short-lived food riots in which local residents objected to the prices they were charged for certain commodities. Another popular way in which persons of less stature made their feelings about town leaders clear was to mock aristocratic customs and displays of authority during parades and on certain ceremonial occasions.

While such displays of incivility concerned many colonial townsfolk, Bridenbaugh found this behavior to be more a nuisance than a threat to the basic economic and social order of colonial settlements. Crimes and disorder, he thought, were "more the natural expression of a rude and lusty populace ... than an indication of widespread viciousness or brutality." Besides, "much of the disorder was confined to the rowdy society of the waterfronts" and crimes such as burglaries and pocket-picking were seen as "the natural resort of the more unfortunate elements of town society."[6] They did not undermine the basic routines of town life. Nor did they challenge the beliefs upon which those routines were built.

There were other reasons why disorderly and even illegal behavior by some town residents and visitors did not disturb colonial town leaders a great deal. Some of these same persons, after all, were profiting from illegal enterprises themselves and could hardly be expected to condemn too loudly the outrages intermittently visited upon their towns by drunken sailors and disobedient slaves. More importantly, perhaps, the vast majority of town residents "still observed the laws necessary for their harmonious dwelling together" and could be counted on to suppress especially egregious displays of behavior when the occasion called for it.[7]

The general prosperity of colonial towns kept down the level of tension that might otherwise have existed between different social classes by providing some hope that persons could improve their situation and enough examples of individuals doing so to affirm their confidence. Other problems related to meeting the needs of town residents or simply keeping up with the physical growth of these settlements inspired a civic consciousness in private organizations and public officials alike. It also prompted them to undertake good works that were supposed to make life more secure in cities than it was in less developed places.[8]

Some portion of the groups that townsfolk created for themselves drew members from several of the respectable classes in colonial society, and this helped to keep the town population more united. These organizations also provided persons who heretofore had not enjoyed the privilege of acting in concert on behalf of a common goal to mimic the ways of better organized and positioned town residents. Among these groups was the first women's club in America, which was formed in Charles Town in 1707. It featured political debates among its members, and Bridenbaugh reported that its discussions sometimes grew quite heated. There also were a number of leisure activities that provided opportunities for persons from several social classes to do things together. Indeed, many clubs that would become political organizations during the American Revolution had their start in taverns frequented by both well-to-do and more modest patrons.[9]

Apparent from the earliest days of colonial town life, then, were many of the social and economic "seeds" that would blossom into a full-fledged urban way of life well before cities became industrial centers in the nineteenth century. Neither the economies nor the social habits of colonial townsfolk were entirely homegrown. American villages were well connected to the outside world, particularly through trade and other commercial activities. Persons earned a livelihood doing a variety of tasks, and they could spend their money on consumer goods that were becoming more available through legal and illegal trading arrangements with that outside world.

Life may have been far from perfect, but many persons found it advantageous to live in towns. These settlements already were acquiring a diverse population, and some groups showed signs of developing a nascent ethnic identity. Social class and religious divisions had appeared. Yet persons were able to soften the hard edges of colonial society at least a little bit by participating in a host of voluntary organizations and leisure activities that appealed to persons from different social classes or groups. All these were early signs that an urban way of life was taking root in colonial villages and towns. It was, at least by Bridenbaugh's account, a society that was "more cooperative and social, less individualistic in its outlook toward problems of daily life ... less aggressively independent than the society of frontier America."[10] It was an urban society whose members were dedicated to prosperity and to conducting their affairs in orderly ways.

Colonial townsfolk began spreading that way of life to new areas and sharing it with additional groups even as they were establishing it for themselves. The diffusion of urban ways was accomplished differently for early suburbs and new settlements that "hived off" from more established towns; and pushing the finger of urban civility into the night proved every bit as intriguing and potentially harrowing as when it reached out to touch the wilderness far to the west of the original coastal settlements. In each case, however, the experiment took hold. Pioneers of various sorts succeeded in extending bourgeois principles and urban ways into new and uncharted territories.

The parties who established suburbs during the first half of the eighteenth century generally came from well-connected and financially secure families. They were leaders in their respective towns, or at least they had profited handsomely from earlier business ventures in commerce or real estate. These persons might have owned country estates that the town gradually grew outward to meet and incorporate. Alternatively, they may have bought large pieces of land on the outskirts of town with the idea of dividing them into smaller parcels and either selling or leasing them to less prosperous individuals or even artisans who sought work and lower living expenses farther away from the town center.[11] Whether these places eventually were incorporated as separate municipalities or were recaptured by a town as it grew toward them is not especially important. It only matters that their development was promoted by persons embracing the very types of bourgeois sentiments and ways of acting which inspired the building of towns in the first place.

If the creation of suburbs was a logical and friendly solution to the problem of congestion near the center of towns, the development of new towns some distance from an original settlement was often prompted by less congenial feelings. Early towns, as I have indicated, were tightly organized and intimate. Life in close quarters created understandable tensions among family members and between different families. While disagreements rarely erupted into fights, "petty hostilities, bickering, property-line disputes, and verbal violence" often led to more formal actions involving the disposition of property, debts, and trespassing charges against one's neighbors. Perhaps economic prosperity, oddly enough, also served to undermine the communal solidarity of early towns. Populations were swelling, and there simply was not enough land to go around. Furthermore, the medieval-inspired habit of fixing wages and prices was quickly eroding under the weight of chronic labor short-ages and competition among merchants. "For all these reasons," Richard Lingeman has argued, "the covenanted utopian town founded by a homogeneous group ... on land given them by the colonial legislature gradually became obsolete."[12] It was simply easier to allow persons to found a new town than to imperil the harmony of the established village by unleashing these feelings upon the entire community for too long.

The revolution against Great Britain changed a great deal in America. One of its more lasting effects on community life was to promote the development of political sectarianism and voluntary associations in places other than the established coastal towns. Urban society was there-by diffused into more rural areas, and newer towns became subject to the same cultural influences found in places like Boston or New York. It also was shared with persons who heretofore had not been able to participate in community affairs. "In the past," Richard D. Brown has said, "such urban society as existed in the countryside had been limited to a very thin layer of elite individuals. Now the proliferation of voluntary association comprehended every social group." A good example of this, after 1790, was the development of voluntary associations exclusively by women or in league with men.[13]

Voluntary associations not only became more numerous and demo-cratic in their membership but also more varied in their mission. Organizations were formed to deal with charity and educational work. Some groups also were dedicated to meeting a host of civic needs like fire protection and political matters. There were many occupational groups and a good number of associations dedicated to worship and fraternal rituals. Also noteworthy were the number of organizations that were founded after the American Revolution whose geographic ambitions stretched beyond the local town to include the county, state, region, or nation as a whole. The models for these organizations were fashioned in larger towns, but they quickly spread into more rural areas and the "hived" villages away from the coast.[14]

The insinuation of bourgeois ideas and customs into new towns had its counterpart inside existing towns as more persons gradually populated the night and introduced habits and ideas similar to those practiced in daylight hours. While this activity greatly accelerated during the nineteenth century, the first signs of bourgeois ways taking over the night appeared in eighteenth-century towns. "With each new year," Carl Bridenbaugh reported, "more men and women went out after dark, and some measure of protection had to be accorded them." This meant that constables had to be more vigilant and streets needed to be lighted. In pursuit of this latter end some "public-spirited citizens" of Philadelphia introduced a few lamps to city streets in 1749. This voluntary effort grew into a more substantial act passed by the colonial assembly in 1751 for the purposes of "enlightening the streets, lanes, and alleys ... and for raising money on the inhabitants" for that purpose.[15] Tax-supported lighting in Boston came a bit later. In 1772 the town Selectmen considered public lighting because so many persons were going out at night "on calls of friendship, humanity, business, or pleasure" and needed protection from "scenes of lewdness and debauchery which are so frequently committed with impunity at present." Some 310 lamps were lit on Boston's streets for the first time two years later.[16]

As with the founding of suburbs, this bourgeois invasion was led by more elite persons who had sufficient money and time to expand their shopping and recreational horizons beyond the daylight hours. The lighting would spread to small towns and into additional parts of cities during the nineteenth century as more individuals could enjoy leisure time after a day at work and they had more money to spend. The night as such was less a wilderness than a logical and readily available point of embellishment for bourgeois ideas and customs.[17] The persons who colonized the nights of eighteenth-century European cities and American towns were the first edge of a bourgeois revolution that already had been firmly planted in daylight hours. They pushed individuals and activities deemed unworthy for inclusion under the tenets of their American creed into corners of the night and certain warrens of the poor and disreputable. The progressive elaboration of that bourgeois revolution by less-than-wealthy persons in nineteenth-century cities stands as testimony to the soundness of its principles and their appeal to a broad array of city residents and visitors.

When Americans settled real frontier areas they were not alone. They did it as townsfolk rather than individual farmers or traders. Indeed, as historian Richard C. Wade has said, "the towns were the spearheads of the American frontier." They were "planted as forts or trading posts far in advance of the line of settlement," and "they held the West for the approaching population."[18] Places like Pittsburgh, Cincinnati, and St

Louis owed their early success to commerce and grew quickly in response to improvements made in long-distance transportation, most especially by way of the steamboat and the efficient trade it brought to what was then the American West. So rapid was their advancement that these pioneer towns were developing their own manufacturing base by the first decade of the nineteenth century and their own suburbs by the third decade. Town leaders also carved out vast trading networks in the unsettled West and "built canals and turnpikes and, even before 1830, planned railroads to strengthen their position."[19]

It was not enough to trade well and prosper. These pioneer townsfolk also had to deal with a host of problems already confronted by coastal towns and cities. Here, too, the bourgeois impulse to encourage orderly ways was fully evidenced from the start, and most of their solutions bore a striking resemblance to those developed by their coastal counterparts. Urban ways were distinguished by their corporate character, particularly when it came to addressing town problems.[20]

Town dwellers created different organizations in pioneer towns for many of the same reasons their counterparts had in coastal towns, now becoming cities, during the latter half of the eighteenth century. Municipal officials simply could not keep up with the demands put to them by a growing populace and economy. It was frequently the case that when this happened "private initiative exerted through voluntary associations frequently achieved better solutions."[21]

There were other reasons for townsfolk to come together. Foremost among them was the growing reality that larger and more diverse populations required greater attention and more elaborate devices to keep them working and living together smoothly. It was thought that "a population derived from such distant sources, and so recently brought together, must necessarily exhibit much ... moral diversity." As a result, town leaders feared that their town would not reach its full potential and could be in trouble. To avoid such a fate, it would be necessary for the "customs, manners, and laws" favored by more established residents to be reasserted. Only then would the "necessary cohesion" of the town's population be assured.[22]

Fortunately, there were many institutions like schools and local government, religious bodies, civic organizations, clubs, and sources of recreation and entertainment that brought persons from the town's various social sets together on a routine basis or, in the case of local newspapers, kept them informed of each other's comings and goings. Though inequality remained a fact of frontier town life just as it was in coastal cities, there was much going on inside towns every day to help blur social distinctions and to soften whatever animosities might have existed between persons who were more and less advantaged than their peers.

This did not stop disagreements from occurring or fights from breaking out either within a given social set or between persons from different walks of life. It was by playing together and working on common tasks or by coming under the influence of persons who did, however, that the "necessary cohesion" among town residents was accomplished and an urban way of life secured.

The pervasive influence of bourgeois values was apparent in the development of early suburbs and in new towns that formed when some members of an established village decided to strike out on their own. Driven by the search for less crowded land just outside of existing town borders, persons brought their aspirations for wealth with them and created places that mirrored the organized and orderly ways that had worked so well for them in the communities they had left. The twin goals of prosperity and order also were seen in the ways that town residents filled the night and the undeveloped lands west of the Appalachian Mountains. An urban way of life predicated on those same bourgeois values was extended to more distant or novel venues, where it met with as much success there as it had when it was offered to less faraway and exotic settings.

It was not welcomed in all places. In fact, many suburban townships were created with the idea in mind that their residents might have the advantage of being in the midst of an urban economy and have services every bit as good as those available to city dwellers without having to put up with all the disadvantages of city living and being around city people. Some early suburban developments were so close to cities that they acquired a residential population almost as varied as that of the city next to them, and their residents readily adopted values and customs that were more like those shared by their big-city neighbors. Some of these places eventually were annexed by cities, and they could not avoid urban people and city ways. Later suburbs tended not to have this kind of mix of people and customs, or they successfully resisted being annexed by their big-city neighbor. Many contemporary suburbs have gradually accepted residents more like those living in the cities near them and have begun to experience problems once thought to stop at the city border. Nevertheless, most suburban townships still do not have populations as large and mixed as those of cities and do not feature an urban way of life with all the rich and varied ways of building a community that go with it.

The view of suburbs advanced here is that they are something of a cultural dead end. It is not that the persons who live there are boring or, for that matter, that all suburban towns are cut from the same middle-class mold. Indeed, suburban townships always have been quite varied in their economic profile. They can hold industrial plants just as easily as they can exclusive residential enclaves. Some even have socially and economically mixed resident populations. It is rather that most suburbs have not developed a varied enough population and economic mix to prompt the development of a vital civic culture in which differences and disagreements must be managed openly as a routine matter. Nor are they likely to have experienced a variety of ways of developing a sense of community among their residents.[23]

One noteworthy example of persons being unable to develop a sense of themselves as members of a viable community was provided by William Finnegan, who wrote about the phenomenal growth of Antelope Valley in northern Los Angeles County during the 1980s and 1990s. The combined populations of Lancaster and Palmdale, the Valley's two main towns, was 60,000 in 1980. By 1994, with their populations estimated to be in excess of 220,000, they went from being suburbs to good-sized cities in less than two decades. In the wake of this rapid and unsettling growth, local residents were unable to establish a set of organizations and habits that would enable them to work together and recognize that they shared a common fate. However disruptive this may have been for the adults who lived there, it was awful for a substantial number of younger boys and girls and adolescents who found themselves growing up without much parental supervision and no good set of institutions to fill the void. They broke into cliques and some formed pretty solid gangs that were organized around a hatred of minority persons (i.e. the Nazi Low Riders) or resistance to such beliefs (i.e. the Sharps or "skinheads against racial prejudice"). Unsupervised parties, drug use, homelessness, irregular school attendance, and frequent fights between members of these groups eventually led to the murder of one of the NLRs by a member of the Sharps and the incarceration of one person.

An observer commented that the "kids [were] left with this intense longing for identification" and the "gangs, race nationalism, and all manner of 'beliefs' arose from this longing."[24] The results for children living in these cities that were not yet communities clearly were terrible. However, many of the same feelings about being unattached and the appeal of violent gang fights and drugs have been observed among minority youngsters in suburban areas outside of St Louis that had gone through some population changes but were not as unsettled as the cities in Antelope Valley.[25] What distinguished both sets of places was that local adults and institutional caretakers were unable to create safe routines and effective organizations to help guide many of their children through some difficult times.

It does not always have to end this way. Monterey Park, another medium-sized city just north of Los Angeles, has come to be populated largely by ethnic Chinese who have created an ethnic enclave outside of the city. Almost two-thirds of the 65,000 persons who live there are of Chinese descent, and they dominate the businesses, churches, schools, and neighborhoods of what is sometimes referred to as the country's first "suburban Chinatown."[26] Residents are bound together in a system of filial and social relations that are reinforced by a common ancestral language, commercial ties, and residential proximity. Although some of the Latino and Caucasian families are not especially pleased with this turn of events, Monterey Park is a community in every sense of the word and it has been built on the back of its residents' ethnic heritage. As effective as this community is, however, it lacks the diversity in persons and civic habits that give expression to a fully developed urban way of life.

Some early suburbs had more mixed populations and their members learned how to deal with differences among their residents in an altogether "urban way." That is to say, they became experienced in dealing with community-building efforts sponsored by business leaders and ethnic groups. They also knew how their local governments could help to shape a viable community life by providing good services, political routines that were congenial, and institutions like the schools which promoted good habits in young persons. They certainly saw the power of the marketplace at work as it helped to shape the tastes and loyalties of local residents and solidify their economic and social standing in the town where they lived. Persons who resided in these early suburbs also developed ways of dealing with each other that simultaneously avoided confrontations and invited active engagement with persons unlike themselves. These places often grew to the point of becoming small cities in their own right. Other "streetcar suburbs" ended up being annexed by cities, and whatever mix of rural charm and urban ways their early residents had known quickly shifted in favor of the city. In either case, these "suburban" developments have retained an urban character that the residents of most suburbs have worked hard to avoid.[27]

Small Towns and Their "Citified" Ways

Much the same has been said of life in smaller towns. Yet a closer inspection of their history shows that in many instances their residents have taken on urban ways of dealing with each other and in handling whatever problems they faced. The main difference between small towns, particularly those which are not part of a larger metropolitan area, and suburbs is to be found in the reasons for their development. Smaller towns and villages often were founded with the idea that they would grow into more vigorous social and economic centers. They were supposed to become the next Athens or New York. Richard Lingeman, who has written extensively about these places, has put it this way. For every town that "took off" and became a city, "there were hundreds of small places ... stamped forever with the identity of 'small town'; yet they had been founded with high hopes that they would become cities."[28]

There were hundreds of additional places whose residents could not wring even that much success out of their hard work and had to abandon their town site altogether. Unlike the residents of most American suburbs, then, the leaders of many small towns wanted to develop their communities into city-like places and yearned to adopt urban ways or at least exhibit urban airs. What is amazing is that so many of them succeeded in reaching that goal.

Notwithstanding their apparent backwoods charm and rural locale, many small towns made more room for different types of persons and styles of life than have modern suburban havens. They have been more receptive to urban customs than one might think, and they have coped with problems and disagreements among their residents in ways that can remind one more of life in cities than of life in suburbs. In fact, it might be argued that persons who live in small towns have figured out how to reconcile different ways of "doing" community that city folk and proponents of so-called "planned communities" would be well-advised to study.

Much of the success that small towns enjoy comes with the effective ways their residents manage the tension between communal idealism and economic energy. Put another way, they work hard to balance the need for order with the drive for prosperity in the daily life of their community, and they often succeed in ways that city dwellers do not. The problems they have may be more manageable and the solutions they fashion may be far less ambitious than those found in cities, but that takes nothing away from the willingness of small-town residents to embrace the American creed or their ability to work effectively and creatively with it.

Economic success and social peace were small-town companions. Yet the covenant that joined persons in their pursuit of prosperity and orderly ways had to be loosened so that they might be free to scratch whatever "acquisitive itch" came upon them in the form of new business opportunities.[29] At the same time, economic expansion seems to have awakened in townsfolk a recognition that they needed to soften the differences among themselves and to mute whatever tensions arose as local businesses grew into substantial enterprises and individuals displayed their wealth more openly. This became harder to do as towns became larger and their populations grew more diverse; and it was especially difficult to achieve in western towns whose early residents had little or no experience together prior to their arrival. They were not always successful in easing such pressures, but they worked hard at it and succeeded many more times than they failed.

Some of the techniques they used were homegrown. Others were borrowed, often quite openly, from coastal towns and cities. All were remarkably "citified" in their own way. There were subscription libraries. The general store, a miniature version of big-city department stores, eventually fell before more specialized retailers who sold only one or two lines of goods. Town politics became better organized. Townsfolk held conventions, and they developed a kind of patronage system common in larger cities. Town governments gradually assumed more responsibility for addressing one or another problem faced by local residents. Residents staged ornate communal celebrations and held grand balls, their cultural activities taken as a sign of civic patriotism or, as it was more commonly called, "boosterism."

The town's barter economy was replaced by a money economy, and increasing numbers of persons participated in it. There certainly were more wealthy persons in town than in the past. However, their number was complemented by a rapidly growing "middle class" that included "grocers, merchants, tradesmen, artisans, shopkeepers, clerks, doctors, lawyers, dentists, ministers, teachers, bookkeepers, [and] petit officials." These persons were "respectable, industrious, God-fearing, early-to-bed-and-early-to-rise, heedful of their neighbors' good opinion, bent on making money and avoiding alien ways," precisely the kind of folks to whom one would turn to keep a community in good working order.[30]

Not everyone prospers even when an economy is doing well, of course, and many residents of nineteenth- and twentieth-century towns apparently found it hard to reconcile obvious differences in material wealth with the idea that any person was as good as everybody else. Some persons improved their material standing over the course of a lifetime by changing jobs and marrying above their station. Others slipped in the town's pecking order by doing poor work, being unsatisfactory businessmen, or simply by being not especially good persons.

Individuals with a real or imagined attachment to the town's "middle class" were especially adept at finding ways to display their own limited wealth by purchasing more goods and embellishing their homes so that they looked something like those of persons who really were well-off. More marginal workers and families would have found it difficult to participate in such displays, even in a modest way. Only later in the twentieth century, and perhaps only in substantial places where credit was more readily available or cheaper goods could be acquired through different means, did less prosperous individuals and families have an opportunity to participate in these same rituals.

Economic differences were not the only ones that became evident to town dwellers. More established leaders often resisted the social climbing of middle-class professionals. Some clubs for men and women became more exclusive. Businessmen increasingly used these clubs for purely recreational purposes; but in many towns these groups also helped to keep businessmen from engaging in unpleasant trading practices or provided owners with assistance when they needed it. Denied access to some of these very groups, many middle-class professionals turned their considerable energy and skills to civic projects so that they might acquire social stature which was commensurate with their economic standing in the community.[31] From time to time these persons also managed to push through civic or political changes that more traditional town leaders did not like.

There were other ways in which persons of different social standing might be made to feel less apart from their better-off neighbors. Small towns still practiced "many traditions, rites of passage, ceremonies, and festivals ... marking birth, marriage, manhood and womanhood, death, each celebrated in ritualized ways before the whole community."[32] Education became an important device for keeping the doors to higher social classes open to persons who historically would not have been part of the town's cadre of leaders. Many organizations, even the most prominent ones in some towns, openly embraced members who came from different levels of the local society. A variety of groups would undertake projects to improve the community. Local churches, "hard-pressed to stimulate interest, took to imitating the social clubs with adult and youth fellowship groups for parishioners." There was less talk about redemption and more about the "social gospel." "In short," Lingeman says, "joinerism was added to boosterism in most modern small towns, replacing the informal sociability of an earlier time when people's relationships ... cut across age, class, occupational, and organizational lines and one's knowledge of all other townsfolk ranged over their entire lives."[33]

The idea of small towns as organically whole and nurturing communities did not survive the nineteenth century. In its place emerged a view of town life that was more complex and fragmented, yet able to sustain a people's faith in themselves and in the place they occupied together. Staying true to their town in effect meant that they were keeping faith with themselves. It now was a place where persons had to work harder at getting along and maintaining democratic pretensions within a tradition-bound hierarchy no longer was an option. The "etiquette of deference" which had made it possible in the past for patently unequal persons in the same town to treat each other with respect and kindness had to be recast.[34] "Joinerism" became the practical expression of their casting about in the nineteenth and twentieth centuries. It also turned out to be the ultimate sign of their success.

The towns in which they lived would never become cities. Still, persons fashioned ways to get along with each other that were decidedly urban in their content and feel. In the process of accomplishing this neat trick, they also managed to build a world around an American creed that they could recognize and embrace.

The people of Jacksonville, Illinois certainly understood the importance of "boosterism" as an expression of their own commitment to enterprise and orderliness. It served as a social glue for the different persons who were migrating to that small town in the decades before the Civil War even as they were pursuing their individual fortunes. Town residents placed great value on building a cohesive community around their churches, political parties, lodges, reform societies, literary clubs, and other voluntary associations; and members were encouraged to adopt a sense of sacrifice and mutual assistance that served the community well.

They created a kind of "voluntary community" that enabled members to "share common institutions and to promote common interests with only limited social and psychological investment" on their part. A person could pass into this community or out of it with relative ease. It was all the organizations they made which brought coherence and a sense of social proportion to the town. One's membership in different groups helped a person to identify the various social boundary lines that crossed the town. It also made easier their effort to define their status relative to other townsfolk by fixing their position on one side or another of those lines.

The network of local groups that they created for themselves worked in much the same way as an ethnic enclave works in large cities. Indeed, even in little Jacksonville, Illinois there were persons who lived in different "ethnic segments" of the town. Within each one of these areas, Don Doyle reports, "a set of institutions, similar in form and function to those of the dominant native American population, was quickly created to integrate the members of each subcommunity."[35] These groups served as the institutional skeleton for each area, allowing persons to pass through it and yet remain integrated in a viable community for as long as they stayed. Those persons who remained for long periods of time, and there were a number who did, kept the organizations running smoothly and provided guidance to individuals who were new to the community.

Important as the organizations were to the enforcement of a rigorous code of good personal and professional conduct, their most active members learned that it would be all but impossible to devise a set of values to which every group in the town would subscribe unconditionally. Public institutions such as the schools or organizations like political parties that openly promoted contacts across the town's several social classes and cultural groups helped to bring a measure of consensus to the town. Yet they worked well only to the extent that their caretakers "recognized the pluralistic nature of the new community" and did not try to impose a single set of standards that covered every situation or set of persons living in the town. Their object instead became "to translate frontier adversity and cultural pluralism into social cooperation."[36]

Cultural uniformity and a singular religious view of the world did not work well for the people of Jacksonville. In truth, the town's different Christian sects found it difficult to get along, much less cooperate on important tasks, until their members embraced more abstract ideas like "piety and fellowship over rigid doctrinal orthodoxy." This discovery enabled otherwise devout sectarians to welcome newcomers and transients into their flocks and to introduce "a sorely needed mechanism for social discipline" to their community.[37] By embracing a mix of civic boosterism, piety, and fellowship the people of Jacksonville managed not so much to overlook their differences as to look beyond them.

They fashioned this solution to the problem of how to get along when Jacksonville was growing, and its residents were able to imagine their town becoming a much larger place. When they thought about the future they did not dream about becoming a major commercial or industrial center, routes to development that other towns latched onto and sometimes worked. They focused instead on plans that would bring them either the state capitol or the main campus of the state university system, two decidedly modern service industries of the sort that would become important to the economies of many cities in the late twentieth century. Jacksonville was not alone in trying to acquire such institutions as anchors for their economic fortunes and signs of their social and cultural accomplishment. Nor was the town unique in its singular failure to realize such a grand scheme.

What is most interesting about Jacksonville's situation was the way in which its residents reconciled themselves to a much smaller future than the one they had imagined once other towns won the race to become state capitol or home to the state university's flagship campus. "Instead of carping about internal failures or denouncing external conspiracies," things they might easily have done, "they adjusted by inverting the boosters' central themes of harmony and collective progress into a tradition of local history that justified small-town failure as chosen success." In much the same way as town leaders did all across the midwest and west when dreams of their towns as magnificent cities came to nothing, the people of Jacksonville "now nurtured the ideal of a small, intimate, self-consciously genteel community."[38]

The people of Springfield, Massachusetts dealt with many of the same problems that confronted residents of Jacksonville, Illinois in the decades immediately before and after the Civil War. The town's economy and population were growing, keeping up with the physical demands of expansion required the local government to become more assertive, and incorporating newcomers into Springfield's social and cultural life was a challenge. Many of their solutions also looked a great deal like those adopted by the people of Jacksonville.

It was not easy to convince many local residents of the need to build new institutions that might address some of these problems, particularly when the solutions required them to pay higher taxes and to accept more government intervention in their lives. Controversies over street lighting and paving showed how their opposition might be overcome, even when these improvements were not being made to all parts of the town. The paving of streets, "like the lighting of the business district, had once been staunchly opposed by those not directly benefited. But now neighborhood jealousy seemed to give way to the generally recognized ascendance of the downtown area, and to the pride that permitted more of the population to identify with Main Street."[39] Much the same approach would have been applied in discussions over many new or expanded services such as extending the water supply, adding a streetcar system, or increasing the number of schools in the town. The strategy did not necessarily work every time it was used; but it did help residents grow accustomed to seeing their private interests enveloped by some larger public good.

On the social front there appeared to be little discord. A good portion of the town population consisted of immigrants, and these persons were producing more children than the white and largely Protestant residents who had founded Springfield. Some immigrants found it easier to fit in than did others, and some experienced prejudice and discrimination at the hands of long-term residents. Yet the expanding economy made their presence less trying than it might have been by providing most persons with an adequate livelihood.

Local residents also increased the number and variety of clubs and voluntary organizations in which they participated. The events sponsored by these groups – some more public and elaborately organized than others – helped both long-time and newer inhabitants of the town to participate in its life more fully. Whether they did this to entertain each other or to do good works is less important than the fact that they did it together. It allowed the social world of Springfield to grow in new and bigger ways "without disrupting the basic social fabric of local life."[40]

It appears that the residents of Springfield did a good job at integrating enough newcomers into the routines and values embraced by more established townsfolk to make overt social conflict less likely or less severe when it did arise. Even in the face of differences in their wealth, background, tenure, and jobs, the people of Springfield found ways for persons on both sides of these dividing lines to participate in the life of the town. Less prosperous or socially esteemed persons could have standing in the community. There were civic tasks to be accomplished that did not require the person doing them to have an impressive social pedigree. A number of local organizations acted in much the same way. Churches managed to hold events that drew in non-members, and political parties invited persons from different parts of the community to become involved in their activities.

This had the effect of moderating whatever disagreements might arise among different persons and made Springfield a place "where status was both readily accessible and yet defined in quite stable, traditional terms."[41] The results of this arrangement were played out on a daily basis, and they seemed agreeable to most persons living and working in the town. Their most severe test came during the 1870s when the nation was experiencing a serious decline in its economic fortunes. Property values were lower in the town. Stores closed. Many persons lost their job. Yet there was no great sense of crisis in Springfield. Nor was there any serious labor unrest. Instead, an organization called the Sovereigns of Labor was formed for the purposes of encouraging fellowship among townsfolk, to hold discussions, and to work together. "Explicitly rejecting the concept of divergent class interests, the Sovereigns recruited members from all ranks of productive enterprises, even including some merchants and manufacturers."[42] The civic culture of Springfield did not fall apart. Persons from different backgrounds who had a stake in the community were invited to consider its long-term prospects and their own shared fate. It apparently worked.

One has the impression that town residents drew on each other for social support in much the same way as a person would draw on a line of credit at a bank where he was known and had done a lot of business. Investors could be reasonably certain that whatever loan was offered would be paid back, because town residents had practiced coming to each other's assistance for a long time. Extending credit in the form of a loan would be just another expression of their faith in each other. It was a belief that persons could be trusted, a faith rooted in hard practice.

In other towns, such as Kingston, New York, it seemed that the creation of a vibrant and varied set of organizations was what made it possible for residents to identify with the community in the first place. These groups, the events they sponsored, and the dealings that members had with each other are what made their local culture viable. Historian Stuart Blumin makes it clear that the lodges, fire companies, militia, and literary societies of that town – many of which were tied to organizations outside of Kingston – grew in response to improvements in the town's economy and changes in its population. Yet it was not at all clear that these changes or groups had disrupted the informal social life of town residents. They added something to the local community. They took nothing away from the more intimate culture that had been there before all the changes occurred.

Many persons, perhaps most of them, did not belong to these organizations. Those who did often came from all over town and, at times, from different social classes as well. Some organizations accepted less prosperous individuals or more settled and entrepreneurial members from one of the town's ethnic populations. On the other hand, many other persons with ties to different ethnic groups did not participate in these community-wide organizations. Some of them became involved with more exclusive organizations belonging only to their own ethnic group. Even these organizations, however, openly participated in events like parades or festivals with persons from other parts of the town. This was a comparatively safe way for longer-term residents to become accustomed to the presence of these "foreign" persons among them and for newcomers to learn the customs of more established townsfolk. Together they made Kingston work and made it possible for themselves to identify with the place, albeit sometimes in different ways. This did not guarantee them success; but it did give them an opportunity "to regard the town more consciously, more seriously, and more often" as their own.[43]

City dwellers and city watchers are accustomed to thinking about lines that divide one group or class from another and of all the real and imagined consequences, most of them on the bad-to-dreadful end of the scale, which flow from these divisions. They do not readily see cities as places where different types of persons, viewpoints, and ways of being together routinely intersect much less complement each other. Yet this is very much the way that life in small towns is portrayed by the persons who have studied it. Indeed, commentators on small-town life have consistently talked about the variety of ways in which persons from different social ranks and groups had frequent contact with each other or opportunities to become familiar with each other's customs and ideas. They speak of easily identifiable classes and differences but also of flexibility and an openness to newcomers and whatever customs and ideas they brought with them.

Obvious yet permeable boundaries made social intercourse and mutual understanding more likely among representatives of the various groups and social sets that filled the town. They also gave substance to the claim that America was somehow a "classless society." Lewis Atherton, who wrote about life in small midwestern towns at the end of the nineteenth century and into the first three decades of the twentieth century, spoke of how town residents openly embraced the idea of "equality" but did not bother to define it. He did not think this a coincidence.

> People seemed to assume that, normally, western society offered complete equality of opportunity. ... On the other hand, equality of ability seems never to have been affirmed or denied by major agencies like the church and school.
>
> On the surface, midwestern faith in a classless society at the very time when people also used the phrase "living across the tracks" seemingly could exist only through a failure to probe the meaning of equality.
>
> Viewed historically, barriers to crossing the tracks and joining the more respectable elements in local society were sufficiently flexible to help explain why individuals held seemingly incompatible views on equality. Moreover, class lines were based on only a limited number of barriers, and less-favored citizens could mingle freely with fellow townsmen in most community activities.
>
> Perhaps this explains why novels of small-town life generally have been inclined to stress relationships between individuals and the community as a whole rather than between classes.[44]

It was not that persons had no code or set of rules by which to live. Rather, "in a new society ... codes of polite behavior were so simple as to require no great ingenuity on the part of ambitious individuals. Churches and lodges were open to all respectable people, and most social life centered in them."[45] The number of activities sponsored by these groups and the degree of organization required to pull them off success-fully anticipated the direction that our social life has taken us in the twentieth century. Nevertheless, many residents did not belong to either of these organizations, "because they preferred to find their social outlets through informal, community activities." Membership "was a matter of choice and not of necessity." Thus, "little stigma was attached to limiting one's participation to affairs involving the whole community."[46] The fact that these activities took place over the course of the whole year only made it easier for persons from different parts of the community to share both the occasion and the town.

Lewis Atherton was more inclined than other commentators to see the proliferation of organizations and clubs in the twentieth century as part of a trend away from the easy informality of small-town life. It was not that he identified this change so much with the growing influence of cities on small towns, though he did make this connection. Rather, he pegged the loss of "togetherness" in small towns during the twentieth century to the "sense of exclusiveness or of superiority" that was engendered by these groups as their members "rushed hurriedly from one stunt ... to another, and reported their meetings at length in local newspapers."[47] There were organizations for men, women, and young persons. Some were service organizations and dealt with specific issues of interest to town residents. Others were broadly cultural in their orientation. Many were religious or dealt with patriotic themes. Some groups seemed to provide their members with an amusing diversion from everyday life. In any case, there were too many of them to mention.

Not everyone found local organizations and especially the lodges as welcoming and democratic as Lewis Atherton described them. Historian Thomas J. Morain discovered that in at least one small town in Iowa at the start of the twentieth century the members of lodges and fraternal orders "maintained a system of highly stratified ranks and offices."

> Local men who dealt with each other as fellow businessmen, customers, or just friends through the day addressed each other during lodge meetings as "worshipful master," "chancellor commander," or "generalissimo." Meetings were conducted in elaborate and formal ritual. However loudly members may have sung the praises of democracy over aristocracy ... they were attracted by the exaggerated ritual and patterns of deference. For one glorious evening a month, they escaped the bland landscape of democracy, equality, the common man, and classless society into a prefabricated world of myth, ritual, exalted rulers, fancy costumes, and noble causes.[48]

It seems that at least some of the organizations which were active and growing during the early twentieth century were looking backward and forward at the same time. Women, to mention one notable popu- lation in the community, became much more active. Not only did they participate more in church groups, but they also founded voluntary associations that spoke to issues of particular interest to them. The memberships of many organizations may have been mixed, but persons apparently still found it useful and valid to act deferentially before persons who were deemed worthy by their peers. There may have been times when members dressed in costumes that looked like something out of a medieval court, but as one newspaper editor said, there was "a valid demand for each and every organization" in town. They connected persons to the workings of a more modern world and to each other. "Association with our fellow creatures," he suggested, "'knocks off the rough edges' and gives us a better perspective of what life should be to all humanity."[49] These organizations did not so much turn their backs on traditional customs and truths as provide a bridge between an older and newer world.

Town residents also found ways of updating traditional events like the county fair so that they fit better in the modern world. Among the most prominent of these inventions were "town days." These festivals – staged variously as "implement day, community day, farmers' spree, poultry show, community mix, ox roast, harvest home, May festival, fiddlers' convention, and so on" – retained agricultural themes and activities. Yet they added all the lights and dazzle of carnival midways and held amusing competitions for the local residents. The leaders of some towns "used national holidays like the Fourth of July and Labor Day for their annual celebration, thus gaining some advantage by exploiting a time-honored but otherwise declining holiday."[50] Other celebrations like Christmas or regular social gatherings like lawn parties and picnics also retained their traditional charms even as new activities and ideas were introduced to them. In this way residents were able to shorten the distance between the informal and intimate practices of small-town life and the more cosmopolitan ideas to which they had been introduced and taken a liking.

This is not to say that the many organizations created by town residents and the good work they accomplished made everyone happy all the time. Progress and comity may have been prominent themes in the history of small towns, but there were disagreeable persons and issues that divided local residents in important ways in these communities just as there are in any place where human beings dwell. These conflicts should be appreciated as more than "disturbing social aberrations to be overcome before further progress could take place." They need not be apologized for as if they were embarrassing instances of social immaturity.[51] They were an integral part of life in small towns and important to the development of some portion of these towns into more substantial cities. Robert Dykstra, who wrote about the early history of cattle towns in the west, found that "social conflict was normal, it was inevitable, and it was a format for community decision-making and thus for change" or progress. Cooperation and conflict were "equally valid aspects of the same social process," he thought.[52]

There was nothing about the development of these towns that was preordained. Success never was guaranteed in the cattle towns any more than it had been for small midwestern farming towns or the early commercial towns on the east coast and their many trading partners in the interior of the country. Persons may have preferred places with which they were familiar when considering where to do their trading, but there was no guarantee that they would return to your town. There were other places with leaders anxious to turn their town into a thriving trading center or port, the county seat, next state capitol, or some latter-day Athens. In terms of the cattle trade and the towns that depended on it, these considerations may have been especially acute.[53]

These campaigns were common to all cattle towns, and they had to be mounted every year. Even as local residents fought to keep their share of the cattle trade, they had to wage another battle among themselves to maintain some degree of control over the less attractive by-products of this trade. Business leaders may have viewed "the brothel, the dance house, the gaming room, and the saloon as necessary adjuncts to the cattle trade." However, there also were persons inside the towns that worked feverishly in behalf of "moral betterment." They wanted all of these less savory elements out of their town, and they did not much care if the cattlemen went with them. Still other residents took a more moderate position, arguing that "gaming, whoring, and heavy drinking" were important to the local economy, while outrages like homicide had to be suppressed.[54] Disagreements among persons holding one or another of these positions were heartfelt and heated. Churchgoing, lodge meetings, picnics, and town baseball games were not going to make these disputes go away. Instead, there remained an uncomfortable stalemate among the contending parties which lasted until the cattle industry itself changed and the residents of towns that had grown along with it found new ways to earn a living.

Town leaders almost always are portrayed as favoring economic development and growth, and nothing in the history of the communities discussed up to this point would contradict this idea. To the contrary, every element of their local culture – from their basic beliefs to their membership in various clubs – that has been talked about or alluded to thus far lends support to the idea that persons work hard to get along so that their community can prosper and grow. The conventional view, for cities as well as towns, is that they are about the business of doing more business. Economic growth is supposed to be good for a community and for the persons who live and work there. Furthermore, as Meredith Ramsay has said, "promoting growth through top-down economic development strategies is politically popular too, because residents can see that their individual interests are tied to the level of commercial activity in their town."[55] This is the way we think the world works.

Fortunately, or unfortunately, the real world is a bit more complicated than that. Not only are growth and development not inevitable, but townsfolk are not always excited by the prospect of getting more business or making their economy more modern. There are occasions when they actively resist these kinds of changes. Surprisingly, perhaps, sometimes they even succeed. When they do, it is because they have drawn on the same cultural traditions and organizational resources that most often are mobilized in behalf of economic expansion. These customs and groups are used by local persons to fight for their community and for a way of life that is precious to them. We know that this has happened in American cities during the last half-century when neighborhood inhabitants resisted plans advanced by business leaders and government officials to redevelop their area or to effectively replace them with new businesses and residents. Now, thanks to Meredith Ramsay, we know that the same thing can happen in small towns in more rural areas.

Ramsay happened onto Crisfield and Princess Ann, Maryland. These were towns whose 1990 populations of 2,880 and 1,666 respectively most certainly would qualify them as being small. Moreover, the villages were locked in Maryland's poorest county and the only county losing residents during a period of state-wide population growth. She was surprised to learn that many citizens were deeply ambivalent about the prospect of bringing new industries and jobs to their communities. After all, Princess Ann was the county seat and commercial center for a declining agricultural industry, while Crisfield was the commercial center in the county for an equally moribund seafood industry. The sorry state of their local economies notwithstanding, local citizens were not at all certain that they wanted new industries moving in and disrupting their time-honored habits, beliefs, and social bonds.

Both the "haves" and "have nots" of Somerset County were threatened by the possibility of economic development. The planters and the packers, Ramsay argued, still had "a stake in maintaining a pool of cheap surplus labor, which, presumably, would dwindle if economic development fulfilled its promise to bring in jobs." Owners of small businesses had reason to fear competition from larger retail stores and the prospect of having to pay higher wages and taxes to support improvements to roads, water systems, and the like. On the other hand, "quality of life was the overriding preference for many newcomers who chose to live in Princess Ann or Crisfield because of the quaintness, charm, and small-town amenities they offered." Many of the more recent inhabitants were retired persons whose fixed incomes also might have been stretched by higher prices and taxes. For a variety of reasons, then, these different groups found it advisable not to promote the development of new businesses in Crisfield and Princess Ann.[56] One might have serious concerns about the longer-term prospects for communities that willfully embrace economies that creak along at a subsistence level. The social and cultural reasons for retaining the life they knew, however, were clear and compelling to many, if not most, of the local residents.

Towns Versus Cities

Buried deep in the stories of towns that opted for growth, or the many places whose residents tried and failed, and even in the few places where citizens ran away from new enterprises, are the telltale signs of an urban way of life and the bourgeois culture upon which it is constructed. A belief in prosperity and social order are the bedrock principles of a bourgeois culture, and most of the towns whose histories were referred to here seem to have been filled with that culture. Crisfield and Princess Ann certainly are not the only towns in the United States ever to have turned their backs on a promising economic venture or failed to capitalize on one that was dropped into their lap. Over the years, many villages and towns across the country have passed out of existence when their leaders committed sins of omission no more serious than those acted out by the residents of these small Maryland communities. If only because they managed to be caught in the midst of their shortsighted act by a perceptive observer, the stories of Crisfield and Princess Ann show us what happens when order is preferred over prosperity. Not much.

Faced with a similar dilemma in the eighteenth century, the founders of early colonial towns had chosen to loosen their grip on the social and economic reins of their communities. They made a self-conscious decision to put prosperity before order. Not to have done so, they feared, would have meant the end of their community, or at least the end of any chance they had to make their community into a larger place and their people more prosperous. If the creaky economies and stagnant or shrinking populations of Crisfield and Princess Ann hold a larger lesson for us, it probably is that colonial town leaders were right. Promoting new economic ventures does not guarantee that a town will grow or that fellow townsfolk will prosper, either as individuals or in a larger corporate sense. The failure to pursue such opportunities when they arise or to create new economic ventures on one's own, on the other hand, all but ensures that one's town will remain small and its residents less than prosperous.

The pursuit of prosperity over order carried its own set of costs for towns and the persons who lived and worked there, and these costs were not borne equally by everyone. It seemed that men and women were forever trying to catch up with their town's growth. To be sure, they were under constant pressure to look after all the roads and alleyways, water and sewerage lines, construction codes and buildings, fire protection and police supervision, and the myriad of other chores that went along with living in a place that was growing. Yet they also seemed to be playing catch-up in a social and cultural sense. Not just for pleasure or the satisfaction of showing off before one's peers, townsfolk filled their world with organizations and ceremonies that affirmed their success and stood as a reminder, to themselves as much as to any outsider who happened to be watching, that they were engaged in an important enterprise and were intending to stay.

It is clear that many town leaders and residents embraced both ends of the American creed. They believed in prosperity and order. However, they usually put prosperity ahead of order and had to work feverishly to keep up with the physical demands of putting a town together and to ensure that most of their fellow townsfolk were marching in the same general direction. This was never easy for townsfolk to do, and much of the time they had to struggle just to come close.

Much of what historians and social scientists do is try to make sense of all that putting together and marching, and they are of the opinion generally that many of the pieces never fit especially well and that most of us are content to follow different drummers. Whether we are bound and determined to follow these drummers over a cliff remains to be seen, but there is that concern, too. Embedded in the history of small towns, though, is a much less gloomy picture. We find persons living in different parts of the country over a period of some 300 years who demonstrated a remarkable capacity for pulling themselves together even as they were pushing each other toward an ill-defined future where they would find something called "progress" in a place they called "home."

We might think less of this accomplishment, perhaps, if it had been done without much forethought and completely on the fly. Yet that was not the case at all. Some townsfolk either were blessed with a certain prescience or were remarkably lucky guessers, setting their sites on institutions and businesses that would fit perfectly in our world today. They were worrying about the mobility of capital and labor and about world markets almost 200 years before politicians, policy wonks, social scientists, and assorted pundits "discovered" these problems at the end of the twentieth century. They also worked on solutions to these problems that we have come to claim as our own. It was the leaders of eighteenth- and nineteenth-century towns who planned and plotted for their communities to become centers of learning and political administration, communication exchange, and financial management. Moreover, they did this decades before heavy industries came and went as a central feature of urban economies and a full century or more before city leaders pursued professional, technical, service, and cultural industries as the key to their future and signs of progress. These people were smart.

They also were good, and their goodness was tied to being productive and orderly. They took the sectarian bite out of moral behavior that was too closely identified with particular churches by pulling most persons into a big tent that had words like "growth" and "prosperity" painted all over it. Not everyone in town would fit in the tent or necessarily want to stay for all the acts; but it was there for everybody to see, draped in bright bunting with fluttering banners and carnival barkers beckoning any paying customer to step in for a time. It was clearly the best show in town. In fact, the town was the show. Its residents were the star performers as well as the show's most appreciative audience.

Hidden behind the smoke, bright lights, and noise of the big show were differences among the performers and audience members. Whatever ill-feelings or disagreements they might have could be put on hold while the show was on and everyone was distracted by circles of entertainers twirling, tripping, or flying before their eyes and over their heads, often at the same time. When the show was over or they were between acts, these feelings and differences became more apparent. It was precisely for these moments, perhaps, that townsfolk devised a variety of customs and put themselves in a number of groups that allowed them to work together despite their differences or to ignore them altogether. They confronted their differences head-on much less frequently. It was their way of turning differences into social cooperation rather than open and protracted bitterness.

This strategy worked for many persons, but it did not work for everyone. Some residents stayed in a given town for a long time. Many others moved from place to place. The populations of eighteenth- and nineteenth-century towns, no less than those of our own towns and cities today, were subject to some pretty substantial changes over comparatively short periods of time. The result was that the hard work of pulling a community together and keeping its members engaged in activities that were meaningful to them became the responsibility of a small number of persons. These individuals and the groups to which they belonged became the community of believers inside every town. They saw to it that opportunities for engagement were available to anyone who might be interested in staying on for more than a little while. They invented the basic customs to which newcomers submitted themselves and the organizations that they petitioned for membership.

Persons participated in these customs and groups, or they did not. In much the same way as town residents and visitors alike could view the big tent and the show going on inside it, however, residents could observe some of their number engaged in the hard work of getting along, or they came under the influence of those who were so engaged. The reality of being part of a community in the making, even if one were not actively involved in the process oneself, had a sobering effect on many persons much of the time. Those who could not be engaged in this way or were unwilling to submit to accepted customs and beliefs even in a purely ceremonial way did not stay around long or led a very lonely and unpleasant life.

Most people were not lonely, or at least they had ways of being engaged by community affairs. At one time or another, they could observe business owners taking a commanding lead in organizing the community. The example they set was crucial to the long-term success of their town,

in large measure because their "personal interests were so tightly inter-
woven with those of the community at large that one [could] not
determine where self-interest ended and public spirit began."[57] Their own
version of practicing piety by osmosis was picked up by other groups.[58]
Among the earliest and most effective practitioners of the American creed
were persons who only recently had come to this country and were not
yet Americans. Members of what we today would call "ethnic groups,"
these persons mimicked the ways of doing business, engaging in politics,
and carrying on social relations that they saw being practiced by representatives of more established groups. They also introduced special
twists to these customs, ceremonies, and codes that were closely identified with the life they had known before coming to America.

Town residents observed local officials trying to bring some unity to
their community. Politics and municipal governance were not yet full-
time callings, but persons took them seriously. These were arenas in
which the corporate mission of their community often was talked about
more openly and loudly than it was elsewhere, and by a variety of persons who might not otherwise have much to do with each other on a
day-to-day basis. Some townsfolk also could help to bring a bit more
unity to the community by shopping or investing in local businesses.
Their number and diversity probably were less than that of the persons
who found themselves embroiled in politics from time to time, but what
they did and the money they spent and invested mattered a great deal.
If nothing else, they showed that the ranks of community's true believers could grow with the economy and accommodate more than the
thinnest layer of the town's traditional leaders, business owners, or
propertied citizens. It probably was easier to be bored in small towns
than it was not to be engaged by the activities going on around oneself
every day.

The residents of eighteenth- and nineteenth-century American towns
were exposed to the rudiments of an urban way of life. Ways of thinking
about oneself and of being together with other persons that we readily
associate with cities were available to townsfolk. They also were tied to
larger economic, political, and social changes occurring outside of their
small town more often than we usually suppose. Their introduction to a
larger market economy, national political themes, and organizations
whose membership included persons living some distance from them may
have been of an elementary sort; but they certainly knew about such
things and had practiced some of them, too.

Life in cities is different from life in towns. The differences between
them have more to do with the number of ideas and ways of being
together that are put into practice every day, however, than in the types of
beliefs that persons hold and manner in which they organize themselves.

There also are more persons who need to be engaged by these practices and ideas, and there is a greater chance in cities than in towns to remain untouched by these same persons, ideas, and practices on an everyday basis. Persons and groups that occupy cities do the same sorts of things that their counterparts in small towns do. City dwellers just do more of them at the same time and in more complex ways than does a small-town people.

Towns have their own built-in tensions and strains just as cities do. Their residents are not immune to conflict, and they can have fights about matters that divide them which are every bit as nasty and protracted as those seen in cities. Townsfolk may be better practiced in ignoring their differences, and city people simply may be too hard-edged to try. This could be so, but I frankly doubt it. Too many careful observers have noted the extreme lengths to which city dwellers go in order to avoid contact with persons and ideas they do not like or have no good reason to know. An equally impressive array of scholars has noted the alacrity with which persons living in small towns and more rural areas sometimes embrace extreme ideas and actions.[59] Historians who write about small towns, as it was noted earlier, simply may not pay as much attention to conflicts and antagonisms in small towns as they do to the equally powerful ways in which townsfolk manage to overlook or move beyond whatever divides them.

It is the habit of looking beyond whatever divides one set of community members from another that might well distinguish life in small towns from what typically happens in cities. The residents of small towns simply may be better practiced in finding ways to accept differences or in not letting them get in the way of more important business. Church leaders in some small towns, it will be recalled, softened their sectarian rhetoric so that they might draw in newcomers and avoid contentious fights with their "fellow Christians." It is a process akin to moving furniture or paintings around a room in order to hide a hairline crack in a wall or applying a thin coat of spackle in the hope that it will not reappear. Townsfolk found ways to live with the social imperfections all around them, or they did the social equivalent of slapping a fresh coat of paint over the cracks in their community. Furthermore, all of it was done in the name of progress and fellowship.

We know that many persons who lived in American cities during the nineteenth and early twentieth centuries tried to look beyond their differences in an attempt to find broader, more inclusive themes that might appeal to a larger number and greater variety of city folk. They were no less attracted to progress or reluctant to invoke the idea of fellowship in order to achieve more unity in their cities. More often than not, unfortunately, the search proved less successful and satisfying than its advocates had hoped it would be.[60] The problem with these efforts may have been that the message reformers were delivering became too abstract and lost all of its moral bite. It also may have been that the geographic breadth of their vision outstripped their capacity to rally all the persons living across ever larger geographic areas like those covered by a big city or a whole metropolitan area. Whatever the reasons, however, city dwellers seemed to enjoy less success in working all the different persons living among them into a credible and self-conscious people. The appeals to progress and fellowship in cities were harder to serve up or more difficult to swallow, and maybe both. In any case, they have not worked as well in cities as they have in small towns.

The real difference between cities and towns on this score may be that cities are large enough to allow some persons to avoid ideas, groups, or customs they find objectionable even as other persons or groups in the same place are confronting them head-on or trying to move beyond them. It is not a question of persons having to make the difficult choice among fleeing or fighting that which is new or objectionable, or remaining true to a bigger, more inclusive community.[61] They can do all three, at the same time.

Much the same probably could be said for the ways in which city dwellers answer the three questions that persons must address as they confront the troubling prospect of making themselves into a self-conscious and effective people, or community. Will they lay down strict criteria for becoming a member of the community, or will they have the equivalent of an open admissions policy? Will they exercise a great deal of control over their members' conduct, or will they allow a variety of customs and beliefs to be expressed? Will they insist that persons take many other groups and interests into account whenever they act, or will they permit individuals to cater more to their own whims and the parochial tastes of the groups to which they belong? The answer in each case will be "yes" or more accurately, perhaps, "both."

Persons who live in small towns are able to come up with more definitive answers to these questions, or they simply may be better practiced at appearing to do so, which for them could work just as well. They may rely heavily on traditional sources of leadership within their business community, and they may allow greater room for the practice of ethnicity than is commonly supposed. They may express a fundamental dislike of government and bureaucratic procedures even as they master the art of bending politics and lawmaking to meet their own particular needs. They may rail against the evils of the marketplace as a corrupter of traditional verities even as they plan for the next town or county fair. They may do all these things, or they may not. Against what goes on in cities, persons and groups in small towns do not appear to do all of these things at the same time. Nor do they seem to find it necessary to do any of them all that openly. A city people does.

The differences between life in cities and small towns may come down to this. City dwellers do not just have the option of practicing small-town ways and more modern bureaucratic stratagems. They do both at the same time. Furthermore, they have found a way to make it work. Cities also are places with a richer and more vibrant public life, just as Plato imagined them to be. Even when their residents pursue purely private ends, they do it more forthrightly and with greater heat than is observed or encouraged in small towns. They are more disarmingly candid in their likes and dislikes, and they are more rambunctious in embracing what they like and in rejecting that which they do not like. They may not be as willing or able to look beyond their differences because it is so much harder to do in the open and so much more entertaining when you try.

The city is one big stage, just like Lewis Mumford said, and its residents are engaged in the longest running morality play ever fashioned by a people. All we have to do is sit back and figure out what they are telling us, even as they are trying to figure it out for themselves. Naturally, that is easier to say than it is to do, and generations of careful, and sometimes not-so-careful, audience members and critics have misread the play and misconstrued the themes embedded in it.

A number of writers, myself included, think that Mumford got it wrong. He saw the modern city as a place where old ways of doing things and imagining oneself had been forever lost. The erosion of civic customs and public attentiveness that he perceived could have taken place only if local institutions and parochial standards no longer were effective, and this is precisely what Mumford and many other persons believe happened. Persons who followed local customs and beliefs, and who ran traditional organizations and institutions were incapable, as Mumford put it, of enlarging the social heritage or transmitting it to a new generation. Instead, they became snacks for the rapacious hatchlings that his "cuckoo bird of capitalism" had set loose in urban nests.

This happened earlier in Europe than in the United States. Once the big, ugly capitalist bird started dropping its eggs all over our country sometime during the middle of the nineteenth century, however, it was all over as far as Mumford and many others are concerned. Humane values and social conduct were swept out of the nest, and they were replaced by avarice and an indifference that wore away at our souls every bit as much as it fouled our civic culture.

Some historians and social scientists are not so sure that the break with our past, no matter how romantically we may now recall it, was all that severe or permanent. Thomas Bender, a prominent and literate advocate of this view, maintains that the old ways of believing and acting together were dwarfed by more bureaucratic habits and turns of mind but not altogether lost in our modern world. New ways broke into cities in much the same way as uninvited guests crash a party. Old ways and invited guests are not forced to leave or even forgotten, but they can be overwhelmed by the strangers who push their way into someone else's house. The invited guests simply stand apart from the party crashers and watch them muscle in on the dance floor, talk too loud, jostle the punch bowl, and grab all the best snacks.

What we have learned from the history of small towns would seem to take us down a path different from the one suggested by Bender, but one that parallels rather than crosses the trail he cut. I would argue that our new-fangled bureaucratic ways, cramped shopping malls, watered-down nationalism, and self-centeredness are built on top of a solid foundation of traditional customs and truths left for us by our town- and city-based ancestors. The modern age has not swept away the past or even overshadowed it. Instead, it is rich with the lessons of the past and not at all hostile to the truths and customs, groups and institutions found in it.[62] Our version of modern-day party crashers turn out to be our younger brothers and cousins rather than a bunch of guys in leather jackets who just moved into the abandoned house at the end of the block.

The effect of all this party crashing, I think, is all right. Or, at least it is not the horrible mess that so many social philosophers, theorists, and critics of modern urban life have imagined that we made for ourselves. We hold open the possibility that the city has remained a place where human beings are capable of making a rich and varied cultural life for themselves, one in which the past has neither been swept away nor overwhelmed by bigger events and more exotic tastes.

NOTES

1   To the extent that this is so, we will have to take a closer look at the connection between urban ways of thinking and being together and the kind of places where these social inventions were hammered out. We once thought of premodern and modern ways of creating a community as being associated with specific kinds of places, with cities being the repository of all modern institutions, customs, and ways of thinking, while towns or villages were places where more traditional habits and beliefs were enshrined. Contemporary thinkers have had a different idea. They have tried to imagine the human community less as a place than as a set of relations that might be practiced in a variety of places, some that are like cities and others that are not at all city-like. This idea has a lot of merit, particularly if it can be shown, as I will try to do here, that important features in our modern urban way of life can be found much earlier than the mid-nineteenth century and

in places a lot smaller and less bewildering than cities. We also will have to look more closely at the parallels between social relations in towns and cities. Historian Thomas Bender believes that social relations in American communities became "bifurcated" sometime during the second half of the nineteenth century. Local ties and ways of communing persisted, but gradually became less important than ideas, customs, and associations imported from the larger outside world. See: Thomas Bender, *Community and Social Change in America* (Baltimore: Johns Hopkins University Press, 1993), pp. 15–43, 80, 108–9, 118, and 122–3.

2 Carl Bridenbaugh, *Cities in the Wilderness: The First Century of Urban Life in America, 1625–1742* (Oxford: Oxford University Press, 1966 [1938]), p. 135.

3 Ibid., p. 138.

4 Academic writers during the 1990s paid a great deal of attention to the emergence of what they called the "delocalized city." According to one of the major proponents of this idea, this is a city whose "development and form ... [are] determined by forces well beyond its bounds. These forces can be rooted in a global context of competition and industrial change, or they may be lodged in larger regional pressures. Whatever the cause, the size, shape, economic structure, and social fabric of delocalized cities depend upon what happens in the outer world." See: Hank V. Savitch, "The Emergence of Delocalized Cities," *Urban Affairs Review*, Volume 31, Number 1, September 1995, p. 137. Delocalized cities allegedly were becoming part of a worldwide economic system whose changing technological and industrial base made them look more alike and develop a more common, and global, culture. These changes were especially evident in so-called "world cities" like New York, London, and Tokyo. However, the implication was that other less grand cities surely would end up being modified by these same changes at some point in the future. See: Susan Fainstein, *The City Builders* (Cambridge, MA: Blackwell Publishers, 1994); Susan Fainstein, Ian Gordon, and Michael Harloe, *Divided Cities: New York and London in the Contemporary World* (Oxford: Blackwell Publishers, 1992); James W. White, "Old Wine, Cracked Bottles? Tokyo, Paris, and the Global City Hypothesis," *Urban Affairs Review*, Volume 33, Number 4, March 1998, pp. 451–77; James W. White, "Half-Empty Bottle Or No Bottle At All? A Rejoinder to Sassen and Smith," *Urban Affairs Review*, Volume 33, Number 4, March 1998, pp. 489–91. The common point of reference for these works seems to be a warmed-over Marxist analysis of crises engulfing capitalist societies at the end of the twentieth century. These crises would include a growing gap between rich and poor persons, unsteady employment patterns, and city residents' attraction to progressive social movements. For our purposes, however, it is important to know that their description of modern cities coming into a world market or coming under the cultural influence of faraway places and peoples is historically groundless. Colonial American villages were well tied into such a market and town residents acquired many goods they could not produce for themselves through a far-flung trading network. Many of the cultural tricks

town residents applied to make a successful go of it in America were borrowed from these same faraway places. Carl Bridenbaugh said almost a half-century ago that "as urban America entered upon its second century of existence, external conditions of a worldwide as well as of a local nature silently and inexorably determined its future, for the cities lay in the center, not on the periphery, of Western civilization." See: Carl Bridenbaugh, *Cities In Revolt: Urban Life in America, 1743–1776* (London: Oxford University Press, 1955), p. 4. American towns were part of a global economy and under the influence of non-local forces long before the end of the twentieth century.

5 Bridenbaugh, *Cities in the Wilderness*, p. 411.

6 Ibid., p. 384.

7 Ibid.

8 Ibid., pp. 231–48.

9 Ibid., pp. 279, 426, 434, 436–42.

10 Ibid., p. 481.

11 Bridenbaugh, *Cities In Revolt*, pp. 24–5 and 232–3.

12 Richard Lingeman, *Small Town America: A Narrative History, 1620–the Present* (Boston: Houghton Mifflin, 1980), pp. 30–3.

13 Richard D. Brown, "The Emergence of Urban Society in Rural Massachusetts, 1760–1820," *Journal of American History*, Volume 61, June 1974, p. 39.

14 Ibid., pp. 40–1.

15 Bridenbaugh, *Cities in Revolt*, p. 33.

16 Ibid., pp. 242–3.

17 Mark Bouman, "Luxury and Control: The Urbanity of Street Lighting in Nineteenth-Century Cities," *Journal of Urban History*, Volume 14, Number 1, November 1987, pp. 7–37; Murray Melbin, "Night as Frontier," *American Sociological Review*, Volume 43, Number 1, February 1978, pp. 3–22.

18 Richard C. Wade, "Urban Life in Western America, 1790–1830," *American Historical Review*, Volume 64, October 1958, p. 14.

19 Ibid., p. 18.

20 Ibid., p. 24.

21 Bridenbaugh, *Cities in Revolt*, p. 98.

22 Richard C. Wade, *The Urban Frontier: Pioneer Life in Early Pittsburgh, Cincinnati, Lexington, Louisville, and St Louis* (Chicago: University of Chicago Press, 1976), p. 104.

23 Mark Schneider, *Suburban Growth: Policy and Process* (Brunswick, Ohio: King's Court Communications, 1980); Peter Muller, *Contemporary Suburban America* (Englewood Cliffs, NJ: Prentice-Hall, 1981); J. John Palen, *The Suburbs* (New York: McGraw-Hill, 1995); Herbert Gans, *The Levittowners* (New York: Random House, 1967); Carol A. O'Connor, *A Sort of Utopia: Scarsdale, 1891–1981* (Albany, NY: State University of New York Press, 1983); Kenneth T. Jackson, *Crabgrass Frontier: The Suburbanization of the United States* (New York: Oxford University Press, 1985); Robert Fishman, *Bourgeois Utopias: The Rise and Fall of Suburbia*

(New York: Basic Books, 1987); John R. Stilgoe, *Borderland: Origins of the American Suburb, 1820–1939* (New Haven, CN: Yale University Press, 1988); M. P. Baumgartner, *The Moral Order of a Suburb* (New York: Oxford University Press, 1988).

24 William Finnegan, "The Unwanted," *The New Yorker*, December 1997, p. 78.

25 Daniel J. Monti, *Wannabe: Gangs in Suburbs and Schools* (Oxford: Blackwell Publishers, 1994).

26 "Chinese Transform Suburbia," *Boston Sunday Globe*, May 3, 1998.

27 Henry C. Binford, *The First Suburbs: Residential Communities on the Boston Periphery, 1815–1920* (Chicago: University of Chicago Press, 1985); Sam Bass Warner, *Streetcar Suburbs* (Cambridge, MA: Harvard and MIT Presses, 1962); Alexander von Hoffman, *Local Attachments: The Making of an American Urban Neighborhood, 1850–1920* (Baltimore: Johns Hopkins University Press, 1994).

28 Lingeman, *Small Town America*, p. 165.

29 Ibid., p. 53.

30 Ibid., p. 170.

31 Ibid., p. 419.

32 Ibid., p. 311.

33 Ibid., p. 411.

34 Ibid., p. 401.

35 Don H. Doyle, *The Social Order of a Frontier Community: Jacksonville, Illinois, 1825–1870* (Urbana, IL: University of Illinois Press, 1978), pp. 13–14.

36 Ibid., pp. 39–40.

37 Ibid., p. 157.

38 Ibid., p. 255.

39 Michael H. Frisch, *Town Into City: Springfield, Massachusetts, and the Meaning of Community, 1840–1880* (Cambridge, MA: Harvard University Press, 1972), pp. 109–10.

40 Ibid., p. 132.

41 Ibid., p. 36.

42 Ibid., p. 219.

43 Ibid., p. 221.

44 Lewis Atherton, *Main Street on the Middle Border* (Bloomington, IN: Indiana University Press, 1954), pp. 100–1.

45 Ibid., p. 104.

46 Ibid., p. 186. For an extensive discussion of the many informal social events that captured the attention of persons throughout the year see pages 190–215.

47 Ibid., pp. 290–1.

48 Thomas J. Morain, *Prairie Grass Roots: An Iowa Small Town in the Early Twentieth Century* (Ames, Iowa: Iowa State University Press, 1988), pp. 22–3.

49 Ibid., p. 23.

50 Atherton, *Main Street on the Middle Border*, pp. 309–10.

51 Robert S. Dykstra, *The Cattle Towns* (New York: Alfred A. Knopf, 1968), p. 364.
52 Ibid., p. 365.
53 Ibid., p. 151.
54 Ibid., pp. 239–43.
55 Meredith Ramsay, *Community, Culture, and Economic Development: The Social Roots of Local Action* (Albany, NY: State University of New York Press, 1996), p. 3.
56 Ibid., pp. 114–15.
57 Atherton, *Main Street on the Middle Border*, p. 23.
58 George Will, "Tale of Two Countries," *Newsweek*, January 20, 1997.
59 Allen W. Trelease, *White Terror: The Ku Klux Klan Conspiracy and Southern Reconstruction* (London: Secker & Warburg, 1972); Seymour Martin Lipset and Earl Raab, *The Politics of Unreason: Right-Wing Extremism in America, 1790–1970* (New York: Harper & Row, 1973); Stanley B. Parsons, *The Populist Context: Rural versus Urban Power on a Great Plains Frontier* (Westport, CT: Greenwood Press, 1973); Richard Maxwell Brown, *Strain of Violence: Historical Studies of American Violence and Vigilantism* (New York: Oxford University Press, 1975).
60 Paul Boyer, *Urban Masses and Moral Order in America: 1820–1920* (Cambridge, MA: Harvard University Press, 1978).
61 Albert O. Hirschman, *Exit, Voice and Loyalty* (Cambridge, MA: Harvard University Press, 1970).
62 John McClymer, "The Study of Community and the 'New' Social History," *Journal of Urban History*, Volume 7, Number 1, November 1980, pp. 103–18.

4

The Civic Culture of American Cities

Sir Peter Hall, the eminent author and urban planner, is certain that cities occupy a prominent place in civilization, but he is not exactly sure why. Unlike Louis Mumford who could find little good to say about the current and future prospects for cities, Hall is mindful of the great artistic, technological, and cultural accomplishments which find their most prominent showcase in these big, human-made places. He chronicles how they came to be in cities and what meaning we might take from having them there. More importantly, for our purposes, he also speaks of order, not merely the physical sort that urban planners like to write about but of a "social and moral order" which animates the lives of the persons who live and work in cities.[1]

Given the caring detail in which Hall describes how cities have been built for over 2,500 years and filled with important artifacts, he is surprisingly mute on what makes the order apparent in city life moral at all and from where the morality comes in the first place. Sir Peter seems to think that it lies somewhere in the spirit of civic innovation that grips city dwellers; but he does not give that animating spirit a name or describe it with nearly the same passion or admiration with which he talks about tall buildings, transit lines, and even sewers. Men and women who live in cities probably were gripped by nothing much more dramatic than the need to get things done in the face of overwhelming problems. "Cities and their citizens," he says, "did what they had to do; they had no real alternative."[2]

I have a different idea, and it is based, in part, on observations first made by Alexis de Tocqueville almost two hundred years ago.

Ever Since de Tocqueville

America was on the verge of becoming a more expansive and urban nation by the first quarter of the nineteenth century. Barely out of its infancy as a nation, the United States was little more than a promising piece of political fiction and a robust venture whose stakeholders as yet had no good sense of what they might accomplish. By any measure, then, 1830 was a good moment for Alexis de Tocqueville to have visited this country and to begin his famous study of its people and their customs. Towns were being planted in new territories, and burgs not much older than these were approaching a size and intensity of social and economic intercourse that would qualify them as cities. These were exciting times for the people called Americans, and de Tocqueville wanted to capture their spirit and habits and to put what he saw and heard on paper.

It is not de Tocqueville's imaginative renderings of America's democratic ethos that concern us here, important as they were and instructive as they are to the subject at hand. Of greater interest is his treatment of how Americans formed "associations." De Tocqueville had in mind what we today call "voluntary" and "non-profit" organizations or, if one were a sociologist, "secondary groups." This would distinguish them from one's family and friendship cliques, social creations that usually are referred to as "primary groups." No matter what one chooses to call them, however, de Tocqueville understood these associations to be "civil partnerships" that enabled Americans to express their interests and to accomplish a myriad of chores which come with keeping house in a democratic state.[3] His aim was to understand these "civil partnerships" and the way they brought Americans together.

One of the more curious features of de Tocqueville's treatment of "associations" is the liberal fashion in which he used the term. He imagined that all manner of groups and organizations which Americans made for themselves, including their businesses and shops, could be thought of in this way. "Americans of all ages, all conditions, and all dispositions," he observed, "form associations."[4]

The "notion of associations" and "the wish to coalesce," de Tocqueville suggested, "present themselves every day to the minds of the whole community" whenever a people has "any knowledge of public life."[5] These ideas form the basis of our civic culture and are the wellspring for all the habits by which we come to know ourselves as civilized beings. They were the stuff out of which America's democratic ethos was fashioned.

Regrettably, this has not stopped cities from being attacked as places where a civilized and cultured existence is difficult, if not impossible, to find. Nor has it protected city dwellers from being perceived as less congenial and moral then their country cousins, as witless conformists and socially aloof at the same time, or being unable to pull themselves together in any meaningful or lasting way.[6] They are far too involved in satisfying themselves and not concerned enough about the production of important cultural goods and values. At the same time, they are unwilling to submit to the tyranny of experts like social scientists and policy makers who would tell them what to do and why they should do it.[7]

De Tocqueville would have expected Americans to make associations that help us be less lonely, if no less strange to each other, and he was right. Persons have found ways to come together, even in this most self-centered of worlds. They just did not do it in a way that de Tocqueville anticipated.

At least around Boston in the late 1990s, one no longer had to be lonely alone. A non-profit organization called the New England Consultants sponsored a day-long seminar on "Loneliness in America." It invited therapists, social workers, clergy, substance abuse counselors, youth workers, and "other helping professionals" to listen to seven experts on loneliness at the Holiday Inn in Taunton, Massachusetts on April 11, 1997.

The brochure I read told persons that they could take the seminar for credit toward their professional certification. For a fee of only $89, participants could hear experts talk about "The Connection Gap: Why Americans Feel So Alone," or everyone's "zones of isolation." They also would be posed rhetorical questions such as "If These are the Best Years of My Life, Why Am I So Unhappy?"

The good news was that we could share the experience of being alone and maybe learn how to deal with it more effectively. The bad news was that feeling out of place, acting like a stranger, or being lonely somehow had become "normal." These states allegedly were endemic to modern society, an unavoidable feature of our daily lives.

Individuals could be whole and happy, but for the disorganized society and alienating customs to which they were subjected. They were not responsible for the misery visited upon them or the unsatisfactory condition of their lives. Society was. The seminar offered the promise of bringing men and women together so that they could work through the trauma of being social.[8] De Tocqueville, I am sure, would have found this a remarkable paradox.

The main ideas behind the paradox were planted in our brains a long time ago. Human beings allegedly do not share a common view of the world and are incapable of working together effectively to make one, unless they foment some sort of revolutionary change. They cannot build a coherent and vital culture for themselves in any conventional sense, however, as long as they remain unknown to each other. Unfortunately, they are not likely to acquire better information about each other, because they are hopelessly divided on the basis of their color, class, gender, religion, and so forth.

Persons who live in smaller communities still may know how to get along and look beyond their differences. City dwellers do not. They have elected, instead, to work out a sophisticated set of rules that allow them to be near each other without having to deal with each other in any sustained or meaningful way.[9] They try not to fight but sometimes cannot avoid it. They make occasional noises about overcoming their differences and uniting under a single moral vision, just like the residents of nineteenth-century American small towns apparently did. Unfortunately, they fell out of the habit of trying some time ago, and many persons doubt that they had the means to succeed even when they still were trying. This is not what de Tocqueville had in mind.

The result is something of a stalemate in which, if we are lucky, we might come to accept each other as "familiar strangers." This may not be an ideal state, but it may be the best that we can do. "Think about it," *Baltimore Sun* reporter Alice Steinbach suggested several years ago. "If, while walking to work, we mark where we are by passing a certain building, why should we not mark where we are when we pass a familiar, though unnamed, person?" These individuals, Steinbach adds, "are important markers in the landscape of our lives. They add weight to our sense of place and belonging." They are "the shopkeeper who nods to you. The bus driver who drives you to work each day. The woman you see walking her child to school."[10] They are all familiar strangers, anonymous but reassuring features on our landscape and in our daily lives. Our contact with them is not long and our knowledge of them is far from intimate, but it is not bad, either.

No one like the "familiar stranger" appears in the literary mural depicting all the characters one might have occasion to see in cities or literally bump into during the typical day. Sociologists and social psychologists, the persons most responsible for painting this mural, make no mention of this idea in their own writing. Their own vision of how different persons can live in comparative peace is suggested with ideas like "communities of limited liability," "ordered segmentation," and "liberated" or "unbounded" communities.[11] These words refer to social groupings and settings in which persons from varied backgrounds are able to live *by* each other without having to live *with* each other, unless they choose to do so; and that presumably does not happen all that often.

Social scientists came up with these phrases to describe a situation in modern society, and especially in modern cities, that finds local communities persisting rather than disappearing. Many studies confirm the idea that persons remain attached to their local community in a variety of ways, even if those ways do not remind us of life in small towns as we have imagined it. "Given the choice," Roger S. Ahlbrandt says, "some people continue to participate in the local community, to give it their time, their loyalty, their energy." They are attached to the place where they live; but "they do so conditionally rather than unconditionally." Their commitment, however real, is not irrevocable. "Communities, like other organizations, must attract participants by positive rewards and gratifications and when they fail to do so people will withdraw their commitment, participation, and investments."[12]

The manner in which residents in an area deal with each other depends in part on the types of persons who live there and the kinds of economic, social, and political resources that are available to them.[13] Their ties to each other can be warm and effective, but they are based on the voluntary commitment of persons to remain in contact with each other and to work together. They cannot be expected to do so simply because someone tells them they should or because tradition dictates that they must. Connections between members of different groups, on the other hand, are marked by a certain restraint and barely hidden animosity that can bubble over into trouble without much effort.

The idea that persons can be close to one another in a physical sense yet remain socially distant is hardly new or something that is acted out only in modern cities. Historians who write about the Ante-Bellum South have often noted that black and white persons shared a physical closeness and, indeed, an intimacy that belied the immense social gulf that separated them on plantations and in towns. The rules of engagement were clear and customary contacts between white and black persons were measured. Violations of those codes and customs were met with strong, often violent, reactions by local residents.

One supposes that something akin to this is thought to be going on inside cities. Yet cities are far more open social arenas; and it is more difficult to monitor the conduct of persons, even when they are members of despised populations like sailors and slaves. That is part of the reason why black and white persons in cities both before and especially after the Civil War found the constraints on their dealings with each other loosened.[14] Blacks were able to develop their own society inside cities, and many of their social inventions were precise replicas of customs and organizations used by white persons. This did not mean, of course, that relations between blacks and whites were congenial. Real and imagined challenges to the dominance of whites were met with severe attacks on numerous occasions.[15]

The point is that physical and social separation inside cities generally was harder to maintain. Persons were reminded about where they could go and what they should do in a variety of subtle and not-so-subtle ways. Much of the time persons stuck with those ways, even when they disagreed with them or did not at all like the idea that members of one or another population would be able to stay. Sometimes they took a different path and were able to ignore rules designed to keep them in line, even if they dared not change those offensive rules.

The situation in which whites and blacks find themselves enmeshed is, of course, an extreme example of what persons in cities generally face and how they are thought to deal with the differences between them. There are occasions when they will forget their differences and act in concert, if only to resist the encroachment of outsiders into their part of the city.[16] Nevertheless, their most intimate contacts are reserved for the persons they know well and to whom they are related through marriage, birth, and their nationality or social heritage.

Today we know that such ties were available to New Yorkers before the Civil War, and they survived even when persons were compelled to move away from their friends and family.[17] One can suppose that similar relations and group ties were present in other large American cities of the period and that these persisted in our time. In fact, there is a substantial body of writing on the role of ethnic enclaves in contemporary cities that speaks to this very point. Persons who had much in common may have been spread throughout a city, but they were able to remain in touch and were drawn back to their old neighborhoods by the shops, organizations, and acquaintances that stayed there.[18] Insofar as this was the case, these "unbounded communities," as Kenneth Scherzer called them, certainly were vital to the social well-being of the persons who were tied to them, and they helped to reduce the anonymity of city life. Still, these places and the relations they sustained did not necessarily provide individuals with the confidence or means to initiate bigger conversations with persons who were not like them.

The picture of cities with which we usually are left is that of a place where persons have few reasons to carry on a meaningful or sustained conversation with different groups and few opportunities to try. The city, under this construction, is more likely to be a place where persons are bombarded with too much social noise, where many encounters between individuals are risky, and each of us tends to retreat to a state of "public privacy." There we put on safe masks and behave indifferently toward each other so that we can make it through the day without being prevailed upon or molested. The norm of "civil inattention" that we practice enables us to acknowledge and avoid each other at the same time when we are among persons who are different from ourselves or in places that do not "belong" to any one group.[19] Our involvement with other persons under these circumstances may be superficial; but social scientists and psychologists believe that city dwellers behave this way to keep their world orderly and their personal identities secure.

A fuller picture of cities and the way that human beings live in them is not quite so anonymous or dispiriting. After all, every city has places where human beings relate to each other in more animated and emotionally satisfying ways. It makes little difference that these sites are neighborhoods where persons from the same background live or simply spots that are frequented by individuals with particular interests and proclivities. Indeed, it is the comparative smallness of these places that makes it feasible for persons with the same outlook on life and a similar array of skills and experiences to find each other and carry on more meaningful conversations.[20] Within the safe confines of these spots, persons are free "to be themselves" and to "do their own thing," no matter how conventional or eccentric a thing it turns out to be.

Cities, owing to their size and diversity, usually are thought to hold many of these safe spaces where persons enjoy the freedom to believe and act as they like. The group or "subculture" that practices these ideas and routines finds room to make its own way in cities. In turn, its members are expected to let persons belonging to other groups or subcultures practice their own beliefs and customs. Much of the time, this arrangement works pretty well.

Again, this might or might not be a bad thing in itself. On the other hand, it certainly does not encourage persons from distinctive groups or subcultures to converse with each other or learn how to reconcile their differences. Nor does it give them any incentive to do so. On those occasions when they try, it is expected that they will talk to each other either too loudly or with too much timidity. Neither of these approaches would be especially helpful in carrying on serious and long-term discussions with persons different from oneself.

Persons in a position to help cannot be counted on to do so. Politicians, for their part, often pander to these groups in different ways, or they may treat one group as an object of scorn in order to get the support of persons from other groups. Social philosophers tell us it is important that we keep trying to talk to each other, but then insist that the conversation be handled in a very "liberal" or "conservative" way. Social scientists point out all the reasons why persons from different walks of life cannot possibly hold a civil conversation, even as they insist that the only way we are going to make it together is by affirming the legitimacy of every group among us. This idea may have merit, or it may not. In neither case, however, are social scientists particularly clear on how this is supposed to happen. It is difficult to imagine how one can learn to embrace another group's values and customs as his own, if the parties in question are not speaking about these matters.

What seems clearer is that life inside cities unfolds in ways that so-called liberal communalists would embrace more readily than would their conservative brethren. Our urban way of life appears to be organized around principles of tolerance and sharing. We seem to accept the presence of persons who are different from ourselves and allow them to pursue their odd and sometimes offensive customs, despite the fact that we do not like them. We also do not put much emphasis on drawing these different groups together or in reconciling their distinctive views of the world. In effect, we act like the private-regarding individuals that social philosophers and scientists have been talking about for a long time.

Persons who know something about cities do not talk about exclusivity very much, except as it is practiced by individuals who are involved with one of the city's many subcultures or find themselves drawn to one of the city's more unique venues. Nor do observers of city life make much noise about piety, except for the many ways in which it is not found in cities. Finally, commentators on the urban scene do not hold out much hope that members of the city's various subcultures will learn to look beyond their differences and adopt standards which take the various peoples around them into account. They are not likely to become public-regarding persons any time soon. Whatever else one might say about cities or the urban way of life practiced there, they do not seem to reflect conservative principles, and their residents ordinarily are not portrayed as acting in accordance with time-honored customs and values.

The problem with building a community around more liberal principles, of course, is that it looks more broken and divided than we would prefer it to be. At the same time, we seem loathe to embrace more conservative ideas and techniques in order to make our cities more united. Our dilemma is that the cities we know do not seem to embrace such values and customs.

Only two explanations seem plausible. Either the absence of such values and customs is real, in which case cities became less congenial places for the cultivation of virtue just as social theorists have said; or, the absence of civic values and habits is more apparent than real, in which case we have not been looking in the right places for an active civic life inside cities or simply ignored signs that one has been up and running all along. De Tocqueville would urge us to look harder.

The Civic Culture of American Cities

There is reason to think that the second explanation comes closer to the truth, and we may have missed or overlooked important sources and expressions of civic life in cities for a long time. Americans are hardly the first people to distinguish themselves as city builders or as creators of an urban way of life. They are, unfortunately, among the most successful builders of cities ever to ignore or dismiss out of hand the value of that way of life or the bourgeois culture produced there. Americans also seem to have an aversion to recognizing or acknowledging the impact that way of life has on everyone else who does not live in cities. There are many reasons why this might be so. One of the more important and ironic sources for Americans' ambivalence about cities, however, may be that cities spread so quickly across the United States and are such a common feature on the country's landscape.

The result, Witold Rybczynski says, should not surprise us. In the United States, he observes, "there never was a sense of cities as precious repositories of civilization." Urban culture spread so rapidly and thoroughly that it "lost its tie to the city, at least in the public's perception. Institutions and customs that elsewhere would have been considered marks of urbanity, here were simply thought of as national traits. Because of this uniformity, there was, as Tocqueville had noted earlier, a less dramatic difference than in Europe between the countryman and the townsman."[21]

There is merit to what Rybczynski says on this score. It certainly helps us to understand why the recent rush of words about the decline of civic life in America has focused on larger national themes and trends rather than on cities.[22] Nevertheless, the heart and soul of our decline, and possible resurrection, remains in cities, just as many persons have said over the years. That is where social critics and reformers have been telling us to look for signs of our discontent with public life. It also is where the impulse to reconstitute a community of believers around religious beliefs and morally upright practices has been expressed most fully.[23] The city has been the place where our national civic life is fashioned most clearly, and it will remain the place where our civic culture will be reclaimed, if it can be salvaged at all.

Having been the site where that good fight has been waged for well more than a century already, we can choose to see cities as places that cannot be saved or as places that never lost their civic capacity or traditions in the first place. Opinion on that matter overwhelmingly favors the former view. Most observers think that American society either has too many ill-fitting pieces and cannot be made whole or, like Humpty Dumpty in the children's nursery rhyme, it has fallen from its high perch and is irreparably broken. I hold the view that American cities have retained their civic capacity and city dwellers continue to make viable and vital communities within their municipal borders.

While many Americans live in cities, it is not the size of these places that captures our attention or shows us how to fill the smaller social worlds that each of us occupies. It also is not the depth of their municipal pocketbooks or the number of artifacts produced in cities that impresses us, favorably or otherwise. Important as such things may be, they are not what makes Americans a bourgeois people that follows an urban way of life.

What is most impressive about cities are the ways that their inhabitants have concocted to be together in the one place they cannot elude each other for too long and are condemned to carry on a dialogue with human beings not like themselves. The life they make there, for themselves and for other persons, is distinctly urban. Cities remain the largest things built by human beings that actually work; and that is not the result of some happy accident or because persons planned it that way. Cities also are the most densely constructed and socially complex of humankind's creations; and that, too, is not a coincidence.

Filling cities with persons and routines that function even passably well so that most everyone gets enough to eat, is clothed satisfactorily, and has decent shelter requires a great deal of hard work. It also takes a lot of cooperation and some amount of good fortune to be realized. All the cooperation, labor, and good fortune that enable cities to operate as well as they do, as often as they do, spring from a common source: the urban way of life that makes it possible for most of us to get along with each other much of the time.

An urban way of life as we have talked about it is not something physical like a tall building or a bridge. Nor is it as familiar to us as our family, neighborhood, or job. It is rather more like a set of public habits or customs that are part of everyday life in cities and at the same time much bigger and more commanding of our attention than most of the events that make up our daily routines. Some of these habits, to be sure, are more grand than others; and like everything else in cities, they were created by earlier city dwellers and willed to us by those persons. As the temporary custodians of these public habits, it is our responsibility to use and change them as we see fit and then to pass them on to the persons and groups that take our place. There is nothing static or necessarily permanent about an urban way of life. Nor is there much about it that has not been borrowed from another people or adapted from an earlier time.

Though the shape and tenor of customary ways of being together may change over time, their ultimate purpose and service to us do not. We call upon them when some of us want to say something important to another group or sometimes even to everyone in the city. We also use these prescribed routines when we simply want to remind everyone, including ourselves, that we are still around. It is through these public declarations, then, that we develop a basic but often unspoken set of understandings about who we are and how we are to behave when we are in each other's presence. It is also the way that we acquire an appreciation for the delicate foundation of mutual trust upon which a predictable and, one hopes, agreeable public order is built. Of such shared understandings, codes, and practices is the craft of citizenship made and the promise of a civic culture realized, whether in our small corner of the city or in the city as a whole. This, too, is an integral part of our urban way of life.

It may be said that the creation and maintenance of a civic culture is the most important accomplishment of an urban people. After all, it is only by observing and participating in activities that bring us together, in more and less homogeneous groupings, that we begin to make sense of all the different persons around us and the ways they combine themselves to accomplish something useful or good. In this manner we learn and come to practice, at least figuratively and sometimes quite literally, how to mind each other's business. It is this quality of minding someone else's affairs that distinguishes the myriad of personal or private acts and little rituals we carry out every day from those events and carryings on which are brought to our attention as object lessons for what is deemed to be typical behavior and an appropriate contribution to our urban way of life.

That part of an urban way of life which becomes accepted or celebrated as a people's civic culture also provides us with ways to frame an explanation about the meaning of big changes that overtake cities from time to time. Our ability and willingness to work with persons different from ourselves is most severely tested on such occasions. The habits, rituals, and beliefs that we package as our civic culture provide us with the means to pass these tests, and to keep passing them for as long or as often as is necessary. There are times when we do a better job of it; and there are moments when we fail miserably. The critical factor would seem to be that we keep trying to get it right.

To the extent that we succeed at all or as often as we do, we are able to build a place called a city that stands as a monument to our way of life. We also find ways to live together that a less persistent people could not hope to match. The best clues to how well a people manages to get along in the world, therefore, are to be found in the ceremonies, customs, and codes for public behavior that constitute a city's civic culture.

Individual city residents, workers, and visitors will find their own way to cope with life in cities, or they will not. Much of the time, of course, they do considerably better than that. Whatever tricks to surviving and thriving in cities they have picked up along the way probably are known to a great many persons. On the other hand, the pet solutions adopted by some persons or groups can bump against those practiced by others and rub raw the sensibilities of everybody involved. Furthermore, even if everyone agreed on what strategies should be used, there is no reason to believe that these solutions would work as well as they had earlier once everybody was using them or some big organization tried to apply these techniques on a wholesale basis.

The private deals we cut for ourselves in order to make our lives better may tell us very little about how large numbers of different persons can be together in cities. Nor do these arrangements guarantee that we will be able to go on with our lives in a predictable and civil fashion. This requires the creation of bigger, more inclusive strategies to make cities corrigible places to live and work. These are the kinds of solutions which are worked out in a city's civic culture and become enshrined as part of our urban way of life.

There are many ceremonies, customs, and codes for appropriate public behavior that become part of a city's civic culture. On one level, they are expressions of how persons in that place have worked out a way to be together in public and still carry on their private lives, peaceably and with at least a modicum of predictability. Nevertheless, though persons in many cities may work at the same jobs, wear similar clothing, or drive identical automobiles, their civic cultures will be different. Cities have a distinctive style and temperament that owe much more to larger pubic rhythms than to the steps of their individual dancers. It is what makes the visitor or newcomer feel immediately ill at ease or comfortable in a city. Indeed, it is what lets us know a place long before we have settled into it fully or acquired much information about the personal lives of those who reside there.

On another level, a city's civic culture retains a mysterious and unfinished quality even for its long-term residents. It never is completely known, much less practiced, by everyone in the city. Although a civic culture is bound by traditional ways of doing things and imagining the world, it is still very much a work in progress. Conditions of life change, and human beings change. If a civic culture is to provide good clues to how a people is to accommodate itself to new circumstances, it too must be able to change.

This is a problem, but it is not a new problem. More than two thousand years ago the Greeks struggled with the question of how to integrate different persons into a polis or political community and to teach them a common set of civic virtues. They did not succeed any more than we seem to most of the time. They found it difficult to incorporate everyone who lived in their cities into the civic culture of those places. They were unwilling or unable to expand their own community of believers to include women, children, slaves, artisans, and many foreigners. They tried to limit the impact of the outside world on their cities and to ignore the divisions built into their own society, but they never succeeded.

The solution for them, and us, was to develop the broad outline of a civic culture and let different groups in the city begin to fill in many of the details of what would pass as good ceremonies, customs, and codes for public behavior. Specific elements of a civic culture remained better or less well known to particular groups in a city. Hence, elements of the civic culture were, and still are, practiced unevenly or not at all in different parts of a city. Some aspects of a civic culture, on the other hand, were more widely shared and able to work across the whole city.

It is hard to compose a neat picture of a civic culture, because all the pieces do not hang together in a uniform way. Some rituals that make up a civic culture give out the same message or convey a similar moral. Other ceremonies and customs make different and even contradictory claims. What they have in common is the ability to serve as an early warning system to outsiders and an elaborate commemorative display for one's own people.

Implicit in the work of a civic culture are ideas that help different parties to make better sense of each other's world, to anticipate problems, and to exercise caution when dealing with persons not like oneself. The stylized displays and messages presented through a civic culture need not be read accurately, of course, or be responded to appropriately. The seriousness of the encoded piece of behavior manages to be related nonetheless by the organized and sometimes dramatic way it is presented. When the group or organization carrying out a prescribed ritual is valued highly, the act carries added weight as an institutional statement. Such displays do not go unnoticed, even when they are not well understood.

Beyond providing the participants with a menu of possible responses to any given problem, a civic culture acts like a map which shows how various ceremonies and customs can be strung together or recombined in order to make any answer more credible, if only to the group that comes up with it. Whatever else is offered in a ceremony or customary display of good public behavior, therefore, the reenactment of pieces of a civic culture binds the participants to each other. It also draws them closer to the place where the rituals are carried out.

The symbolic seeds of a civic culture are planted in the soil, then, every bit as much as they are put into the people which grows them. In this way a civic culture makes it possible for different groups to claim the same piece of land as their own and to become part of a more inclusive community. They gradually develop something that comes closer to being a common view of the world and they figure out better ways to be in it together. This remarkable accomplishment might be realized in many settings. However, it occurs most often in cities. This is because a city, even in a country where the influence of an urban way of life is felt in many smaller communities, remains the best place to find different types of persons engaging in many activities that are not known as well or in such variety outside of the city. The city also is the best place to find the elements of a civic culture being displayed and tested on a routine basis.

The Paradoxical Community

It rests with us to describe the nature of the bonds that hold us together and the mutual sacrifices and beliefs which give those bonds their rightful feeling. I already have alluded to the moral view that informs the way we put the world together. It is built around the principles of prosperity and orderliness, and it is decidedly urban in its temper and tone. The nature of the social bonds that hold us together – the way we create and maintain our communities as viable and vital places – is every bit as interesting but more difficult to describe.

We are fortunate that the everyday people who fill the world and give it meaning are not social philosophers. They are practical men and women who must find ways of being together that work and are accepted as good by a large number of their fellow community members. Their answers to the questions I posed earlier fall somewhere between the jumbled social mess we fear is all around us and the comfortable certainty that is guaranteed by liberal communalists or their conservative counterparts.

Persons who follow an urban way of life have fashioned a world that mixes principle with the need to make practical accommodations. Their brilliant solution to the problem of order draws heavily from both the liberal and conservative brands of communalism. In fact, each of the four basic ways that everyday people use to make their world brings together elements of liberal and conservative communalism. These ways of "doing" community will be described in great detail later in the book. For the time being, I only will highlight the main features that each of them possesses.

Commercial communalism entails the kind of community building that we associate with the business leaders of a city. Its operating principles are sharing, piety, and public-regarding behavior. When business leaders try to organize the world they usually find it necessary to openly accept more and different persons into the community than they otherwise would admit. On the other hand, they put renewed emphasis on the kind of behavior that persons are allowed to demonstrate in public and they insist that behavior serve the commonweal.

The finest examples of commercial communalism in American cities are found in voluntary subscription campaigns that business people use to drum up money and support for projects they deemed to be in the interest of the whole community. These campaigns have long been used to promote a variety of initiatives within cities. Projects in whose behalf subscription campaigns are undertaken sometimes are geared to meet more public ends such as constructing a municipal park or providing charity. On other occasions the campaign can serve more private ends like the promotion of a joint stock company that would bring more industry and jobs to the city. Much of the time, however, it is difficult to tell where the dividing line is between the public and private benefits that will result from the successful completion of a subscription campaign.

Ethnic communalism is the kind of community building that one finds, not surprisingly, inside ethnic enclaves and among persons who can trace their origins to a foreign land. Its champions organize their part of the urban world around belonging, tolerance, and privacy. Unlike business people who try to run a community, ethnic group leaders in most cases have been able to retain their strict membership criteria. Within the confines of their own group, however, they promote a lot of self-seeking behavior and accept beliefs and actions that can be much different from those embraced by persons in the larger society.

The quintessential examples of ethnic communalism are found in rotating credit associations and mutual trade associations. Both take advantage of the trust and regard that fellow ethnic group members have for each other. The former requires participants to share a little of their disposable wealth in order to capitalize the purchases or investments of their fellow ethnic group members. They usually are used by less well-to-do persons. Mutual trade associations are created by ethnic business people in order to protect their markets inside a given territory and to help them reduce some of their costs by collaborating in the purchase of materials and goods at better rates. There are obvious parallels between these types of activities and the voluntary subscription campaigns under-taken by more prosperous business leaders. Indeed, rotating credit associations and mutual trade associations are the ethnic versions of voluntary subscription campaigns.

Consumer communalism is achieved through the spending habits of shoppers and investors. Persons are supposed to become more alike through the power of the marketplace. To a certain extent this strategy does work. Individuals certainly are able to share both more goods and the experience of acquiring them. Self-seeking behavior is encouraged, and many different persons are encouraged to participate in activities that reflect such pursuits. At the same time, though, this is supposed to be done under carefully laid out rules. Failure to abide by the rules governing shopping and investing prudently is supposed to limit or stop one from participating in this kind of communal activity.

The central ritual in consumer communalism is shopping. However, it is the extension of credit to more and different types of persons which makes it possible for them to act and look more like each other by shopping and investing in similar ways. Principles embedded in voluntary subscription campaigns are broadly applied here as well. Individuals voluntarily give up a portion of their wealth in order to get something for themselves even as they contribute to the well-being of the community as a whole by circulating more money through it and showing their loyalty to local businesses. In effect, consumer communalism gives persons who are not rich an opportunity to participate in rituals that once were the special province of only wealthy individuals. It also enables less prosperous individuals to adorn themselves in a manner that mimics but cannot replicate the ways that truly wealthy persons display themselves.[24] You may not be rich, but this does not preclude you from acting like you are.

Finally, *government communalism* combines the idea of belonging with tolerance and public-regarding behavior. One observes this kind of community-building activity whenever government agents do something that draws citizens together or extends the rights and prerogatives of citizenship to more persons. Rules are not ignored once individuals gain admission to the community as citizens, but the same rules may not be enforced as rigidly as they were before citizenship was granted. Government officials sometimes try to encourage certain groups by passing rules that favor these parties, or they may subsidize into existence groups that are deemed useful to the commonweal. More often than not, however, government agents build better communities indirectly by assisting larger numbers of citizens or by involving them in officially sponsored ceremonies such as voting.

The central rituals in government communalism are not elections and voting. They are paying taxes and getting special favors. The act of paying taxes is akin to a mandatory subscription campaign, and the revenues that are generated are supposed to be used to serve a broad public good. It is the way that both more well-off persons and less than well-off persons extend credit in amounts that are roughly proportional to their wealth to agents who are supposed to represent their interests. More often than not, though, these benefits are not spread all that broadly and end up benefiting some types of persons more than others. The general good accomplished under government communalism is of an indirect sort, as it is in shopping, whereby improvements in the condition of life for some persons among us is deemed a good thing for all of us.

We shall see that each of these types of communalism was in use well before Americans staged their revolt against Great Britain. There has been no great evolution since then in the way that Americans use these different techniques to make communities or to transform themselves into a more united people. One form of communalism may be more popular for a while, but it never dominates the other approaches to building communities for too long. It is more likely that persons will put these ways of "doing" community together in different combinations in order to address a new or especially nagging problem. If I have done my math properly, there are fifteen ways in which these four types of communalism can stand alone or be brought together. The residents of American cities can experiment a long time with different ways to improve their communities before conceding defeat; and they have not done that yet.

It often is said that we live in a more liberal age. If this were so, it would mean that elements of liberal communalism should be more apparent in our dealings with each other. Persons who have studied cities and the urban way of life practiced there far longer than I have certainly write about cities as if they were sinkholes of sharing, tolerance, and private-regarding behavior. Still, I am not at all sure that they are right or that cities are best understood in terms that more liberal commentators would find agreeable. Indeed, I am pretty certain they are wrong and that it makes at least as much sense to imagine cities as repositories for conservative ideas and customs.

The recipe for community life that persons in small towns have put together over the years reveals an interesting mix of more liberal and conservative themes. It is something of a paradox, because one is not supposed to be able to blend these two ways of organizing communities. In fact, social philosophers of a more liberal or conservative bent are fully convinced that they alone know what a good community looks like and how to put one together. The types of communalism I have identified reflect the idea that a good community is likely to have both conservative and liberal themes built into it. The civic culture of cities, I hypothesize, should have more of this mixing going on than is apparent in small towns. It is that feature of community life which should best distinguish the civic culture of small towns and suburbs, even a suburban enclave of the sort created by Chinese Americans just outside of Los Angeles, from that of larger cities.

It may be that our period of history has been tagged as being more liberal because we try so many ways of mixing and matching different ways of building communities at the same time. I am afraid that this explanation is no more satisfactory than the one that would have us using more liberal ways to build communities today. No less an authority on these matters than historian Paul Boyer has shown that many groups in nineteenth-century American cities experimented continuously and sometimes frantically in the hope of finding some new way to keep their communities together and to transform themselves into a united people.[25]

We shall have to find a better explanation for why we are living in a liberal age or abandon that idea altogether.

I suspect that we shall not have to abandon this idea. Our liberal bias is plainly seen in the many ways we use the marketplace and government to encourage more of us to stay orderly and behave as if we were prosperous, even when we are not. Customs and beliefs surrounding *consumer* and *government communalism* can help to make us happy and whole, but only in an indirect way. They accomplish this by featuring individuals as the parties who are responsible for building a coherent world and making meaningful sense of ourselves as a people.

Citizens and shoppers can make the world a better place, but only one person at a time. In principle, there is nothing to stop them from becoming more organized. Yet the basis for doing so among shoppers is not readily apparent, unless they belong to a group with some outstanding grievance against a particular product or the company that manufactures it. The reasons for citizens to do so, on the other hand, are difficult to sustain, even when the means are available. It is hard to mobilize large numbers of citizens for extended periods of time to achieve anything except during periods of national calamity, and sometimes not even then. While government officials and political rituals can encourage citizens to accomplish certain ends or to build a particular kind of community, there are times when leaders do not find it advantageous or desirable to encourage their constituents to become part of a larger political or consumer movement.

Commercial and *ethnic communalism*, on the other hand, both feature corporate solutions to problems. The hard work of making a people and building a community is done primarily by groups of like-minded persons and is undertaken principally for their own betterment. The dilemma for business people and ethnic leaders is figuring out how to translate what is better for them into something that is good for the rest of us. They certainly have not been the only parties in cities who were sympathetic to this way of making a good community or, for that matter, the only ones that practiced it. They simply did more of this kind of community building than did other groups.

More corporate ways of building communities and a united people have their own limitations and quirks. For instance, there is no guarantee that all the members of ethnic and commercial groups will cooperate with each other all of the time. Nor is it clear that all members benefit equally from the labor of their larger group or that outsiders will not take some advantage from the success that these groups enjoy. It means only that the chief reason for undertaking all this hard work is the advancement of a self-conscious group or the community as a whole, not the material well-being or personal satisfaction of individuals.

Business leaders and ethnic groups can use their influence to promote change or to keep the world as we find it. Agents of government and the marketplace likewise can work in the service of change or to maintain the world our ancestors made. The liberal character of our time has virtually nothing to do with changing or maintaining the world. It has everything to do with using individuals to do the hard work of building communities and in helping us to develop a finer notion of ourselves as being part of a larger, more inclusive people.

Given the attention we give to governments and the marketplace as the institutional pillars of the modern world, none of this should come as much of a surprise. We might be more surprised by the fact that corporatist strategies for making communities and ourselves into a people retain as much authority and effectiveness in the modern world as they do. The point of this extended discussion is to encourage us to divorce our talk about liberals and conservatives from any idea that one of them is more interested in promoting social change or that change, in whatever form it takes, is at the base of our unease about the future. What may be more central to our malaise is a reliance upon individuals as world builders and the carriers of our culture.

Even if this is so and we are about to "rediscover" the joys of working through smaller groups and doing it closer to home, this does not mean that we will abandon or forget the lessons we learned through the government or marketplace. Indeed, urban dwellers rely upon a mix of more distant and immediate obligations in order to put together their communities and to make a whole people out of a disparate collection of persons and groups. In two of these ways – *commercial* and *ethnic communalism* – groups are given more responsibility and credit for building communities and making a united people. In the other two ways – *consumer* and *government communalism* – individuals are given more of the responsibility and credit for achieving these goals.

None of these approaches to making a community and a people is perfect and can stand alone. Each contributes something to our urban way of life, particularly as it is practiced inside cities. No small part of their contribution is tied to the fact that they combine both liberal and conservative ways of "doing" community and making cities good places to live and work. In fact, it is possible to combine these different types of communalism in such a way as to advance contradictory ideas about the right way to build communities. When ethnic leaders and business people promote a community-building activity, for instance, they have to reconcile the ethnic leader's responsibility to their own group with the business person's interest in framing the initiative so that it appeals to the broadest possible constituency. In principle, this should be very difficult to do.

Their union is not logical. It has big contradictions built into it.

Nevertheless, these two ways of conducting civic life may not be as irreconcilable as political theorists have maintained.[26] In fact, their union may bring a certain vigor to whatever action is taken under their joint sponsorship precisely because it shows how different groups and interests can be reconciled when important issues are raised. City dwellers who come from different walks of life are not supposed to be able to carry on serious discussions with each other, much less initiate significant ventures together. It is precisely this feature, however, which gives community building activities in the United States the paradoxical quality of being liberal and conservative at the same time. More importantly, it may actually work.

The problem, of course, is that we do not see the urban world working all that well. At the very least, there are many persons or groups that do not benefit from much of the hard work which is undertaken. Generations of urban reformers have worried about this and experimented with ways to make an urban way of life work more smoothly, if not more equitably. Notwithstanding their good intentions, many thoughtful persons today believe that something is fundamentally wrong with cities and the way of life practiced there. We are not certain how to turn this situation around, or even that it can be turned around.

One possible solution may be to look less often to government agencies and the marketplace for answers to our problems. It may have been unrealistic to expect individual citizens and shoppers to take on much of the responsibility for solving our pressing social, economic, and political problems. It also may have been unfair. We may be better advised in the future to use more corporatist strategies to make our communities better places to live and work. In the past, these have been activities that featured the work of business people and ethnic groups and reflected the influence of *commercial* and *ethnic communalism.* For reasons that are obvious, however, this solution would not be warmly embraced by many Americans who are interested in creating the impression that we are more alike than we are different and that individuals matter more than groups. Many urban reformers and virtually all the social philosophers who write about community life do not like paradoxes. They prefer that we package our solutions to problems in neat boxes decorated in colors that do not clash.

In Celebration of Us

It is regrettable but nonetheless true that the world usually does not present itself to us so cleanly. Indeed, if there is one thing about cities on which both their boosters and detractors can agree, it surely is that cities are an odd, I would say paradoxical, mix of the best and the worst that life has to offer. Unmistakable wealth and grinding poverty are posed like ill-matched relatives forced together at a family reunion. Parks that once were lovely and full of children are now unkempt and littered with broken bottles and worse. Homeless persons who murmur and sing to themselves or bark obscenities at passersby stand defiantly in front of grand public buildings or panhandle for change from neatly dressed men and women on their way home after a long day at work. A short ride on a trolley or bus can take you from elegant downtown offices and department stores to neighborhoods with tired buildings and nasty-looking tenants. They are distinct but inseparable pieces of the same big puzzle. When we think of cities in this manner, it becomes less difficult to imagine that they can be made more prosperous and orderly by the equally paradoxical coupling of liberal and conservative ways of "doing" community.

Earlier in the book I told a story about Dayton, Ohio and the apparent lapse in civic memory that its people had experienced as a result of unsettling changes in their local economy. Their problems, it will be recalled, were visited upon them by the closing of the National Cash Register Company and the economic aftershocks that rippled through the city when other businesses suffered because of its closing. Other jobs eventually became available for many out-of-work persons. In the meantime, however, the people of Dayton apparently had forgotten a great deal of what made them special. It was their support for organizations that were not at all like businesses but also did a lot to sustain the community in good times and bad. De Tocqueville might say that the "civil partnership" among Dayton's residents had weakened. Yet it was weak less because a business "association" had folded than because Dayton's citizens had abandoned other "civil associations" and modes of civic engagement.

The people of Dayton may have snapped out of their dazed state and figured this out by now, or they may still be stumbling around in search of solutions to problems that persons used to take for granted. In either case, it is clear that they had lost their civic memory at least for a while and that the consequences were not good.

I will end this chapter with a different kind of story, one showing that not all cities suffer from lapses in their civic memory. Even when life is not great, the people of some cities set aside special occasions that remind them about what is important, or they use such moments to signal a change in their understanding of what is important. The effect in either case is the same. Through such events they display ideas and ways of being together that may help them better meet the challenges of a new day. Such occasions are important in their own right, if only because they make a great many persons stand up and take notice of what is being done and said. They are more important, though, for all the hard work and shaking out of priorities and loyalties that take place as groups put the bigger show together. Recent changes in the celebration known as Mardi Gras in New Orleans provide a good illustration of how this process works and of a civic memory in action. The changes also demonstrate how different parties bring their way of "doing" community to the same event and give expression to the tensions or paradoxes built into their local society.

Most of us know Mardi Gras as the big party in New Orleans that precedes Lent every year. The people of New Orleans certainly know it in this way. They know it, too, as an economic windfall that each year brings several hundred million dollars into the local economy, 27 million dollars to the city in tax revenues, and an additional 15 million dollars in state taxes.[27] They also experience the event as a civic ritual to which many groups across the city, and increasingly in the surrounding suburban parishes as well, dedicate much spare time throughout the year.

There are many ways in which one could make sense of all the work and showmanship that goes into making Mardi Gras a success. The most provocative and informative treatments of the celebration, however, have been provided by a pair of writers who see it as a noisily staged contest between socially prominent individuals and those for whom civic accomplishment is valued highly. While the two commentators agree on this point, they draw remarkably different conclusions about what all the changes mean to the persons who live in and around New Orleans.

Calvin Trillin, writing for *The New Yorker* early in 1998, tried to capture how the balance between social prominence and civic accomplishment had shifted over the years. He noted that in 1991 members of the city council finally took up the issue of whether the old line krewes that marched in the Mardi Gras parades had to be integrated. A variety of different persons were represented on the city's 29 krewes, but each krewe tended to have only certain types of persons among its members. A krewe might be composed of white or black persons, men or women, and more wealthy individuals or common folk. The black members of the city council decided that it was time to change this arrangement. Many persons in New Orleans, black as well as white, were not so sure this was a good idea. The leaders of the most prominent krewes, each of which drew its members from the highest rungs of New Orleans society, were especially incensed. "As people who thought they had been doing a good deed by putting on a parade," Trillin observed, "they felt hurt at being cast as selfish, and even racist. They were forced to defend themselves with studies showing – of all things – how much tourist money their parades brought in."[28]

Representatives of less elite groups and populations in the city took strong exception to even this kind of pedestrian defense of the old-line krewes. There were strong arguments to be made against the krewes with higher social pedigrees, Trillin pointed out. Certainly, persons could not have missed the irony of having the black mayor of a major American city paying "ritual respects to an explicitly white king of a segregated private club." Trillin also noted, however, that "Carnival had traditionally been replete with incongruities."[29] One of these anomalous incongruities was the all-black krewe known as "Zulu" which had been marching in Mardi Gras for many years under its own special banner.

Trillin reflected on his own impressions of the Zulu krewe and the parade's more exotic participants:

> When I saw the Zulu Social Aid and Pleasure Club parade on Shrove Tuesday thirty-seven years ago ... it was widely considered a sort of moving 'Amos 'n' Andy' show that would eventually crumble under the pressure of respectable black people. But Zulus still parade in blackface and grass skirts every Shrove Tuesday; their parade has grown more lavish and, somehow, more acceptable, with the inclusion of black professionals and politicians and a number of white people. In New Orleans, it had always been assumed that people would celebrate Carnival in their own way, whether it was by riding in the parade of an all-woman krewe or holding a ball-gown contest for men in drag.[30]

Thus, while the krewe organizations themselves were anything but democratic, a variety of groups always managed to participate in the parades. James Gill, taking a more academic view of the proceedings, observed that "every formal parade attracted hordes of 'second-liners' performing impromptu dances as they follow the floats. Less formal parades were everywhere, from the marching clubs that proceeded from bar to bar to the 'gangs' in the black neighborhoods who dressed up as Red Indians on the warpath."[31]

There was a great deal of what kindergarten teachers call "parallel play" going on in the parades. Persons representing different parts of New Orleans' diverse population may not have been in the same groups, but they did play next to each other in the same sand box, share the toys left for them, accepted each other's presence, and, most importantly, did not throw sand at the other children.

> No class ... had an exclusive claim on Carnival and several parades were staged by men and women who had no social pretension but did have a fierce dedication to their cultural inheritance. Black society had its own cotillions and debutante parties (and) the predominantly black krewe, Zulu, preceded Rex along the parade route. ... After Rex came the poor

man's floats ... with scores of riders unloading tons of plastic beads ... not infrequently caught at earlier parades and hoarded for redistribution.[32]

A number of persons feared that much of this democratic spirit would be lost in the rush to integrate the private clubs which sponsored the different parades. Their concerns were not unfounded. Attempts by the mayor and krewe captains to reach an accommodation that would satisfy council members did not succeed. By 1993, three major krewes – Momus, Comus, and Proteus – had canceled their parades but not their private balls, leaving Rex as the remaining old-line krewe to carry on its traditional parade, albeit with some new black members.

Calvin Trillin looked upon these changes with a favorable eye, believing that they breathed fresh democratic air into an otherwise antiquated celebration. New Orleans, he suggested, became a little more "American" and a little less aristocratic with the passing of the Comus, Momus, and Proteus parades. Indeed, the emergence of a group called the "Krewe of America" and its parade featuring a large number of out-of-towners who have enough money to buy their way into the celebration added, for Trillin, a distinctly cosmopolitan and commercial flavor to what had remained a parochial affair for far too long.

James Gill generally shares Trillin's assessment that the public meeting between Rex, the unmasked civic leader, and Comus, the masked aristocrat, openly acknowledged the importance of social eminence over civic accomplishment in New Orleans society. Yet he is not so quick to condemn such practices or to embrace the celebration's new democratic trappings. He recalls the origin of krewes and their gay floats after the Civil War as expressions of protest against outsiders and their ideas, especially their progressive racial views. Such vivid but otherwise muted protests had given way over the years to more explicitly social celebrations. Still, a number of groups felt the sting of being excluded from many events.

There is much to admire in the Trillin and Gill treatments of Mardi Gras, and perhaps the white and black citizens of New Orleans should have found more important civic tasks to work on together long before now. The fact is they had not, and these changes in Mardi Gras might have been the first sign that the people of New Orleans were waking up to that reality. They may have been working out a new way of talking to each other.

I hope this is the case, because in pulling apart the old way of doing Mardi Gras the citizens of New Orleans were also undermining a venerable custom that urban folk from different social stations have long used to "talk" to each other. Historians who look at parades, celebrations, protests, and even occasions of mob unrest as "street theater" tell us that these engagements serve a variety of purposes for the persons who put them on and for the larger community that attends to them. There are times when participants in these affairs come from most corners of the community and moments when only narrower portions of the population are involved. Some of the engagements are more rowdy than others, and there has been a general trend toward making the events more "commercial" by attaching them to shopping more than making noise, disrupting traffic, or breaking store windows.[33]

Who participates in these events and how they act on any given occasion can tell us a great deal about the temper and content of civic life at a particular moment in history. In general, historians have been of two minds when trying to make some sense of these public engagements. On the one hand, they correctly note that some events are more "democratic" than others in the sense that a broad segment of the population actually participates directly in putting the affair before the public. While there never is an occasion when all groups and ideas are presented for wider public viewing, historians have observed that groups with less social standing in the community play a less prominent part in well-organized public demonstrations. Their involvement often is limited to more raucous and violent public displays. On the other hand, there is no getting around the fact that many parties with questionable social pedigrees and little wealth have collaborated with more prominent and well-to-do groups in planning and executing many of these affairs in the past. This would include outbursts of popular unrest against a host of disreputable persons and obnoxious policies and business practices. The point that each was trying to make with its involvement might be different, but over the years persons from different social groups and classes in cities have worked together in ways that go way beyond "parallel play" in many episodes of public commemoration and condemnation.

In the case of New Orleans and the controversies over racially segregated krewes and social clubs, I suppose the message that lower-class persons depended upon the charity of their social "betters" was clear enough in the old Mardi Gras and maybe demeaning to some persons. At the same time, except for the failed legal challenge to segregated luncheon clubs, the condition of life for minority and poor persons does not appear to have been a concern for the individuals trying to break into the higher levels of New Orleans society. Indeed, as a result of all the arguing over Mardi Gras the idea that individuals blessed with good fortune have an obligation to help those who are much less well-off might well drop off the city's civic radar screen in the future or not be acknowledged in so public a way by other groups.

In the end, all of the legal fuss and principled fury over Mardi Gras turns out to have been about the insistence of meritorious persons to receive more social recognition than they had gotten in the past. Although the specter of ancient tribal or sexual stigmas was waved in front of everyone to justify their claims of unfair treatment, we will have to see how many accomplished persons from these despised castes actually end up being invited to join the elite luncheon clubs whose parades they helped to end. The successful challenge to the old-line krewes appears to have had nothing to do with making life a little better for the poor, the lame, and the mute who live in New Orleans. Furthermore, it does not seem that anyone initiating the controversy thought about the important changes that had taken place in Mardi Gras. It had once been an event in which the cream of New Orleans society railed against evolution and mocked black persons. Now it was an occasion when civic-minded Rex was sandwiched between the Zulu krewe and poor man's floats from which loot pilfered from the rich was redistributed to the masses. The protesters only ensured that accomplished persons got the public approbation they deserved without also having to take on the responsibilities that formerly had come to persons who wished to climb to a higher spot in New Orleans society.

Whatever else one might say about the new and improved Mardi Gras, it certainly is a less parochial celebration today. It shows how an important "local" event continues to be shaped by ideas and groups introduced from outside the city. The celebration also draws on all the different ways in which Americans traditionally have tried to build their sense of community. Elements of commercial, ethnic, consumer, and governmental communalism are all apparent in the conflict over Mardi Gras or in the celebration itself. Business and social leaders in New Orleans have used Mardi Gras not only to celebrate themselves but also to draw attention to ideas about how the larger community should be organized around them. They came to rely on the appeal of Mardi Gras to outsiders who came to the city and spent a great deal of money to participate, however indirectly, in this communal event. Shoppers reinforced whatever messages were being aired by members of the local business and social elite. Representatives of imagined or would-be ethnic groups used the event to organize themselves and to push for changes in the social makeup of New Orleans "society." Government officials did their best to work with these various parties in an unsuccessful effort to broker a deal that would keep the celebration more like persons recalled or at least make its passage into something new less fractious.

The outcome of all these deliberations and fights, from our perspective, really matters less than the fact that Mardi Gras draws on ideas about how to build a better community which are not supposed to be found together, much less mesh so vividly. Mardi Gras embraces both tolerance and piety. Within certain well-marked limits, anything goes. Persons may drink too much and engage in behavior that on another day would land them in jail, and sometimes still does. Yet the whole town does not suffer from the excesses of Mardi Gras revelers, and the police are never so far away or out of sight that they cannot be called upon to keep the festive ravings and rants of persons in check. There is a healthy mix of private-regarding and public-regarding behavior in the work of the various groups that participate in Mardi Gras. They are able to re-affirm their status and share a very public moment with each other to make sure that everyone gets the point about where in the city's social and economic food chain each of them stands. Finally, the whole argu-ment over who could be a member of the krewes participating in the parade speaks powerfully to the question of how open or closed member-ship in the New Orleans branch of the community of believers was to be. Some persons who have been a part of that group forever were reluctant to open their arms (and luncheon clubs) to persons who not only felt excluded but were in fact kept out of the kind of deliberations that made New Orleans move in one direction or another. Other persons who had lived and worked in the city for a long time wanted to play a bigger role in making those kind of decisions, or at least get the chance to play more often in the same sand box with the older kids.

Our brief discussion of changes in Mardi Gras also should remind us that we can make too much of one event and read too much into changes that take place in it. After all, the Rex Carnival ball and its debutantes still are put out for public viewing by the media, and Comus still receives Rex, however discretely, at the Municipal Auditorium. Clues to how society in New Orleans once worked, and maybe still does, have not been eliminated. No matter how muffled or amended, important features of the old ways remain intact and available to remind us how we used to put together a "proper" society.

The day for remembering these lessons may come sooner for New Orleans than anyone imagines. The well-born and plebeian may again find common cause and try to reassert some of the old ways. They will do it, if only to beat back the drunk and rowdy crowds in the French Quarter whose members today beg less for plastic beads and more for a show of flesh from the young women who stand on the floats during the parades.

What happens in an event like Mardi Gras does hold some clues to the character of a people and to the compact or "civil partnerships" they have made among themselves. Yet Mardi Gras is no more New Orleans than Father's Day is Spokane, which happens to be where that particular custom was invented. Bigger public demonstrations merely provide a convenient window through which one can glimpse a bit more of the routine work that goes into maintaining a community and something of what its members think of themselves or what they aspire to be.

Most of the clues to understanding a city's civic culture or the messages conveyed by groups trying to shape that culture are embedded in their routine work. Pedestrian as most of our days may be, they consist of many small moments whose union, however seamless or patched together it may appear, has integrity and value. Personal as so many of these moments are, sometimes intensely so, they take on a broader significance when brought to the attention of a larger audience. It is in this way that private acts, the typical comings and goings of everyday life, become public events and the accomplishment of an everyday people. The cumulative effect of all these acts makes an urban way of life real to those who live it and reveals to the rest of us the set of understandings and foundation of trust upon which they fashion a workable social order. It is this set of understandings, the sense of mutual regard it implies, and the customary ways that groups put this rough consensus into action that are a people's and city's civic culture.

Conspicuous events can usher in new understandings and help to establish opportunities for collaboration that had, until recently, been missed. Reviews of the event, once it has taken place, become part of the stored public memory for conducting this or similar affairs. They are much more than a pleasant recollection. They form a kind of social capital that can be saved or reinvested in new activities, much as one would draw on a line of credit to start or expand a business venture.

What is apparent from events like Mardi Gras is that every city has its own quirky ways and interesting stories to tell. Persons who occupy cities, even those who stay for only a little while, do a whole lot more during their tenure than take up space. They are unwitting collaborators in making a world that works, and indeed works better than most of us recognize or are willing to acknowledge.

City dwellers are neither passive nor ineffective. Though they may be compelled to cope with events and conditions not of their own making, they make things happen. Furthermore, what they do makes a difference not only to each other but also for persons and in places far removed from where they are. We are, after all, much less the inventors of our own world than borrowers and sometimes thieves of other persons' worlds. We take what we need from the available store of cultural goods, put these items to some good use, and either pitch the remnants or tuck them away for safe keeping. The effect, in either case, is the same. Our urban way of life is energetic and at times even wildly creative, but it remains fundamentally parochial.

This is why so much of what passes for everyday life in different American cities can be both familiar to us and can make us feel oddly "out of place" at the same time. Our urban way of life is not practiced exactly the same way in all cities. There are many variations in what is valued and how persons give expression to those values. It is time, I think, to turn our attention more fully to the stories that Americans have told each other as they made themselves into a bourgeois people who practice an urban way of life in the cities they call home.

NOTES

1 Sir Peter Hall, *Cities in Civilization* (New York: Pantheon Books, 1998), p. 612.
2 Ibid., p. 933.
3 Alexis de Tocqueville, *Democracy in America*, Volume II (New York: Vintage Books, 1945), p. 124.
4 Ibid., p. 114.
5 Ibid., p. 123.
6 Rowland Berthoff, *Social Order and Disorder in American History* (New York: Harper & Row, 1971); Larry Lyon, *The Community in Urban Society* (Chicago: Dorsey Press, 1987), pp. 93–112.
7 Manuel Castells, *The Urban Question* (London: Edward Arnold, 1977); Norton Long, "Territoriality and Citizenship," *American Review of Public Administration*, Volume 23, Number 1, March 1993, pp. 19–27; Thomas Bender, "The Erosion of Public Culture: Cities, Discourses, and Professional Disciplines," in Thomas L. Haskell (ed.), *The Authority of Experts: Studies in History and Theory* (Bloomington, IN: Indiana University Press, 1984), pp. 84–106; David A. Hollinger, "Inquiry and Uplift: Late Nineteenth-Century American Academics and the Moral Efficacy of Scientific Practice," in Thomas L. Haskell (ed.), *The Authority of Experts*, pp. 142–55.
8 John Rice, *A Disease of One's Own: Psychotherapy, Addiction, and the Emergence of Co-Dependency* (New Brunswick, NJ: Transaction Books, 1995).
9 David Karp, Gregory Stone, and William Yoels, *Being Urban: A Sociology of City Life* (New York: Praeger, 1991), pp. 82–105.
10 Alice Steinbach, "Those Strangers We Know," *Reader's Digest*, October 1993, p. 138.
11 Morris Janowitz, *The Community Press in an Urban Setting* (Chicago: University of Chicago Press, 1967); Gerald Suttles, *The Social Order of the Slum* (Chicago: University of Chicago Press, 1968); Gerald Suttles, *The Social Construction of Communities* (Chicago: University of Chicago Press, 1972); Albert Hunter, *Symbolic Communities: The Persistence and Change of Chicago's Local Communities* (Chicago: University of Chicago Press, 1974); Barry Wellman, "The Community Question: The Intimate Networks of East Yorkers," *American Journal of Sociology*, Volume 84, March 1979, pp. 1,201–31; John R. Logan and Glenna D. Spitze, "Family Neighbors," *American Journal of Sociology*, Volume 100, September 1994, pp. 453–76.

12 Roger S. Ahlbrandt, Jr., *Neighborhoods, People, and Community* (New York: Plenum Press, 1984), p. 3; Avery Guest and Barrett Lee, "The Social Organization of Local Areas," *Urban Affairs Quarterly*, Volume 19, Number 2, December 1983, pp. 217–40; Carol Silverman, "Neighboring and Urbanism: Commonality Versus Friendship," *Urban Affairs Quarterly*, Volume 22, Number 2, December 1986, pp. 312–28; Edward Crenshaw and Craig St John, "The Organizationally Dependent Community: A Comparative Study of Neighborhood Attachment," *Urban Affairs Quarterly*, Volume 24, Number 3, March 1989, pp. 412–34; Meredith Ramsay, "Redeeming the City: Exploring the Relationship Between Church and Metropolis," *Urban Affairs Review*, Volume 33, Number 5, May 1998, pp. 595–626; Logan and Spitze, "Family Neighbors."

13 Donald I. Warren, *Black Neighborhoods: An Assessment of Community Power* (Ann Arbor, MI: University of Michigan Press, 1975); Curt Lamb, *Political Power in Poor Neighborhoods* (New York: John Wiley, 1975); Matthew A. Crenson, *Neighborhood Politics* (Cambridge, MA: Harvard University Press, 1983); Howard W. Hallman, *Neighborhoods: Their Place in Urban Life* (Beverly Hills: Sage, 1984); Ahlbrandt, *Neighborhoods, People, and Community*; Robert Jay Dilger, *Neighborhood Politics: Residential Community Associations in American Governance* (New York: New York University Press, 1992).

14 Richard C. Wade, *Slavery in the Cities: The South, 1820–1860* (New York: Oxford University Press, 1972), pp. 143–79; Howard N. Rabinowitz, *Race Relations in the Urban South: 1865–1890* (New York: Oxford University Press, 1978), pp. 198–254; Julie Winch, *Philadelphia's Black Elite: Activism, Accommodation, and the Struggle for Autonomy, 1787–1848* (Philadelphia: Temple University Press, 1988).

15 Kenneth T. Jackson, *The Ku Klux Klan in the City: 1915–1930* (New York: Oxford University Press, 1971); Robert P. Ingalls, *Urban Vigilantes in the New South: Tampa, 1882–1936* (Knoxville, TN: University of Tennessee Press, 1988).

16 Jonathan Rieder, *Canarsie: The Jews and Italians of Brooklyn Against Liberalism* (Cambridge, MA: Harvard University Press, 1985).

17 Kenneth A. Scherzer, *The Unbounded Community: Neighborhood Life and Social Structure in New York City, 1830–1875* (Durham, NC: Duke University Press, 1992).

18 Mark Abrahamson, *Urban Enclaves: Identity and Place in America* (New York: St Martin's Press, 1995).

19 Karp et al., *Being Urban*, pp. 89 and 92.

20 Ibid., pp. 107–31.

21 Witold Rybczynski, *City Life* (New York: Simon & Schuster, 1995), p. 114.

22 Alexis de Tocqueville, *Democracy in America*, Volume II (New York: Vintage Books, 1945); Norton E. Long, "Seeking the Polity's Bottom Line," *Administration & Society*, Volume 24, Number 2, August 1992, pp. 107–14; Michael J. Sandel, "America's Search for a New Public Philosophy," *The Atlantic Monthly*, March 1996, pp. 57–74; Michael Schudson, "What if Civic Life Didn't Die?" *The American Prospect*,

Number 25, March–April 1996, pp. 17–20; Theda Skocpol, "Unraveling From Above," *The American Prospect*, Number 25, March–April 1996, pp. 20–5; Robert Putnam, "Robert Putnam Responds," *The American Prospect*, Number 25, March–April 1996, pp. 25–8; Ann Swidler, "To Revitalize Community Life, We Must First Strengthen Our National Institutions," *The Chronicle of Higher Education*, May 16, 1997. Andrew Greeley has an unpublished manuscript entitled "The Strange Reappearance of Civic America: Religion and Volunteering" which has been available on his web page for a few years. In it he criticizes Putnam's thesis that civic life in America is declining and offers evidence from social surveys to bolster his own argument that volunteering, especially through religious groups, is especially high in the United States. Further evidence along this line is provided by Everett Ladd, "The Data Just Don't Show Erosion of America's 'Social Capital'" in *The Public Perspective*, Volume 7, Number 4, June/July 1996, pp. 1, 5–22.

23 For an interesting treatment of the idea that we need to pay closer attention to "the domain of Obedience to the Unenforceable" and the sound moral footing upon which all humane and civic behavior must rest see: The Right Honorable Lord Moulton, "Law and Manners," *The Atlantic Monthly*, July 1924, pp. 1–5. More recent and explicit treatments of the role of religious values and conduct grounded in good Protestant teachings for communities generally and cities in particular can be found in several sources. John Higham, "Hanging Together: Divergent Unities in American History," *Journal of American History*, Volume 61, Number 1, June 1974, pp. 5–28; Patrick J. Hill, "Religion and the Quest for Community," in Leroy S. Rouner (ed.), *On Community* (Notre Dame, IN: University of Notre Dame Press, 1991), pp. 149–61; and Stephen Kalberg, "Tocqueville and Weber on the Sociological Origins of Citizenship: The Political Culture of American Democracy," *Citizenship Studies*, Volume 1, Number 2, July 1997, pp. 199–222. The most thorough and useful treatment of this subject, however, remains Paul Boyer's book *Urban Masses and Moral Order in America: 1820–1920* (Cambridge, MA: Harvard University Press, 1978).

24 Juliet B. Schor, *The Overspent American: Upscaling, Downshifting, and the New Consumer* (New York: Basic Books, 1998).

25 Boyer, *Urban Masses and Moral Order in America*.

26 For a discussion of why these four ways of "doing community" might not be reconcilable, see: Christopher Lasch, *The Revolt of the Elites and the Betrayal of Democracy* (New York: W.W. Norton, 1995). I cannot do justice here to the extensive and finely textured argument that Lasch lays out in the book. However, it really is a critique of how traditional elites abandoned their obligation to be community leaders and how certain traditional institutions like "the church" have been supplanted by things like self-help groups and personal therapy. He does not hold out much hope of finding a cure for what ails America in the marketplace, government, or in the "tribalism" one might associate with ethnic groups.

27 James Gill, *Lords of Misrule: Mardi Gras and the Politics of Race in New Orleans* (Jackson, MS: University of Mississippi Press, 1997), p. 19.

28   Calvin Trillin, "New Orleans Unmasked," *The New Yorker*, February 2, 1998, p. 41.
29   Ibid.
30   Ibid., p. 41.
31   Gill, *Lords of Misrule*, p. 12.
32   Ibid., p. 20.
33   Paul A. Gilje, *The Road To Mobocracy: Popular Disorder in New York City, 1763–1834* (Chapel Hill, NC: University of North Carolina Press, 1987); Susan G. Davis, *Parades and Power: Street Theatre in Nineteenth-Century Philadelphia* (Berkeley, CA: University of California Press, 1986); Stephen Nissenbaum, *The Battle for Christmas* (New York: Alfred A. Knopf, 1996); Mary P. Ryan, *Civic Wars: Democracy and Public Life in the American City during the Nineteenth Century* (Berkeley, CA: University of California Press, 1997).

5

Belonging and Sharing

It was the custom of eighteenth- and nineteenth-century editors to read each other's newspapers and to publish stories about what was going on in towns and cities some distance from their own. One such story out of Richmond, Virginia that was published on January 21, 1825 found its way to the *Boston Daily Advertiser* eight days later.

> *Singular Discovery* – A gentleman has just arrived in town, who asserts that he has discovered a certain, simple and easy method of resuscitating drowned persons, and says he means to give exhibitions once a week during his stay in Richmond; but cannot commence immediately in consequence of having had the misfortune to lose his servant at his last exhibition ... where by an unforeseen accident the man was left too long in the water or perhaps from the obstinacy of the fellow who wanted to go to a frolic that evening, and wished his master to get a substitute. The discoverer therefore gives notice that he wishes to hire, by the year, any healthy, well behaved white man or woman that may be relied upon for sobriety. He gives them good wages and assures them it is not the least painful and perfectly safe. None need apply without a good recommendation. Drowning is rather a pleasant sensation.

Inasmuch as the ill-fated assistant was unable to offer any credible testimony of his own, it is not immediately apparent how the editor of the newspaper or the man who discovered how to resuscitate drowning victims could be so certain that the experience was painless and pleasant. This question actually may have been important to readers in Boston and elsewhere in 1825, because reports of persons drowning were common fare in newspapers of that time and town residents openly expressed their concern over such deaths. It also is an important story, however, because it tells us something of how persons from different levels of society – in this case a "master" and his obstinate "servant" – might go about the delicate task of negotiating their relationship in an urban world where ideas like fealty and obligation no longer carried as much social weight as they once did.

Good wages, comfort, and safety awaited those who were healthy, sober, had solid work habits – the ability to hold one's breath for long periods not being one of them – and came well recommended, or so the story says. This certainly sounds like a good deal, perhaps even a great deal. The secret to this special arrangement, in any case, surely had something to do with faith and keeping one's promises. However, it also had something to do with the ability and willingness of persons to behave in a way that conveyed faithfulness and showed promise. Trust could not be taken for granted. It had to be earned, in a manner of speaking, or at least attested to by better known or more believable persons.

Prior to the American Revolution, and going back to medieval times according to historian Carl Bridenbaugh, the "protection of business and trades had been afforded to town dwellers by the requirement that all newcomers desiring to open a shop in a community take out a 'freedom,' which was granted upon payment of a certain sum of money."[1] Today prospective business people and professionals would have to buy a license before they could practice their craft or sell their products. At least in early America, however, these sums of money did little to establish one's credibility as a craftsman or business owner, and not everyone wishing to work in a particular town or city bought these communal indulgences. American towns typically needed more individuals to open shops than were available, and town leaders did not want to discourage any aspiring business person. Newcomers apparently became freemen largely for the purpose of voting in municipal elections, another act which helped to stamp them as credible persons in their town.

More important to the fixing of one's identity as a trustworthy person, apparently, was one's admission to a congregation or religious sect. In fact, acquiring membership in this kind of group, or in lodges or fraternities which had many religious trappings, served as an effective means of distinguishing worthy persons from less worthy individuals long after universal suffrage was introduced to America. It was, as sociologist Max Weber would later observe firsthand, "an absolute guarantee of the moral qualities of a gentleman, especially of those qualities required in business matters. Baptism secure[d] to the individual ... unlimited credit without any competition. He [was] a 'made man.'" Weber also found that "when a sect member moved to a different place, or if he was a traveling salesman, he carried the certificate of his congregation with him; and thereby he found not only easy contact with sect members but, above all, he found credit everywhere." The same was true of lodge members. Membership was a ticket into the community of believers.

One's affiliation with one or more of these organizations obviously did not guarantee success. Nor did it mean that congregation members or fraternal "brothers" would pay off one's debts should one fail in a business venture. It only meant that one could be trusted. What mattered most to prospective investors "was the fact that a fairly reputable sect would only accept for membership one whose 'conduct' made him appear to be morally *qualified* beyond doubt." Admission to a sect was not a piece of insurance that could be cashed in for a sum of money, but it did serve as "a certificate of moral qualification" which could be drawn against as one would draw on a line of credit at a bank.[2]

Weber and others have rightly noted that being certified as "morally qualified" made it easier for entrepreneurs and craftsmen to establish themselves in a local market, even when they were not permanent residents. Furthermore, certification stuck to a person as long as he continued to behave in a commendable fashion. What has been missed or not emphasized enough up to this point, however, is that the "conduct" which made a person morally qualified was not necessarily tied to making money, either for oneself or for others. It certainly had nothing to do with ostentatious displays of wealth or self-aggrandizement. It was more important to be a good person, someone who was humble and could be counted on to do the right thing. This could be demonstrated in a number of ways, but being helpful to others less fortunate than oneself was particularly valued.

A column published in the *Burlington Free Press* on March 27, 1849 does a good job of laying out the features that distinguished a person who was humble and worthy of admiration from one who was merely prosperous and dedicated only to himself or herself. A portion of it is reproduced below.

How Some People Get Into Society

There is a class of ultra fashionables ... people grown rich by speculation, who having lived all their life time in a vulgar manner, are very anxious to make up for lost time. They live extravagantly ... and give themselves airs which to all sensible and well-bred people are perfectly ridiculous. Conscious that they have nothing but their wealth to recommend them, they make the greatest possible display of it on all occasions, and naturally entertain the greatest contempt for all who are destitute of their only claim upon public attention.

There is above all these a small class of unobtrusive, pure and gentle aristocracy, dependent upon education, taste and refinement, which, without any display, is everywhere observed, and is the special envy of the parvenus and fashionables.

As the rank of this society does not depend on riches, the poor, to a great extent, as well as the rich, belong to it, and it is by its qualities and constitution the most exclusive of all societies, since it is quite impossible for any one to join it without possessing the proper qualifications. Besides, the ambition of the aspirants is generally directed to the more lowly sets of fashion and flash.

Those being ridiculed in the column were not part of the natural aristocracy of good persons who, regardless of their rank, carried themselves in an honorable and modest way whenever they were in public. They were vulgar individuals who had come into some money and used it to show off. They contributed to nothing greater than themselves.

This attention to manners and the approval that flowed to persons who were attentive to the condition of others were not peculiar to the residents of Burlington, Vermont. Nor was it new. A century earlier, Carl Bridenbaugh reports, a member of the New York Council had observed "that Riches are not always acquired by the honestest Means, nor are they always accompanied with the greatest Integrity of Mind ... or with the most generous Sentiments and publick Spirit." The speaker heaped praise on what he called "the middling Rank of Mankind" who "have justly obtain'd the Character, to be generally the most honest." The councilor concluded by saying that he was "fully perswaded that we may much more safely trust our Liberty and Property with our neighbors of a middling Rank than with those of the greatest riches who are thereby tempted to Lord it over their neighbors.'[3]

To truly be a person in good standing meant that you were obligated to share some of yourself or what you possessed with other persons. If one had behaved in this way, he might be memorialized in almost saintly terms at the time of his death and be held up for all would-be claimants to the community of believers as an object of veneration. An especially fine illustration of this is found in a "tribute of respect" that was composed by three members of the Franklin Lodge, No. 3, I.O.O.F. in honor of a deceased "Brother." A portion of the story as it was published in the *Wheeling Intelligencer* on October 15, 1867 is reproduced below. It reveals that the death of William Taylor was both unexpected and painful to his friends.

For sixteen years he has been an active member of this Lodge ... engaged in all our labors to "relieve the distressed, to visit the sick, to bury the dead and to educate the orphan." He has been so long regarded as the leader of every good and benevolent object ... that we know of no one who can supply his place. His love for Odd Fellowship, his regular attendance amongst us, the interest he maintained in every subject that claimed our attention, the judicious words he spoke ... and his deportment in the Lodge room, gained our confidence and regard.

William Taylor apparently had been a very good man. His passing left a big hole in his lodge and in the larger community. It would be easy, perhaps, to make too much of one group's loss and to claim that what its members felt and did somehow reflected on all of Wheeling, West Virginia. Yet this kind of testimonial was not unique to the Franklin Lodge or to Wheeling. "Brother" Taylor's life and good works spoke to a way of belonging to a people and a place that was admired by many persons who knew him and worked with him. His death did say something about the whole community.

Insofar as the sentiments and deeds conveyed in this heartfelt tribute were shared by any sizable portion of Wheeling's residents, whatever prosperity and order the people of Wheeling knew in the years immediately following the Civil War rested upon a solid moral foundation. Being certified as a morally qualified person was not just about business. It also was about making a contribution, of tithing oneself so to speak, so that other human beings could see and come to understand what it meant to be part of a good community.

The fact that the organization which afforded Taylor such privileges and obligations had branches in different towns did not hurt his chances to secure credit or a legacy. Nor would it have mattered that he used such attachments for the purpose of making social and business contacts while away from home. Membership in the larger organization became the means through which William Taylor and many persons like him would have created a small but effective "solidarity group" for themselves inside a town or city that had an affiliated sect or group in it. Historian Thomas Bender has said that membership in such "translocal" groups actually "drew people together into a community" wherever it was that they happened to be.[4] It did not remove them from the life of the local community. It brought them further into it. To the extent that this happened at all, and it apparently happened a great deal, the persons and groups that were joined together in this way became early subscribers to the community of believers in the town or city where their church, sect, or lodge was located. Whether one belonged to these groups mattered a great deal back in the nineteenth century.

This is not to say that everyone who was part of the community of believers always was on good terms with every other communicant or that they all took the same position on significant matters brought before them. Conditions inside the town and nation conspired against such an outcome as the nineteenth century wore on, and life inside towns and cities simply became bigger and more complicated. More residents gradually became actively engaged in the economic and political life of their hometown. This was especially true and important for "ordinary citizens" who now participated in economic activities "that were formerly thought to be strictly in the province of the elite" and who now treated political office holding as more than an entitlement for their better-heeled neighbors. Thomas Bender says that these ordinary persons "were no longer willing to give a broad mandate to an acknowledged local elite who would then be free to do what they thought best for the whole community."[5] More common folk were making a claim for membership in the community of believers, and they were doing things to make the claim stick.

Elite persons may have been unable to lead as they had in the past. It also was not clear, however, that more ordinary persons were equipped or even willing to take on all the traditional obligations which established leaders had customarily assumed as their birthright and special burden. Who would constitute the community of believers was undecided and, perhaps, even unknowable in a growing and busy urban world. In themselves, neither the conservative's preference for tighter entrance criteria nor the liberal's desire to let in many more persons and groups would offer a workable solution to how one might make a better, more inclusive community. Before there could be greater prosperity and more order in American towns and cities, therefore, residents would have to find novel ways to balance the right of a person to belong to the community against his or, only somewhat later, her obligation to spread its bounty and many responsibilities more broadly among their fellow townsmen. Individuals from the several levels of local society had to work out a new or more flexible hierarchy and a social compact that would make sense to them. Only then would persons, having been satisfactorily rearranged on their new social ladders, learn how to pass along whatever materials and information were needed either to build their house higher or to put out fires that flared up from time to time during the course of their ambitious climb.

Taking Care of One's Own

Carl Bridenbaugh, the chronicler of early-American city life, has said that "a belief in a hierarchy of classes based on status" was never fundamentally challenged by the American Revolution.

> A mercantile aristocracy had rooted itself in the cities and ... presumed to control in its own interest public policy, organizations of many kinds, religious bodies, and social life ... exercised a determining influence on education and the entire range of urban intellectual activities, and, on the whole, had evolved a very promising and fruitful culture.

He found ample evidence of "these aristocracies in action," but, he cautioned, "one could also detect the rise of their Nemesis, the up-and-coming middle class."

> The craftsmen and shopkeepers, men of middle rank, shared in the new prosperity, and as their class moved upward in numbers and strength, they came to sense their importance as a group and to entertain ambitions for political power commensurate with their economic status. They had no wish to overthrow the gentry but rather they desired to move up into their ranks and share the power and prestige.

Members of this nascent middle class were not the only ones inside cities making noise about being taken more seriously. Another, albeit much smaller and less articulate, set of potential claimants was found among the "citizens of the lower class" consisting of seamen, day laborers, and negroes who had "little to say in municipal affairs." Notwithstanding their marginal economic and social position inside cities, at least "their white members were not a depressed group. Many of them rose to middle-class standing and not a few became property-owners. Along with the tradesmen and artisans they had hopes of improving their status and their fortunes."[6]

The society inside American towns and cities was more open than its counterpart in most European communities of the period, and many persons from the middle and lower ranks of society did improve their social and material standing. Nevertheless, differences in the amount of wealth controlled by individuals from the several levels of society inside cities did not shrink markedly before or after the American Revolution. If anything, the distribution of wealth among city and town residents seemed to grow more exaggerated and unequal as American society matured and generally became more prosperous.[7]

The absence of any direct challenge to the social hierarchy that had been established inside towns and cities was perhaps all the more remarkable for this reason. It was only the particular array of actors who currently stood higher or lower than their peers that was openly questioned. The answer that residents devised to this dilemma required them to identify new ways for a person to become worthy in the eyes of his fellow townsmen and to acquire meaningful roles to play inside the community. This was something that persons from different levels of the local society were able to do and, indeed, sometimes even did together. It became a consuming passion for an ever larger number and more varied mix of individuals in towns and cities throughout the nineteenth century. Participation in the many organizations they created was the single most important expression of their growing social status and certification as morally qualified human beings in the place where they lived.

The first priority of those individuals and groups that already belonged to the community of believers was to take care of their own; and they worked hard at it. Taking care of others who were not yet members of this social confederation, or who might never be, was never far from their minds. However, their foremost concern was to watch out for each other and to ensure that current members did nothing to jeopardize their standing as credible or credit-worthy human beings.

Men and women could find any number of ways to lose their standing in the community. That is why so much time was spent alerting townsmen of a new way one might fall from grace or be subjected to the corrupting influence of someone who already had. It was incumbent on persons, for instance, not to participate in wild gatherings or to exhibit a looseness of character. Persons kept particularly close tabs on public displays of religious fervor in this regard, because such events held great potential for releasing individuals from the constraints imposed by a well-disciplined congregation that usually met indoors.[8]

This new way to demonstrate that one belonged to a group of religious believers, however, usually turned out to be less of a threat than persons feared.[9] Readers of the September 9, 1858 edition of the *Carolina Spartan* learned, for example, that there had been a series of "camp meetings" or revivals in Spartanburg, South Carolina over the course of the previous week. Although these events sometimes drew skeptical looks from local citizens because of their expressive character, the newspaper reported that all those attending the revivals had behaved well. "Nothing reflects more credit upon communities," the editors noted, "than respectful, decorous conduct at religious meetings." An almost identical series of revival meetings in and around Spokane, Washington was reported in the January 13, 1882 edition of the *North-West Tribune* with equally unspectacular reviews of the participants' behavior. Conventional persons thrown into gatherings that might bring out decidedly unconventional feelings and conduct tend to soften the event rather than their commitment to community standards.

Expressions of concern about decorous behavior on the part of local residents nonetheless riddled local newspapers throughout the nineteenth century and were subject to much public discussion. Readers of the May 17, 1810 edition of the *Boston Gazette*, for example, were advised to be judicious in selecting the concerts they might attend. The success of a recent concert held at a local coffee house was bound to encourage other groups to sponsor similar events, according to the editors of the newspaper. It was important, therefore, for persons to be certain that the events they attended united "pleasure with improvement, innocence with recreation, and the promotion of health with the amelioration of the heart and mind."

There were many public events, of course, that managed to do this. Two such occasions also took place in Boston, this time just before the start of the Civil War. Both were reported in the *Boston Daily Advertiser*, and both fit comfortably in the local cultural scene. The first occurred on May 12, 1860 and marked the thirteenth anniversary of the Boston Society of Natural History. Details of the program were not revealed, but it really did not matter. It was reassuring enough then, just as it is today, to know that the public meeting had been crowded "by an audience containing most of the Brains of Boston." The second meeting did not take place on June 2, 1860 when it was reported, but it was set into motion then and would have attracted a substantial audience when it was held. A Daniel Pratt, Jr., who was also known as the "Great American Traveller," challenged William Lloyd Garrison and Wendell Phillips to "literary combat." A 25 cent admission fee would have allowed ticket holders to take in a spirited debate on "the virtues of the Abolition Party and Political Platform."

Similar debates and public meetings were held in towns and cities across the country in the years before the Civil War, and in each case local citizens had to think hard about their commitment to each other and to some much larger ideals. The *Wheeling Daily Intelligencer* reported on January 8, 1861, for instance, that the "working men of Wheeling" had voiced their displeasure with secessionist noises coming from their neighbors in Virginia and South Carolina. They declared their support for the Union, passed several patriotic resolutions, and sang the Star Spangled Banner four times. Less than four months later Union meetings were being conducted at school houses and the Court house, a military company was being organized, and residents from three wards in the city were busily preparing themselves to do "Union business."[10]

There were many more occasions both before and after the Civil War when members of the various churches, social clubs, debating societies, and charity organizations found in a city came together simply for good fellowship and to carry on the work of their group. What follows is a small sampling of events tied only to religious meetings that took place in communities across the country in the three decades following the Civil War. Beyond the sheer number of occasions that persons affiliated with one or another religious group apparently met, one is necessarily impressed by the array of services that churches provided to their members at an early date and the variety of groups which kept themselves within the orbit of their respective congregations.

The editors of the *Pine Bluff Press* reported on April 8, 1869 that the Jewish citizens of this Arkansas community had erected a beautiful and expensive synagogue. "In doing this," the editors noted, "they displayed not only their taste and liberality of feeling, but also exemplified their sentiment of devotion." All citizens, regardless of their religious affiliation, were invited to attend services held in the new building. This feeling of tolerance apparently did not disappear. A little more than four years later, it was reported in the September 25, 1873 edition of the *Pine Bluff Weekly Press* that "the Hebrews of Pine Bluff" had gathered at their synagogue in celebration of Rosh Hashanah, and that they had been joined by many non-Hebrew citizens who came to view the ceremony.

The July 10, 1875 edition of the *St Louis Dispatch* reported that only a portion of the German young people in the city were attending Sunday school on a regular basis. All denominations in the city had these schools, and each church could be counted on having a number of qualified teachers available for the children who showed up. The report went on to detail how many schools, teachers, and students were enrolled in classes for the Evangelical, Baptist, Methodist, Presbyterian, Independent Evangelical Protestant, and Lutheran Churches. The same paper dutifully reported on August 23, 1875 that 209 young girls had received their first communion at St Michael's Church. It also was observed that the girls had marched in a procession from St Philomena's convent to the church and were wearing white dresses with veils enveloped by floral wreaths.

Eleven different churches published notices for upcoming services in the Sioux Falls, South Dakota *Daily Argus* on July 7, 1886. There was a gospel temperance meeting at the Presbyterian Church and a "social" sponsored by the Women's Christian Temperance Union at the Baptist Church on the same day. A man from Minneapolis gave a temperance speech at the Methodist Church on August 25, 1886, and the entire Presbytery of South Dakota met in Sioux Falls on September 8, 1886. The Presbyterian, Methodist, Reform, and Congregational Churches had special Christmas celebrations, and the Norwegian Lutheran Church held two services on New Year's Eve of that year.

The *Carolina Spartan* reported on November 11, 1891 that 120 families in Spartanburg, South Carolina had said that they would take in two or more visitors scheduled to attend the December gathering of the Baptist Convention in their city. Another 11 families declared that they would happily take women conventioneers into their homes. After the Convention was over, the Spartanburg Baptist Church issued a public thanks to all the persons and other churches in the city that had helped to make the gathering a great success.

There was nothing special about these events or the towns and future cities where they took place. One could find just as many testimonials to the religious bent of townsmen and city folk in communities all over the country in the decades following the Civil War. More importantly, perhaps, so far as I have been able to tell, there has been no appreciable drop-off in the number or variety of activities sponsored by different religious bodies in this century. What might have changed is the number of occasions when churches from different denominations actively collaborated in a larger religious or community event. It actually may have increased.

If inter-denominational activities have increased in the twentieth century, it only is because church leaders in the nineteenth century had begun to explore ways in which their different religious views might be reconciled or at least temporarily set aside so that they could work together on important projects. At other times, church leaders looked for occasions when members of their congregations simply could enjoy each other's company. An example of the latter type of meeting was reported on in the January 3, 1865 issue of the *Manchester Daily Union*. The Methodist Episcopal Society of St Paul and the Lowell Street Universalist Society put on a New Year Social party at Smyth's Hall for the benefit of their members. A similar event in Wausau, Wisconsin was reported in the *Wausau Daily Record Herald* almost a half-century later on November 25, 1908. It entailed a Thanksgiving service held in the First Presbyterian Church which was sponsored by that congregation as well as the Methodist, Universalist, and Baptist Churches in Wausau.

A report in the *Sioux Falls Argus* for November 11, 1886, on the other hand, hinted at the more serious work that was undertaken when representatives from different religious bodies came together. It detailed how all clergy in the town had held their weekly meeting the previous day. They were not alone. Religious leaders in a number of communities were involved in this kind of activity during the nineteenth century. Nor was the feeling of religious tolerance that such meetings engendered trivial. It encouraged persons to look upon each other's churches in a familiar and friendly way and to view their activities as making a valuable contribution to the whole community.

Joseph B. Cottrell, D.D. used his column on "Churches and Creeds" in the October 31, 1888 edition of the *Carolina Spartan* to express this kind of sentiment. He began by criticizing a statement made by the Presbytery of Charleston, South Carolina against Roman Catholicism. His words were far more noteworthy, however, for their solicitous representation of other denominations and his embrace of religious pluralism.

> The Presbyterian Church is a grand, old historic Church. I've the same respect for her that I have for the Roman Catholic Church, the Protestant Episcopal Church, or the Baptist Church. They are all Churches of God – *and man*.

The Kingdom is catholic. No one of the churches is, nor are all them combined, catholic. They are scaffolds round about "the structure which we raise," and not a little cometh to the help of the scaffold workmen ... I am well aware of the offense I give in speaking of the Roman Catholic Church as among the Churches of God; but it is sincere. It is in spite of much, and because of much more, I so class her.

The ability of church leaders to embrace the principle of religious tolerance and to work with their fellow ministers, rabbis, and priests enabled them to come together when they thought community problems were too large for any one of them to address alone. This was the case in San Diego in 1895, for example, when the Civic Association asked local clergymen to preach in support of municipal reforms which would have made it easier to revoke the licenses of businesses deemed immoral or disreputable. Several ministers responded favorably to the request, and the comments that five of them made from their pulpits were reproduced in the February 18, 1895 edition of the *San Diego Union*. The subject of the Reverend Mr Knapp's sermon at the First Baptist Church was "The Duties of the Citizen." Parts of it are reproduced below.

In the last analysis the citizen is the ruler of the country, or the republic is a failure. His representatives are not his masters, but his servants. ... His patriotism should be part of his religion.
The citizen should assume the responsibility. He should be the politician. If political affairs are unclean, it is the fault of clean men who hand them over to unclean men.
Good men should be willing to give some of their time and strength by holding office. It is a duty. ... Do not be selfish.
Should we not unite and make this the ideal residence spot which God intended it to be. This city can well dispense with any class of men to whom the slums are a necessity.

It is clear from the sermon that questions about morality, civic improvement, duty to one's fellow townsmen, and public accountability were all bound together and given a solitary focus in the person of San Diego itself. The city became a vehicle through which many good things could be realized and a lot of bad stuff like gambling, boozing, and whoring could be defeated, or at least kept in check. The possibility of making one's city a better place was greatly enhanced when local religious leaders set aside their differences and undertook good works of both a secular and sacred sort together.

The cast of characters in each city was different. For the residents of Fairbanks, Alaska in 1919 it involved a discussion at St Matthew's Church on the question of union among the various religious bodies in

Christendom. In the case of Valdosta, Georgia in 1925, it meant that the
Business Men's Evangelical Club of Valdosta had arranged a series of
speakers for all the city's churches, and that the town's Ministerial Union
was deciding to have pastors switch pulpits again so that congregations
could hear from different ministers. In 1927 the Federal Council of
Churches of Christ in America was helping Protestant churches in
Pittsburgh attract more members through an evangelical campaign. The
YMCA in Burlington, Vermont in 1936 collaborated with the local
Methodist Church in offering a dinner and evening of entertainment
including demonstrations by the Boy Scouts and a basketball game. Plans
were made to invite other local churches to work with the YMCA on
similar projects. A few months later seven Protestant churches held a
service in the city's Memorial Auditorium in honor of the Boy Scouts. In
Waltham, Massachusetts, a small city just outside of Boston, the
Waltham Council of Churches held a rally in the social hall of the First
Congregational Church on Sunday January 30, 1955. Women from three
other churches put together a buffet dinner for everyone attending the
University of Life rally. A local Jewish Temple honored two Methodist
pastors in February of that same year for embodying principles of
brotherhood in their ministries. Almost 15 years later in Columbia,
Maryland, a new club called The B'nai B'rith Women initiated
"Operation Bookstrap" which was intended to encourage persons to
donate children's books that would be given to youngsters who could not
afford to buy books.[11]

The point is that different religious groups were working together or
on parallel tracks in order to accomplish something that would help their
respective cities, and that they all could recognize the contribution that
other bodies were making to the well-being of their community. One did
not become a better person by accident. Nor did a community become
better simply because its people wished it to be so. Reverend Mark B.
Strickland of the First Congregational Church in Manchester, New
Hampshire thought that it would take a lot of hard work. In the case of
his own city, he believed that many of the problems that persons faced
during World War II could be attributed to ignorance. The "30 different
religious groups and a great many more churches, as well as some 10
racial units or national units large enough to have a limited amount of
social cohesion" could live better in Manchester, he thought, if they knew
each other better. This would not come easily. "We are not inherently
good, nor do we naturally acquire goodness," he said. "All that is good,
noble and beautiful is obtained only through effort, labor, cultivation
and perseverance."[12] This is precisely what different churches and religious denominations in towns and cities across America had been doing
for more than a century. They had been working at it.

They still were working at it in Cleveland when the National Conference of Christians and Jews celebrated the 36th anniversary of National Brotherhood Week in 1968. They also were working at it in Boston in 1968 when Cardinal Cushing made the first appearance of a Roman Catholic prelate at the King's Chapel Unitarian Church. They continued to work at it in 1973 when the American Jewish Committee urged all civic and community groups in Pittsburgh not to meet in clubs that discriminated against any racial, religious, or ethnic groups. Some residents of Louisville certainly worked at it as well when the First Unitarian Church invited the head of the local NAACP chapter to talk about the merger of the city's schools with those of Jefferson County during the desegregation controversy in 1975.[13]

There is an important lesson embedded in these episodes of interdenominational cooperation. It is that the presence of so many denominations and church bodies in American towns and cities has produced a "religious economy" which is both competitive and pluralistic.[14] The energy of that economy has sometimes fractured the religious marketplace. It also has led some mainstream religious leaders to complain that conventional churches were losing ground to denominations which were strange to most Americans. They decried the fact that religious rituals, rhetoric, and symbols were not as much a part of our everyday lives as they had been, even as they looked askance at the proliferation of new churches and religious beliefs embraced by their fellow Americans. Many persons embraced newer faiths that offered them "an association of loving individuals" instead of a traditional church which seemed to put the "religious community over the individual."[15]

The difference between these two approaches of making a church or "religious community" is real, even if the practical results of working with other like-minded persons who share similar beliefs and a common theological orientation to the world are indistinguishable. A more traditional or conservative approach is predicated upon the prior existence of a community of believers into which the individual is born or put. A more liberal approach draws on the idea that individuals make a thoughtful and voluntary commitment to a group that is constructing its own theology or gladly accepts a variety of orientations to believing and acting religiously. Some traditional religious leaders have a problem with this more liberal way of imagining and building a community of believers.

It may be true in some communities, but certainly not in all, that traditional religious ideas and customs have a more subdued presence in our daily routines today. At the same time, there also may be more collaboration among mainstream religious bodies than at any time in our history. These two conditions complement rather than contradict each other. They would not have occurred without all the reaching out and compromising that nineteenth-century religious leaders did with each other and all the good work that came from their meetings. The muting of sectarian differences which took place time after time in American towns and cities allowed church leaders to become partners in creating more inclusive communities even as they were satisfying the varied religious needs of their followers. It also encouraged a certain flowering of different religious ideals and practices to take place.

Belonging to rather select communities of believers did not necessarily make it harder for the members of different congregations or faiths to reach out to other persons. Each group had worked from a comparable position of moral worth, if not social standing, in their respective hometowns. Their struggles and accomplishments were similar. An interest in building a good community for their own members had drawn them closer to persons practicing other faiths. It seems that religious pluralism had ended up working surprisingly well for these and other Americans, enabling persons from different social circles to collaborate more readily and effectively than they otherwise might have. We may see that lessons learned in America's religious marketplace were applied in other domains of social intercourse as well. To the extent that this proves to be the case, the eventual benefit of belonging to distinctive communities of believers would have been shared with a larger number and more varied array of persons.

Dealing with Newcomers

The problem was that there always seemed to be more persons wanting to make a town or city their home than there was room to accommodate or any interest in welcoming. Some intended to stay and were able to make a go of it in their new surroundings. Others were simply passing through on their way to another destination or, in some unfortunate cases, to no place in particular. Still others would remain for a while and try to make a life for themselves. They failed and either stayed on as a permanent and painful reminder that not everyone can belong or fit in, or they moved on to some other place. Alternatively, they may have accomplished what they set out to do and returned to their homeland. All the persons who made their way to different American towns and cities fit into one of these categories, and all these persons had to be dealt with in one fashion or another by the more permanent residents of these same communities. It was not easy for any of them.

The whole matter of restricting immigration to towns and cities had been settled pretty quickly in colonial America. Leaders figured out that it was impractical to limit how many of what kinds of persons who had which skills were allowed to enter and stay in their town. More importantly, enforcing such restrictions would only have held back their plans for economic expansion and dampen their dreams to become wealthier and more prominent than they already were.

This did not mean, however, that every potential visitor or resident and worker was equally welcome. Some persons, most notably slaves and sailors but also religious dissenters of one or another sort and persons of dubious moral worth, were not welcomed at all. Or, they received what might today be viewed as an unwarranted amount of attention during their short stay in town. These individuals and groups were so queer, off-putting, or offensive that they never could have been brought into the local community of believers. Accepting them as honorary guests, giving them a temporary pass as it were, much less embracing them as dues-paying members was out of the question. Indeed, they were so "out of place" that they might have been construed as a threat to the community. At one time or another, a good number of these outsiders were thought of in just this way and found themselves treated in an unfriendly and even hostile manner by a community's better-established and accepted residents.

Transient persons were the least likely to register on the civic radar screen of American towns and cities. Most of them found their way in and out of a place without causing too much of a stir. They stayed long enough to earn the money they needed to go somewhere else, or they pushed on with little or no cash reserve. Sometimes, as I already noted, they returned to the foreign country from which they had emigrated. Such was the case for the eleven members of the Williams family in 1850. A black family, the Williams managed to raise $1,000 to pay for their passage back to Liberia. This may not have been their homeland, but it was a place that a number of Americans were willing to help black persons to return in the years prior to the Civil War. This probably is why the Williams's story was published in the *Boston Evening Transcript* on October 3, 1835, while local citizens never heard about most sojourners.

Most individuals who passed through a town or city probably never were touched by any organized effort on the part of local residents to help them or push them on to their next destination. Those who did come to the attention of community leaders had markedly different experiences. Some of the reactions to the arrival of newcomers were positive, even uplifting. Other responses by public institutions and private organizations established by residents who had money were far less agreeable.

Those newcomers who fared best found their way to a town or city whose economy was robust and whose leaders were eager to have new residents join them in what they fully expected would be a glorious future. Local residents worked hard to meet the needs of newcomers who often arrived with little money and in bad health after enduring a long and sometimes quite dangerous trip. The residents of Portland, Oregon were alerted to the possibility that the number of immigrants they had anticipated arriving in their city had been greatly underestimated. All citizens were asked to "show their benevolence" to these immigrants in the September 25, 1852 edition of the *Oregonian*. Some portion of the population held a series of meetings over the course of the next few months in order to deal with these persons as they began to arrive. At one such meeting the plight of "sick immigrants" was considered and a committee was formed to deal with the problem. One resident offered to turn a house that he owned into a hospital. There apparently were not enough buildings in the whole city to house all the immigrants. As a result, a good number of them were forced to camp out. The local churches proposed to take a special collection for the relief of the destitute travelers and to help pay for the new hospital.[16]

A situation not unlike that described for Portland, Oregon emerged in Omaha at the conclusion of the Civil War. It was reported in the March 3, 1865 edition of the *Nebraska Republican* that wagon loads of immigrants from the East were arriving daily. The atmosphere was described as "welcoming" and there was a prediction that the population of the city would double by the end of the year. The July 28, 1865 issue of the newspaper mentioned that over 50,000 miners had passed through the community on their way to gold fields farther to the west. The deluge was largely over by August, but the October 27, 1865 edition of the *Nebraska Republican* reported that Omaha was "overflowing" with residents and that vacant lots would have to be turned into business buildings in order to accommodate all of the city's new residents. Three years later the *Omaha Republican Weekly* was reporting that more "pilgrims" had again been arriving in the city. The newspaper subsequently announced that local citizens had provided "care and acres" to a family of poor Irish immigrants who had just arrived and that an immigration society was being established in the city. Scandinavians were becoming a large element of the city's population and, happily for the editors of this newspaper, also Republican voters. Trains and "prairie schooners" brought so many newcomers to Omaha that all the city's hotels were expected to remain crowded throughout the fall and winter. Conditions were so good, in fact, that a band of Winnebaego Indians may have left their reservation just to seek winter employment in the city's "hearty, vigorous industries."[17]

When economic conditions were good, newcomers were presented in a favorable light. In conversation with a newly arrived group of settlers from Missouri, for instance, a reporter from the *Billings Herald* noted on May 5, 1883 that the 26 individuals had come with "considerable ready capital" to raise cattle. "Young, intelligent, energetic and anxious to help themselves they are just the class our people will unite in welcoming to Montana, and who will abundantly prosper with ... this growing country." Even with the warm endorsements that were thrown their way, however, it was not easy for newcomers. They sometimes banded together in order to ease their movement into a new town or city. What was reported in the January 28, 1891 edition of the *Argus Leader* in Sioux Falls, South Dakota happened in a number of communities. It seems that 125 members of the "Sons of Maine" and the "Ladies of Maine" had their second banquet on that date. They spent some time talking about their memories of life in their home state before dining and being entertained. Judge Park Davis, president of the "Sons of Vermont," then spoke of the possibility of joining the two groups in a move that would enhance "the prosperity of our city." Additional testimonials followed the judge's speech to conclude the evening's festivities.

There were many more persons whose reception and treatment were not nearly so congenial. The *Boston Evening Transcript* of October 3, 1835 carried an announcement regarding two sets of persons who were consistently viewed as potential troublemakers: homeless transients and children. Individuals speaking in behalf of the Committee on Public Instruction alerted citizens that this body wished "to secure the attendance of vagrants and idle children" at the public schools.

Black persons also were a favorite object of concern and a target for nasty pieces of commentary. The unfriendly treatment accorded to blacks has been apparent in many places and at many different times. It became more public in northern cities during the Civil War when white and black persons began to compete for the same jobs. The editors of the *Bergen Democrat* published the following advice to white persons of more modest standing on November 21, 1862:

> How to get employment: White men and women in want of employment are advised to black themselves with burnt cork rubbed in with lard, and make immediate application to government, or any of the noisy abolitionists. Ebony is all the go now, and who would not prefer a black skin to an empty stomach! Try it white trash.

An article published in the January 18, 1865 edition of the *Cleveland Daily Plain Dealer* went further by expressing more sympathy for white Southerners than for former black slaves. "Our people," the author stated, "seem to be too much concerned in the condition of the African race to spare a thought on their own color." Southern "refugees" were facing great hunger and terrible living conditions. "Does any one know of such destitution among the colored race? On the contrary, they are fat, hearty, and saucy."

Some residents of Pittsburgh reacted similarly to the proposed housing of "loyal Japanese Americans" in a local orphanage nearly 80 years later near the end of World War II. It was reported in the June 29, 1945 edition of the *Pittsburgh Post-Gazette* that a protest would be issued at a "citizens' meeting" held in the offices of American Legion Post No. 81 in the northside neighborhood where the orphanage was located. Residents were complaining despite the fact that local ministers had approved of the plan and representatives of the War Relocation Authority had held a public meeting at the Chamber of Commerce auditorium on the subject earlier the same month.

A person did not have to be a member of a despised population to be treated in this way. It was reported in the *Louisville Daily Democrat* on October 9, 1868, for instance, that a crippled man and his two daughters had been denied admission to the poor house despite having walked all the way from Illinois to reach this city. The City Marshall of Fargo, North Dakota was complimented in the April 19, 1879 edition of the *Fargo Times* for having kept the streets free of tramps. He apparently told them that he would put them to work sweeping the streets, if they did not leave town. A similar pitch was made to the citizens of Cleveland who were told in the August 31, 1885 issue of the *Cleveland Plain Dealer* that transients should be put to work in the new woodyard established by the Bethel Associated Charities. Readers of the *San Diego Union* on December 20, 1885 were told that 11 men already working as part of a "chain gang" cleaning the streets would soon be joined by "all the tramps ... on the way to San Diego."

Arrests of transients often coincided with changes in the seasons and the start or finish of a harvest. Readers of the *Idaho Falls Post* were informed on November 14, 1926, for instance, that these persons were being incarcerated much less frequently since the fall harvest had been completed. In subsequent years, the citizens of that city softened their approach to transient laborers and their families. The November 30, 1930 issue of the newspaper declared that city funds would have to be expended on unemployed transient laborers, if local groups did not help out. On December 1 of the following year, it was reported that the Boy Scouts, city firefighters, and a local paint company had joined together in an effort to repair toys for the children of itinerant laborers. Donations from city residents also were requested.

Even when outsiders were not arrested they often were treated inhospitably. It was reported in the July, 23 issue of the *Burlington Free Press* that "nonresidents" no longer would be given treatment at the city's Free Dispensary. One year later, readers of the July 18 edition of that newspaper were informed that the Police Headquarters no longer would be treated as a "lodging house" for transients. It was said that they could find housing in empty box cars at the railroad depot and that this would greatly assist local officials in ridding the headquarters of bugs and lice.

Who was able to find a place and part to play inside American towns and cities made a great deal of difference in the history of these places. It had a determining effect on the composition of the groups which constituted the local community of believers. It also helped to give more precise shape and texture to the bourgeois civic culture that persons created in different places. Historians have given some thought to the question of who remained in American towns and cities. They also have tried to figure out how those who stayed put were different from the persons who either could not make a go of it or were simply passing through on their way to some unknown destination. No small part of their concern was for the apparent discrepancy in wealth and general well-being between those who left and those who stayed. However, they also worried about the effects of transience on the social order and sense of comity inside American towns and cities.

These are important questions, and individual historians have exhibited a great deal of creativity in trying to address them. Unfortunately, we still have only the barest outline of an answer after examining these issues.[18] Our failure in large part can be attributed to the difficulty of studying large numbers of persons who did not stand still long enough to leave a detailed record of their actions or a legacy to appreciate. Nonetheless, historians have been able to identify several features that distinguished the lives of persons who were relatively more mobile from those who moved less frequently or at least stayed in the same municipality for longer periods of time.

It bears repeating at the outset that the fabled mobility of the American people is not new. With the possible exception of the first few years of settlement along the Atlantic coast, it has been the habit of persons who lived in this country to move around. Even those who remained in the same place for a decade or more tended to change their residence every few years. The phenomenon known as "moving day" was a common feature of life in American cities. Readers of the *Wheeling Intelligencer* on April 2, 1867 probably did not need to be reminded that "yesterday was preeminently a moving day:"

> We doubt if one-half the population who are in the habit of at all changing their local habitation, know where to find the other half this morning. An old citizen remarked to us that he had never seen in the city so many people

moving in one day. All day long there was a constant stream of drays and other vehicles loaded with family fixins pouring along every street in the city, and more household rubbish was subjected to the wholesome influence of light and air than at any one period in our recollection. Although the morning promised very unfavorably for those under the necessity of changing, nobody seemed daunted, and the work went bravely on ... feather beds and such suffered nothing beyond the wear and tear incident to the great moving day.

Persons who stayed in the same town or city longer tended to do better than those who moved from place to place. Surprisingly, perhaps, it was not just older and more skilled workers who did better by sticking around longer. Younger or less trained persons also could improve their material and social standing over the course of their working lives. It apparently was not the promise of great wealth that kept persons in one spot and comparatively satisfied. They might buy property or see some marginal gains in their own lives, but the distribution of wealth inside American communities was growing more unequal over time. Persons of what was called the "middling ranks" may have done better, but their share of the city's wealth was not growing. What mattered was that they could see the possibility for greater advances in their children's lives. They also could participate in the life of the town more fully. It was this promise and their involvement in the social and cultural life of a community that usually was more settled than they were which renewed their faith in the American creed.[19]

This was important because the prosperity that towns and cities experienced did not lead to the elimination of poverty for many of their residents. Life remained hard for a great many persons. Furthermore, it was harder for persons who were not a fixture in the community than it was for those who were.

Those who claimed to be permanent residents of a particular city could count on some charity during the course of the typical year, particularly around the Christmas holidays. Tucked among all the announcements about parties and church services every year there were sure to be notices about special gatherings and offerings made to the poor, and particularly for children whose families were indigent. Sometimes business people made contributions directly from their store of goods. This was the case in Sioux Falls, South Dakota in 1893 when Mr Barney McCrosen invited all boys who had not been visited by Santa Claus to appear at his warehouse. Santa was there to greet them, and he gave them apples, oranges, bananas, and nuts.[20] On other occasions, local organizations provided gifts and food to area residents in need of some holiday comfort.

Towns and cities always set aside funds to help their poorer neighbors or turned to local churches and charity organizations to help indigent persons through hard times. The aid may not have been enough and it may not have come as often as it was needed, but local institutions and agencies did try to meet the needs of those most severely touched by disease, the loss of a job, or the failure to secure housing. More predictable sources of assistance for larger numbers of persons was slower in coming and did not arrive until government programs were set up to maintain persons at some minimal levels of subsistence. Even then it often was important to certify persons receiving aid as being "worthy" of assistance and to tie whatever food or resources they got to established ways of conducting the community's business.

A good example of how this was accomplished in the days before government agencies transformed small amounts of temporary assistance into more permanent entitlements was found in Pittsburgh's "Bundle Day" program. The idea for Bundle Day was reported to have come from a St Louis minister who was present during the Pittsburgh event and who later applauded it. According to the report published in the December 10, 1914 edition of the *Pittsburgh Post*, donations were to go to a particularly worthy class of impoverished families.

> In Exposition Machinery Hall this morning are enough clothing and provisions to stock a department store, the result of Pittsburgh's generosity yesterday in the observance of Bundle Day. Small mountains of wearing apparel are flanked by great piles of groceries, bedding and furniture and the analogy to a department store will be completed next week when all of this merchandise will be "sold" to the poor of the city in exchange for "credit checks" furnished them by charity investigators and sent in mail order consignments to poverty-stricken families of European soldiers.
>
> The activities of the day were surprisingly well organized ... (with) each wagon ... assigned a route and two or three Boy Scouts or Holy Cross guards ... on every one to help the driver in making collections. Persons who had bundles ready hung flags from their houses. ... Others carried their bundles to the nearest police station or fire engine house, each of which was a collection station.

This event was significant on a number of levels. Of particular importance was the extension of "credit" to families making a great sacrifice for the well-being of the whole community and nation. Also worth noting was the way in which the organizers had made this novel, if not extraordinary, event more conventional by letting the recipients "spend" their credits like money in a setting that resembled a department store.

Persons today might offer used or "pre-owned" clothing and household goods to agencies like the Salvation Army in exchange for "credits" or deductions on their federal income taxes. No one ever checks the quality or monetary value of the items being donated. They are accepted on faith, just as the value declared on one's income tax forms is accepted as a faithful representation of the donor's sacrifice. By the time federal tax officials certify the value of the contribution and the donated goods have reached some needy person, a whole range of persons would have acquired financial or social credits and been certified as morally upright. They would have been extended membership in the community of believers, if only under these limited and prescribed conditions.

In the case of the Pittsburgh families whose principal wage earner was in Europe fighting a war, they had given something precious to the community and were in a position to get something back for their sacrifice. Whatever social stain might stick to persons receiving charity was greatly diminished by certifying them as "morally qualified" beings and allowing them the honor of "shopping" for goods as if they were just like everyone else. Indeed, that was the point of the whole exercise. Those accepting aid were just like their more prosperous neighbors and, given the nature of the circumstances, probably even more deserving of a share of the community's stock of goods and good will.

Between Natives and "Minorities"

Persons who could not pass this kind of moral residency requirement were "outsiders," their presence taken on sufferance. Their long audition for acceptance, if received well at all, probably would have been marked by hard feelings and no small amount of fighting with more established groups. It has become accepted practice in the United States to speak of such persons as "minorities."

The treatment of minority peoples at the hands of more established groups has been studied for a long time. No small part of the attention paid to them has focused on conflicts and controversies which arose as a result of their arrival or their efforts to participate more fully in the life of their adopted town or city.[21] Native and minority residents may have found many occasions to cooperate on important tasks and to extend an open hand to each other in the past. Yet one would be hard put to find this good will recorded by academic researchers. We have been much more efficient in tracking down and chronicling the nastier exchanges between the representatives of minority populations and a community's better established residents.

What emerges from the picture left by writers is incessant bickering and some full-fledged battles over jobs, housing, access to local institutions, and social eminence in the communities where newcomers and old-timers bumped too hard into each other or crossed each other's path too often. Old-timers generally won these fights, but not always or for long. What is more interesting is that the fights waged by the minority newcomers usually were a great deal more limited and conservative in their goals than one might suppose. Furthermore, divisions and ill-feelings within minority populations probably were every bit as important to their defeats as were the presumed power and antagonism of their opponents.[22] Almost as surprising, perhaps, government inter-vention in behalf of one side or the other often did not help to settle disputes in a mutually agreeable way. In fact, federal agencies and programs, even more than state or local initiatives, often served to ex-acerbate tensions and make an accommodation between established groups and minority newcomers less likely and more costly.[23]

A good example of political, if not governmental, complicity in making relations between natives and newcomers worse off was provided by the residents of St Louis in 1854. According to a report issued in the August 10 edition of the *Daily Missouri Democrat*, the "spirit of mobocracy [had] trampled down all law and order" for three days in the city. Aroused by "demagogues" who had appealed "to native prejudices," the riot "originated in the effort made to array foreign born and American citizens against each other in a political contest, and in the still more unfortunate introduction of religious differences into partisan struggles." A committee was appointed to determine whether Irishmen had barri-caded themselves behind the doors of the Catholic College with weapons and ammunition sufficient to carry on a prolonged struggle. Having found none, the newspaper reissued its plea for calm and the mayor mobilized a volunteer police force of some 1,000 men to restore peace to the city.

Another violent engagement tied to political agitation and social tension, this time between white and black persons who disagreed on the issue of slavery, was reported in the *Boston Daily Advertiser* on December 14, 1860. What was called a "John Brown meeting" at the "colored people's church" was disrupted by a large crowd assembled outside the building. "Negroes were hunted to their holes like rats," and when one "showed his teeth, his chin was barked with bricks and stones and sometimes clubs." White men cried "down with niggers and up with ourselves." Blacks responded by hollering "up with ourselves and down wid de white trash." The violence did not last long, but it was memorable.

Often the attacks were more limited but targeted more precisely. A story in the July 12, 1884 edition of the *Arizona Champion* described how during the course of the previous evening two neighboring saloons in Flagstaff had their front windows blown out by a mysterious explosion. A second report on August 16 detailed an anonymous letter that was sent by the bomber who said that either the bar's owner or his "Chinamen" would have to go. A small group of men from San Diego met a little more than one year later in their own city for the purpose of forming an anti-Chinese society whose objective was to expel all Chinese persons from California. As reported in the *San Diego Union* on December 20, 1885, the group failed to draw more than a dozen men.

Black Americans have long been viewed poorly by their fellow countrymen. A particularly interesting illustration of just how far white persons would carry their prejudice was found in Fairbanks, Alaska in 1910. A fair held for the benefit of St Joseph's Hospital in the city Auditorium was described in the October 12 issue of the *Fairbanks Daily News-Miner*. It was reported that the ladies of the city already had been visiting the many booths at the fair with the idea of purchasing one of the many bargains offered there, but that "the big rush" would come this evening when husbands and beaux joined their ladies "with the expectation of loosening their purse strings." The author of the story went on to describe each of the booths in some detail. In the middle of his walk around the fair, he offered the following picture of one such booth.

> Down by the right hand box is the nigger baby attraction, where those sufficiently skilled may be able to make the aforesaid baby eat a large rubber ball. The ball must, however, strike the nigger's chin or he will refuse to be fed.

What is both disturbing and enlightening about this particular episode is not that it took place in a town that had few, if any, black residents in 1910. Rather, it was the comfortable way in which the "attraction" was put right in the middle of a charity fair that received a great deal of public approbation and financial support from community residents. Mention of the "nigger baby" drew no more attention than the descriptions of any of the other booths, items, or cultural attractions laid out for persons attending the event. It was just there.

All of this we have come to expect. We are less accustomed to hearing about moments when natives and minorities struck more thoughtful poses or were observed struggling with some other group's discomfort. We can and should admire the tentative efforts by minority persons to poke and chisel away at the social restraints that held them back or to think out loud about what their obligations were to persons who were not like them, even if we find their answers outdated and patronizing. The point is that both partners in this union were trying to figure out better ways to approach each other and waltz across the dance floor that was their community without tripping over their own and each other's feet.

Readers of the *Carolina Spartan* on December 27, 1882 were treated to an interesting editorial on relations between white and black persons that spoke to this idea. It began with a story about a "colored man" who occupied "a high position in our government" and happened to be passing through the county where Spartanburg was located. Denied entry to a hotel restaurant at one train stop, his white companion was compelled to bring his friend's meal back to the train.

> Now, such little incidents as these bring us face to face with this great question of social equality between two distinct races. Germans, Irish, Italian ... may mingle and live together ... but when the African ... would seek perfect social equality ... then comes the war of colors.
>
> Our country now has to meet the social question ... and settle it in some way or other. There is a general feeling of security on the part of both races that this matter has been pretty fairly adjusted. The negro has equal political rights ... but when it comes to hotels, schools, churches and places of public amusement ... a sharp dividing line is drawn.
>
> To the student of sociology this question is most interesting. It is doubtful whether two races ... can live together long in the same country ... without some social links binding them together. The history of the next hundred years will throw some unexpected light on this dark subject.

The writer of this editorial was right and wrong. There would be much light thrown on relations between black and white persons, but it would not take a century for the fire or light to be lit. The author of the piece was not sure what would happen, his ready embrace of sociologists being the surest sign of his confusion. The social links which bound the races together would make sharp dividing lines all but meaningless well before then; but the author clearly anticipated that some sort of struggle was in the offing.

Less than a quarter century later, it was reported in the March 8, 1905 edition of the *Charlotte Daily Observer* that Emanuel M. Hewitt, "a negro justice of the peace," and another black man had demanded to be served lunch in the city hall lunch room. They would not cross the hall and eat in the section reserved for black people and threatened to take the whole matter to the US marshal.

> After some hesitation Hewitt and his friend were served with lunch. While all this was taking place the lunch-room was crowded with members of the bar. Miss Margaret Sisson, the young woman who was directed by the proprietors to wait on Hewitt and his friend, said she was not accustomed

to waiting on negroes, and at the close of the work hours today would give up her job.

We do not know what effects this solitary act of defiance may have had on the residents of Charlotte, North Carolina. What is known, however, is that the editors of the *Charlotte Daily Observer* took the opportunity in the March 24 edition of the newspaper to comment on the negligence of white persons toward the black people who lived among them. On many matters of interest to their fellow residents, white persons had little knowledge and even less experience. They were urged to correct that oversight and develop a broader understanding of what the black man needed and wanted.

> It is within the power of white men of standing to do much for the brother in black ... without derogating aught from their own dignity or waiving any view they hold with regard to the proper relation of the races. The negroes will not misunderstand them upon this point nor seek to take advantage of the friendly manifestation. It is said, truly, ... that the negro is with us, and to stay, and the dominant race in doing its duty by him, is only doing its duty to itself.

Persons who draw strength from better-regarded groups often find the members of a minority population objectionable. Nevertheless, it is possible to search for more agreeable and effective ways to bring minority residents closer to the community of believers, even if they cannot yet be brought into it. In the case of Charlotte, North Carolina at the turn of the twentieth century, it would be by discovering a higher duty to their "brothers in black" that white leaders would better apprehend and serve their own people. This is precisely how a community of believers seeks to balance its members' need to maintain an identity and institutional presence against the demands of other groups to be accepted into their company. It is the way they practice belonging and sharing at the same time.

Call it paternalism, if you like, but this attitude has characterized the tentative and uncertain attempts by established groups in many communities to reach out to a variety of newcomers, but most especially to their minority neighbors. The citizens of Pittsburgh, for instance, were encouraged to view newly arrived Irish immigrants in this way. One local politician took the position that the Irish had come for the same reasons the English had. His comments were recorded in the *Pittsburgh Daily Morning Post* on October 22, 1842. He said, "the Irish part of our community are fast assuming their just grade in public estimation. They should be looked upon to be what they really are, a worthy and industrious class of people." He then went on and implored his fellow citizens to "lend every assistance to disseminate, among them, just and upright principles, and teach them to love this, their adopted country."

A similar sentiment was recorded in the *Argus Leader* on January 20, 1891 in relation to the native American people around Sioux Falls and South Dakota generally. The newspaper noted that the recent war with the Indians was nearing its end, and that citizens would have to decide how best to deal with these people. "It is cheaper, in dollars and cents," the author noted, "to civilize the Indians than to exterminate him. ... And above all come the considerations of humanity, and justice, neither of which a civilized people like ours can afford to violate."

The question of whose ways and ideas should have precedence was rarely asked. The social and moral integration of the city as it was currently constituted was the preeminent concern of even the most progressive city leaders. Additional room for newcomers could be made near, if not yet entirely inside, the community of believers.

Readers of the *Boston Herald* on March 2, 1860 learned, for example, that the state Senate had revised the statutes pertaining to the militia so that "colored persons" would now be allowed to train next to their white fellow citizens. Members of the Freedman's Association met at the Second Presbyterian Church in Wheeling, West Virginia, according to a report in the *Wheeling Intelligencer* on February 6, 1865, with the idea in mind to provide newly freed slaves "with food and clothing, and, in time, education." On August 10, 1893, the *Florence Gazette* reported that Professor W. H. Council of the Huntsville Normal School had de-livered a lecture at the AME Church of Florence, Alabama on the subject of relations between the races. A generation later, the Louisiana Con-gregational Conference gathered in April of 1925 for its 56th annual meeting in New Orleans. It issued a statement against the migration of blacks to the North, hoping instead that they would stay in the South. Part of the declaration, as it was published in the April 2, 1925 edition of the *New Orleans Times-Picayune,* held that "the white people of the South" were the "Negro" community's "best friends." A great many black persons did not accept the suggestion or the friendly idea that allegedly laid behind it.

There certainly have been many recent examples of this idea being applied to a community's less esteemed and accomplished minority resi-dents. It was reported in the July 31, 1964 edition of the *Boston Globe,* for instance, that Cardinal Cushing had summoned a committee to unite in fighting the "evils of racism.' This call went out following a series of violent incidents that had taken place in northern cities, including one in East Boston only one week earlier. "No true citizen who cares for civil rights and a respect for the law can stand aloof," the Cardinal declared. "No true Christian who sees every man as his brother can turn away unmoved."

During that same period of urban unrest, the *Cleveland Plain Dealer* reported on August 20, 1968 that the city's Welfare Federation had spent $145,000 to sponsor an intercultural and interracial Summer Campership Project for a number of children. The Superintendent of the Pittsburgh school system declared his hope in the November 9, 1973 issue of the *Pittsburgh Post-Gazette* that he could end the "white stranglehold" on contracts for school construction and supplies. Finally, the Germantown Ministerial Association made a special request in the February 15, 1990 edition of the *Germantown News*. The members asked residents of this small Tennessee city to support a campaign to rebuild a church belonging to a black congregation that had been burned down by arsonists. The reconstruction of the facility was completed by October of that year thanks in part to the effort of local churches and the Germantown community at large.

Between the Generations

Accompanied sometimes by violent clashes between natives and newcomers, the process by which one or another minority population is brought into "the American mainstream" has rarely been easy or accomplished quickly. Indeed, the estrangement and redemption of minorities has been a crucial theme in the story that Americans tell about themselves. Important and dramatic as that story has been, it pales in significance to a story told much less often about the incorporation and exclusion of younger and older Americans into the community of believers.

Older persons today rarely are portrayed as active and effective agents for the communities in which they live. It was not always so. Particularly in towns but also in early American cities older residents continued working beyond what we would call their "retirement age." What historian Carl Bridenbaugh referred to as the "greybeards" were seen as community patrons who were engaged in a number of economic, cultural, and political ventures.[24]

Today many older persons volunteer their time to "good causes." Some continue to work in low-paying jobs on a part-time basis in marginal sectors of the economy. Most others spend a large portion of their waking hours socializing with other persons their age. If they are mentioned in newspaper accounts, it usually is as the guests in some community-sponsored activity held "in their honor."[25] However satisfied they may be with their lives, the vast majority of older Americans would entertain no illusions about exercising much authority in their community. There is no place for them on a council of wise and experienced elders that serves as the community's memory and guide on matters of taste and manners, as Plato imagined there would be inside his good city. Nor are they often consulted or made to feel much a part of their community. What political power they exercise will more likely be seen frustrating rather than embracing community initiatives, just as any school official frustrated over the loss of a school bond at the polls would testify. Older persons have become socially disenfranchised in this century and increasingly dependent on government largesse to keep themselves fed, housed, clothed, and in some semblance of good health. Having been pushed into retirement and lost control of the land and public chores that made them credible and useful, they became candidates for charity rather than contributors to the commonweal.[26]

The view of older persons as vital contributors to their communities contracted along with the role they played in local economies. A connection between these states seems unmistakable, particularly in light of a campaign on the part of business people, charity reformers, and opinion leaders at the end of the nineteenth century to push older workers to accept mandatory retirement. The "enthusiastic belief in the redeeming promise of youth" was expressed by nearly everyone, it seems, but older persons themselves. It was a calculated move in many ways, set as it was against a sudden concern on the part of employers about the health and efficiency of their most senior employees.[27]

The irony, of course, was that young persons were becoming a smaller part of the industrial workforce at the end of the nineteenth century and the beginning of the twentieth century, even as their energy and strength were being heralded as good reasons to hire them. More teenage boys and girls were staying away from full-time employment or delaying their entry into the job market and attending school longer than they had in the past. This change, like many innovations in social customs and ideas about what constitutes appropriate behavior, was apparent earlier in middle-class and more well-to-do families than among poor and working-class families. Parents from more prosperous households had the luxury of not needing their children to work. It was literally the case that they could afford to extend their children's dependence upon them for a longer period of time.[28] Greater numbers of children, and this really means more children from less prosperous families, would take fuller advantage of these same opportunities as the twentieth century unfolded.

Adult concern about the precocity of children and the necessity to keep their youthful exuberance in check was an interesting corollary to all these changes. One read little about boys and girls in the newspapers of nineteenth-century towns and cities except in relation to their church groups, school commencements, and occasional misadventures involving snowball fights or escapes from families and businesses to which they had been indentured. Readers of the *Boston Chronicle Gazette* in 1820 would have learned about several schools being opened for "young ladies" or "young men," a school of dance for children, and an effort by the caretakers of Boston's asylum for indigent boys to place some of their youthful charges with local businesses as apprentices.[29] The citizens of Norwich, Connecticut entertained a Young Men's Lyceum in their town, according to the *Norwich Evening Courier* on October 5, 1850. This group met every Monday evening at the Apollo Hall and was in need of funds to pay for their lecturers. An advertisement placed in the *Bergen Democrat* on March 28, 1862 offered 30 boys or girls who were about 15 years old a chance to earn five or six shillings daily while learning how to polish silverware. The June 13, 1862 issue of that newspaper carried an offer from a Mr Zingsem of "the most liberal inducements to boys and girls to learn a very respectable occupation enabling them to earn large wages."

These efforts, while successful up to a point, did not provide a way to deal with the large number of children who belonged to immigrant families and the poor or who were staying home longer and not going to work. There was understandable concern about how they would fit into the local community and use all the free time made available to them. Adults had two answers for these concerns. They invented a kind of behavior that was called "delinquent" and meant to apply only to bad things that young persons did. In reality, this entailed little beyond attaching the term "delinquent" to many activities that had long been popular among children and teenagers but were now viewed as "troublesome." It had the advantage of giving adults a way to talk about their children's behavior that drew a clearer, albeit arbitrary, line between what they would accept as conventional behavior in their world and what they would not tolerate.

Adults also introduced a mass system of public education to their towns and cities, setting aside land for schools sometimes even before other public buildings had been erected. Schools were supposed to accomplish many things for communities, including serving as a sign that citizens were serious about making their town into a civilized and more urban kind of place. High on the list of what schools were supposed to offer children would have been a "middle-class outlook" on the world. In practical terms, this meant that young persons would not act like "delinquents" and would adopt standards more in keeping with the bourgeois civic culture into which they had been born or dropped.[30] They would learn about self-restraint, thrift, and the responsible use of independence and free time, even if there was little in their everyday lives to reinforce these lessons.

One of the more interesting and revealing ways in which well-meaning adults attempted to handle the many children left free to roam city streets without the advantage of much guidance or oversight was to take them from the streets altogether. The plan, as it was imagined and executed by a number of organizations in east coast cities, was to bundle the unwanted children off to a place where they would be safe and no longer a threat to themselves or the public. Tens of thousands of children, most of them not of immigrant stock, were "placed out" with families throughout the midwest during the second half of the nineteenth century and into the first decades of the twentieth century.[31]

An early report of one such group's activities was conveyed in the *Boston Daily Advertiser* on April 18, 1860. "No charitable association among many of our city," the article stated, "does so much good, according to the amount of money expended, as the Children's Mission to the children of the Destitute." It was noted further that the Children's Mission, which was run by the Unitarian Association, had been hard at work placing children in "good, wholesome, healthy homes in the country" for the last two or three years. The reporter had attended "interesting exercises" the previous day in which 36 children started their westward trek to Warren County, Ohio. "The children were neatly dressed, and looked remarkably cheerful and well pleased with the prospects of their journey." The Mayor of Boston, several members of the local clergy, and a judge all attended the ceremony. "Many who parted with them with tearful eyes," the reporter concluded, would "anxiously watch their progress through life, and unite with them in blessing the Association which built them this highway to comfort, prosperity and success."

This was an extreme step. Nevertheless, it was a step that leaders took and many adults apparently favored during the second half of the nineteenth century when the population of most eastern cities swelled dramatically. Basic changes in the way that young persons were thought about and treated were slow in coming. Against the alternative of continuing to remove large numbers of children from cities, however, the prospect of dealing with local "delinquents" and larger school systems does not seem all that severe.

It also was during the decades after the Civil War that more young persons began to organize "Societies" not unlike those to which many adults belonged or to hold events like balls and concerts designed specifically for themselves. Some of these groups were affiliated with churches and schools or were sponsored by adults, just as they had been in the past. This would have included organizations such as the Boy Scouts or

Girl Scouts, Junior Chambers of Commerce, athletic leagues for girls and boys, youth orchestras, and the like. Others appeared to be independent of adult-run organizations; but it sometimes is hard to tell from newspaper accounts just how independent these groups were from adult oversight or control. What is clear, however, is that young persons in twentieth-century towns and cities continued to organize themselves into groups or enjoyed the attention of adults who saw to it that children and teenagers got a taste of what could be accomplished by voluntary organizations.[32]

Newspapers after the start of the twentieth century generally paid more attention to children and teenage boys and girls. A number of newspapers set aside whole pages of one or more issues during the course of a week to cover events and issues germane to younger persons. Part of the reason no doubt was that childhood and adolescence were emerging as distinctive social categories within American society. The persons put inside those bins increasingly became objects of curiosity and concern on the part of their parents and the larger community. Experts wondered aloud about the best way to deal with young persons under a variety of circumstances. Some of the topics were serious. Readers of the *Cleveland Plain Dealer* on March 30, 1885 were asked to consider, for example, what effects recent state legislation limiting child labor might have on school enrollments. Other questions, while taken seriously by adults at that time, appear a little less forbidding to us today. A good illustration of this was also found in the *Cleveland Plain Dealer*. Parts of the story as it appeared in the February 28, 1885 edition of the newspaper are produced below.

TOO MUCH STUDY
Required of Children Attending the Public Schools
What Well Known Physicians Have to Say About It
Something is radically wrong in the pubic school system when pupils are required to take their books home to study nights and holidays. ... Children are questioned every day ... as to whether they studied the evening before and if they did not they are kept at work after school hours.

Many parents have been obliged to take their children out of school to preserve their health and very many more seriously think of doing it.

Dr. G. C. Ashmun, health officer: "Nightwork as a rule is hurtful. I have seen children seriously injured by worry over studies and approaching examinations."

Dr. J. F. Isom: "I did lots of night work in my younger days and it didn't hurt me ... The time to be devoted to study depends upon the constitution of each pupil."

Dr. F. H. Clark: "The child gets all the brain work it ought to have in the day time ... I have known nervous troubles and congestion of the brain to result from night study."

Dr. C. B. Parker: "Girls at certain periods of growth should not be urged to the same tasks as boys, as the latter have a decided advantage. Tasks should be lighter for girls."

The idea that children should not be pushed so hard or constrained by adults was picked up in another column offering advice to parents in Idaho Falls nearly 50 years later. Alice Judson Peale's "Talks to Parents" column appeared in the October 9, 1931 edition of the *Idaho Falls Post* and extolled the virtues of children's "free association" with their peers. The "stimulation of new play ideas ... helps make up a child world, where the child's realities are the realities that count," Ms Peale stated. "Plenty of casual association ... will help correct faults of character and aid him in his later adjustment." Furthermore, it is when he is "subjected to the impartial treatment of a crowd where he must make his own way on his own merit" that he feels more comfortable and makes greater progress.

It is hard not to conclude that children were being cut loose and expected to mold into miniature adults too early in life. Researchers who have looked at childhood and adolescence in the nineteenth and twentieth centuries make it clear that young persons were supposed to be learning how to fit into an adult world that was organized around bourgeois principles like orderliness and civility. School was not supposed to be fun. It was child's work. The authors of the two newspaper stories cited above had a different view; and they were not alone in the view they held.

It appears that there was a great deal of ambivalence about when children should be introduced to the adult world and uncertainty as to how this should be accomplished. All things considered, it had proven easier to take the rights and obligations of adulthood from older persons than it was to give them to children. Removing the option of gainful employment from more children at the end of the nineteenth century clearly made it harder to accomplish this goal. That is why ever more attention was paid to the school as an important site where children could learn some of the skills and acquire experiences like those which conventional adults might have.

Children undoubtedly did things with their parents in the nineteenth century and learned a great deal from the adults who lived and worked around them. That same kind of learning goes on today, and it is vital to the well-being of the children exposed to it but also to the community as a whole which benefits from having young persons who are better prepared to become adults. Yet today we seem to make more fuss about doing things with our children. We now have a special day, for instance, when mothers take their daughters to work with them, just so the child can see her parent as a professional and a wage earner and not just as "Mom."

One could say a lot of nice things about such a day. The importance of the event comes at least as much from the fact that daughters (and sons for that matter) have less chance to see mom in action, though, as it does from seeing how she fills the day away from home. Grown-up persons in the twentieth century increasingly have gone out of their way to create moments when children were made very much aware of the fact that they were being treated like adults or having an adult-like experience. A good part of the reason, I suggest, is that more children are less familiar with what adults do on an everyday basis than they once were. As a result, we need to make a bigger show of introducing them to our lives on those occasions when we let them sneak a peak.

Most of the moments are gentle and even fun. It was reported in the *Sparks Tribune* on May 19, 1913, for instance, that the high school track team had defeated members of the school faculty and alumni organization in their annual meet. Fathers and sons of the Idaho Falls stake, a Mormon territorial jurisdiction consisting of several church bodies, had held their annual outing at Big Springs on August 8, 1926. According to the story in the *Idaho Falls Daily Press*, everyone had enjoyed a day's worth of fishing, biking, and other sports. "Lads and Dads" dined together in their first annual father–son banquet in Burlington, Vermont on May 20, 1936, according to a report in the *Burlington Free Press*. And a story in the *Tupelo Area Journal* told how fathers and sons in Tupelo, Mississippi were organizing a golf tournament in their city on July 9, 1963.

Some of the moments are more serious or are intended to convey a clearer and more dramatic message to young persons about the obligations and problems they will have to face as adults. Most of these occasions are set up as "rituals of reversal" in which a person is allowed to do something he would not ordinarily have the chance or right to do. Anthropologists who have spent time with so-called "primitive" peoples are familiar with ceremonial moments when the world is seemingly turned upside down. The inequities or built-in stresses and strains that are part of any community are played out in a ritualistic way. Women take up arms and men flee from attacks which injure and sometimes kill one of them. Women go into labor and their husbands isolate themselves in a hut and roll around as if they, too, were about to give birth. The switch in roles does not last long. No one stays pregnant forever, after all, and a tribe would not expect to win a battle being led by a bunch of screaming women wielding pots and pans.

Rituals of reversal can be amusing because they make the world look familiar and strange at the same time. They last only a little while, however, and are carried out in ways that become traditions in themselves. No real "harm" is done to the world when persons are subjected to these periodic trials. Indeed, the legitimacy of the world as everyone knows it is reinforced by seeming to have been put through so severe a test. We recognize the arbitrary way in which the world is organized and acknowledge that some persons get the bad end of that deal. Yet we persist in embracing the fiction that the way we do things is really the only reasonable alternative. All other ways of being in the world bring confusion and discord. The truth is that women could do many things ordinarily assigned to men, and men also would have little trouble learning how to carry out most of the things that women do. We all know it; and the stylized exchange of roles shows that we know it.

Children are introduced to several of the more serious features of adult life in their community through just such rituals of reversal. On one occasion reported in the *San Diego Union* on May 5, 1905, the Order of the Eastern Star held its annual "Children's Night" when "tots from the homes of the members ... are waited upon like kings and queens by their elders." The children were given a firsthand introduction to lodge life and the ritualistic reenactment of deference to those persons standing on a higher rung of the community's social ladder. Rituals of reversal also could help children learn about politics and government service. The Boy Scouts of Valdosta, Georgia held a general election among their members in 1937 to see who among them would serve in all the official positions that adults filled in their city's government. According to a story in the *Valdosta Daily Times* on February 1, 1937, city officials had agreed to "step down" so that "the boys might take over the government of the city for one day."

Although there certainly was a play-like quality to these exchanges, there also were important messages being given to the children who participated in the ceremonies. Foremost among these messages was the idea that someday they would be assuming responsibility for running organizations and ensuring that the local government worked well. They had to learn how to do this, and it was not too soon to begin this lesson.

Just how quickly children could be thrust into more adult-like roles in the workforce and political scene is amply demonstrated by three events that took place in larger cities during this century. It was reported in the *Pittsburgh Post* on December 19, 1914 that local newsboys had petitioned the city government to rescind a ban on their right to sell Christmas toys and garlands. City officials relented. Their position was that the youthful vendors created "a yuletide atmosphere and spirit that should not be discouraged." A group of 45 students from the Rayen School in Cleveland, Ohio was reported to have marched two miles from their school to the downtown area in order to protest the closing of all the public schools because of financial problems that the city was experiencing. The story appeared in the December 3, 1968 edition of the *Cleveland Plain Dealer* and indicated that the youngsters had chanted "Education not vacation!" as they proceeded on their march. Finally, it was reported in the September 11, 1975 edition of the *Boston Globe* that 18 students in white jackets with blue arm bands had been instrumental in cooling tempers at Hyde Park High School during a luncheon break. The group consisted of white and black youngsters called "student aides" who were trained to mediate disputes between their fellow classmates. Inasmuch as their work was conducted in a desegregated school and in a city where school desegregation was hotly contested, the teenage students had taken on a great deal of responsibility and performed well.

There was nothing play-like in the work of the newsboys or students. It was serious, and the young persons made a difference in the life of their communities. Moments when they had a chance to act like adults or saw adults behaving competently would have been instrumental in teaching them how to act like competent persons and effective stewards of their city's affairs. This, too, is part of the service that rituals of reversal provide to a community. They show a city's children how to belong and how to share. They also give young persons an opportunity to practice the rights and obligations that come with being a trusted person, that is, a "made man" or a "made woman" who was worthy of membership in the community of believers.

NOTES

1   Carl Bridenbaugh, *Cities in Revolt: Urban Life in America, 1743–1776* (London: Oxford University Press, 1971), p. 85.
2   Hans H. Gerth and C. Wright Mills, *From Max Weber: Essays in Sociology* (New York: Oxford University Press, 1958), p. 305.
3   Bridenbaugh, *Cities in Revolt*, p. 148.
4   Thomas Bender, *Community and Social Change in America* (Baltimore, MD: Johns Hopkins University Press, 1993), p. 97.
5   Ibid., p. 102.
6   Bridenbaugh, *Cities in Revolt*, pp. 420–1.
7   James Lemon and Gary Nash, "The Distribution of Wealth in 18th Century America: A Century of Changes in Chester County, Pennsylvania, 1693–1802," *Journal of Social History*, Volume 2, Number 1, Fall 1968, pp. 1–24; Edward Pessen, "The Egalitarian Myth and the American Social Reality: Wealth, Mobility and Equality in the 'Era of the Common Man'," *American Historical Review*, Volume 76, Number 4, October 1971, pp. 989–1,034; Gary Nash, "Urban Wealth and Poverty in Pre-

Revolutionary America," *Journal of Interdisciplinary History*, Volume 6, Number 4, Spring 1976, pp. 545–84; G. B. Warden, "Inequality and Instability in Eighteenth-Century Boston: A Reappraisal," *Journal of Interdisciplinary History*, Volume 6, Number 4, Spring 1976, pp. 586–620; Craig Buettinger, "Economic Inequality in Early Chicago, 1840–1850," *Journal of Social History*, Volume 11, Number 3, Spring 1978, pp. 413–18; John Alexander, "Resurrecting the 'Progressive' Interpretation of the Coming of the American Revolution: Committees, Crowds, and the Urban Crucible," *Journal of Urban History*, Volume 8, Number 2, February 1982, pp. 217–29.

8   Richard Carwardine, "The Second Great Awakening in the Urban Centers: An Examination of Methodism and the New Measures," *Journal of American History*, Volume 59, Number 2, September 1972, pp. 327–40.

9   Benton Johnson, "Do Holiness Sects Socialize in Dominant Values?" *Social Forces*, Volume 39, May 1961, pp. 309–16. In this small yet classic piece of sociological analysis, Johnson demonstrated that certain religious sects embraced values and ideas about hard work that are similar to those held by persons in the larger society and more mainstream religious groups. Dramatic revival meetings and services masked conventional norms and real-world practices that belied the other-worldly exhortations of the holiness sect worshipers.

10   *Wheeling Intelligencer*, April 18, April 26, May 4, 1861.

11   *Fairbanks Daily News-Miner*, June 10, 1919; *Valdosta Daily Times*, February 3, 1925 and February 27, 1925; *Pittsburgh Post-Gazette*, September 8, 1927; *Burlington Free Press*, March 3 and June 27, 1936; *News Tribune*, January 29, 1955; *Boston Globe*, February 23, 1958; *Columbia Flier*, January 10, 1970.

12   *Manchester Union*, October 15, 1945.

13   *Cleveland Plain Dealer*, February 18, 1968; *Boston Globe*, October 7, 1968; *Pittsburgh Post-Gazette*, March 2, 1973; *Louisville Courier-Journal*, January 11, 1975.

14   Rodney Stark and Laurence R. Iannaccone, "A Supply-Side Reinterpretation of the 'Secularization' of Europe," *Journal for the Scientific Study of Religion*, Volume 33, Number 3, 1994, pp. 230–52.

15   Robert Bellah, Richard Madsen, William Sullivan, Ann Swidler, and Steven Tipton, "Religious Individualism and Fundamentalism," in Garth Massey (ed.), *Readings for Sociology* (New York: W.W. Norton, 1996), p. 334.

16   *Oregonian*, October 2, 1852, October 23, 1852, and October 30, 1852.

17   *Omaha Republican Weekly*, March 11, April 15, May 13, June 10, August 26, and December 21, 1868.

18   Richard Alcorn, "Leadership and Stability in Mid-Nineteenth-Century America: A Case Study of an Illinois Town," *Journal of American History*, Volume 61, Number 3, December 1974, pp. 685–704; Bruce Dancis, "Social Mobility and Class Consciousness: San Francisco's International Workmen's Association in the 1880s," *Journal of Social History*, Volume 11, Number 1, Fall 1977, pp. 75–98; Edward Kopf, "Untarnishing the Dream: Mobility, Opportunity, and Order in Modern America," *Journal*

of Social History, Volume 11, Number 2, Winter 1977, pp. 206–27; John Cumber, "The City and Community: The Impact of Urban Forces on Working-Class Behavior," *Journal of Urban History*, Volume 3, Number 4, August 1977, pp. 427–42; Joel Schwartz, "Tenant Unions in New York City's Low-Rent Housing, 1933–1949," *Journal of Urban History*, Volume 12, Number 4, August 1986, pp. 414–43; Kenneth Winkle, "The Voters of Lincoln's Springfield: Migration and Political Participation in an Antebellum City," *Journal of Social History*, Volume 25, Number 3, Spring 1992, pp. 595–612; Stephan Thernstrom, *Poverty and Progress: Social Mobility in a Nineteenth-Century City* (Cambridge, MA: Harvard University Press, 1964); Howard Chudacoff, *Mobile Americans: Residential and Social Mobility in Omaha, 1880–1920* (New York: Oxford University Press, 1972); Stephan Thernstrom, *The Other Bostonians: Poverty and Progress in an American Metropolis, 1880–1970* (Cambridge, MA: Harvard University Press, 1973); Clyde Griffen and Sally Griffen, *Natives and Newcomers: The Ordering of Opportunity in Mid-Nineteenth Century Poughkeepsie* (Cambridge, MA: Harvard University Press, 1977).

19   "It is not equality of *condition* but equality of *opportunity* that Americans have celebrated." Stephan Thernstrom, *Poverty and Progress*, p. 256.

20   *Evening Argus-Leader*, December 25, 1893.

21   See, for example, John Higham, *Strangers in the Land: Patterns of American Nativism, 1860–1925* (New Brunswick, NJ: Rutgers University Press, 1955); Nathan Glazer and Daniel Patrick Moynihan, *Beyond the Melting Pot: The Negroes, Puerto Ricans, Jews, Italians, and Irish of New York City* (Cambridge, MA: MIT Press, 1967); Elmer Clarence Sandmeyer, *The Anti-Chinese Movement in California* (Urbana, Il.: University of Illinois Press, 1973); Daniel J. Monti, *A Semblance of Justice: St Louis School Desegregation and Order in Urban America* (Columbia, MO: University of Missouri Press, 1985); Daniel J. Monti, *Race, Redevelopment, and the New Company Town* (Albany, NY: State University of New York Press, 1990); Peter Skerry, *Mexican Americans: The Ambivalent Minority* (New York: Free Press, 1993); August Meier and Elliott Rudwick, "The Boycott Movement Against Jim Crow Streetcars in the South, 1900–1906," *Journal of American History*, Volume 55, Number 4, March 1969, pp. 755–75; Christopher Wye, "The New Deal and the Negro Community: Toward A Broader Conceptualization," *Journal of American History*, Volume 59, Number 3, December 1972, pp. 621–39; Lee Finkle, "The Conservative Aims of Militant Rhetoric: Black Protest During World War II," *Journal of American History*, Volume 60, Number 3, December 1973, pp. 692–713; Ira Berlin and Herbert Gutman, "Natives and Immigrants, Freemen and Slave: Urban Workmen in the Antebellum South," *American Historical Review*, Volume 88, Number 5, December 1983, pp. 1,175–200; Elliot Barkan, "Vigilance Versus Vigilantism: Race and Ethnicity and the Politics of Housing, 1940–1960," *Journal of Urban History*, Volume 12, Number 2, February 1986, pp. 181–90; W. Edward Orser, "Secondhand Suburbs: Black Pioneers in Baltimore's Edmondson Village, 1955–1980," *Journal of*

Urban History, Volume 16, Number 3, May 1990, pp. 227–62; Thomas Linehan, "Japanese American Resettlement in Cleveland During and After World War II," *Journal of Urban History*, Volume 20, Number 1, November 1993, pp. 54–80; Kenneth Goings and Raymond Mohl, "Toward a New African American Urban History," *Journal of Urban History*, Volume 21, Number 3, March 1995, pp. 283–95; Kenneth Goings and Gerald Smith, "'Unhidden' Transcripts: Memphis and African American Agency, 1862–1920," *Journal of Urban History*, Volume 21, Number 3, March 1995, pp. 372–94; Arnold Hirsch, "Massive Resistance in the Urban North: Trunbull Park: Chicago, 1953–1966," *Journal of American History*, Volume 82, Number 2, September 1995, pp. 522–50; Thomas Sugrue, "Crabgrass-Roots Politics: Race, Rights, and the Reaction Against Liberalism in the Urban North, 1940–1964," *Journal of American History*, Volume 82, Number 2, September 1995, pp. 551–78.

22 Daniel J. Monti, "Patterns of Conflict Preceding the 1964 Riots: Harlem and Bedford-Stuyvesant," *The Journal of Conflict Resolution*, Volume 23, Number 1, March 1979, pp. 41–70; Daniel J. Monti, "Intergroup Conflict and Collective Violence: The Case of New York City, 1960–July, 1964," *Journal of Political & Military Sociology*, Volume 6, Number 2, Fall 1978, pp. 147–62; Meier and Rudwick, "The Boycott Movement"; Orser, "Secondhand Suburb"; Finkle, "The Conservative Aims of Militant Rhetoric."

23 Eugene J. Meehan, *Public Housing Policy: Convention Versus Reality* (New Brunswick, NJ: Center for Urban Policy Research, 1975); Jonathan Rieder, *Canarsie: The Jews and Italians of Brooklyn against Liberalism* (Cambridge, MA: Harvard University Press, 1985); Ronald P. Formisano, *Boston Against Busing: Race, Class, and Ethnicity in the 1960s and 1970s* (Chapel Hill, NC: University of North Carolina Press, 1991); Scott Cummings, *Left Behind in Rosedale: Race Relations and the Collapse of Community Institutions* (Boulder, CO: Westview Press, 1998).

24 Bridenbaugh, *Cities in Revolt*, p. 366.

25 On most occasions this turns out to be a banquet or concert of some sort. See: *Wisconsin River Pilot*, February 13, 1869; *San Diego Union*, May 10, 1877;

26 W. Andrew Achenbaum, "The Obsolescence of Old Age in America, 1865–1914," *Journal of Social History*, Volume 8, Number 1, Fall 1974, pp. 48–62; Carole Haber, "Mandatory Retirement in 19th-Century America: The Conceptual Basis for a New Work Cycle," *Journal of Social History*, Volume 12, Number 1, Fall 1978, pp. 77–96.

27 Achenbaum, "The Obsolescence of Old Age in America", p. 59.

28 Joseph Kett, "Adolescence and Youth in Nineteenth-Century America," *Journal of Interdisciplinary History*, Volume 2, Number 2, Autumn 1971, pp. 283–98; William Graebner, "Outlawing Teenage Populism: The Campaign Against Secret Societies in the American High School, 1900–1960," *Journal of American History*, Volume 74, Number 2, September 1987, pp. 411–35; Stephen Lassonde, "Learning and Earning: Schooling, Juvenile Employment, and the Early Life Course in Late

Nineteenth-Century New Haven," *Journal of Social History*, Volume 29, Number 4, Summer 1996, pp. 839–70.

29 *Boston Chronicle Gazette*, January 6, March 16, June 12, and September 14, 1820.

30 David Allmendinger, "The Dangers of Ante-Bellum Student Life," *Journal of Social History*, Volume 7, Number 1, Fall 1973, pp. 75–85; John Gillis, "Youth in History: Progress and Prospects," *Journal of Social History*, Volume 7, Number 2, Winter 1974, pp. 201–7; R. P. Neuman, "Masturbation, Madness, and the Modern Concepts of Childhood and Adolescence," *Journal of Social History*, Volume 8, Number 3, Spring 1974, pp. 1–27; Joseph DeMartini, "Student Culture as a Change Agent in American Higher Education: An Illustration From the 19th Century," *Journal of Social History*, Volume 9, Number 4, Summer 1976, pp. 526–41; Janet Riblett Wilkie, "Social Status, Acculturation and School Attendance in 1800 Boston," *Journal of Social History*, Volume 11, Number 2, Winter 1977, pp. 179–92; Daniel Rogers, "Socializing Middle-Class Children: Institutions, Fables, and Work Values in 19th-Century America," *Journal of Social History*, Volume 13, Number 3, Spring 1980, pp. 354–67; Jeffrey Mirel, "From Student Control to Institutional Control of High School Athletics: Three Michigan Cities, 1883–1905," *Journal of Social History*, Volume 16, Number 2, Winter 1982, pp. 83–100; Janice Weiss, "Educating for Clerical Work: The 19th-Century Private Commercial School," *Journal of Social History*, Volume 14, Number 3, Spring 1980, pp. 407–24; Stephen Norwood, "The Student Strikebreaker: College Youth and the Crisis of Masculinity in the Early 20th Century," *Journal of Social History*, Volume 28, Number 2, Winter 1994, pp. 331–49; Joel Pearlmann, "Who Stayed in School? Social Structure and Academic Achievement in the Determination of Enrollment Patterns, Providence, Rhode Island, 1880–1925," *Journal of American History*, Volume 72, Number 3, December 1985, pp. 588–614.

31 Marilyn Irvin Holt, *The Orphan Trains: Placing Out in America* (Lincoln, NB: University of Nebraska Press, 1992). For a more elaborate treatment of how the process worked in Boston, see pages 83–6.

32 For a few examples of each type of young person's organization see: *Manchester Daily Union*, April 24, 1875; *Tupelo Journal*, February 3, 1877; *San Diego Union*, October 22, 1881; *Sparks Tribune*, November 4, 1914; *Argus Leader*, August 8 and December 22, 1891; *Wilmington Morning News*, January 25, 1922 and February 2, 1925; *Valdosta Daily Times*, December 15, 1925; *Lawrence Daily Journal-World*, December 1, 1926; *Idaho Falls Post*, November 16 and November 24, 1928; *Fairbanks Daily News-Miner*, November 28, 1939; *Boston Daily Globe*, March 1, May 21, and August 31, 1945; *Pueblo Star-Journal*, January 20, 1950; *Manchester Union Leader*, January 27, 1951; *Bergen Evening Record*, January 2, 1960; *Oregonian*, January 15, 1960; *Boston Globe*, June 27, 1962; *Pittsburgh Post-Gazette*, May 4, 1973; and the *San Diego Union*, March 15, 1976.

6

Piety and Tolerance

Piety is all about the business of making, enforcing, and acting in accordance with rules. When persons show their fidelity to conventional standards *and* better known or more believable parties attest to their good acts and values, we may say that they are being pious. *Tolerance* is all about stretching rules, fiddling with standards, or applying sanctions in an uneven or tentative manner. When individuals break rules or try to introduce new standards for judging what is right or wrong, then the limits of *piety* are being tested or redefined and *tolerance* is being embraced.

Only rarely do persons behave as if no rules were in effect. On the other hand, there are many instances in which persons act as if rules do not apply as much to them or rules are enforced weakly. It is as if we were uncertain about how seriously a given rule should be taken or how severely individuals who violate rules should be punished.

Many persons today are likely to say that we are much too tolerant. Rules are not enforced consistently, and there is much disagreement about what constitutes appropriate and inappropriate behavior in too many places or types of gatherings. Other persons are quite certain that we have too many rules or that our rules are applied in ways that discriminate against one or another group. We punish some types of persons more frequently or severely for the same offense than we do other kinds of people.

The history of towns and cities surveyed for this book indicates that there is validity to both these positions. Americans flop around a great deal on matters related to making and breaking rules in the places where they live. They are tough on some issues and soft on others. They do not like to talk about repressing any group, but they manage to do something that looks a whole lot like repression to a number of persons. We prefer to talk about repairing our communities when they suffer damage at the hands of destructive individuals or returning the victims of crimes to the situation they enjoyed at an earlier and happier time. Yet we are slow to carry out these promises and sometimes appear to forget them altogether.

It seems right to conclude that Americans like to have it both ways, usually at the same time. They mix piety and tolerance, sometimes favoring one over the other, but usually keeping them in some rough balance to each other. There are times when piety is enforced in the most severe ways imaginable. On other occasions, persons will make a lot of noise about upholding standards, even as unconventional practices and values are played out right in front of them. This may seem hypocritical. Nevertheless, this approach is likely to work better within the city's bigger borders and more open social spaces than if residents had taken a hard position in behalf of piety or tolerance and refused to budge from it. Of course, the very mixing of pious and tolerant ways can create the impression that cities are morally bankrupt places with a lot of confused persons running around inside. The results may not be pretty in every case, but they appear to have worked well enough for the last three hundred years.

No Place to Run, No Place to Hide

One was never too young or too old to be reminded of the importance of piety. Nor was the appeal of illicit acts and criminal adventures confined to the community's more marginal members or to outsiders. It did not matter how mundane or macabre the act was. A portion of the community was bound to be offended by it for one reason or another, and residents were sure to reflect upon the meaning of the act and those persons who carried it out. It may not have been the case that wrong-doers had no place to run or no place to hide inside American towns or cities. It just seemed that way much of the time.

Persons who engaged the services of indentured servants in the nineteenth century were loathe to lose their investment; and children who ran away from the families for which they worked were a constant source of irritation. One Boston family in 1810 offered a reward of six cents to the person who returned an 11-year-old girl named Sarah Graham to them, while another family was willing to pay two dollars for the return of an 11-year-old black girl who had run away from their house. Yet a third household was searching for a 12-year-old boy who had run away. Two of these advertisements carried the threat of legal prosecution for anyone who provided shelter for these children.[1]

Boston residents that year also were extremely concerned about runaway carriages and carts. Complaints filed against persons driving their carriages too quickly on the Lord's Day and disrupting church services led to the imposition of two dollars for anyone whose carriage went faster than a "foot's pace." A few months later "public feeling" again was "very much alive on this subject" after two children were killed by carts going too fast on city streets.[2]

Boston authorities had a suspect in the murder of Timothy Kennedy on March 6, 1820, the same day the event was reported. A reward of $200 was offered for the capture of Michael Powers, "an Irishman," and two weeks later he was taken into custody as he tried to board a ship headed back to Dublin. He denied murdering Kennedy, but he was found guilty at his trial less than one month later all the same. Days later he made a public declaration that rumors about his killing other men, too, were not true. He was executed on May 25, 1820, two and one-half months after Mr Kennedy's body had been found in the cellar of a house.[3]

"Led on by the flesh and the devil" in February of 1845, a starving Irishman stole a piece of meat and was caught by Boston policemen as he tried to escape. He explained his situation to the butcher, and the shopkeeper gave him a good meal. Two months later an inquiry was launched into the severe flogging of a Boston school boy at the hands of his teacher. The boy had provoked his tutor by whispering in class. The same teacher was reported to have kicked a little girl earlier in the year.[4]

Readers of the *Carolina Spartan* on March 18, 1858 were treated to a pair of stories that the editors thought said something important about their community and life in the South generally. A burglary into the store of Mr A. Tolleson netted the robbers $27. That would have been bad enough, but it was carried out on a Sunday evening. This prompted the editors to declare that Spartanburg was "throwing off its verdancy and donning city airs." In the other story, "the trial of Patrick, slave of Miss Lucy Tanner, on a charge of poisoning, with intent to kill, Peter, slave of Col. S. N. Evins" was recounted. A jury brought in a verdict of "not guilty" following four hours of deliberation, in large measure because the evidence against Patrick was so skimpy. The editors noted that the trial was "another refutation of the abolition slander that a negro cannot get justice in the South. Garrison sometimes copies items from us. We commend this to him as a selection for the enlightenment of his readers."

Five years later at the height of the Civil War, the City Council of Spartanburg took several steps to protect members of the community.[5] They passed an ordinance that was intended to punish citizens who allowed their goats to run free. To this they added a law which prohibited any "colored man" from using a horse or mule to make money for himself. It did not matter that the man were slave or free, the animal would be seized and his profits "appropriated for the public good of the town." A further ordinance called for any slave left occupying a house without his owner or without the company of a responsible white man to be "impounded." His owner would be fined five dollars for every day the slave had been left to roam around freely.

The editors of the *Bergen Democrat* in Hackensack, New Jersey had their own Civil War troubles.[6] No fewer than two attempts were made to arrest them for making "treasonable expressions" and condemning Lincoln's prolonging of the war. On one occasion, the friends of the editor were compelled to fight off his would-be attackers in what was described as a "considerable scrimmage."

Louisville had interesting problems of its own after the Civil War was concluded. Two brothers were arrested for distributing opium in 1868. One worked for a city drugstore and stole over $12,000-worth of the drug from the store's stock which came from Turkey. The other brother sold the drugs in over a dozen cities, including New York. Both pleaded guilty to the charges against them. Shoplifting had become a serious problem, and women were caught stealing far more often than men. A federal soldier shot two black men who refused to let him into a house where a black woman he would visit was staying; and a black teacher and his black female companion filed assault and discrimination charges against a dockkeeper who would not allow them to stand near a group of white women.[7]

It was reported in the March 21, 1882 edition of the *San Diego Union* that all saloons were shut down in faithful observance of the Sunday-closing law. A two-horse wagon also was said to have careened through the town on that day and crashed into a store. The wagon, according to the newspaper account, "was considerably demoralized." Eight days later the newspaper reported that a number of saloon keepers had paid fines for violating the Sunday-closing law. Charlie Daynes, who was described as an "infamous wretch" was arrested, tried, and sentenced all in a matter of two days for beating his wife and step-daughter. The "brute" got a 180-day sentence for assaulting his wife and 90 days for striking the little girl.[8]

The San Diego newspaper reprinted an interesting editorial out of San Jose on September 23, 1882. It dealt with the causes of insanity. The editors of the San Jose paper attributed it to bad breeding and related "violations of moral law." It was reported in the January 27, 1883 edition of the San Diego newspaper that a man was found guilty for stealing some charcoal and sentenced to spend ten days in the city jail. Suspicions about his sanity led him to be committed to the county hospital where he would be given a psychological exam. On March 1, 1883, it was reported that a stranger to San Diego was taken to the hospital by a police officer. A doctor declared the man "insane by reason of alcohol."

The town of Rochester, Minnesota experienced a few interesting transgressions and crimes in 1886.[9] A drunken man accepted a payment of $100 for his wife from his drinking partner. The man who took the wife was not expecting to receive the children as well, and the woman was none too pleased about the deal herself. The sheriff was reported to have settled the affair by returning the woman and her children to the husband and $90 to the swindled friend. No accounting was made of the remaining ten dollars. One month later, a 20-year-old woman was charged with choking and stabbing her newborn child to death.

The citizens of Spartanburg, South Carolina in 1891 continued to wrestle with questions involving relations between black and white persons. The murder of one black man by another at an encampment just outside of the city provoked editors of the *Carolina Spartan* to call for strong actions to be taken against the settlement and the "degraded white women" who lived there.[10]

> One of these, Nancy Pearson, who has several negro children, was arrested and imprisoned as an accessory before the killing. It may be that this murder will break up the disreputable state of affairs in that neighborhood. If it does not, a stronger and more sudden power than organized justice may suddenly appear one of these nights and clean out the whole neighborhood.

This call for vigilante action against the settlement did not lead to an immediate attack. The editors made a second and seemingly more humane statement on the same matter the following week. They continued to declare the "Howard Gap colony of white women" a "standing menace to good order" and "a danger that threatens society at the bottom." At the same time, they also asked if something could be done to help the women in question.[11] "Is any one bold enough, or good enough, to hold out a friendly hand, or speak a kind or helpful word to them? It is a social condition that confronts us. How shall it be managed?"

Two years later, on January 5, 1893, an equally strong but quite different position was taken by the editors of the *Florence Gazette* in response to the murder of a black man.

> A white man killed a negro man on Saturday night before Christmas. The colored people were having a Christmas tree, when the white man deliberately fired into the house from his yard nearby, killing the man instantly. This caused a stampede from the house of the crowd. The murder caused great indignation among all classes and they will see that the crime is avenged.

Residents of Southern communities were not the only persons who called for tough and even violent reaction when a particularly heinous crime was committed or an important point of morality was being openly repudiated. Local businesses and citizens in Fairbanks, Alaska responded quickly to a call on December 17, 1909 by the editors of the *Fairbanks Daily News-Miner* for funds to aid in the apprehension and conviction of a man who committed a "brutal assault" on a young cashier. Over $1,400 was donated in less than one day.

Fortunately, the man had run away before "carrying out his purpose." This did not assuage the good people of Fairbanks, however.

> The boast of Alaska has always been that in spite of the fact that men of all classes have been attracted to the North the women have been safe to walk the streets at day or night without fear of being insulted or molested. The crime last night was the first ... ever committed in Fairbanks and as far as known, the first in Alaska.
>
> When the news of the assault spread, a large crowd gathered ... at the scene of the crime and indignation reached such a stage that had the assailant been captured last night attempts to lynch him would undoubtedly have been made.

There were other strategies that city residents and officials adopted to maintain a sense of decorum in their hometown or to enforce standards for appropriate behavior which seemed threatened. The Grand Jury responsible for Sparks, Nevada in 1911 was reported to have turned "its eagle eye" upon the town's "resorts." The charge was that "one of the saloons in this city allows gambling in the house and that this same saloon is in the habit of permitting women to frequent their resort."[12]

What happened in Sparks was hardly a unique occurrence in the history of urban politics in this country. Similar bodies have been impaneled by communities throughout the nineteenth and twentieth centuries to make investigations into particularly messy issues that citizens thought would not be addressed satisfactorily or needed a high-profiled group to handle. This has been especially true when public officials themselves were under investigation or some human-made or natural calamity had befallen a city like a riot or great fire. One such investigation was launched in Pittsburgh in November of 1915 when a Police Magistrate was accused of selling "vice privileges" in his part of the city to a pair of men from Chicago.[13]

Another story out of Pittsburgh on that same day showed that public officials sometimes tried to anticipate problems or counter expected breeches in public order before they took place. Police were reported to have been "strict in suppressing roughness" during Halloween celebrations several days earlier.

Fifth avenue was the scene of the biggest celebration, many from the adjoining boroughs and townships coming to the city to join with the revelers in the one night of the year when "almost anything goes" with the police.

The revelers took cognizance of the police order barring the throwing of rice, corn, lampblack, flour and other injurious substances, and none of the banned articles were in evidence. Merchants ... took precautions against the crowd by boarding up plate glass windows in front of their stores to prevent breakage.

The report went on to add that smaller street celebrations had taken place in districts across the city and in many of the surrounding suburbs. In several cases, the festivities were sponsored by local business groups or were held in public buildings so that children could have a good time without being out on the street.

A "noted minister" from Valdosta, Georgia in 1915 declared liquor to be a "minor evil" in comparison to "dope" which, he said, made men evil. One imagines that his speech was a response to the unusually heavy "traffic in cocaine" that authorities had been tracking over the past few months.[14] Other events at that time were not quite so dramatic. A "suspicious dog was shot dead" on a city street because it had been "acting very queerly." Seventeen incandescent lights were stolen from the Grand Theatre one evening. A doctor's office also was robbed of "valuables" and a white man was arrested for that crime. A train conductor stopped a train so that a local colored preacher could catch a thief who also was colored. An alleged chicken thief made the mistake of trying to sell the purloined fowl to a police officer. Grand jurors were looking into several larger matters, including the murder of a black man at the hand of several masked men. The recorder's court, in the meantime, was pursuing a number of interesting "blind tiger" cases in which illegal liquor was being smuggled into local establishments. One month later, Frank Baker, a white man, was arrested for selling whiskey. He had previously been arrested for assault and battery.[15]

There seemed to be few changes in the types of crimes Valdosta residents were committing ten years later. During an argument about the weight of some meat at the local Piggly Wiggly store, one man was reported to have "playfully" slapped another. The victim of the assault picked up a meat cleaver and cut the other man over his eye. He then fell to the floor and died from a heart attack. Two men who were due to be hung for murder in the jail yard had their execution temporarily postponed, even as a crowd of local residents was gathering outside the jail to see "the boys drop." The injunction was lifted four days later, and the sheriff had a roof put over the yard so that spectators could not witness the hanging.

Police announced in March of 1925 that they were starting a campaign against "loafing Negroes." Later that month the police had an extremely busy weekend and made 20 arrests, largely for drunk and disorderly conduct. In April they kept busy with the "more rigid enforcement of the radiance against bright lights on automobiles" within the town limits. Two black men were taken into custody on April 22 on suspicion of being "slickers." It was reported that they "were well dressed and rode in a handsome touring car." In May, two more black men were taken into custody on suspicion that they were going to stage "one of the old pocketbook flim-flam games." They were charged with loitering and loafing in order to "keep them quiet." An automobile driven by a white woman crashed into a furniture truck on that same day. She claimed that her brakes had failed. Later that month, police found a large still and destroyed it.[16]

Some of the crimes reported to have taken place in only three days in Pittsburgh that same year revealed that life in that city was becoming rougher. More than a score of saloonkeepers protested a law that led to their businesses being closed because of illegal liquor sales. A Chinese laundryman claimed for a second time that his son had been kidnapped by members of a rival tong. A man staying at a hotel was murdered, and his roommate was held for the crime. Two murder trials were concluding; but other cases were being prosecuted for battery, embezzlement, manslaughter by automobile, possession of stolen goods, and employee theft. A victim of a street robbery died from wounds to his head and body. Three boys, two with Italian-sounding names and one who was black, were arrested as members of the "panel gang" and accused of robbing a store. They were brought before the city's Morals Court. They were 13 and 14 years old.

Five men and a woman were arrested for disorderly conduct right after a disturbance had broken up an anti-Soviet meeting at the Labor Lyceum. Federal rather than local prosecutors were assigned to handle the case. A former police officer was killed after confronting a group of black men in front of a pool hall. More than 100 residents were arrested as other city policemen searched local "haunts of Negroes" in the area in an attempt to capture the murderers. All but three of the black persons arrested were subsequently released. Police stopped a riot at a Duquesne basketball game, and another basketball game between Catholic schools was stopped because of a row.

Five youths were arrested for stealing and later wrecking a car. They were between 16 and 23 years old. A man who had been stabbed was arrested for being a "suspicious person." An Italian man was arrested for possessing illegal firearms. A "Negro" man was accused of setting his home on fire after arguing with his wife. Both were arrested as "suspicious persons." Finally, the star witness in a tong murder case was herself murdered before she had a chance to testify in court.[17]

Crime and punishment in Burlington, Vermont during 1935 was less dramatic but more personal. Emily Mercer was the first bootlegger to be convicted since a new law against prohibition had been enacted. She was sentenced to spend up to one year in jail for possessing alcohol with the intention of selling it. Gordon Wiggins, aged 19, was convicted of shooting and raping Francis Shea. Margaret Parent received a sentence of between 12 and 18 months for prostitution. Emmet Armstrong was fined $100 and court costs of $13 at his trial for vehicular homicide in the death of Donald Halpin. Two men were arrested for selling liquor on which the tax had not been paid, and a druggist had his license suspended for selling spirituous liquor without a prescription signed by a doctor. Frank Dubie and Florabelle Beaupre were arrested for adultery and sentenced to between one and two years in prison. Charles Hawkins was arrested for killing his six-year-old son. Two fishermen had a fight. One of them, Joe Witz, was arrested for sending the other man to the hospital. Finally, two women were given small jail sentences after they had a street brawl.[18]

It is likely that persons in larger cities were doing some of the same things that residents in smaller cities and towns were doing in the years following the Depression and World War II. We certainly know that rule-breakers in smaller cities were committing some of the same offenses as their big-city peers. In fact, the spread of violence and crimes like those witnessed in larger cities into smaller cities, suburban municipalities, and even some out-of-the-way towns in more rural areas turned into one of the bigger unpleasant surprises of the late-twentieth century.

The real difference in rule-breaking between smaller cities and towns, on the one hand, and larger cities, on the other, was in the kinds of rules that warranted some sort of public airing when they were broken. Newspapers in smaller cities and towns continued to make a bigger deal over smaller crimes. Malefactors were more likely to be named and victims embraced in these places. Well into the 1970s, for instance, the *Germantown News* published the names and addresses of every resident who was fined for parking or driving violations. Newspapers had printed the names of wrongdoers, delinquent property taxpayers, and even hotel guests throughout much of the nineteenth century. Only smaller cities and towns persisted in this practice into the twentieth century; but even their newspapers gave up trying to keep track of who was dropping into the local hotel.

Newspapers in larger cities tended to ignore smaller violations of rules and pay more attention to particularly nasty or better-organized expressions of rule-breaking. On just one day in 1977, for example, readers of the *Chicago Tribune* were treated to the following stories dealing with crime and punishment. A foster parent who had been arrested months earlier on drug charges continued "to live with five foster children and to receive state child-care payments of more than $2,500 a month." The Chicago police department's intelligence unit, having admitted earlier in the year to spying on political and civil rights groups, acknowledged that it also had targeted the Independent Voters of Illinois for over 30 years. A federal grand jury indicted a man for mail fraud, "charging he talked 26 Chicago area persons into investing $750,000 in a nonexistent shopping center." Finally, "a carnival worker from Alabama was raped and her husband pistol whipped ... by a gunman who invaded their room in a South Side motel."[19] Crimes, like the persons who perpetrated them, tended to be bigger and more anonymous. At least it would have appeared that way to members of the community in larger cities who read the daily newspaper at the end of the twentieth century.

"Extreme Piety Does Not Often Kill the Average Californian"

Individuals who broke the rules in American towns and cities during the nineteenth century usually did not make a public declaration of repentance or offer any sign of their moral reclamation. Such demonstrations, if they occurred at all, apparently were better left said to ministers or shown in church. Their neighbors showed no great need to hear a wron-doer's confession or to witness his act of contrition. Adults were supposed to know how to act and were expected to fit in as best they could.

If a person was unwilling or unable to meet this standard, community members had any number of ways to make their displeasure known. In general, however, they counted on three tried-and-true techniques to protect themselves and their community. The first of these were "paybacks." The least severe consisted of monetary fines or services "paid" to the community in general or as compensation to the victims of a crime. More severe paybacks entailed a temporary or permanent removal from the community. This usually meant that a person was put in jail; but sometimes a man or a woman simply was run out of town.

This was no small rebuke. A person without a place to call his own or to take him in, after all, does not matter. He is not a real person. In the most extreme cases, his execution constitutes a "final solution" of a particular kind, a formal dissolution of any tie that he may have had to a community and a rejection of any claim to the presumptive rights that membership would have afforded him. It was not about preventing other persons from committing the same or even worse offenses. Nor was it about exacting vengeance, no matter how heartfelt the cry for it may have been. It was about removing the stain of one person's existence from a community and reflecting upon the tentativeness of our own claims to its memory and tender mercies.

The second technique involved "shaming" a wrongdoer. Ordinarily, this was accomplished by naming persons in the local newspaper who had committed an offense and sometimes including their address in the report. We only can guess at the effect such public revelations may have had on the named persons in the nineteenth century. In our own time, however, efforts to publicize the names and pictures of men who have tried to pick up prostitutes or molested children or to otherwise mark persons who have broken rules so that everyone else might know them have provoked a great deal of public discussion. If nineteenth-century men and women were anything like us, they would not have liked having their names paraded before the public as wrongdoers any more than we do. Some towns today still publish the names of malefactors on a routine basis, but there appear to be fewer that do this than was once the case. Shaming seems to have fallen out of favor.

The question of when persons should not be condemned in public was managed a little bit differently in every American town and city. Like the matter of dealing with crime generally, there were no hard or fast rules on how public shaming should be handled. In one particularly revealing case, editors of the *Wheeling Intelligencer* on February 22, 1867 laid out their reasons for not publishing the proceedings of the Police Court any longer. A portion of their comments is reproduced below.

[The] scally-wags who form the generality of those who come before that court, have little or no sense of shame, and rather regard the notoriety thus obtained as something to be proud of, so low is their sense of honor.

[We] would like to deal with strict impartiality, and publish all or none. Yet if a man or the son of a man of social disposition gets into a difficulty which brings him before ... Judge Good, the local is requested not to publish the matter.

Our theory is, that the first offense should be handled severely, and the ... pretended respectability of the party is only a reason that he should be made to feel that a respectable standing in a community is a something to be guarded with sacred care; a something that is to be maintained in its purity as a moral standard and that cannot be used as a cloak to screen offenders from publicity. We have always noticed that people who presumed upon the general good standing of themselves or their relatives ... to commit occasional breeches ... soon become the most troublesome offenders known to the community.

This is all very well and good. Keep in mind, however, that the editors already had decided not to publish the proceedings of the Police Court, and hence the names of wrongdoers, in the newspaper. In good democratic form, they extended the cloak of anonymity to the low-born as well as those with "the influence of a moneyed position" behind them, but only up to a point. Circuit Court cases still had their defendants named.[20] These cases tended to be more serious and dealt with crimes like murder, forgery, assault, horse-stealing, rioting, and bastardy. Assuming that some high-born persons eventually would be caught committing one of these offenses, their names still would have appeared in the newspaper with all of Wheeling's most serious miscreants.

A good public shaming was called for in some cases, of course. Boys and young men who committed an offense, usually of a comparatively minor nature, sometimes received a public reprimand and were expected to make a contrite showing. Just how badly they really felt, as any parent would testify, was difficult to assess. On those rare occasions when newspaper accounts carried such a story, however, the reader was left with the impression that youthful wrongdoers had been dealt with firmly but fairly and probably would not commit another offense. A good example of this was reported in Sioux Falls, South Dakota in 1886 when several boys were caught stealing watermelons. They were brought to municipal court where they were said to have been "scared straight by the judge" and "frightened about as badly as the Chicago anarchists."[21]

The third and by far the most common response to crime was to use the violation as an excuse to rally good persons and have them, not the wrongdoer, show just how committed they were to living within the rules. Community members accepted the fact that some persons were just plain bad and could not be salvaged. They also knew that everyone was capable of acting badly at least once in a while. So, they were not especially surprised when persons did something wrong, and it was not a big deal if they were punished for their misdeeds. Members of the community were much more interested in ensuring that the overwhelming number of persons around them who were good most of the time stayed that way.

The idea that crimes can be prevented or that we should work harder to bring wrongdoers back into the fold is a peculiarly modern conceit. It is borne of the same Progressive-era idea that "society" is poorly organized and somehow makes us do bad things. Society can be made right, the argument goes, if we listen to experts who ask for more programs to heal and renew our troubled brethren. Rather than the bad guys having to learn how to fit in with us, somehow it has been turned around so that we are supposed to learn how to fit in with them.

For all our caterwauling about "reforming" persons who have done something bad, however, we really do not spend much time or money trying to make them better. They are locked up and forgotten by everyone except the victims of their heinous acts. All that changes when they are released, of course, and they visit their old haunts and commit some more crimes. Then we become all riled up again, rally ourselves, and try to throw the perpetrator away a second time, or a third time. Perhaps we are more tough-minded than we think.

"Extreme piety does not often kill an average Californian," replied a reporter from Topeka, Kansas when asked for his impressions about San Diego back in 1881. He was not impressed with the moral standing of Californians, and he shared his thoughts with a fellow newsman who was writing a story for the September 9 edition of the *San Diego Union*. The Topeka reporter was supposed to be commenting on the small number and modest size of churches in San Diego, but he used the moment to make a much bigger point.

Had the local reporter wanted to take issue with his colleague, he might have noted that the Unitarians, Methodists, Episcopalians, and Presbyterians already had churches in town and held regular services. He also might have mentioned that a Ladies' and Pastors' Christian Union dedicated to doing charitable works had been formed earlier in the year or that a "tent" revival less than one month earlier had drawn good crowds.[22] The San Diego reporter could have rebutted his colleague from the midwest, but he was more taken by the tartly worded barb aimed at the character of his fellow Californians.

These reporters were far from the only persons in the United States who thought that the residents of nineteenth-century American cities were impious and that we should do something about it. It is not much different today. We are not inclined to think of cities as places where human beings behave in accordance with time-honored customs and values any more than the reporters did. We are more likely to imagine cities as places where a variety of views are openly expressed and where no one is pressured to subscribe to a particular dogma or set of standards. That is to say, we see cities as places where groups practice tolerance more often than they do piety.

If one equates piety with churchgoing, a common but understandable error, then the moral countenance of Americans had slumped long before they ever settled in California. "Several influences, chiefly of an urban nature," Carl Bridenbaugh tells us, already had undermined "the power of the church for the enforcement of social discipline" in seventeenth-century American villages. The chief competition for colonial churches apparently was the local tavern. One minister, Dominie Backerus, complained as early as 1648 "that his hearers rushed to tap houses as soon as church was out, for further fortification against evil."[23] He was far from alone in noting the frayed moral fiber of American colonists. Nevertheless, different religious groups continued to set up churches and promoted a variety of social activities from within the confines of their parish halls during the colonial era and throughout the nineteenth and twentieth centuries.

Piety and profanity have coexisted well in American towns and cities, even though cities usually are dismissed as moral sinkholes and towns are popularly viewed as bastions of religious probity. Despite the real and imagined differences between towns and cities, they have two important features in common that play into a larger discussion about piety and tolerance in American society. First and foremost, their residents and workers practice an urban way of life. They embrace a bourgeois creed predicated on progress and order, or at least they act that way much of the time.

Conventional religious groups in this country tend to reinforce the American creed and give it a nice theological spin, even when it seems ill-advised. For instance, when the national secretary of the Christian Endeavor Society visited San Diego in 1905 he tried to show parents how important it was to keep Sunday schools up and running. He also wanted to inspire young people to stay with God. In drawing his listeners to these important ideas, he observed that "ninety-eight percent of the prisoners" in one facility he knew "claimed at one time to have been members of a Sunday school."[24] This, he assured his audience, was evidence of the continuing need for Sunday schools and religious training for children.

The second feature that towns and cities have in common is that everyone who lives or works there does not have an equal say in running the place. Only some persons fashion the American creed that guides everyone else's life or directs the civic rituals and social routines which provide the muscle for bourgeois ideals. That special duty falls to a confederation of persons and groups which constitutes a "community of believers" in any given town or city. The members of this special community bear primary responsibility for determining who will be let into their confederation, the kinds of rules that are made and how strictly they are enforced, and how much of everyone's behavior is dedicated to public or private pursuits.

Fourteen years after Californians were declared safe from the ravages of excessive piety and ten years before the good people of San Diego were shown that the Sunday school door almost always opened to the penitentiary, the Reverend J. Frederic Dutton spoke about "the higher needs" of that city.[25] In his sermon at Unity Hall, the Reverend Mr Dutton declared that his city needed a new library, a series of public concerts and lectures during the winter season, more literary and science clubs, and a good college. More than anything else, however, the people of San Diego needed to create "an intellectual and moral aristocracy."

> An aristocracy of some kind we are sure to have. Sooner or later every community divides into higher and lower. People who would keep all upon a level, level down not up. Aristocracy is to most people a hated word, but it simply means, "the rule of the best," and who does not desire that? But we do not want an aristocracy of money or of birth, but of character, i.e. of knowledge, wisdom, virtue.
>
> A certain amount of material prosperity is generally necessary to the highest spiritual activity of an individual or a community. The sad truth is, however, that too often our material prosperity outruns our spiritual activity and ease and luxury are sought as ends in themselves.

Plato might have turned such matters over to a council of elders. Responsibility for carrying out this kind of mandate in San Diego would have been passed to the local chapter of the community of believers.

A tension exists between members of the community of believers and persons or groups that could be called "non-believers" or outsiders. Whether the rights and obligations that come with membership should be shared with any or all outsiders and non-believers is a serious matter. We have seen that a great deal of time and energy is spent working out the details of how and when outsiders can assume the privileges and duties that come with membership in this select confederation. It is not a tidy process or something that comes without pain and hard feelings.

Outsiders and non-believers have to demonstrate their worthiness. The burden of proof, as it were, falls on them. It does not on their neighbors. Persons and groups already in the community of believers set the standards for membership and lay out the rules that outsiders must follow, if they are to gain entry to this club. This may not be fair or nice, and the results may not be pretty or even agreeable to would-be members. Nevertheless, it is the way the process works.

There certainly are times when community members act clearly in behalf of piety. The assault of a young Louisville woman by a black man in 1868, for example, prompted an estimated 200 black residents and smaller number of whites to hunt for the perpetrator in a nearby swamp.[26] When the man finally was caught, he confessed to the crime. According to the newspaper account, it was his black pursuers who gathered wood and burned him at the stake. Local authorities tried to interfere with the execution, but they were threatened by both the black and white members of the crowd.

Assaults upon persons who are viewed as particularly vulnerable, like women, provoke especially swift and definitive reactions by community members. Children have been treated in much the same way. Parents, teachers, and most certainly strangers who abuse children are seen as committing an almost unpardonable act. Calls to punish them tend to come quickly and hold out little hope for the perpetrator's survival or salvation. On the other hand, if an otherwise heinous act can be recast in a less harsh light, then the punishment can be softened. This was the case for a St Louis woman in 1875 who was accused of throwing her newborn child into a stove and burning it alive.

The woman's attorney argued that the child may have been alive after its birth, but only for a short time. He made no excuses for disposing of the child's body in this way. However, he argued that a verdict of manslaughter would be more appropriate in light of the failure to prove that the infant was full-term and healthy. The prosecuting attorney concurred, but only in part.

> Should the child have met death ... by the instrument of abortion, then ... the offense is only manslaughter in the second degree. But if you find ... that ... the child ... was cast into the stove still alive, and met death by the flames that she kindled around it, then ... the accused is guilty of ... murder in the first degree.
>
> You must feel an oppressive weight in the air you breathe with her, a repulsive shudder with which we instinctively shrink from a being abhorred, as ... when God affixed his blighting brand on the brow of Cain.
>
> I think I can see those little arms lifted above the flames, that I can hear the feeble voice raised in helpless suppliance.
>
> Protect the little ones from the abortionist, for they cannot protect themselves. Guard the domestic hearth from desecration. ... Arrest the tide of infant blood ... or lechery will stalk abroad in our midst until chastity becomes the scoff of the town and society sinks to the level of the Seraglio.[27]

Despite the prosecutor's impassioned speech, only a portion of which was reproduced, the defendant was found guilty of manslaughter in the second degree and sentenced to spend five years in the penitentiary. Before the end of August that same year, another woman was arrested in St Louis after being identified to the sheriff as a mother who had thrown her newborn baby into a privy in Sparta, Illinois in 1874.[28] Child murder was not at all uncommon in the nineteenth century, and citizens then seemed just as troubled as we are today by the prospect of ending a life prematurely and in dealing with the consequences of such an act.

From time to time, community members also can decide that it would be better to forget that something unseemly had ever happened or simply to let bygones be bygones. Just such an opportunity arose in St Louis in February of 1875, one month after the murder trial was completed, when "the furniture and fixings of Madame Kate Clark's *maison de jore* at

Sixth and Elm streets were sold at auction."[29] By all accounts, Madame Clark was a successful madam.

> Some of the most wealthy ... tried with Mrs Toodles from uptown for this or that article of *virtu* not virtue, as they passed in turn beneath the hammer ... inviting enough to seduce an Eastern potentate ... knocked down to Smith, Brown, or Jones, as the case may be.
>
> Brown smiled and looked happy as he thought of the story he would tell Mrs B. and the girls, as to where the elegant set came from, and how the Snifkins across the way would be dying with envy as they saw it delivered at his own proud mansion.
>
> And why this sale of earthly splendor? Not because the slaves of vice and passion have ceased to patronize this mansion of misery. Not because the wages of sin ... were not still at the command of the sharp and shrewd managers of the place, but because simply she is going to be married. A plain business arrangement has been entered into with a gentleman of New York ... and somewhere in an uptown neighborhood of Gotham the penates will be set up and Mistress Kate will enter upon her new life.

There are occasions when a crime has been committed, of course, that allowances are made for extenuating circumstances. At those moments it sometimes is appropriate, and maybe even necessary, for the members of a community to make a more public declaration of forgiveness for the wrongdoer. This was the case, for instance, in Idaho Falls in 1932 when a local woman was accused of murdering her husband.[30] He still was alive when the authorities found him lying in his bed. He had been shot once in the back, and the gun was on the floor next to him already cocked and ready to be fired again. Oddly enough, the victim declared that he had tried to commit suicide. If that was so, then he proved successful. Still, the special prosecutor felt compelled to bring his wife to trial on the charge of murder after the husband died.

The widow provided no explanation for the act or her part in it, except to say that her husband might have hired someone to kill him. In the end, the jury accepted the victim's deathbed declaration and found his wife not to be responsible for the crime. Spectators in the courtroom applauded. The prosecutor was philosophical about losing the case. He stated that there was but one explanation for the way it all turned out, "and that is that the dying man, with all his faults, was a good sport."

There were limits to sportsmanship and to a community's willingness to be forgiving. The trial of a man from Fairbanks, Alaska in 1909 provides a good illustration of how piety can be asserted, even when someone accused of a crime claims to have been driven to act by forces outside of his control.[31] This particular defendant, whose "general bad reputation, too, was against him," claimed that he should not be held liable for assaulting and trying to rob a man of $1,000 because he was temporarily insane at the time. The source of his passing insanity was an epileptic fit allegedly brought on by an injury that he had suffered as a child. He declared that he really was defending himself from his alleged victim, a Mr Hale. It was Hale himself, the defendant claimed, who had gone mad while they were talking about "whether life in Alaska was likely to drive a man insane." An expert called to testify on this particular matter found it hard to believe that the defendant's condition would reveal itself in this way 50 years after the original blow had been inflicted. The judge ruled the claim of epileptic insanity immaterial to the proceedings, declared the defendant guilty, and eventually sentenced him to serve 15 years in the state prison.

Piety often is asserted before an act deemed immoral or unseemly has a chance to be committed. These judgments are offered in the form of laws, and they can be spelled out in great detail. The residents of Germantown, Tennessee discovered just how numerous and detailed their "miscellaneous" crimes could be when the Mayor and Board of Aldermen reviewed a draft of a law at a public hearing on May 5, 1980.[32] "Miscellaneous" offenses covered everything from protecting children to disorderly behavior, lewd public acts, gambling, and fortune-telling. Persons would be barred from predicting the future "by any means of possession of an occult or mysterious power for hire or reward."

Had the ordinance passed, it would have become illegal "to dig, take or carry away earth, soil, shrub or other planting from the land of another or from public lands." Children would not be allowed to play games "on streets or other public places with the city – excepting parks and playgrounds – or the playing on any lot or yard if such play annoys others." Persons would be prohibited from smoking in many public offices and businesses, and spitting was to be banned nearly everywhere. Finally, it would have become illegal "to keep a disorderly house" within the city limits.

In most communities, this would be understood to mean a house of prostitution. For the good people of Germantown, however, this referred to any house in which "loud or improper noises or collecting drunken ... and disorderly persons ... to the annoyance of others and disturbance of neighborhoods" were apparent. As the reporter who composed the article said, "there seems to be a law for everything, with every fine in its place."

There also are many instances, on the other hand, when residents openly display a more tolerant attitude toward human frailties and behavior otherwise considered inappropriate by conventional standards. City officials in Spartanburg, South Carolina approved a tax law in 1888 that treated "gaming" or any place where a form of gambling was occurring like any other business. It was licensed and kept under government supervision rather than banned and driven underground.[33] The citizens of Casper, Wyoming did the same thing with carnivals in 1919. Rather than banning them outright, the town sheriff raised the daily license for parties presenting such entertainment to $100.[34] Persons who needed such licenses or who violated this or other local ordinances in Casper were not shunned or incarcerated, only fined. It was reported in the May 5, 1919 edition of the *Casper Daily Tribune* that the police department had earned $7,622.50 during the preceding month in this way. Individuals who could not afford to pay their fines were put to work cleaning the city's streets. Criminal behavior did have value. Persons who broke rules and community standards paid for the privilege in one or another way.

A slightly different tack, this time against the evil of alcohol, was taken by the bishop assigned to the Sioux Falls diocese in 1891.[35] Acknowledging that the law prohibiting alcohol consumption had failed to stop persons from drinking, he proposed to start a National Catholic Total Abstinency Society. It would not have been "composed of reformed drinkers, but of youths and maidens, men and women, who had never indulged or who had no acquired taste for drink." No one pretended that bad things and weak persons could be avoided. The only viable option was for good persons to remain vigilant, protect the community whenever possible, and to take comfort in each other's company.

The idea that deviant or illicit acts could be managed or have their effect on the public limited was popular in the nineteenth century.[36] Community members acknowledged that persons sometimes behaved improperly or made mistakes that offended their neighbors and damaged lives or property. Human vulnerability, corruption, and mendacity were regrettable facts of life. Still, there had to be some sort of accounting for bad deeds and a way for persons to earn their way back into the good graces of the community. Wrongdoers needed to be constrained. The effect of bad deeds had to be contained or at least explained away, and the community had to remain alert to the corrosive influence that bad persons could have on everyone else. Vulnerable but otherwise good citizens might nibble away at the edges of immorality and take an occasional bite out of crime, but they were unlikely to purify local society or keep bad things out forever.[37]

There were many instances, however, when local reformers worked too hard at purifying their local society or assumed that they could keep the forces of darkness from their threshold. While not exactly a failure, these efforts obviously did not rid cities of bad persons or noxious influences. They were much more important in making middle-class persons self-conscious about their growing importance inside towns and cities.

Would-be reformers became acquainted with the range of public and private resources at their disposal as well as the means to use them. They also were instrumental in introducing large social-welfare agencies and better public health and safety measures to cities.[38] These were not trivial accomplishments.

More often than not, though, aggressive efforts on the part of civil authorities or citizens to remove questionable persons and practices from their midst not only failed to accomplish that end but sometimes made problems worse. They often ended in ugly street battles in which persons were killed and property was destroyed. Nasty confrontations between long-term residents in cities and newcomers, as I noted in the previous chapter, have a long and sometimes sordid history in United States cities. Rioting and looting, particularly when it was directed at newcomers and perpetual outsiders, could last days and take many lives.

What is surprising about many of these engagements is that the violence and destruction of property were not more extensive. The objectives of rioters and vigilante groups usually were modest. Indeed, both the groups that engaged in violence and the parties which were lined up against them or were the targets of violence often went to great lengths to limit the amount of carnage that took place.[39] They did not succeed on many occasions; but they did try and were successful more often than we appreciate today. Furthermore, persons who engaged in collective acts of violence usually were trying to defend local prerogatives and customs rather than to establish a new social and economic order in cities. The result in either case was that violence ordinarily was used to achieve more limited and conservative goals. It reinforced piety and traditional rights and prerogatives more than it represented a push for big changes and greater tolerance in cities.

The conservative and often reactionary quality of much social unrest in American cities sometimes is viewed as a queer exception to what has occurred in many other countries. In particular, this would apply to some European nations where a more "progressive" and at times even radical strain of organized political violence allegedly has been in evidence for the last century.[40] Without taking issue with those persons who view urban violence in Europe as being more evolved or politically sophisticated than its American counterpart, there are several good reasons why outbursts of popular unrest in America would reveal a conservative bias. As I argued in another forum some years ago, it all started with the American Revolution. More precisely, it was the conflicts leading up to the great revolt which "vindicated the use of violence in behalf of locally prescribed economic and political practices."[41] Thanks to the revolution against Great Britain, American civil violence was politicized relatively earlier than it was in Europe. Unlike what is supposed to have happened in European towns, American city dwellers who took up arms in defense of local customs actually won. American colonists beat a big national government and stopped it from enforcing its will on them. Furthermore, it took Americans from all levels of society to join together in order to beat back the British challenge to their authority.

It made a difference that more prosperous individuals in some cities like New York continued to participate in displays of popular violence during the first third of the nineteenth century. When they finally ceded control over the timing and uses of popular unrest to less prosperous or esteemed groups later in that century, wealthier persons often quietly endorsed violence when it was used to support ideas they liked or punished a group they did not like.[42] This, too, helped to keep violence within certain limited and acceptable bounds.

It was not just wealthy patrons who supported the use of popular unrest in behalf of local customs. More organized groups and political parties also used violence to defend established routines inside cities, or they used local gangs to make this point for them. They usually did not turn to violence in order to topple the status quo or to make new claims on wealthy or more powerful groups inside cities. American civil violence, therefore, combined two features of civil unrest that were not supposed to be seen together. A more "modern" type of organization often used violence to achieve parochial or "pre-modern" goals instead of pushing for new resources and political rights for its members.

There was a final reason why I thought American civil unrest might be used for more conservative ends than its European counterpart. It was that violence in American cities seemed to have been used "only when alternative methods of addressing problems were unavailable or had been shown to be ineffective."[43] When groups had disagreements, it was customary for them to turn to violence only as a last resort. This, too, may have been a holdover from the way in which American colonists used various types of civil disobedience and unrest in their campaign to get a fair hearing and more independence from Great Britain.

More recent research undertaken by American historians, however, points to two other explanations for the apparently conservative nature of American civil unrest.[44] Groups that used non-conventional acts to make a point, especially when those actions could turn violent, needed to become comfortable with the idea of expressing their anger in less oblique and more instrumental ways. Part of this learning process entailed gradually reaching out to groups different from one's own or to a different part of one's own community. This took time and required a good deal of experimentation and soul-searching on everyone's part. Their violence was tentative or narrowly focused, designed to drop really big hints about their displeasure rather than to provide the solution for their problems. Violence was not something that groups did on a whim or without having first tried different ways of making their case clear both to their antagonists and to themselves. Alternatively, groups found ways to adapt traditional expressions of popular discontent so that they might better fit more contemporary targets.

Good examples of how violence was used in these ways are not hard to find. One came during the conflicts leading up to the American Revolution as traditional English rituals associated with "inversions" of authority or what we have called "rituals of reversal" such as tarring and feathering or putting on a mock trial for one's antagonists were put to new uses. In this case, they helped colonists of different social ranks grow accustomed to working with each other even as they were "punishing" despised British officials.

Approximately one century later in Memphis, Tennessee white persons were outraged after the Civil War by signs that black residents were growing more powerful in the city. Many of them took to the streets and attacked black individuals and institutions that seemed to embody that rise to power and respectability. Irish firemen and policemen were involved in the riot, in part because the appearance of armed "Negro soldiers" had constituted a singular challenge to their own recent advancement in the city. Their participation helped to demonstrate that most of the rioters were not rowdies. They were artisans, proprietors of small shops, and even some professionals.

It is interesting to note in this case that black business people and soldiers presented a picture of "the world turned upside down" that white persons found intolerable.[45] Moreover, the threatened inversion promised to be permanent and far-reaching. There was nothing ritualistic about the changes in question.

It was customary on these occasions for the party whose position was most tenuous to temporarily assume rights and prerogatives that otherwise would be denied them. The right to use violence against those in a superior, or in this case an increasingly more equal, position to one's own was one of those temporary privileges. That so much violence has been directed against "minority" populations and usually failed to stop them for too long, then, speaks less to the bigotry often expressed during these engagements and more to the implicit recognition that the world was changing in important, if not fundamental, ways. Oddly enough, ritualistic displays of violence against minorities in American cities certified their claim to membership in the local community of believers, even if it could not guarantee an invitation to join it. No one would have bothered them, much less taken such strong actions against them, had they not become more credible.

The so-called "race riots" instigated largely by minority persons in many American cities during the second half of the twentieth century were neither "protests" nor acts of rebellion. They extended the tradition of ritualistic violence, only this time against a world that was not changing quickly enough to suit them. One can make a case that this violence was no more successful in achieving big changes for blacks than organized attacks against them had been in stopping minority residents in the long run from making a place for themselves in their new, big-city homes. Violence in both cases served as a kind of acknowledgment of the changes occurring in cities just as ritualized rebellions in so-called "primitive" cultures celebrated the stability of those worlds.

"Bad Boys"

The single most important challenge to the community of believers has not come from minorities. It has come from teenagers. Adolescents emerged in the twentieth century as surly but important petitioners to the adults who organize and run their town or city. They have taken on responsibilities and assumed privileges typically reserved for older persons, or had such rights and duties ceded to them by adults who were too lazy or distant to care. The result in either case, sadly, is the same.

Teenagers have asserted themselves as workers and consumers, as active sexual beings, and in matters of life and death in ways that many adults never do. Having presented themselves as adults and tried to enter the conventional grown-up world without really knowing what they were doing, many adolescents have had to substitute aggressiveness for experience and bravado for wisdom. If there were a ritual or ceremonial occasion in which Americans celebrated the premature emergence of teenagers as full-blown adults, it would entail taking a loaf of bread out of an oven when it was only half-baked.

In the process of coming out this way, teenagers have participated in the largest inversion of social roles ever witnessed in American towns and cities. The grandest or most exaggerated expression of this ritualistic reversal may be found in contemporary big-city gangs like the Crips, Bloods, Vice Lords, and Disciples and in the children who emulate them. In their stylized dress, ritualistic declarations of brotherhood, indecipherable graffiti, and crude capitalization of home-grown entrepreneurs, contemporary gangs are a cruel and sometimes violent parody of eighteenth- and nineteenth-century male fraternities. To be a "made man" in this world requires adolescent boys, and increasingly also young women as well, to stand the criteria for certification as a morally qualified human being in the conventional world on their head, or maybe to turn them inside out. They are not against the conventional world so much as they are mimicking it with the few tools they have at their disposal in communities that have forgotten them.

All of this started much more modestly and innocently in towns and cities sometime during the middle of the nineteenth century. An early and eerily prescient warning to the adults of Wheeling, West Virginia came in 1860.

> Bad Boys – It is a fact which there is no use disguising that this city is educating a very large lot of bad boys for the penitentiary and so forth. The following may be recommended to parents as a proper course of training. Give the boys the unrestrained liberty of the streets at night, until such hours as they choose to return to the parental roof, allow them money to spend when they do not know its value, let them form such associations as dark hours and the desire to see "fun" suggest, permit them to do as they please without fear of being corrected for misdemeanors and they will be almost sure to become, in time, candidates for the penitentiary.[46]

It probably is not a coincidence that widespread expressions of concern about teenagers emerged around the time of the Civil War. Towns had been growing quickly in number and size. Cities also were on the verge of becoming the kinds of industrial and commercial centers that would have been familiar to our parents and grandparents. The newspaper in Wheeling that year contained a number of stories about children and young men as laborers and independent beings who needed to be watched more or held to higher standards of public decorum than they had in the past. Some young men complied. Others did not.

The situation facing older children and teenagers would become even more problematic during the Civil War. This is so because a war turns the world we know on its head in many serious and far-reaching ways all at once. The unimaginable suddenly becomes palpably real and unavoidable, and communities are transformed into sets where old expectations and routines are reworked by persons whose only stage experience up to now has been watching someone else do the acting.

That war is a singularly awful experience for men is easily demonstrated. It also is bad for children and young persons who are left with comparatively fewer healthy and competent adult males around from whom to learn the tricks and hard work that go into being a full-time father, family head, provider, and community leader. War has been much better for American women. Roles ordinarily reserved for men become available to women when wars take place, and American women have taken advantage of every war this country has fought by moving into these roles and performing them every bit as competently as men. Children have not been so fortunate. They are left more to their own devices than is customary or good for them and the community. The ritual of inversion for boys and girls simply could not be as well fixed in the conventional routines of their towns and cities as it was for the women who were left behind.

After a war has been concluded, we know life does not revert to the way that persons recall it before the men went off to fight. Women, as we shall see in the next chapter, never go back completely to being the kind of daughters, sweethearts, and wives that men remember. Nor do boys and girls give up all the freedoms they have come to take for granted after their fathers come home. Some of the more riveting moments one can have when reviewing the local histories of different cities comes immediately after a war is over and persons are seen struggling to right the world and make sense of what they have lost and gained. The names and pictures of sons and husbands who died appear on pages that also carry announcements of weddings long delayed and many marriages that could not withstand the strain of separation or change. It is all very sobering and sad.

What happened or did not happen to young persons was an important part of this picture. Newspapers in the decades after the Civil War published many more stories about misbehaving teenagers and children than they had in the past. Community leaders also were seen taking more frequent and serious steps to gain some measure of control over their young charges.

Sometimes the problems were small but nonetheless serious in the eyes of local adults. This was the case in Rochester, New York when local residents in 1887 mounted a boycott of local shops that sold toy cannons and pistols because they viewed these items as being too dangerous for children.[47] Other issues were big enough to engage the attention of institutions whose caretakers had a special role in seeing to it that children and teenagers were reared properly. One such incident was recorded in San Diego in 1895 when boys were being unruly at the Little Sherman and Sherman Heights schools. The Board of Education declared that it would support any arrests of these children that were initiated by the Principals.[48]

Police or reform schools came to be viewed by many persons as the last best hope to save boys from themselves and to protect the community from their misdeeds. On October 2, 1909, two incidents of this sort that took place in Oregon were reported in the *Fairbanks Daily News-Miner*. The first event involved a group of 12-year-old boys in Portland who planned to cause a trolley car to crash by greasing the rails on a piece of track that ran down a steep hill. Editors of the Portland newspaper believed that the only solution for such "idle, revengeful, vicious creatures" was to pack them off to a reform school. On the other hand,

Allen Olson of Astoria, Oregon was only nine years old when the police caught him selling stolen goods to a "second-hand dealer." The youngster, who was turned over to his family, claimed to have been driven to commit house burglaries by watching a movie that featured just such an operation.[49]

Boys in Idaho Falls during the Depression may not have been angels, but on March 19, 1931 the editors of the *Idaho Falls Post* waxed poetic when describing the opening of "marble season" in their city and the importance of this annual ritual. To them, "spring wouldn't be spring without marbles to officially inaugurate the season. From time in memorial this has been so, and will probably continue to be so." This may well have been the case in Idaho. Or, the editors may have been hoping to keep their boys from turning out like the young men from New York City whose exploits they had recounted in the February 23rd edition of their newspaper. One young man from New York died in a fight when "'The Hooligans,' a gang from the Red Hook section of Brooklyn, battled with 'The Hudson Avenue Boys' in a Brooklyn dance hall." The story indicated that "a siren placed on the roof of the dance hall for such emergencies was the signal which brought police swarming into the place." There was much gunfire in the darkened hall, and the police had to detain 60 persons, 40 of whom were women. It was not a good scene. Indeed, "when the place finally was cleared the floor was strewn with clothing, blackjacks, revolvers, and vanity cases."

Teenagers became no less rowdy or threatening in subsequent decades. Juvenile delinquency in Cleveland during World War II, for example, apparently became dramatically worse than it had been. Dr Henry Ollendorf from the Friendly Inn Social Settlement Center thought that delinquency among black youths and children of the "underprivileged class" had less to do with breaking laws than violating social standards. The problems they have come from being "banned from participation in those cultural associations wherein are taught and practiced the accepted social standards." Another story a few months later drew an even closer connection between the war and the juvenile "crime wave" that was overtaking the city in 1943. The cause of all these juvenile misadventures, according to its writer, was the failure of mothers to properly monitor their children. The "hand that rocks the cradle is now running a drill press," the reporter dutifully noted. Too many women were working in war-related industries and not attending to their important duties at home.[50]

Parents in Pittsburgh at the end of the war also were blamed for their children's bad behavior. At least that was the opinion of leaders drawn from civic, religious, and law enforcement agencies from across the city who met in the Center Avenue YMCA in August of 1945. "Eighty

percent of the cases [he saw] were traceable to conditions in the home,"
one representative said. Several other persons, perhaps making too
obvious a point, "stressed that gambling houses, cabarets, and all night
places ... which lure youths are run by adults. Stricter law enforcement,
penalizing parents when juveniles break curfew regulations, and closing
all-night spots," were deemed to be good ideas. These proposals sound
oddly familiar. The main thing to come from the meeting, however, was
a suggestion to set up a permanent committee "to plan and put into operation a positive program to further democratic aims and ideals."[51] This
was very much in keeping with rhetoric at the end of the war and many
of the efforts by leaders in other towns and cities to deal with their own
juvenile delinquency problem.

Yet the problem did not go away. If anything, juvenile delinquency and
organized violence by gangs grew worse and the array of causes grew
larger. Judge John J. Connelly of the Juvenile Court of Boston in 1952
attributed the 120 percent increase in juvenile problems in his city to
television, the economy, and "a postwar psychology." He wanted
parents to supervise their children better and to promote more organized
recreational activities. The following year all public and private agencies
in Boston were called on to form a "united front" against the dramatic
increase in teenage gang and racial "incidents" that was being experienced in the city at that moment. The Greater Boston Council for
Youth later launched a three-year $210,000 project that was intended to
help control the city's juvenile delinquency problem.[52]

Whatever they did with the money failed to stop teenagers from
behaving in dangerous and reckless ways. The social and political
upheaval associated with the Vietnam War and city school desegregation
conflicts did not help Boston leaders calm their children during the 1960s
and 1970s. Nor did all the population changes taking place in the city
make it any easier to address, much less stop, the use of violence and
intimidation by teenage groups and better-organized gangs. By the
1990s, the social fabric of Boston seemed to be raveling as a result of all
these changes. Uncontrolled teenage violence was one of the more
dramatic outcomes of these unsettled times.

The first shooting at a Boston high school football game in twelve years
prompted school officials in 1991 to post security guards at subsequent
contests. Teenagers from the rival schools had milled on the field during
the half-time routines of the two cheerleading squads. Taunts and jeers
between them led to one youngster shooting another.[53] Two women and
one man were injured in 1992 when gunmen opened fire on a group of
persons standing on a city street corner.[54] This drive-by shooting, like
others over the next few years, created an enormous amount of anxiety
in the city and increased homicides among teenagers to frighteningly high

levels. A particularly brutal murder by eight members of one street gang was recounted in great detail during the trial in which a younger member acted as a witness against two of his older partners. Several other witnesses were intimidated by friends of the defendants; but testimony about the rape and murder of an innocent woman that were told by persons still willing to step forward were chilling.[55]

Street gangs populated largely by minority adolescents and young men were not the only sources of unrestrained violence that Boston residents had to face during the 1990s. An open-air concert in City Hall Plaza "erupted into violence" one evening in 1992 when unruly persons attending the event provoked the police to end the music after only three acts had performed. Fifteen persons were injured during the melee and 24 were arrested. "The acrid smell of smoke," the reporter wrote, "hung in the air over Boston Common, a byproduct of the blazes set in garbage cans along Tremont Street. Broken glass from bottles and car windows lay strewn across City Hall Plaza." "Newspaper boxes lay on their sides ... in a gnarled tangle of metal ... kicked over by groups of rampaging youths."[56]

The Police Department's Community Disorders Unit had to visit public housing sites in South Boston, a predominantly Irish-American enclave much troubled during the school desegregation controversies. The reason was that young white males were attacking minority persons who were moving into the projects. Relations between white residents and the police grew increasingly strained. At one point a community meeting attended by several hundred residents led to calls for the disbanding of the special unit. Work also done by the Police Department's Drug Control Unit in another neighborhood plagued by drug sales and other illicit business operations put several of its officers in a tough spot when they arrested another cop during one of their raids. Community activists were more concerned about the fact that it had taken so long for the police to begin their clean-up of the area. No one took much note of the fact that the arrested men had their names and addresses mentioned in the story about the neighborhood sweep. Residents did take strong exception, however, to delays in the trial dates for the persons who were arrested.[57]

Something quite remarkable happened in South Boston in March of 1996. Several young men broke into the rectory of St Brigid's Catholic Church, almost injured one of the priests with a gunshot, and robbed the church of $2,724 in receipts from the parish bingo games. A young man from the neighborhood was later arrested for committing this un-precedented crime.[58] Problems with drug sales and overdoses and violence against minority tenants also continued to plague several public housing developments in South Boston well into the 1990s. The leader of a tenants task force at one of the developments, Maureen Berry, said that she used to go to meetings "to yell and scream." "Now I sit and cry with the other women. We talk about the people we've lost. I don't have any solutions anymore."[59] This neighborhood as well as others in the city seemed to be falling apart.

City officials, residents, and parents did not sit idly by and watch several troubled neighborhoods and a whole generation of children fall into some enormous hole. Instead they began the hard work of taking back and rebuilding their neighborhoods and protecting their children. While by no means an unbridled success or close to being finished, many persons and groups have labored mightily in what they viewed as a last-ditch effort to save places and persons that were important to them.

Nothing good would have happened had they been unable to rekindle a sense of trust among themselves or reassert a degree of orderliness in the everyday activities that persons observed. In effect, they had to learn how to become good neighbors and establish, as the headline of one newspaper story declared, "their own rules of the game."[60] There was less "new" about these rules than persons imagined. Residents became less tolerant of some kinds of persons and activities, and they reintroduced the idea that following rules was a good and necessary thing to do.

Most of these neighborhood initiatives were undertaken by residents who worked with little or no outside support for a number of years. They sponsored community activities such as picnics and sporting events, anything that might create a presence for their organization and a safe place for children and adults to congregate. Some groups set up "neighborhood watch" teams that kept an eye on who was in their area and on what these persons were doing. At least one of these groups also worked with public officials in order to establish programs for teenagers. Other groups worked with less desirable persons in order to find them jobs or to continue their education.

These renewed signs of life helped to push drug dealers and troublemakers to other corners, sometimes blocks away. In a few cases they also served to convince some of these same troublemakers to shape up so that they did not have to leave. More important to the long-term viability of these neighborhoods, however, was the creation of partnerships with public and private agencies that were in a position to funnel money to these areas now that they were safer. Now organized as community development corporations, these neighborhood groups applied for loans from foundations or grants from different public agencies to expand their reclamation efforts. Beyond providing some social services to persons who needed them, several of these organizations and at least one church group also developed housing projects for low- and moderate-income residents in their area.[61]

Slowly, sometimes painfully slowly, business people began to open shops and retail centers that had not been seen in some of these areas for many years. Part of the reason may have been that suburban areas had all the commercial shops they could handle, and business people wanted to find new markets. On the other hand, a number of inner-city neighborhoods that have been reclaimed were now much more attractive as investment sites for all types of businesses. Government officials in charge of city agencies do what they can to promote further economic development activities in these areas. Sometimes the new supermarkets, pharmacies, and department stores are welcomed. On other occasions they are viewed as a threat to small retail shops that have been in the area for a long time. In at least one notable instance in Boston, local activists and their state legislator successfully stopped a powerful family from constructing a new facility in their neighborhood.[62] The important point, of course, is that now investors and entrepreneurs are running toward these neighborhoods instead of running away from them. Order begets prosperity, and the organizing principle behind order is piety.

The hard and sometimes thankless work that is required to promote piety never ends, particularly when adults are trying to introduce the idea to younger persons who have been left to fend for themselves for much too long. Many groups in Boston, including the city police department and a coalition of local ministers, took to the streets during the 1990s in a concerted effort to reduce the indiscriminate violence that was taking so many young lives and hurting so many neighborhoods. Their hard work paid off.

An organization known as Teen Empowerment celebrated its fifth annual Youth Peace Conference on May 11, 1997.

> For at least one day, peace was officially cool. Approximately 800 teenagers converged ... to celebrate the dramatic drop in violence among Boston's youth – no one under age 18 has been killed by a gun in almost two years – and to hang up their most well-worn attitude: the jaded veneer of tough indifference.

One year later at the sixth annual gathering of this group, almost 750 young people "from across the city came ... to participate in interactive workshops, listen to other teenage speakers share stories of teen pregnancy, the importance of an education, and the dangers of drugs and gangs."[63] Other organizations in the city such as the Boys and Girls Club in the Dorchester neighborhood, a group known as Gang Peace, and the aforementioned group of black Protestant ministers known as the 10 Point Coalition also were doing their part.[64]

Sometimes their magic worked. Sometimes it did not. One of the persons for whom it did not work was a 16-year-old named Eric Paulding who was killed in what police believed to be a feud between rival neighborhood gangs in Dorchester.

> Paulding's slaying ... ended a stretch of 29 months without a juvenile slaying in Boston. And it prompted civic leaders to renew calls for community involvement and cooperation with law enforcement agencies.
> "We must make sure we use this occasion to transform our future and our circumstances," the Rev. Eugene Rivers, pastor of Azusa Christian Community ... told about 800 mourners at the New Covenant Christian Center in Mattapan.
> Before the noontime funeral, the mourners – mostly teenagers – spilled outside into the parking lot of the Christian center ... where there was a strong police presence.
> Counselors handed out pink slips of paper noting the locations and ... hours of community centers, where clergy and counselors will offer aid.[65]

Some adults finally were listening and trying to help. Unfortunately, it was not at all clear that enough youngsters were doing their part. Gangs and the violence they embraced continued to flourish in Boston at the end of the 1990s. The anti-gang initiative was "just holding its own."[66]

> Although the organizers expect to reach nearly 1,000 at-risk youths by the time the school year ends June 23, levels of gang activity, in general, are on the rise and Asian youths, in particular, are emerging on the local gang scene.
> So sensitive has Boston become to the problems that it has quietly decided to change the red T-shirts traditionally worn by participants in its summer job programs to gray to avoid potential problems with either Bloods, whose gang color is red, or Crips, whose color is blue.
> Asians ... have been set upon by bigger, tougher, more aggressive black kids, and are asking "how long are we supposed to take this?" They are doing what most adolescent males will do in this situation in the absence of effective adult assistance.
> "Black kids are playing with fire and don't know it" because they are unaware of the power and sophistication of older Asian gangs, and "are overestimating their power to subordinate these kids."

The sense of frustration expressed by adults who were working so hard to limit gang activity in the city was understandable. It certainly had been nice for the President of the United States to fly to Boston in 1997 to compliment their work and announce a plan to spend $500 million to deter juvenile violence.[67] Yet they knew that the chances of stopping gangs from spreading were small. With all the hard work they had done, they still were just holding their own. It has seemed on many occasions that church leaders, social service providers, school officials, police officers, and other concerned adult volunteers were not making much headway in their campaign. They were reaching children and teenagers who could still be brought over by the message they preached, but they could not save all of the youngsters who needed their help with gangs or the other problems that teenagers face.[68]

It has always been so. Community members in nineteenth-century cities had no illusion about saving every soul. They paid more attention to managing crime and limiting the effect of misdeeds on the good persons who lived among them. Piety worked, but only for those who were prepared to be received into the community of believers. Everybody else was more or less on their own.

NOTES

1 *Boston Gazette,* January 1, March 26, October 4, and November 26, 1810.
2 Ibid., August 6, October 22, and October 29, 1810.
3 *Boston Chronicle Gazette,* March 6, March 20, April 13, April 17, and May 25, 1820.
4 *Daily Evening Transcript,* February 3 and April 25, 1845.
5 *Carolina Spartan,* September 3, 1863.
6 *Bergen Democrat,* June 13, 1862 and August 5, 1864.
7 *Louisville Daily Democrat,* September 5, May 11, and May 22, 1868.
8 *San Diego Union,* March 21, March 29, and April 5, 1882.
9 *Rochester Post: Official Paper of the City and County,* April 16 and May 21, 1886.
10 *Carolina Spartan,* November 4, 1891.
11 Ibid., November 11, 1891.
12 *Sparks Tribune,* October 27, 1911.
13 *Pittsburgh Post,* November 11, 1915.
14 *Valdosta Daily Times,* April 19 and February 18, 1915.
15 Ibid., February 4, March 12, March 27, April 8, May 5, May 19, June 15, and July 28, 1915.
16 Ibid., January 9, January 13, March 7, March 16, April 14, April 22, May 7, and May 25, 1925.
17 *Pittsburgh Post-Gazette,* February 26, March 3, and March 11, 1925.
18 *Burlington Free Press,* January 1, January 9, January 17, January 25, February 2, August 15, August 27, and October 26, 1935.
19 *Chicago Tribune,* May 19, 1977.
20 *Wheeling Intelligencer,* April 15, 1867.
21 *Daily Argus,* September 1, 1886.

22 *San Diego Union*, June 5, May 6, and August 10, 1881.

23 Carl Bridenbaugh, *Cities in the Wilderness: The First Century of Urban Life in America, 1625–1742* (London: Oxford University Press, 1966), p. 105.

24 *San Diego Union*, September 27, 1905.

25 *San Diego Union*, October 14, 1895.

26 *Louisville Daily Democrat*, January 7, 1868.

27 *St Louis Dispatch*, January 20, 1875. In what was headlined as a "supposed case of abortion" in Wheeling, West Virginia, the *Daily Intelligencer* published a story on July 27, 1861 about a newborn child whose body was found by some workmen on the grounds of a Catholic graveyard. They buried the body, not thinking too much about it. The Reverend Bishop Whelan heard about the affair and notified the city coroner. A jury was called to the graveyard to examine the body, but nothing could be done about the situation.

28 *St Louis Dispatch*, August 26, 1875.

29 Ibid., February 4, 1875.

30 *Idaho Falls Post*, January 12, 1932.

31 *Fairbanks Daily News-Miner*, November 18, 1909.

32 *Germantown News*, May 8–14, 1980.

33 *Carolina Spartan*, November 7, 1888.

34 *Casper Daily Tribune*, June 24, 1919.

35 *Argus Leader*, August 10, 1891.

36 Eric Monkkonen, "From Cop History to Social History: The Significance of the Police in American History," *Journal of Social History*, Volume 15, Number 4, Summer 1982, pp. 575–92; Neil Shumsky, "Tacit Acceptance: Respectable Associations and Segregated Prostitution, 1870–1910," *Journal of Social History*, Volume 19, Number 4, Summer 1986, pp. 681–98; Jeffrey Adler, "Streetwalkers, Degraded Outcasts, and Good-for-Nothing Huzzies: Women and the Dangerous Classes in Antebellum St Louis," *Journal of Social History*, Volume 25, Number 4, Summer 1992, pp. 737–56; Eric Monkkonen, "A Disorderly People? Urban Order in the Nineteenth and Twentieth Centuries," *Journal of American History*, Volume 68, Number 3, December 1981, pp. 539–59; Eugene Watts, "Police Response to Crime and Disorder in Twentieth-Century St Louis," *Journal of American History*, Volume 70, Number 2, September 1983, pp. 340–58; John Schneider, "Public Order and the Geography of the City: Crime, Violence, and the Police in Detroit, 1845–1875," *Journal of Urban History*, Volume 4, Number 2, February 1978, pp. 209–38; Jeffrey Adler, "Vagging the Demons and Scoundrels: Vagrancy and the Growth of St Louis, 1830–1861," *Journal of Urban History*, Volume 13, Number 1, November 1986, pp. 3–30; Gilles Vandel, "The Nineteenth-Century Municipal Responses to the Problem of Poverty: New Orlean's Free Lodgers, 1850–1880, as a Case Study," *Journal of Urban History*, Volume 19, Number 1, November 1992, pp. 30–59.

37 David Johnson, "The Origins and Structure of Intercity Criminal Activity, 1840–1920: An Interpretation," *Journal of Social History*, Volume 15, Number 4, Summer 1982, pp. 593–606; Pamela Haag, "The 'Ill-Use of a

Wife': Patterns of Working-Class Violence in Domestic and Public New York City, 1860–1880," *Journal of Social History*, Volume 25, Number 3, Spring 1992, pp. 447–78; Neil Larry Shumsky, "Vice Responds to Reform: San Francisco, 1910–1914," *Journal of Urban History*, Volume 7, Number 1, November 1980, pp. 31–48; Marilyn Thorton Williams, "New York City's Public Baths: A Case Study in Urban Progressive Reform," *Journal of Urban History*, Volume 7, Number 1, November 1980, pp. 49–82.

38   Gregory Singleton, "Mere Middle-Class Institutions: Urban Protestantism in 19th-Century America," *Journal of Social History*, Volume 6, Number 4, Summer 1973, pp. 489–504; J. Joseph Huthmacher, "Urban Liberalism and the Age of Reform," *Journal of American History*, Volume 49, Number 2, September 1962, pp. 231–41; Raymond Mohl, "Humanitarianism in the Preindustrial City: The New York Society for the Prevention of Pauperism, 1817–1823," *Journal of American History*, Volume 57, Number 3, December 1970, pp. 576–99; Mark Haller, "Urban Crime and Criminal Justice: The Chicago Case," *Journal of American History*, Volume 57, Number 3, December 1970, pp. 619–35; Robert Buroker, "From Voluntary Association to Welfare State: The Illinois Immigrants' Protective League, 1908–1926," *Journal of American History*, Volume 58, Number 3, December 1971, pp. 643–60; Kenneth Kusmer, "The Functions of Organized Charity in the Progressive Era: Chicago as a Case Study," *Journal of American History*, Volume 60, Number 3, December 1973, pp. 657–78; Richard Weiss, "Ethnicity and Reform: Minorities and the Ambiance of the Depression Years," *Journal of American History*, Volume 66, Number 3, December 1979, pp. 566–85; Daniel Bluestone, "'The Pushcart Evil': Peddlers, Merchants, and New York City's Streets, 1890–1940," *Journal of Urban History*, Volume 18, Number 1, November 1991, pp. 68–92.

39   Harvard Sitkoff, "Racial Militancy and Interracial Violence in the Second World War," *Journal of American History*, Volume 58, Number 3, December 1971, pp. 661–81; Thomas Hammett, "Two Mobs of Jacksonian Boston: Ideology and Interest," *Journal of American History*, Volume 62, Number 4, March 1976, pp. 845–68; Michael Hindus, "Black Justice Under White Law: Criminal Prosecutions of Blacks in Antebellum South Carolina," *Journal of American History*, Volume 63, Number 3, December 1976, pp. 575–99; Elliot Gron, "'Good-Bye Boys, I Die a True American': Homicide, Nativism, and Working-Class Culture in Antebellum New York City," *Journal of American History*, Volume 74, Number 2, September 1987, pp. 388–410; David Grimsted, "Ante-bellum Labor: Violence, Strike, and Communal Arbitration," *Journal of Social History*, Volume 19, Number 1, Fall 1985, pp. 5–28; David Roediger, "'Not Only the Ruling Classes to Overcome: but also the So-Called Mob': Class, Skill and Community in the St Louis General Strike of 1877," *Journal of Social History*, Volume 18, Number 2, Winter 1985, pp. 213–40; Lynne Taylor, "Food Riots Revisited," *Journal of Social History*, Volume 30, Number 2, Winter 1996, pp. 483–96; David Grimsted, "Rioting in Its Jacksonian Setting," *American Historical Review*, Volume 77, Number 2, April 1972, pp. 361–97; David Stowell, "Small Property Holders and the Great Strike

of 1877: Railroads, City Streets, and the Middle Classes," *Journal of Urban History*, Volume 21, Number 6, September 1995, pp. 741–63; Herbert Gutman, "The Tompkins Square 'Riot' in New York City on January 13, 1874: A Re-examination of its Causes and Aftermath," *Labor History*, Volume 6, 1965, pp. 44–70; Allen H. Grimshaw, *Racial Violence in the United States* (Chicago: Aldine, 1969); Elliot Rudwick, *Race Riot at East St Louis* (Carbondale, IL: Southern Illinois University Press, 1964); Richard Wade, "Violence in Cities: A Historical View," in Roger Lane and John J. Turner (eds), *Riot, Rout, and Tumult* (Westport, CT: Grenwood Press, 1978), pp. 349–63.

40 Charles Tilly, "Collective Violence in European Perspective," in Hugh Graham and Ted Gurr (eds), *Violence in America* (Beverly Hills: Sage, 1979), pp. 83–118.

41 Daniel J. Monti, "The Relation Between Terrorism and Domestic Civil Disorders," *Terrorism: An International Journal*, Volume 4, Numbers 1–4, 1980, pp. 132–4.

42 See: Bruce Nelson, "Organized Labor and the Struggle for Black Equality in Mobile During World War II," *Journal of American History*, Volume 80, Number 3, December 1993, pp. 952–88; Shane White, "'It Was a Proud Day': African Americans, Festivals, and Parades in the North, 1741–1834," *Journal of American History*, Volume 81, Number 1, June 1994, pp. 13–50.

43 Monti, "The Relation Between Terrorism and Domestic Civil Disorders"; Sitkoff, "Racial Militancy"; Also see: Cheryl Greenberg, "The Politics of Disorder: Reexamining Harlem's Riots of 1935 and 1943," *Journal of Urban History*, Volume 18, Number 4, August 1992, pp. 395–441.

44 Herbert Gutman, "Work, Culture, and Society in Industrializing America, 1815–1919," *American Historical Review*, Volume 78, Number 3, June 1973, pp. 531–88; Altine Waller, "Community, Class, and Race in the Memphis Riot of 1866," *Journal of Social History*, Volume 18, Number 2, Winter 1984, pp. 233–46; Kevin Hardwick, "'Your Old Father Abe Lincoln Is Dead and Damned': Black Soldiers and the Memphis Race Riot of 1866," *Journal of Social History*, Volume 27, Number 1, Fall 1993, pp. 109–28; Robin D. G. Kelley, "'We Are Not What We Seem': Rethinking Working-Class Opposition in the Jim Crow South," *Journal of American History*, Volume 80, Number 1, June 1993, pp. 75–112; David Waldstreicher, "Rites of Rebellion, Rites of Assent: Celebrations, Print Culture, and the Origins of American Nationalism," *Journal of American History*, Volume 82, Number 2, September 1995, pp. 37–61; Graham Hodges, "The Decline and Fall of Artisan Republicanism in Antebellum New York City: Views from the Street and Workshop," *Journal of Urban History*, Volume 18, Number 2, February 1992, pp. 211–21.

45 Hardwick, "'Your Old Father Abe Lincoln,'" p. 110; Waller, "Community, Class, and Race"; Waldstreicher, "Rites of Rebellion."

46 *Daily Intelligencer*, July 14, 1860.

47 *Union and Advertiser*, July 5, 1887.

48 *San Diego Union*, March 12, 1895.

49 *Fairbanks Daily News-Miner*, October 2, 1909.

50 *Cleveland Plain Dealer*, February 20 and May 1, 1943.
51 *Pittsburgh Post-Gazette*, August 22, 1945.
52 *Boston Daily Globe*, April 22, 1952; February 24 and October 7, 1953.
53 *Boston Globe*, October 12, 1991.
54 Ibid., February 21, 1992.
55 Ibid., March 5 and March 8, 1992.
56 Ibid., June 19, 1992.
57 Ibid., March 31, 1992.
58 Ibid., March 7, 1996.
59 Ibid., February 25, 1997. Also see the editions for March 4 and March 8, 1997 for additional stories on this subject.
60 Ibid., September 17, 1991.
61 Ibid., October 19, 1991; February 9, 1993; June 19, 1995; March 24, 1996; May 12, 1996; February 19, 1997; February 23, 1997; February 25, 1997; February 27, 1997; May 7, 1997; May 12, 1997; August 5, 1997; and August 6, 1997.
62 Ibid., August 17, 1995; October 9, 1995; July 28, 1996; November 30, 1996; December 15, 1996; January 7, 1997; January 26, 1997; February 23, 1997; June 22, 1998.
63 Ibid., May 11 and May 10, 1997.
64 Ibid., December 20, 1997; December 21, 1997; and May 26, 1998. The ministerial alliance called the 10 Point Coalition was launched in the early 1990s as a way to mobilize churches to fight against gang violence. See the *Boston Globe* for May 19, May 20, and May 22, 1992 for a description of the genesis of this coalition and its early plans.
65 Ibid., December 20, 1997.
66 Ibid., May 26, 1998.
67 Ibid., February 20, 1997.
68 Ibid., June 29, 1992; August 14, 1997; August 17, 1997; November 16, 1997; November 20, 1997; and January 26, 1998.

7

Private Lives and
Public Worlds

Mrs Grace Palmer Craig was scheduled to give a lecture on the evening of April 24, 1918 in Casper, Wyoming. The subject of her speech, "Learning the Fine Art of Minding Your Own Business and Being Happy," was part of a series of "free lectures" presented by her over the course of a week. Much to the delight of the local business people who sponsored her visit, the lectures apparently had "aroused the greatest interest and enthusiasm" from local residents.[1]

Not unlike itinerant preachers, showmen, and peddlers, individuals like Mrs Craig crisscrossed the country during the nineteenth and early twentieth centuries plying their own special trade: public speaking. Their tours were booked in advance and often subsidized by leading citizens who wanted to provide the locals with a little culture and a good night out. The response to these presentations by persons in the audience generally was positive.

The speeches covered a wide variety of subjects. Discourses on foreign countries and national issues like temperance or slavery were sandwiched between more mundane talks like the one presented by Grace Palmer Craig. The interesting thing about Mrs Craig's speech was not the recognition that each of us has a private life, but that we have an obligation to leave each other alone.

Historians have found different ways and times for dating the emergence of the individual as an object of veneration or a vehicle through which the whole of American society could be improved. One certainly can make a strong case for connecting the rise of individualism with the prosperity enjoyed by a growing class of middle-class persons during the nineteenth century. About this period and class, E. Anthony Rotundo has said, the opportunity for material advancement "encouraged a boundless optimism about the effects of self-cultivation."[2]

This enthusiastic embrace of the "self" was its foremost accomplishment and was manifested in many ways. Included among them were different forms of "self-analysis" and therapeutic regimes, abstinence from liquor, a fondness for athletic displays, and control over impulses ranging from gambling and shoplifting to sex. Regrettably, it also showed up in the retreat of middle-class fathers as a presence in the home and in the lives of their sons. This suggests that the oft-criticized parenting style and disengagement of some lower-class fathers from their sons in our own time had more privileged roots in the nineteenth century.

Many religious services and reform activities today are no less moralistic than those found in eighteenth and early nineteenth-century towns and cities. There was a corporate quality to those earlier engagements, however, that more contemporary activities seem to lack. Signs that such exercises would develop a pronounced secular twist and help the individual more than a larger communal group were in evidence well before the twentieth century.[3] We remain united by more than our technology and toys. To many observers, however, it seems that improving the quality of one's *private life* and solitary achievements are more important than dedicating oneself to communal goals and the larger *public world* they would edify.[4]

That Mrs Craig's speech was endorsed by some of the community's top leaders made it even more special, because traditional business people in American towns and cities always had insisted that persons watch out for each other. Now they were embracing a speech in which the individual's presumptive right to some privacy and happiness depended on his or her doing just the opposite. Grace Palmer Craig was elevating the practice of civil inattention, of "minding one's own business," to the level of a civic ideal. To the extent that her views were consistent with ideas that many other persons had in their own heads, it was becoming acceptable public practice for individuals not to pay attention to what was going on in the larger world around them.

We are not quite so enamored with this idea today. If anything, many community leaders would be happier if we returned to the days when minding each other's business was considered a good thing to do. Our lack of involvement in each other's affairs, they would say, has brought us nothing but trouble.

"We Regret to Have Seen ... a Spirit of Indifference"

As if to make the point stick, a National Commission on Civic Renewal was appointed in the late 1990s just to assess the effect of public apathy on civic life in America. This "high-powered panel of academics, business executives, and Washington insiders" issued its report card on the civic health of America in June of 1998. We flunked.

"This should be a time of hope for Americans," the 20-member commission declared, "and when we consider our economic circumstances, it is. But when we assess our country's civic and moral condition, we are deeply troubled."[5] Americans were cynical about public life, especially the parts that involved politics and their elected officials. Citizens were voting in ever smaller numbers, not contributing to political campaigns, and not putting themselves up for elected office.

This was not what the founding fathers had in mind when they fashioned America's political system as a republic. What made matters worse, as far as the commission members were concerned, was that we had the time to be interested and to participate. We just chose to spend our spare time on ourselves.

The commissioners noted the existence of "a new movement of citizens acting together to solve community problems" and endorsed it. They also admitted, however, that the tiny effort had "gone largely unnoticed, unappreciated, and unsupported" by the American public. Composed largely of non-traditional groups with few resources or small volunteer groups, churches, and foundations, this movement was able to produce only a few local success stories in the places where groups were working. Our national government and the political parties whose prosperity depend upon its good reputation and purse were not held in high regard. Civic routines built around the work of political parties and large public agencies were similarly devalued.

Americans, it seemed to the commission members, were much too wrapped up in their private lives. They were not paying nearly enough attention to their neighbors or trying to help make their own town or city a better place to live. The larger public world that lay all around them and really needed their help was languishing.

This was a pretty grim pronouncement. Yet as the reporter who wrote about the National Commission on Civic Renewal stated, "analyzing and abhorring the end of a civil society has become one of Washington's most popular academic pursuits" in recent years. This was an accurate observation, but it also trivialized what many observers of American civic life had come to see as a really serious problem. If the experts were right, we no longer were carrying the "national malaise" which former President Jimmy Carter diagnosed back in the 1970s. Our vague sense of moral ill-health had since erupted into full-blown cases of "me-firstitis" and the "go-find-your-own-lifeboat" pox.

There surely is some merit to what the experts have said about American civic life. Grace Palmer Craig's prescription for making it through life by remaining blissfully unaware of what persons were doing around you may have reached back and bitten us. Still, it was hard to take their dire predictions all that seriously. Even a casual review history reveals that civic lethargy is not a new concern for the leaders of America's towns and cities. Observers worried about the crumbling infrastructure of America's civic culture long before shopping malls allegedly made us slaves to our credit cards and television supposedly turned our children's minds to mush.

As far as some persons were concerned, we showed signs of being lazy early on in our history. Readers of the *Norwich Courier* on June 1, 1825, for instance, were admonished to participate in the upcoming 4th of July celebration. "We regret to have seen, on former occasions, a spirit of indifference prevailing on the part of many of our citizens," the editors solemnly declared. They thought this "little creditable to the feelings of those concerned and an evil omen to our free institutions."

If they were right, the good people of this Connecticut town were on the verge of forgetting about their country's most important national holiday less than a half-century after the conclusion of the American Revolution. It is no small irony that this turn of public ill-health was declared several years before Alexis de Tocqueville happily observed Americans enjoying a rich and vibrant civic life. Sometimes it is hard to know which expert to believe.

None of this is to say, of course, that Americans have always done a good job watching their neighbor's behavior and minding their community's business. Furthermore, part of our concern over the depressed state of American civic life today is no doubt due to the fact that we can afford the luxury of sitting around and worrying about it more than we could in the past. The amount of time we have away from the places we work has grown dramatically over the last century, and there has been no shortage of commentary about how well or poorly we have spent it. The conventional wisdom, as articulated by the National Commission on Civic Renewal and other parties, is that we have not put that spare time to good public use. We have expended too much energy buying more stuff or collecting new experiences for ourselves and not enough on improving our communities. Moreover, we have shown little inclination to engage in a serious dialogue about our public obligations.

These concerns are not trivial, and the observations on which they are based are not ill-founded. It really does take a lot to pull us away from our daily routines and to draw a serious breath about anything much beyond our last bank statement and catalogue order. At the same time, when problems do arise we usually find ways to muddle through these bad times together. Things work out, maybe not as neatly as we would have liked but certainly well enough for us to get by.

The real crunch on our civic routines comes when we are faced with an especially tough problem or cannot avoid groups that trouble us. When confronted with such difficulties we have been known to treat each other poorly and sometimes even fight. Our displeasure at those moments is real enough. So, too, is our desire to win whatever argument we are having.

Fortunately for us, a good many of our fights follow a prescribed sequence of events and conform to rules that most everyone has learned and accepts as binding. We do not have to make up guidelines for fighting at the same time we are trying to figure out how to settle our disagreements. There is much more than good luck at work here. The ritualistic quality of these conflicts is not an accident. It is a tribute to civic routines that work so well that we do not even have to think about them.

This is no less true of those occasions when our fights turn terribly violent. When some portion of our people has turned against another in the past, they often have done great harm to each other and to the places where they live. No matter how enraged or destructive we became, however, Americans rarely used violence to feed a grand ambition. It has not been our custom to tear down the world we knew or to replace it with a better world in a violent flourish. Our anger more often masked an ill-tempered reckoning with changes that we were not yet willing to acknowledge. Disgruntled activists and paperback radicals will be disappointed to learn that violence is not as American as apple pie. It is more like a marinade, helping bad news taste better and making it at least a little easier to swallow.

Important as our fights sometimes are and dramatic as the violence can be, this is not the most important way in which persons have learned to communicate with each other. Town and city dwellers are much more likely to try to stay out of each other's way and adjust, however grudgingly, to the ill-feelings they share. From time to time, the historical record shows, these groups even manage to discover that they have some common interests and learn to cooperate on important tasks.

All of this takes a great deal of hard work and patience on everyone's part, and this is fine as far as it goes. Yet many observers would have liked to see more moments of accommodation and greater success coming from these joint ventures. To the extent that our reading of history has been thorough and fair, however, it is clear that Americans usually go about the business of building a world in fits and starts, particularly when they have to deal with persons who are different from themselves. We probably should be pleased that we have done as well as we have so much of the time.

Social philosophers and activists who worry about such things are far from satisfied with this outcome. They want more successes. They also believe that the business of making a world which works well need not be so messy. That is why their models of what goes into a good community build on two tidy views of the world. The problem, as I noted earlier, is that most human beings are not philosophers or well-read reformers. They do not think clearly all the time, and they are prone to fits of sloppiness. Thus far we have seen that blurred visions and messiness work well enough most of the time. We either are suspicious of elegant and neat answers or too lazy to make them work.

The models served up by the social philosophers called "communalists" are helpful, even when they turn out to be impractical. They drive us to ask sharper questions about how things actually work out in "the real world." In the context of the present chapter, we are trying to determine how persons balance their *private lives* with a larger *public world*. Their task is made much harder by virtue of the world being filled with persons who are not like themselves.

It is not immediately apparent how all these different persons residing in the same place figure out that they can work together or at least do not have to fight all the time. There are many signs that they manage to do this and, regrettably, sometimes just as many signs that they may never get it right or do not really want to try. The explanation for both outcomes is the same. Kindergarten teachers call it "parallel play." We will too.

It works like this. Children left on the same playground or at the sandbox play near but not with each other. Their clumsy attempts at negotiating the proprietary rights to a soccer ball or shovel rarely yield a happy or long-lasting peace. Nevertheless, these are the first crude but necessary steps children take toward recognizing each other's legitimate claim to the place where they are playing and to the tools of play that always seem to be in someone else's mitts. It is the way in which parallel play sometimes grows into collaborative play. More importantly, perhaps, it is how their little private lives begin to mesh into a bigger public world where other persons must be taken into account, if anyone is to be happy or get along with anybody else.

Parallel play operates in a similar way in cities where different and sometimes quarrelsome groups must stumble into a state of mutual regard, if not admiration and affection, before they have much hope of getting what they need. We know that cities teem with persons who do not know one another well or may not like each other. When one set of them puts together groups of their own or watches how other persons do it, this is how they learn about each other. It also is how they come to see the possibility and necessity of working together at least part of the time. At the risk of making too much of school-yard imagery, cities are really big parallel playpens.

The most distinctive feature of group life in cities is that there is so much of it and so much to learn from it. All manner of groups fill the day with their activities, and organizations leave many tantalizing clues as to their intentions and needs. Sometimes they can be found working off in a corner on their own special projects. On other occasions, they literally parade their work and ideas before their fellow residents. They may or may not find common cause with other groups in the city, but this is how their hard work and commitment to the place where they all live become more apparent to everyone.

Whether they end up collaborating on future projects remains to be seen. It is enough in the short term that they come to see each other as legitimate claimants to the small space they occupy in tandem and to consider the possibility and potential benefits that would accrue to working together. This is parallel play, and city dwellers are serious parallel players.

Important as parallel play may be to the smooth and effective operation of cities, it does not make the civic culture of these places valuable to us in the long run. Parallel play was not enough to secure the blessings of liberty for us during the American Revolution, and it will not be equal to the task of keeping Americans together in the twenty-first century. If we are to make viable and vital civic cultures in the places where we live, we will need to do something more. We have to learn how to work together.

If one takes seriously all the hard work that goes into parallel play, we can see how it contributes to the commonweal by acquainting different groups with what other persons are doing and seeing whether it works well for them. This is the first step to learning the rules to the civic culture game and how they actually work. Without knowing those rules and having a chance to practice them before a sympathetic audience, no group has a realistic chance of joining the community of believers. To the extent that parallel play is necessary for a city's civic culture to work at all, our public world may be in better shape than we thought.

Learning by Doing

In 1821 some local physicians met and established a Medical Society of Pittsburgh. They decided to hold monthly sessions and to have one of their colleagues present "a dissertation on some medical subject" at each meeting. Any person who failed to make his appointed speech would be fined 50 cents for every meeting he attended until such time as the speech was made.[6]

It was reported in the January 16, 1822 edition of the city newspaper that a number of persons had met at a private residence with the idea of establishing an organization "for the relief of distressed emigrants from the island of Great Britain." One of the members of this new group declared that they were obliged to help, but the work of the group also would bring them closer together and make them better persons.

A decade later, local Irish residents from Pittsburgh held a St Patrick's Day dinner. Thirteen formal toasts were made by leaders of the event and at least three times that many were offered from the floor. Local Democrats and Republicans gathered to nominate their candidates for the upcoming gubernatorial election, and the Presbyterian General Assembly met in special session for a few days. Finally, a number of groups finished their preparations for the city's July 4th celebration. Among them were "The Friends of Martin Van Buren" and the "Mechanics and Working Men" of Pittsburgh.[7]

There were signs from other nineteenth-century towns and cities that persons we would call "blue collar" or "working class" today were organizing and being accepted in their respective communities. The creation of a Mechanics Society in Norwich in 1825 was looked upon as a positive development, but only as long as it worked for the benefit of its members and included persons of "an unimpeachable moral character." The annual meeting of the society that year was held at the district school house.[8]

In 1840 the Franklin Association of Boston posed the question for their next meeting: "Are the laboring classes in our community enjoying their full share of influence?"[9] On March 29, 1843, the editors of the *Pittsburgh Mercury Post* encouraged the "workingmen" of that city to form "an institute for the discussion of the social and political measures which now agitate the public mind." They also promised that space would be set aside in their newspaper to report on actions and positions taken by the members of such an institute.

A "co-operative association" was organized in Wheeling, West Virginia in 1867 for the purpose of building a foundry. It was announced that all laborers would be stockholders in this new venture.[10] A similar effort was launched in San Diego in 1871 with the founding of an association whose members hoped to provide housing for less well-to-do families, add to the city's population, and increase its taxable property.[11] Funds for the association would be derived "from a fixed payment of one dollar per month on each share subscribed" and invested in land secured by a mortgage. The association would sell houses and lots to shareholders, "giving deeds and possession on payment of ... small monthly installments extending over a long term." Families of "limited means" would be spared the expense of securing money to buy the land and to put a house on it.

Boston residents were greeted with organizational news of a different sort on November 11, 1860. They learned that the Bunker Hill Wide Awakes had held a meeting the previous evening at which time they made arrangements for a parade and supper. The Rail Splitters and other Republican organizations of Charlestown planned to join the demonstration. This political challenge did not go unheeded. At a meeting two weeks later, the Conference Committee of the Union and Democratic Conventions selected their candidates for Aldermen. "The list gave the Committee much satisfaction," party stalwarts were proud to report, "as the gentlemen are all known to the business community ... and have the confidence of our citizens." Among their number were a "hotel keeper, marble dealer, auctioneer, and merchants."[12]

A citizen in Pine Bluff, Arkansas calling himself "Equality" complained in 1873 about a decision made in the last meeting of the school board. It seems that a woman was given permission to use empty space in the school building for music classes she would teach, while a man was denied space to conduct night school classes. "Equality" was not bothered by the prospect of private parties using public facilities. He only wanted the school board to apply the same standard for all petitioners.[13]

Residents of Spokane, Washington woke up to the news in 1882 that the Cheney Academy was receiving its finishing touches. It was built with funds provided by Judge Cheney of Boston who also donated $3,500 to the academy and hired two Boston residents to teach in the school. There was some concern that the judge spent all this money just so the building would be named after him, which probably was true. Some persons also wondered whether the academy was a private or public institution inasmuch as it was "free to all" in this district and only charged $6.50 for a student who was from outside the district. The town also dedicated itself to raise $1,400 to help maintain and run the facility.[14]

It was reported in the *Wilmington Morning* News on January 3, 1881 that the Lenape Tribe of Red Men of Wilmington, Delaware had celebrated its 13th anniversary by putting together a lovely banquet and listening to inspiring talks given by "visiting sachems and chiefs." On that same date, the "colored people" of the Bethel AME Church put on a fair at the National Hall to benefit that religious body. The newspaper reported on February 20 that the Wilmington theatrical season would be unusually active until the end of the month and that the Mattahoon Tribe, No.1, IORM, had appointed a committee to make a date for an excursion to Atlantic City. On February 28 it was announced that the Popular Micks' Association was giving its third annual reception at the Masonic Temple dancing rooms and that the Young People's Literary and Musical Society of the First Presbyterian Church would be giving its usual free monthly entertainment on the following Thursday evening. Finally, on March 16 it was recorded that the Philharmonic Club had held a rehearsal last evening and would give its fourth concert on March 24. The Ladies of the Auxiliary Corps, GAR would have a meeting this evening, and the Wilmington Athletic Association announced that it would give an exhibition some time early in April. The proceeds from that performance would be used to purchase new equipment.

Among the social events mentioned in the January 5, 1885 edition of the *Cleveland Plain Dealer* were the installation of new officers for the Buckingham Council of the Royal Arcanum, the Rothschild Lodge of the Kesher Shel Barzel, the Commodore Perry and Memorial Post chapters of the Grand Army of the Republic, and the Hungarian Aid Society. Local musicians proposed to form their own social organization, and Cleveland bakers announced that they planned to form a union. The Dorcas Society, a charity group, received a generous donation from a show that had been produced by a "company of young society ladies." Races and competitions were held at the Casino Roller Rink, and a Burlesque Polo Game was staged at the Olympian Roller Rink for the benefit of the Firemen's Relief Association. The East End Conversational Club announced that it would meet at a private residence. The Phoenix Lodge, IOOF and the faculty of the Homeopathic Hospital Medical College held memorial services for deceased members, and public dignitaries attended the funeral of a fireman. Finally, Drew's Dime Museum declared that it would show "Nubians" who could trace their ancestry to Adam through Ham, the son of Noah, and display their weapons, which they would be using in eight weeks upon their return to Africa and the Soudan War.

It was announced in the April 26, 1887 edition of the *Charlotte Chronicle* that "colored" voters were going to have a mass meeting at the courthouse that evening in order to nominate a candidate for mayor. Everyone knew that person would stand in opposition to the Democratic nominee. On June 3, 1887, the same paper announced that the captain of the Fearless baseball club, the city's "colored" team, would be holding a meeting that evening.

Rochester, New York started that same year with a flourish of club meetings and formal balls. The Ladies Auxiliary and Young Men's Christian Association thanked persons for participating in their New Year's reception. Members of the Marshall Post Drum Corps enjoyed a ride in E. F. Higgins's new sleigh called "Northern Light." The Human Society had its annual meeting in the Power Block building, while the Sons of Veterans planned their annual ball on February 7 at Wood's Academy. Ten other dress balls, all sponsored by different organizations, were planned for the evening of January 17. The Knights of the Golden Eagle publicly installed its new officers at the New Osman house. Dancing and music followed the ceremony. A free concert was given at the Main Street skating rink, and the New York Poultry and Pet Stock Association was scheduled to hold its first exhibition.[15]

Looking back at the end of the nineteenth century, we can begin to see why so many persons today fret about the state of our civic life. Daily newspapers were awash with announcements about what the different groups in their town or city were doing, planning to do, or had just done. Churches were prominently mentioned for all that their members were doing. However, there also were many clubs, lodges, sororities, literary groups, political meetings, and what we today would call "single-issue" organizations dedicated to ending one social malady or another.

We see nothing like this in contemporary newspapers. There still are whole pages dedicated to community announcements and the like, but the groups whose activities are prominently displayed are not like those which were active at the tail end of the nineteenth century and the front end of the twentieth century. They are much more likely to be self-help groups for persons suffering from a physical affliction, going through some sort of personal crisis, or coming to terms with some unpleasant event in their current or past lives.

Although there are lodges, political organizations, labor unions, choral societies, and social clubs still out there doing whatever it is they do, it is unlikely that there are as many of them as there once were and little doubt that they are making much less noise about their activities than they once did. We look back at all the groups that were active near the end of the nineteenth century and wonder how much better off we would be today if our voluntary associations were as busy and noisy as the "old-time" groups obviously were.

Not everyone at the end of the nineteenth century, however, thought that all this organizing and going to meetings was a great idea. It seemed to some observers that there were times when no one was doing anything but joining organizations and attending meetings. The editors of the *Carolina Spartan* certainly thought so. That is why they reprinted a blistering attack on clubs and meetings in the October 7, 1891 issue of their newspaper. Part of the article is reproduced below.

Meetings! Meetings! Meetings!
by Amos R. Wells, in Christian Union
Every victim of our modern civilization knows just how it may feel to be fattened for home consumption by a tasty gourmand of the Cannibal Islands. For the prince of these fuming times, whose meat is men, must be ... Meetings! Meetings! Meetings! I am dying of them.

There they come rushing up red faces and flashing eyes. They are the people with a mission ... and of great hearts palpitating for all mankind. Hear their indignant outcry: "The Tweedledom Question! The Tweedledee

Cause! The Thingumbob Reform! American Citizenship! Social Amenities! Christian Duties!"

Never was there such a highly organized century. Never has an age so reveled in by-laws, honorary members, and roll calls ... so many ... meetings.

We cannot love our poets in fireside peace. We must draft a constitution and love them together, in Browning Club ... and Tupper Society. We cannot ride our intellectual hobbies in decent privacy, but must trot them out before Theosophic Coteries, Societies of Christian Socialists. ... Our recreations must be by platoons, in bicycle clubs, chess clubs ... and so on to infinity. We must save our sociability to eke out the monthly church social ... and there are the prayer meetings. I wish I could do something about the prayer meetings.

Every year adds to the number of those people ... whose business it is to get up meetings. Preachers, editors, politicians, reformers, missionaries, YMCA secretaries, evangelists, lecturers, WCTU organizers, labor unions, Sunday school workers – all these are hourly devising fresh schemes to "get us to come out." Come out for what?

Today our leaders and leading thinkers wish that more of us would "come out" and join a group that does something we could construe as being in the "public interest," even if that only meant joining a bowling league.[16] Is it possible that there was a time when Americans had too much of a good thing when it came to joining clubs or attending events sponsored by different organizations? Some Americans certainly thought so at the end of the nineteenth century and the top of the twentieth century.

In fact a great many Americans commented upon the organizations and meetings that seemed to sprout like weeds in towns and cities during the last third of the nineteenth century and right through the Great Depression of the 1930s. They probably did not feel as strongly about it as Amos R. Wells obviously did. Nevertheless, the sentiment that "there were too many organizations taking up too much of one's spare time" was held by more than a few town residents.[17] No matter how many Americans may have felt this way, however, there were always more who wanted to join established groups or start brand-new ones.

The Druids Hall was the most popular place for lodges, unions, and other organizations to hold their meetings in Wausau, Wisconsin shortly after the turn of the century. It also may have been the only spot in town where groups of any size could have met. It was reported in the January 14, 1909 edition of the *Wausau Daily Record-Herald* that this facility was the headquarters for 15 organizations, and one or another of them met there almost every night. The United Order of Druids met there on the first and third Friday of every month. The Bartender's Union met on the first Monday. The Wausau Krieger Verein met on the second Sunday. The Electrician's Union met on the fourth Wednesday. The Beavers Reserve Fund fraternity met on the second and fourth Monday. The Gegenseitige Unterstuefung Geselschaft Germania held meetings there on every second and fourth Tuesday. The German-American alliance met on the third Sunday. Finally, the Wausau central labor union met there every second Friday.

It was reported in the *Sparks Tribune* on March 26, 1913 that the Volunteer Fire Department of Sparks, Nevada was going to hold an important meeting the next evening at City Hall. All members were requested to attend. It also was noted that this evening the Pythian Sisters of Sparks would meet at Robinson's Hall and the Executive Committee of the Sparks Progressive Club would meet at the Tribune office.

If you happened to be living in Pittsburgh in April and May of 1915, you could hardly have avoided attending a meeting or being swept up in some kind of public-spirited event. On April 22 a meeting of the Pittsburgh Vacant Lot Garden Association was held to consider how lots around the city could be made to look pretty or be used for small fruit and vegetable gardens so that individuals could reduce their expenses and improve their diets. In only its second day of campaigning, the Boy Scout Fund was able to attract $40,000 in subscriptions. Their goal had been to raise $50,000. Persons who were planning to move on the traditional May 1st Moving Day were encouraged to contact the Duquesne Light Company and change their address so that they would have electricity when they moved into their new apartment. The College Club and Rotary Club both had meetings. The Criterion Club held its annual elections, and the Pittsburgh Male Chorus announced that it would end its season with a final performance that evening.

Among the items noted in the May 30, 1915 edition of the *Pittsburgh Post Gazette* were detailed accounts of social activities, membership drives, and a few building campaigns for 25 fraternal, patriotic, and benevolent men's associations. The Hibernians of Western Pennsylvania also were making final plans for their 56th anniversary and the 11th annual Irish Day celebration. More than 30,000 persons attended the previous year's celebration. An estimated 3,500 women volunteers and business people led a campaign to raise funds for Belgian war victims. Mayor Armstrong came out in support of the effort. R. J. Heinz opened a new settlement house for children of the 23rd ward and dedicated it to his wife. Many men and women were prepared to serve as leaders and coaches for the 400 boys and girls who already had signed up to become members. A German organization in the city proclaimed that its members were loyal to the United States. The Total Abstinence Convention opened its meeting of more than 400 persons by hearing a commendation sent to them by President Wilson. The Shriners announced that they would hold a parade in celebration of laying the cornerstone for its new temple. A minister speaking at Carnegie Music Hall denied that prosperity was bad and poverty a blessing, and another man of the cloth stated that Jesus had approved of the banking system created by the Jews.

After the conclusion of World War I, the Army and Navy Club became a popular organization to join in Casper, Wyoming. Over 100 persons might be served dinner there on any given evening, and for a while in 1919 almost two dozen persons were added to the roster of members every day. Not wanting to show any disrespect to former Marines, the Army and Navy Club called on all who might be living in the area around Casper to use its facility for the purpose of organizing their own special organization called the "Devil Dog Club."[18] It would be both a social club and a mutual aid association for the veterans.

The July 21, 1926 issue of the *Lawrence Daily Journal-World* contained notices about several interesting events. The local Ku Klux Klan meeting provoked a great deal of interest coming as it had so close to the date that political parties were scheduled to choose their candidates for several elected offices. A local insurance company announced that it would give a concert. Members of the Elks club lost to the "Odd Fellars" in a baseball game. Local delegates to the National Editorial Association were invited to attend an all-state picnic. Finally, local boys who showed interest in developing farm products met at a private residence for a regular session of the Corn Club.

Readers of the *Valdosta Daily Times* on September 5, 1936 were informed that the "Negroes of Valdosta" planned to hold their annual Labor Day festivities at the Cypress Street Tabernacle where those in attendance would be treated to a speaking program on current political issues. St Paul's AME Church also was planning a special program for men. There was going to be a 50-man spiritual singing group. The pastor from the First Methodist Church and County School Superintendent also were scheduled to speak at the gathering. The citizens of this Georgia city also learned that local members of the United Daughters of the Confederacy had received an angry letter from an officer of their organization who lived in Fayettville, Arkansas. The letter drew attention to the fact that Governor Talmadge had appeared on the Lincoln program in Springfield, Illinois this past February 12 and "prayed for another Lincoln in the White House to take the place of President Roosevelt." Local members were urged to vote against Governor Talmadge in the September 9 primary as a protest "against a sentiment so repugnant to the principles of our organization, and the traditions which it is designed to perpetuate."

The Great Depression of the 1930s seemed to barely put a dent in the activities of local clubs and associations. If anything, groups were pushed to work harder and do more for persons who needed their assistance and, one supposes, also to help convince themselves that their community would make it through this terrible ordeal. Fewer groups run exclusively by men remained active during World War II, in large measure because so many potential conscripts were off fighting in Europe or the South Pacific. Local groups continued to dedicate themselves to projects on the home front which would help bring the war to a successful conclusion. Many of their initiatives, however, were coordinated by federal agencies or taken up as a result of government encouragement. Those clubs and associations which ascended to positions of leadership were now more likely to be run by women.

This did not change after the war was over. Men's organizations did not reassert themselves at the conclusion of World War II as they had after previous wars. The war in Korea just a few years later really seemed to mark the end of men's leadership and, in some cases, even their active engagement in clubs and associations that took the lead in community affairs. This change was especially clear in larger cities and less strong in small cities or larger towns. Nevertheless, it was apparent that men were prepared to cede much of the routine work ordinarily done by groups affiliated with the community of believers to organizations whose membership was composed largely or entirely of women.

The "golden age" of American volunteerism and civic life, to the extent that we had one at all, probably ended with this country's entry into World War II. This ending had less to do with the emergence of women as central players in the civic culture of their town or city than the withdrawal of men from the ranks of the community's most ardent defenders. Men did not stop being involved in organizations dedicated to good public works, and they still found ways to form satisfying attachments to each other. They simply did not assume as much responsibility for maintaining the community of believers inside their city as they once had.

Of course, none of this takes anything away from women or the groups they organized and ran. By the early 1940s women were hardly novices in campaigns to improve their community or to sustain institutions whose mission was to keep most of us pulling in the same direction rather than pushing against each other. Many of their number had been working diligently toward these ends long before the "golden age" of American civic culture was launched in the latter decades of the nineteenth century. No, something else had been going on that helped to change Americans' civic habits in big ways by the time this country entered World War II.

Commenting on the social habits of town dwellers in the five or six decades preceding that war, Richard Lingeman has said that "joinerism" had added its considerable weight to "boosterism" as one of the distinguishing features of life in American towns. He argues further that "joinerism" was particularly important because it replaced the easy "sociability of an earlier time" with more modern forms of association and amusement. Everything had become bigger and more commercial. Even small towns were now part of a "mass society." It simply was not easy any longer for individuals to develop relationships that "cut across age, class, occupational, and organizational lines" or to have "knowledge of all the other townspeople" that "ranged over their entire lives."[19] The easy informality and organic wholeness of life in small towns was gone. Substituted for it were "associations" which attempted to re-create the fabled intimacy of towns on alternate Thursday nights down at The Hall.

He was not the first person to hold this view. The idea that American society became a "mass society" in which local attachments had grown feeble and ineffective was popular in the years following the Civil War. The problem, of course, was that our romantic attachment to small social worlds filled with spontaneity, mutual respect, and active engagement was projected onto both small towns and ethnic enclaves in cities much too casually. Persons who lived in these places did not necessarily know or much like everyone else who lived there. They often had serious disagreements among themselves. Furthermore, our entanglement in bigger organizations and more commercial types of amusements was more "urban-like" than "mass-like" in character. It also reinforced more "traditional" and intimate ties among townsfolk and started a lot earlier than we are accustomed to thinking. After all, we have seen that an urban way of life insinuated itself into the daily routines of small towns a full century before most commentators believe it did. More importantly, perhaps, it met with little or no resistance when introduced there. In fact, persons who lived in towns often embraced big-city customs shamelessly.

The movement toward more "top-down" forms of association in which local chapters of national organizations were opened in many cities and towns was already in force before the American Revolution. This was especially the case for several charity organizations that were trying to meet the needs of poorer colonial townsfolk and the Freemasons which had chapters in several towns prior to the revolt against Great Britain. Commercial recreation in the form of popular entertainment and shopping surely was given a substantial boost from persons of more modest means during the second half of the nineteenth century. Yet it, too, was already a well-established habit among better-off persons in cities at the end of the eighteenth century.[20] Finally, the alleged turn to more "private" forms of home-based socializing and entertainment also had been in the works for a long time. It was prompted by community leaders who tried to discourage their neighbors from showing too much enthusiasm in public whenever there was a holiday, and sometimes even when there was not.

The latter half of the nineteenth century found more Americans taking advantage of these cultural opportunities, but there was nothing all that novel in the activities and groups themselves. Persons working through these "newer" forms of association certainly did a great deal in their communities and are viewed as an integral part of American civic culture's "golden age." Yet they did not replace older ways of having fun or getting along with one's neighbors. They added to our approved stock of voluntary organizations and ways of relaxing. Now we could do a lot more than go to a church social or take a pint at the local pub.[21] Persons still went to church, of course. Or they did not. They also visited family members and their neighbors, attended community picnics, got drunk and rowdy with their friends, and joined clubs that had no national pretensions. They just had many other things they now could also do.

Men and women who lived in larger cities after World War II had more of these outlets than did individuals who resided in towns; but persons who lived in towns certainly knew about these diversions and had access to some of them. Persons who lived in towns still joined local clubs, fraternized with men or women who shared a common ancestry, volunteered to help sick or luckless souls, and contributed their labor or donated money to worthwhile causes and projects in their community. So, too, did men and women who lived in cities.

There were differences. City dwellers no longer paid as much attention to smaller pieces of do-gooding and simple social gatherings as they once did. They also appeared content to let more of the routine work of keeping their community together fall to someone else. To the extent that this was so, it only was because they had grown accustomed to having city-wide organizations and public agencies do good things for them or for persons in need. All the grassroots organizations and churches working in cities today show us that city residents never forgot how to do good things for themselves. Over the course of the last 50 years, however, there had been increasingly fewer persons reminding them to do so and fewer occasions when they could not turn to someone else first.

The National Commission on Civic Renewal may have come closer to describing the condition of civic affairs in bigger cities, but even there they missed a great deal of what was going on with regard to volunteer work, neighboring, and group life. Boston residents in 1950, for instance, were greeted with the news that over 40 women's groups would meet during the last week in March. The 27th annual session of the New England Hospital Assembly began, and over 4,200 health care specialists were expected to participate in the three-day meeting. Dorothy

Thompson, a *Boston Globe* columnist, was the keynote speaker at the Greek Independence Day dinner which over 4,000 persons attended.

During the month of April, it was announced that the Spring Music Festival would be held at the Hatch Shell in conjunction with the city's Mid-Century Jubilee. Clarence E. Smith, head of the "40 'n' 8 Club," pledged his support of the American Legion's membership drive and programs in behalf of veterans and children. Coordinators of the Easter Seal drive acknowledged that subscriptions were running $140,000 short of what they had hoped for, and they made one last appeal to the public for support. One thousand volunteers were expected to meet on Boston Common for the start of the Boston Jubilee "Clean–Paint–Fix Up" campaign that was scheduled to start on Patriot's Day. The event was sponsored by the Chamber of Commerce. A record turnout was antici-pated for the Knights of Columbus Patriot's Day Dinner. Mrs Bradford Washburn, the only women to date to have climbed Mt McKinley, was the guest speaker at the 17th annual banquet of the Boston Women's Business and Professional Clubs. Finally, the Beacon Hill Residents Association announced that Mayor Hines would attend its upcoming meeting in order to discuss the Charles River Embankment Project.[22]

March and April of 1954 found the people of Odessa, Texas looking forward to a different set of activities. Ranchers from Texas and other states were converging on Odessa for the annual Sand Hills Hereford and Quarter Horse Show. A reception was held to honor two young pianists after the Civic Music Association concert. The Women's Christian Fellowship saw a film on farm life in India during their monthly luncheon. It was declared that Christianity would make the lives of those farmers better. Representatives of the Odessa Federated Clubs organ-ization attended a district meeting. The season's basketball finale pitted the city's top male team against the best female team. The Alpha Omega chapter of Epsilon Sigma Alpha hosted a dinner and dance. At their last meeting, the Odessa Garden Club presented a book to the Ector County Library. Members of the Pioneer Study Club discussed "Texas Women, Life, and Heritage." Fifteen members of the Amicae Chapter of Tri-Hi-Y were presented at a hotel dance. Finally, the "Society Schedule" reported activities undertaken by the Sam Houston Parents Club, Pythian Sisters, the Women's Society of Christian Service, the American Business Women's Association, and the Odessa Music Study Club, among other groups.[23]

In January 1963 the Masons of Tupelo, Mississippi installed their new officers. The Junior Auxiliary met at the Citizen's State Bank Community Room. Musicians from Mississippi, Tennessee, and Alabama attended a music clinic at the Calvary Baptist Church. Registration for adult ball-room dancing was held and classes were scheduled for a six-week period.

A companion set of classes for young people was offered at the Tupelo Youth Center. The Friday Bridge Club played at the home of Mrs Jack McCullar. The Newcomers Club of Tupelo met at the home of Mrs R. H. Turner in order to plan activities for the upcoming year, while the Tupelo Legal Secretaries Association met at the Hotel Tupelo. Members of the WSCS of the First Methodist Church met in the Chapman Boble room. During the session, Mrs Milam announced that the recent clothing drive had succeeded in bringing in 16,000 articles of clothing. It all was sent to Hong Kong where missionaries would distribute items to the poor. Finally, the ladies of the Order of the Eastern Star held a lovely reception following the installation of their new officers, and Girl Scout leaders met at the First Presbyterian Church in order to prepare their program for the upcoming year.[24]

A local soothsayer predicted that Las Cruces, New Mexico would have a good year in 1979. Its residents certainly had a busy January. Among the groups that had formal meetings were the Welcome Stranger Club, Las Cruces Horsemans Association, the Progress Club, Dona Ana Council of Garden Clubs, the United Way of Dona Ana County, Parents Without Partners, Easter Seal Society, the Las Cruces Social Club for single, divorced, or widowed persons, and the Las Cruces 800 Toast-Mistress Club. It also was announced that the Munson Senior Center was hosting belly dancing classes.[25]

Historians have been surprisingly mute on the importance of sooth-saying and belly dancing in American communities, but they have studied how persons from different social classes come to share a more common outlook on life. Their version of parallel play is captured in the term *embourgeoisement*. It refers to the process by which working-class persons take on habits and ways of looking at the world that might be construed as bourgeois, such as a belief in security, property, and smaller families.[26]

In a world where backwardness was equated with being part of the last group off the boat and persistence may have mattered more than skill when it came to improving one's life chances, it was necessary for less well-off persons to learn how better-established groups viewed the world and managed their affairs. It was no less true for newly arrived foreigners.[27] Fortunately for newcomers and hard-working artisans, most communities were open and solicitous enough for them to make modest material gains and to acquire some status in the eyes of their better-off neighbors.[28] The distribution of wealth in American towns and cities may not have become more even, but persons from different social ranks and backgrounds still found ways to gain acceptance in each other's eyes and to collaborate when it was deemed necessary or desirable.

The process of becoming a bourgeois person has been laid out most clearly for individuals with real or imagined claims to what in the nineteenth century was still a nascent middle class. These middle-class aspirants, according to Sam Bass Warner, "enjoyed a number of important advances in everyday consumption" over their peers in the artisan class.

> The bare floors, whitewashed walls, and scant furniture ... gave way to wool carpeting, wallpaper, and all manner of furnishings. The houses themselves became relatively cheaper and grew in size. ... The children slept one to a bed, and indoor toilets became common in their homes.
>
> Mid-19th-century families of the new middle class did not need to put their children to work ... they could take full advantage of the new grammar school education. Finally, they had grown prosperous enough to attend the increasing variety of offerings of commercial downtown entertainment.[29]

The speed and manner of their ascent was marked by the acquisition of values dealing with home life, hard work, and thrift. Their rise also was distinguished by a move into a wider social universe in which voluntary associations played an important part. These groups – "lyceums and literary societies, music societies and dancing assemblies, militia and fire companies, baseball and cricket clubs, brass bands and lodges" – were not reserved for the wealthiest individuals in a community.[30] Yet a connection between these classes was clear nonetheless. Some of the philanthropic and literary groups which middle-class persons created were fashioned in the image of organizations founded by wealthier persons. Middle-class individuals also participated in some of the community activities sponsored by their more well-to-do peers in much the same way as artisans and laborers sometimes participated in middle-class groups.

Some of the dedication to following rules that was promoted by upper-class and middle-class leaders no doubt rubbed off on the working-class individuals who became affiliated with different voluntary organizations. However, a good many artisans, laborers, and poor persons did not participate in these groups or accept all the sweet music played by groups that stood ahead of them in the community's pecking order. Indeed, as I mentioned earlier, control over the nature and timing of unruly street demonstrations, brawls, parades, and riots was ceded to workingmen and the poor during the middle of the nineteenth century. They made good use of it, but they were not revolutionaries. Much of their unruliness actually conformed to time-honored customs involving popular unrest and was used to defend their vulnerable position in the community's hierarchy rather than overturn it.

Be that as it may, the process of becoming familiar with the bourgeois civic culture of American towns and cities proceeded unchecked. It seems clearer now that the growth of clubs and other groups helped to certify or validate, if you prefer, the successful planting of a bourgeois civic culture inside American towns and cities. They did so in at least two different but complementary ways. Voluntary associations reinforced more traditional ties among long-time residents, but they also facilitated the introduction of newcomers or would-be claimants to the community of believers to its more established members.

Most groups that cared to attend to its messages and tricks or that wanted to participate in activities advanced under its flag were welcome to do so, even if their members were not especially liked. Would-be claimants to the community of believers may not have been able to pronounce "embourgeoisement," much less describe what it means, but they sure could learn how to parallel play.

This much seems clear. Persons whose wealth, occupation, or social standing put them at the top of a community's hierarchy took the proper training and treatment of those behind them as their special obligation. They set standards and established ways of dealing with each other that were shared with groups further down the queue. At the very least, those other groups were able to observe what their social betters believed in and how they acted. Persons often referred to as "the middling sort" took some of these lessons to heart, but they also developed ways to engage in community affairs and each other that were more their own. Some of their ideas and strategies were shared with groups that stood ahead and behind them in line.

Those individuals and groups closer to the end of the line may not have wielded much influence in community affairs, but they were neither deaf nor dumb. Their private actions and beliefs were of interest to persons who stood ahead of them, just as the habits and values of more esteemed groups inspired a curious mix of admiration and ridicule on the part of less well-to-do residents. It was in the manner of their communication with each other, both obvious and stylized, that their private acts became a source of public speculation and a prod to open collaboration between them. The mimicry and embellishment which laid near the heart of this process were what made parallel play so popular and effective for existing and would-be members of the community. It was how they learned about each other and themselves.

What was not so readily apparent until now is just how extensive and elaborate the process of parallel play was inside American towns and cities. It seems that almost every set of persons could and did act as both teacher and student at one time or another. It was not just persons who came from different social classes who taught and learned from each other. So, too, did groups representing different religions, races, generations, and, as we will shortly see, genders and ethnic peoples.

Some embraced the goal of becoming a full-fledged member in the community of believers more quickly or earnestly, but every group had to take it seriously. Those that did not were shunned or left town. Even their "sacrifice" served the greater community in the long run by reminding everyone who stayed what would be required of them.

Parallel play also took place in a host of venues and for a variety of reasons. Some of it was purely social, as in the case of clubs that met in private residences and did nothing more exciting that play cards or discuss a book. Other groups mixed social motives with more obvious appeals for assistance to fellow members. Lodges, sororities, and church-related groups were especially good at doing this. They also participated in community-wide campaigns to help address whatever problems seemed to be troubling their fellow residents at the time. Still other organizations had a more instrumental focus and a permanent set of part-time volunteers or paid helpers to do their work.

The point is that town and city residents had many moments when they could learn about what other persons were doing. They also could put what they were learning to good use on many topics or problems of interest to their members. Helping others or working on a project outside of one's immediate neighborhood became a way of helping oneself and one's closest acquaintances. It was, as I said earlier in the book, a way to show that one belonged to a community even as one was sharing something important with persons who did not and maybe never could be a member. Much relief work for victims of war or natural disasters in distant places or charity for the poor certainly falls into this category of parallel play.

Quite apart from all the good or even not-so-good work that is accomplished through parallel play, one sees that the line we put between private and public acts is easily crossed and frequently irrelevant to groups that are trying to do something. Public school officials allow private groups to meet in school buildings or individuals to provide services there in exchange for a fee. Hotel owners, banks, and church congregations donate space for citizens to discuss topics of broad public interest, or they rent rooms to a number of different groups that cannot afford to build their own clubhouse. Homes become places where public campaigns are hatched, and public parks or streets are transformed into platforms where the disenfranchised and aggrieved give expression to their private dreams. And everybody can hear about it from their neighbors or local radio station, read about it in the newspaper, or watch it unfold on television in the privacy of their home. It is messy, but it works.

The ultimate contribution of parallel play is to strengthen the community of believers by encouraging different groups to follow rules and established customs. Included among them would be those all-important rules and customs which prescribe how antagonistic groups are supposed to fight and reach an accommodation. This can have the effect of reinforcing inequities that are built into the world as we know it. Thus, the hierarchy of merit and prestige that is embraced by lodge "brothers" and sorority "sisters" does nothing to undermine the distinctly un-brotherly or un-sisterly way in which wealth and power are distributed outside of the clubhouse. Nor does the inverted brotherhood and sisterhood of contemporary youth gangs do anything to fundamentally alter their impoverished status in the eyes of conventional adults.[31]

On the other hand, parallel play does not guarantee that everyone can be like everybody else or that the world we know will never change. It only ensures that we will have had practice looking at the world the same way others look at it and acting on the world in much the same way other groups do. A community in which groups have this kind of shared perspective certainly can change, but it is unlikely to change quickly or in fundamental ways.

"Disregarding the Tenderness of their Sex"

One finds no better illustration of how private lives blend almost imperceptibly into a larger public world than by tracing the changing role of women in the civic culture of American towns and cities. As in many matters related to the development of urban life in America, our appreciation for the contribution of women has been limited by the absence of good information for the years prior to the Civil War. The attention paid to upper-class and middle-class women in much academic research probably is attributable to the fact that better records were kept about what these women did. Nevertheless, it is clear that all sorts of women have been busily engaged in the hard and often thankless task of pulling communities together and keeping them in good working order for a long time. Whether serving as volunteers, learning skills like public speaking and bookkeeping, or simply by keeping a watchful eye on their neighbors and strangers, women have always made a difference in the public life of their community.[32]

Women never have been *just* wives and homemakers, although a great deal of their early service to the community has been portrayed as a logical extension of these roles. It certainly is true that much of their informal socializing on the street, at shops, or inside their residences had the effect of developing a network for themselves. At the same time, it also made the social life of their whole neighborhood more coherent and stable.[33] Women who came from working-class or lower-class immigrant families carved out their own sphere of influence and organizational life inside the burgeoning ethnic enclaves of nineteenth-century American cities. They participated in both church and more secular organizations which helped to accustom them to life in America and tied them into voluntary associations that were active in their neighborhoods.[34]

Their contribution in this regard was every bit as substantial as that of men, who also met informally during the course of the day and exchanged news and gossip. In fine democratic fashion, men of all classes might congregate at the "public house" for a drink or at some other decidedly male venue like a cockfight as they still did in Charleston during the early 1700s. Friendships between men or women made it easier for both to create voluntary associations that reflected their interests. Early women's groups may have been tied more closely to churches and charity work than those of their male counterparts; but that was not always the case. America's first women's club apparently was founded in Charleston, South Carolina in 1707 "shortly after 170 male Dissenters had organized a political club, and while the town's only accused witch was still in prison." The group apparently caused quite a stir among men in the town. "What is most singular," a dismayed parson reported, is that "the women of the town are turned politicians also and ... meet weekly among themselves, but not without falling out with one another."[35] In short, they were behaving like men or engaging in activities that until then had been the special province of men. The important point, however, was that both made contacts and groups which were vital to the community's well-being in the long run.

Not to be outdone, women of decidedly less standing in the community also left their mark. Bridenbaugh relates the story of "two young sparks" out to meet their "mistresses" on a Saturday night in Boston back in 1736. They were set upon by a "troop of young Ladies or Foot pads, who instantly surrounded them and attacked them." One escaped, but the women held onto the other, "strip't down his Breeches and whip't him most unmercifully."[36]

Some women in colonial America found a measure of security through more conventional routes. Carl Bridenbaugh reports that "much urban retailing fell into the hands of women, for it was one of the few means for the sex to earn a living. Merchants' wives ... frequently retailed for their husbands, and during long lonely periods the spouses of sea captains kept shop with silks, yarns, shoes, pins, ribbons, threads, buttons, and yard goods." Misadventures at sea and on the battlefield also made a number of widows who "turned to keeping store, often with considerable success." While "millinery, dry goods, and groceries were the favorite lines for women, they were to be found conducting a surprising variety of small retail enterprises."[37]

These initial forays by women outside of the home may appear narrow or limited to us. Nevertheless, their involvement with other women and groups provided them with opportunities to organize, do noteworthy things outside the home, and display their skills to the broader public.[38] With the exception of the female footpads, of course, it made little difference that much of women's work in behalf of charities or their church was viewed as an extension of their "natural" roles as nurturing and decorous souls. They still did the work. Furthermore, it prepared women for the day when they performed services that were no different than those carried out by men. This, in turn, would make their claim for membership in the community of believers far more credible.

There were early indications that women would make a contribution every bit as great as the one made by men. A large fire that consumed one whole block of business structures in Pittsburgh on November 25, 1823 even showed that they could do the same hard work. Though several fire companies did their best to contain the fire, much property was lost and several persons died during the conflagration. Editors of the *Pittsburgh Mercury* declared the many men who stood by and watched the fire or tried to act like commanders rather than water carriers to be "lamentable and shameful" creatures. At the same time, they observed that it was "but justice to state that a number of females, disregarding the tenderness of their sex, and the inclemency of the night, joined in the lines" to fight the fire.

There were other signs that men's and women's roles inside cities might converge sooner than anyone expected. A Female Employment Office was opened in Boston on November 26, 1829 for four hours every day, and by 1850 it could be reported that the Boston Female Medical School was beginning its fifth term with 20 to 30 ladies. Besides the baseball games and temperance addresses that were held on Boston Commons in 1870, there also was a public meeting for the city's "workingwomen."[39] The purpose of this initial gathering was to consider the needs of women in the labor force. They wanted pay equal to that received by men so that they would not have to resort to crime in order to care of their families. Apparently, all manner of women were beginning to take more active public roles by the first third of the nineteenth century.

Historian Anne Boylan has written that each organization founded by women in New York and Boston during this period had its own particular mix of members. Prior to 1830 it seemed that upper-class women as well as the wives of middle-class merchants, shippers, professionals, and ministers were more involved in women's groups. After 1830 women who were the wives of shopkeepers, who were supporting themselves, or who were drawn from more liberal wings of several religious denominations began to take a more active role in different women's groups. Ruth Alexander has shown that women from families which were economically secure continued to champion benevolent causes and charity campaigns. Those who came from working-class households or the lower end of the middle class were seen joining temperance societies more often, both as a means of self-improvement and to help women who abused alcohol.[40]

By all accounts, the last 60 years of the nineteenth century was an especially rich moment for the history of women in American cities. The rise of great industrial enterprises, political agitation tied to the Civil War, widespread immigration, and the expansion of businesses that provided a variety of goods or services to growing urban populations all played a part in the development of new women's roles. Not all women had the same experiences at the same time. Women in the northeast tended to be ahead of their counterparts in other regions of the country both in terms of the jobs they held and the public obligations they assumed.[41] Still, for women all these changes meant that an unprecedented number of new opportunities and challenges awaited them.

By and large, women met the challenges of this period in much the same way as men might have. They pushed and pried their way into less skilled jobs which had been held by men up to that point, or they broke into newer white and pink-collar jobs in service and retail businesses which were expanding at the time. Although their movement into these realms was contested, they persevered.

Women's organizational life also expanded in new and dramatic ways. They retained an interest in charity work, but they also became more active in unions, politics, and educational institutions. More women joined associations in which men were members; but they also continued to develop formal and informal groups populated exclusively by other women.[42]

Topics of particular interest to women now were debated openly. The question of whether a fair should be held to raise money for the Women's Christian Home in St Louis was discussed in 1875. Persons who believed that there should be a place for young ladies to live and be protected from the evils of city life won the debate.[43] The editors of the *Tupelo Journal* came out in favor of establishing a "Society of Public Improvements" in the May 17, 1877 edition of their paper. This committee would be responsible for considering whether the city should construct a large public park. They observed that in the North such a committee would have been populated exclusively by women, but that Southern women did not "push themselves forward" as much as their Northern sisters do.

Plans for the society and park were implemented in the weeks that followed.

Their reluctance to step forward did not last long. Women in Charlotte, North Carolina were invited by leaders of the Tryon Methodist Church to attend a meeting in 1887 at which the question of establishing a "reformatory home" for women would be discussed. In the same March 3 issue of the *Charlotte Chronicle*, it was announced that arrangements to establish a "House of Refuge" for the benefit of "reclaimed fallen women" also were proceeding nicely.

Laboring men of Sioux Falls, South Dakota were active in the city during March of 1890. At the same time, however, the Women's Industrial Society also was meeting regularly. They may have been too successful in helping women get jobs, because less than one year later the Women's Benevolent Association had to announce that it was searching for girls to look after children and for women to clean homes.[44]

The march of women into the workforce and their involvement in more civic organizations at the end of the nineteenth century prompted a great many men and women to think about the changes they were witnessing. Nothing captures the ambivalence of men toward this movement better than a series of stories and commentary pieces that appeared in the *Daily Picayune* between May 6 and May 12, 1895. Parts of these items are reproduced below.

DUSTY DELILA IS ON THE WAY
The Other Side of the New Woman Crusade
Odd Things May Happen When Women Try to be as Men Are
Vast waves of enthusiasm have deluged the nation over the new woman.

It has been abundantly shown what she would be if she jumped into the industrial and professional fields of masculinity. But there is another side to manhood, and if women are going to gobble up all the prerogatives ... at one swoop they must take the bitter with the sweet. They can't all be doctors, lawyers, ministers, etc., and even the receptive capacities of the army, navy, the mechanical pursuits, police forces, fire departments and other similar things will not be able to accommodate all the new women.

[A] certain percentage of them will invade the pleasant pathways of trampdom. ... There will be "Dusty Delilas" ... and "Weary Winnies" without number. When any of these ladies call at a house occupied by the Coming Woman and a Gone Man, the former, of course, will be out hustling to maintain a meal ticket in the family, while the latter will be unprotected at home minding the babies.

Street corner loiterers will find themselves forced into an ignominious background when the New Woman gets into her stride. ... All the tough gangs will be made up of women, and ... young men will be constantly complaining to the police about the cruel treatment they receive at the hands of these ruffianesses while on the way home from sewing school.

The labor unions will be all officered by women. ... Any daring man who remains at the head of a corporation will speedily be frozen out, and there will be nothing but strikes and bylaws passed giving each employee half a day on Monday to attend bargain counter sales.

This is merely an outline sketch of what will happen when the New Woman is in control.

To a certain extent, women who were making advances in the economy of New Orleans were viewed as an amusing distraction. Their inversion of traditional male roles was treated as a joke. Yet there are ideas in the story which were serious and seem oddly familiar to us. The joke had bite to it.

Women were asserting themselves in ways that men found disconcerting but quite powerless to stop. As mute testimony to this point, the newspaper published a story on the same day that related the proceedings of the annual meeting of the Business Woman's Exchange. Though celebrating only its first birthday, the organization had made good progress during the preceding year. All 18 chapters of the King's Daughters, a local women's society, not only supported the work of the Exchange but also had been responsible for launching the business group in the first place. Sometimes when the world is turned upside down it stays that way.

At some point during the last 30 years we lost sight of how much the world has been turned on its head with regard to women's roles. Historians have shown some interest in describing how women edged their way into industrial and clerical jobs in the early twentieth century, even to the point of chronicling their willingness to strike for better working conditions more than men.[45] They left social scientists to describe how women became more deeply involved in the work of their community and to examine the current status of women in the workplace. A few of these authors have described the ways in which low-income and ethnic women help to anchor their neighborhoods and support each other.[46] (They are good at it. Indeed, they often translate the social capital they acquire inside a neighborhood into limited political influence outside of it.) In general, however, social scientists have not attended to how women shape the urban world around them or collaborate with each other. They have looked at the way cities are designed with an eye to highlighting everything that allegedly frustrates women or limits their ability to do important cultural work.[47]

That many women in this century have struggled to break into occupations formerly dominated by men or scrapped their way to political respectability as candidates for elected office or as policy advisers and heads of important agencies is at once important and quite beside the point. Their ascension to the community of believers certainly did turn a part of the world on its head; but it was not much of a surprise, either.

There was no magic here. As the economy of urban areas grew larger and more varied during the second half of the nineteenth century, it was able to draw in more persons. Ethnic immigrants and, somewhat later, black sojourners from the South were part of the population that was accommodated. So, too, were women.

The magic for women, if there was any, came from all the hard work they had done in towns and cities *before* the economies of these places were robust enough to accommodate many of their number. Women have always been identified with bringing more decorum and higher values to the places they lived and to the people residing there with them. Their preparation for membership in the community of believers was meticulous, their contributions as private persons to the larger public world around them incalculable.[48]

Order begets prosperity. Prosperity, in turn, makes it possible for the community of believers to be expanded and its current members receptive to persons who, under other circumstances, might not be viewed as morally qualified beings. Such was the case for black persons and many of the immigrants who came to this country during the nineteenth and twentieth centuries. Women, for all the difficulty they have had in getting a seat at the table, were not similarly burdened.

The other major lesson to be taken from the experience of women is that while they may have taken on new civic roles they did not withdraw or excuse themselves from other obligations they had assumed in the past. A major point of contention became how they would reconcile these additional public duties with their private lives. As with most of the stresses and strains built into our urban way of life, this one is never fully or satisfactorily resolved. It is managed.

Dr Charlotte Baker was chosen once again to lead the San Diego chapter of the Equal Suffrage Association in 1905. Other officers for the organization also were elected and it was announced that a public meeting would soon be held on the subject of "What Women Can Do for Civic Improvement." Within ten years, women from San Diego were engaged in many other activities. On October 15, 1915 the National Secretary of the Women's Peace Party from Boston came to speak on defense matters. She was preceded by the woman who had been declared the Vice Presidential candidate for the Prohibition Party. Women hosted "shut-ins day" at the San Diego Exposition. The Ladies Aid Society of the First Methodist Episcopal Church met. It was reported that women of the Wednesday Club had met on Thursday this past month and that Mme Katherine Tingley would be lecturing on "Justice and Freedom" at the Isis Theater. Music was to be provided by the Raja Yoga Girls String Quartette and Girls Chorus.[49]

Leading women from Valdosta, Georgia still would take a leading role in directing their city's "cleaning-up day" in 1914, and the whole town would be treated to a talk by Dr Geisel entitled "Home Behind the Man" which was presented at Valdosta College. In his presentation, Dr Geisel argued that education was detrimental because women were being trained out of being wives and mothers.[50] A similar message was left for the citizens of Las Cruces, New Mexico on October 8, 1915 when the editors of the *Rio Grande Republic* called upon women to volunteer or be paid to teach girls how to cook, do housework, sew, and wash laundry.

Representatives of women's organizations from the Boston area in 1920 urged members of a state legislative committee on metropolitan affairs to appoint special women police officers for the protection of girls who frequented local beaches and amusement centers. One month later, working girls from across New England met at the opening session of the New England Conference of Trade Union Women to consider pressing for legislation that would benefit them. By the end of that year, 94 women were taking exams to become police women.[51]

Twenty years later women had ascended to the highest levels of community responsibility inside Cleveland, Ohio. They organized a campaign to mobilize 40,000 women to work in war industries, sponsoring public discussions on the war, and running the Red Cross Drive.[52] By the end of the war men and women were trying to sort out all the changes they had gone through. Women had assumed great responsibility for not only keeping important civic routines in good order but also for working in a variety of industries whose products were crucial to the war effort. An interview provided by Miss Katherine Butler, who was liaison officer of the War Manpower Commission in Pittsburgh, gave some indication of just how difficult a transition this was going to be.

"When the boy friend is in town, a woman worker isn't worth a nickel."
"Women may master men's work, but as long as women are women their hearts, homes and emotions will rule them," she declared.

Women's inherent love of bargain-chasing is a bug-a-boo to attendance records, too, Miss Butler said. An astounding number of women take suddenly "ill" every time a big sale is advertised.

"Employers must realize that women, most of them, do have responsibilities other than their jobs and must make allowance for them if they continue to work after the war."

As far as absenteeism goes, the rate is slightly greater among men workers. Miss Butler has an answer for that, too. "Men can't stand to be 'topped' by women ... it drives them to drink and of course, with the wife's working, they have more money to spend and less feeling of responsibility. The place for married women, after this war, is in the home. But it's going to take a lot to convince them of that."[53]

Women had grown accustomed to doing things they never had been allowed or encouraged to do in the past. What had once been unimaginable had become palpably real thanks to the war. Public subsidies for day care services were merely one small part of that picture.[54] The Pittsburgh city council was petitioned by 75 members of the Council of Working Mothers who did not want to leave their jobs now that the war was ending. Officials decided that they had better look hard to find the $6,400 it would take each month to keep eight nurseries open for the 269 children whose mothers had been employed in war-time industries. Yet now that the "emergency" was over, they were uncertain as to whether city tax revenues could be spent on such a service. They would investigate the question but decided that it would be prudent to approach the private Community Fund for assistance in the meantime.

While reports like these were piling up in cities across the United States, there were other indications that women were still volunteering to do charity and church-related work in their towns or cities. Between 500 and 600 members of the Junior Catholic Daughters of America and the Catholic Youth Organization participated in a Vocation Day program in Manchester, New Hampshire on June 22, 1951. The story in the *Manchester Union Leader* indicated that girls marching in a procession at St Joseph's Cathedral would be "dressed to represent many of the lay and religious vocations open to youth today." It may be hard to believe today, but in 1960 rural girls from the area around Omaha, Nebraska were trying to regain the title of "Miss Farm Implement" at the 69th Farm Equipment Association Convention. The organization had been under some pressure to pass the crown back to a small-town girl after it had allowed city girls to enter the pageant in 1958.[55] Finally, on January 29, 1969 readers of the *Bergen Evening Record* learned that a representative from the League of Women Voters would speak before the Hackensack Women's Club on the subject of "The Urban Situation and How It Affects Us." They also read that the local chapter of Women of the Moose was honoring Elyse Engels at the Moose Lodge on February 14th of that year.

The various roles contemporary women play in their homes and in the world outside their homes strengthen both places. It also solidifies their claim for membership in the community of believers. We have known for some time that women as such never were completely stuck in narrowly framed private lives any more than men enjoyed exclusive access to the advantages and obligations that came with being a public figure. Individual women have been making notable contributions as private caregivers and/or public servants from the time they arrived. We also know, however, that it has not been easy for women in this century to balance the competing demands put to them by persons who would have them attend exclusively to one or the other of these two domains.

What we have not appreciated until now is how artfully women have balanced their growing obligations in both realms. Some women have concentrated more on caregiving within the confines of their homes and immediate neighborhood. A second collection of women has flourished in more public endeavors and the workforce.[56] Still others have tried to split the difference and do a bit of both. None of them has had an easy go of it. Each has made a different contribution. It was not always neat, but it worked. That outcome, as we have seen, has served us pretty well so far.

In small places and in earlier times it was not so difficult to strike a balance between one's private life and one's role in a larger public world, because no great gulf separated them. Who you were and what you did in one domain carried over to the other. That is why newspapers once routinely published the names of persons who committed crimes inside their city's borders, and why in some smaller cities and towns they still do. It also is why persons who have done something commendable are named and the part of town where they live is mentioned in newspaper stories. We become object lessons for other persons in the community. Our experiences, successes, and failures become their own.

During the second week of January in 1979, the Women's Resource Center in Germantown, Tennessee urged local women to attend a program that would be presented on January 18th. The story in the *Germantown News* mentioned that a pot-luck supper would be served and would be followed by a film entitled "You Pack Your Own Chute." The film's female producer and star was a management consultant who presumably wanted to empower women by helping them to confront and overcome their worst fears. The film showed her facing her own worst fears of heights and water by parachuting into the ocean.[57]

One week later the same newspaper carried a story about a man who had given up his career as director of public relations for the Memphis division of the National Hemophilia Foundation in order to teach disco dancing. He thought that his background in counseling and public relations would be "an invaluable tool in teaching dance." "In many ways," he said, "I work against the image that John Travolta created in 'Saturday Night Fever.' Disco in its pure form is both enjoyable and therapeutic." He was hopeful that disco dancing was not a passing fad, because he wanted to help bring this "joyful form of expression" back to men and women on the dance floor.[58]

We should be grateful that the parachuting hydrophobic did not have an eating disorder, and we can only hope that therapeutic disco dancing makes a comeback in the next millennium. The point to their stories, however, is not that they were funny or that the public display of one's private hang-ups is endearing. Their tales are more broadly instructive than that.

We have drawn a clear line between our private lives and a larger public world only in more recent times. This has not come because we wanted to abandon the public realm or drop any pretense that we were obligated to watch out for each other, whether on the dance floor or when falling from the sky. There are too many good examples of men and women still working to improve the towns and cities where they live and the quality of each other's lives for that to be so. Rather, it has come from our insistence that each of us is precious, if only to ourselves, and that what happens to us matters more than what happens to the person next door. It is the odd elevation of individual expression as a civic virtue that makes our arms sore and heads ache. The lesson, I think, is clear. We cannot hope to lift each other if we insist on patting ourselves on the back every time we try. That is not the way our ancestors built communities with viable and vital civic cultures, and it will not be the way we sustain them in the future.

NOTES

1   *Casper Daily Tribune*, April 24, 1918.
2   E. Anthony Rotundo, "Body and Soul: Changing Ideals of Middle-Class Manhood, 1790–1920, *Journal of Social History*, Volume 16, Number 4, Spring 1983, p. 25.
3   Richard Carwardine, "The Second Great Awakening in the Urban Centers: An Examination of Methodism and the New Measures," *Journal of American History*, Volume 59, Number 2, September 1972, pp. 327–40; James Moorhead, "Between Progress and Apocalypse: A Reassessment of Millennialism in American Religious Thought, 1800–1880," *Journal of American History*, Volume 71, Number 3, December 1984, pp. 524–42; John Patrick Diggins, "Comrades and Citizens: New Mythologies in American Historiography," *American Historical Review*, Volume 90, Number 3, June 1985, pp. 614–38.
4   John Higham, "Hanging Together: Divergent Unities in American History," *Journal of American History*, Volume 61, Number 1, June 1974, pp. 5–28; Donald Scott, "The Popular Lecture and the Creation of a Public in Mid-Nineteenth-Century America," *Journal of American History*, Volume 66,

Number 4, March 1980, pp. 791–809; Robert Fisher, "Organizing in the Modern Metropolis: Considering New Social Movement Theory," *Journal of Urban History*, Volume 18, Number 2, February 1992, pp. 222–37.

5   *Boston Globe*, June 25, 1998.

6   *Pittsburgh Mercury*, August 22, 1821.

7   Ibid., March 19, April 9, May 28, and July 2, 1835.

8   *Norwich Courier*, August 31, 1825.

9   *Boston Daily Evening Transcript*, October 20, 1840.

10   *Wheeling Intelligencer*, July 15, 1867.

11   *Daily San Diego Union*, July 9, 1871.

12   *Boston Daily Advertiser*, November 17 and November 30, 1860.

13   *Pine Bluff Weekly*, September 11, 1873.

14   *North-West Tribune*, January 27, February 17, and April 14, 1882.

15   *Union and Advertiser*, January 4, January 13, and January 19, 1887.

16   Robert D. Putnam, "The Strange Disappearance of Civic America," *The American Prospect*, Winter 1996, pp. 34–48.

17   Richard Lingeman, *Small Town America: A Narrative History, 1620–The Present* (Boston: Houghton Mifflin, 1980), p. 407.

18   *Casper Daily Tribune*, September 20 and September 22, 1919.

19   Lingeman, *Small Town America*, p. 410. Also see: Claude S. Fischer, "Changes in Leisure Activities, 1890–1940," *Journal of Social History*, Volume 27, Number 3, Spring 1994, pp. 453–75. Fischer provides a nice review of what was supposed to happen to our social lives as America was transformed into a "mass society" in the years between the Civil War and World War I. He also is able to demonstrate why persons who hold this view were reading too much into the changes that were taking place in Americans' social habits and ties to voluntary associations.

20   Carl Bridenbaugh, *Cities in Revolt: Urban Life in America, 1743–1776* (London: Oxford University Press, 1971), pp. 162–3.

21   Fischer, "Changes in Leisure Activities, 1890–1940," pp. 453–4.

22   *Boston Globe*, March 26, April 2, April 16, and April 23, 1950.

23   *Odessa American*, March 1, March 9, March 17, and March 25, 1954.

24   *Tupelo Area Journal*, January 2, January 10, and January 18, 1963.

25   *Las Cruces Sun News*, January 1, January 9, January 17, and January 25, 1979.

26   Daniel Walkowitz, "The Shuttle and the Cross: Weavers and Artisans in the Kensington Riots of 1844," *Journal of Social History*, Volume 5, Number 4, Summer 1972, p. 487.

27   Herbert Gutman, "Work, Culture, and Society in Industrializing America, 1815–1919," *American Historical Review*, Volume 78, Number 3, June 1973, pp. 531–88; Gordon Kirk and Carolyn Tyirin Kirk, "Migration, Mobility and the Transformation of the Occupational Structure in an Immigrant Community: Holland, Michigan, 1850–1880," *Journal of Social History*, Volume 7, Number 2, Winter 1974, pp. 142–64; Douglas L. Jones, "The Strolling Poor: Transiency in 18th-Century Massachusetts," *Journal of Social History*, Volume 8, Number 3, Spring 1974, pp. 28–54; William Harris, "Work and Family in Black Atlanta, 1880," *Journal of Social*

History, Volume 9, Number 3, Spring 1976, pp. 319–30; Michael Urban and Anthony Boardman, "Economic Growth and Occupational Mobility in 19th Century Urban America: A Reappraisal," *Journal of Social History*, Volume 11, Number 1, Fall 1977, pp. 52–74; Rowland Berthoff, "Peasants and Artisans, Puritans and Republicans: Personal Liberty and Communal Equality in American History," *Journal of American History*, Volume 69, Number 3, December 1982, pp. 579–98; Paul E. Johnson, *A Shopkeeper's Millennium: Society and Revivals in Rochester, New York, 1815–1837* (New York: Hill and Wang, 1978).

28 Charles Olton, "Philadelphia's Mechanics in the First Decade of Revolution, 1765–1775," *Journal of American History*, Volume 59, Number 2, September 1972, pp. 311–26; Kenneth Kusmer, "The Functions of Organized Charity in the Progressive Era: Chicago as a Case Study," *Journal of American History*, Volume 60, Number 3, December 1973, pp. 657–78; Richard Brown, "The Emergence of Urban Society in Rural Massachusetts, 1760–1820," *Journal of American History*, Volume 61, Number 1, June 1974, pp. 29–51; Gary Nash, "The Social Evolution of Preindustrial American Cities, 1700–1820," *Journal of Urban History*, Volume 13, Number 2, February 1987, pp. 115–46; Roy Rosenzweig, *Eight Hours for What We Will: Workers and Leisure in an Industrial City, 1870–1920* (Cambridge: Cambridge University Press, 1983).

29 Sam Bass Warner, *The Private City: Philadelphia in Three Periods of Its Growth* (Philadelphia, PA: University of Pennsylvania Press, 1968), p. 66. Although Warner and others make a strong case for dating the emergence of a self-conscious middle class at sometime in the middle third of the nineteenth century, no one really is certain when this class actually emerged inside American towns and cities. According to Carl Bridenbaugh, for example, "the very conditions that made possible the rise of a bourgeois aristocracy in the cities concurrently lifted up the middle class, who by 1760 had become numerous and prosperous as a class and stood ready to demand a voice in the determining of affairs affecting them in the society to which they had contributed so much." "The American tradesmen and artisans were rapidly acquiring a feeling of self-confidence issuing from a self-respect not yet evident in their European counterparts. More of the great intellects of the cities came from this group than from any other; now it was Benjamin Franklin ... who set the tone of urban culture and provided leadership for the citizens." They were not "levelers" in the sense that they wanted everyone to be equal. They only "insisted that no ... obstacles be thrown in the path of a man making his way to eminence and fortune by talent and hard work." Bridenbaugh, *Cities in Revolt*, p. 350.

30 Stuart M. Blumin, *The Emergence of the Middle Class: Social Experience in the American City, 1760–1900* (Cambridge: Cambridge University Press, 1989), p. 206; Stuart Blumin, "The Hypothesis of Middle-Class Formation in 19th-Century America: A Critique and Some Proposals," *American Historical Review*, Volume 90, Number 2, April 1985, pp. 299–338.

31 Blumin, *The Emergence of the Middle Class*, p. 223; Daniel Monti, "Gettin' Right With Humpty: Or How Sociologists Propose to Break Up Gangs,

Patch Broken Communities, and Make Scary Children Into Conventional Adults," *Free Inquiry in Creative Sociology*, Volume 24, Number 2, November 1996, pp. 133–44; Daniel Monti, "On the Relation Between Gangs and Social Organization," *Free Inquiry in Creative Sociology*, Volume 25, Number 1, May 1997, pp. 3–8.

32 Julie Plaut Mahoney, "Women in Cities," unpublished manuscript, Boston University, July 1998.

33 Judith DeSena, "The Gatekeepers of Urban Neighborhoods," *Journal of Urban Affairs*, Volume 16, Number 3, 1994, pp. 271–83; T. L. Haywoode, "Working Class Women and Neighborhood Politics," in J. N. DeSena (ed.), *Contemporary Readings in Sociology* (Dubuque, IA: Kendall-Hunt, 1989), pp. 77–91.

34 Carol Groneman, "Working-Class Immigrant Women in Mid-19th Century New York: The Irish Woman's Experience," *Journal of Urban History*, Volume 4, Number 3, May 1978, pp. 255–74; Janice Reiff Webster, "Domestication and Americanization: Scandinavian Women in Seattle, 1888–1900," *Journal of Urban History*, Volume 4, Number 3, May 1978, pp. 275–90; Corinne Azen Krause, "Urbanization Without Breakdown: Italian, Jewish, and Slavic Immigrant Women in Pittsburgh, 1900–1945," *Journal of Urban History*, Volume 4, Number 3, May 1978, pp. 307–30; Julia Kirk Blackwelder, "Working-Class Women and Urban Culture," *Journal of Urban History*, Volume 14, Number 4, August 1988, pp. 503–9.

35 Bridenbaugh, *Cities in Revolt*, p. 279.

36 Ibid., p. 382. For some insight into the ways headstrong young women were handled in subsequent years, see the following works: James McGovern, "The American Woman's Pre-World War I Freedom in Manners and Morals," *Journal of American History*, Volume 55, Number 2, September 1968, pp. 315–33; Mary Odum, "Single Mothers, Delinquent Daughters, and the Juvenile Court in Early Twentieth Century Los Angeles," *Journal of Social History*, Volume 25, Number 1, Fall 1991, pp. 27–44.

37 Bridenbaugh, *Cities in Revolt*, p. 78.

38 Nancy Cott, "18th-Century Family and Social Life Revealed in Massachusetts Divorce Records," *Journal of Social History*, Volume 10, Number 1, Fall 1976, pp. 20–43; Nancy Cott, *The Bonds of Womanhood: Women's Sphere in New England, 1780–1835* (New Haven, CT: Yale University Press, 1990); Mary P. Ryan, "The Power of Women's Networks: A Case Study of Female Moral Reform in Antebellum America," *Feminist Studies*, Volume 5, Number 1, Spring 1979, pp. 66–85; Mary P. Ryan, *Women in Public: Between Banners and Ballots, 1825–1880* (Baltimore, MD: Johns Hopkins University Press, 1990); Ann Firor Scott, "On Seeing and Not Seeing: A Case of Historical Invisibility," *Journal of American History*, Volume 71, Number 1, June 1984, pp. 7–21; Estelle Freedman, "Separatism as Strategy: Female Institution Building and American Feminism, 1870–1930," in Penny A. Weiss and Marilyn Friedman (eds), *Feminism and Community* (Philadelphia, PA: Temple University Press, 1995), pp. 85–104.

39 *Boston Daily Evening Transcript*, November 26, 1829 and November 11, 1850; *Boston Herald*, July 2, 1870.

40 Anne Boylan, "Women in Groups: An Analysis of Women's Benevolent Organizations in New York and Boston, 1797–1840," *Journal of American History*, Volume 71, Number 3, December 1984, pp. 497–523; Ruth Alexander, "'We are Engaged as a Band of Sisters': Class and Domesticity in the Washingtonian Temperance Movement, 1840–1915," *Journal of American History*, Volume 75, Number 3, December 1988, pp. 763–85.

41 Marjorie Murphy, "Gender Relations on an Urban Terrain: Locating Women in the City," *Journal of Urban History*, Volume 13, Number 2, February 1987, pp. 197–206; June Sochen, "Myths and Realities About Urban Women," *Journal of Urban History*, Volume 8, Number 1, November 1981, pp. 107–16; Mary Lou Locke, "Out of the Shadows and into the Western Sun: Working Women of the Late 19th-Century Urban Far West," *Journal of Urban History*, Volume 16, Number 2, February 1990, pp. 175–204. For a treatment of the way these regional differences played themselves out for some women in the South at the start of the twentieth century, see James Leloudis II, "School Reform in the New South: The Woman's Association for the Betterment of Public School Houses in North Carolina, 1902–1919," *Journal of American History*, Volume 69, Number 4, March 1983, pp. 886–909.

42 Leann Whites, "The Charitable and the Poor: The Emergence of Domestic Politics in Augusta, Georgia 1860," *Journal of Social History*, Volume 17, Number 3, Spring 1984, pp. 601–16; Lisa Fine, "Between Two Worlds: Business Women in a Chicago Boarding House, 1900–1930," *Journal of Social History*, Volume 19, Number 3, Spring 1986, pp. 511–20; Susan Levine, "Labor's True Woman: Domesticity and Equal Rights in the Knights of Labor," *Journal of American History*, Volume 70, Number 2, September 1983, pp. 323–39; William Leach, "Transformations in a Culture of Consumption: Women and Department Stores, 1890–1925," *Journal of American History*, Volume 71, Number 2, September 1984, pp. 319–42; Mark Peel, "On the Margins: Lodgers and Boarders in Boston, 1860–1900," *Journal of American History*, Volume 72, Number 4, March 1986, pp. 813–34; Linda Kerber, "Separate Spheres, Female Worlds, Woman's Place: The Rhetoric of Women's History," *Journal of American History*, Volume 75, Number 1, June 1988, pp. 9–39; Jodi Vandenberg-Daves, "The Manly Pursuit of the Partnership Between the Sexes: The Debate Over YMCA Programs for Women and Girls," *Journal of American History*, Volume 78, Number 4, March 1992, pp. 1,324–46; Maureen Flanagan, "Gender and Urban Political Reform: The City Club and the Woman's City Club of Chicago in the Progressive Era," *American Historical Review*, Volume 95, Number 4, October 1990, pp. 1,032–50; Joanne Meyerowitz, "Women and Migration: Autonomous Female Migrants to Chicago, 1880–1930," *Journal of Urban History*, Volume 13, Number 2, February 1987, pp. 147–68; Heather Frazer, "Labor, Reform, and Feminism in Chicago During the Progressive Era," *Journal of Urban History*, Volume 16, Number 3, May 1990, pp. 312–18; Daniel Eli

Burnstein, "Progressivism and Urban Crisis: The New York City Garbage Workers' Strike of 1907," *Journal of Urban History*, Volume 16, Number 4, August 1990, pp. 386–423.

43   *St Louis Dispatch*, October 1, 1875.

44   *Argus Leader*, March 19, 1890 and January 5, 1891.

45   Patricial Cooper, "Women Workers, Work Culture, and Collective Action in the American Cigar Industry, 1900–1919," in Charles Stephenson and Robert Asher (eds), *Life and Labor: Dimensions of American Working-Class History* (Albany, NY: State University of New York Press, 1986), pp. 190–204; Valerie Quinney, "Office Workers and Machines: Oral Histories of Rhode Island Working Women," in Stephenson and Asher, *Life and Labor*, pp. 260–81.

46   DeSena, "The Gatekeepers of Urban Neighborhoods"; Haywoode, "Working Class Women and Neighborhood Politics"; Ida Susser, *Norman Street: Poverty and Politics in an Urban Neighborhood* (New York: Oxford University Press, 1982); Nancy Naples, "Activist Mothering: Cross-Generational Continuity in the Community Work of Women from Low-Income Urban Neighborhoods," *Gender and Society*, Volume 6, 1992, pp. 441–63; Daniel J. Monti, "The Organizational Strengths and Weaknesses of Resident-Managed Public Housing Sites in the United States," *Journal of Urban Affairs*, Volume 11, Number 1, pp. 39–52.

47   Julie Plaut Mahoney, "Women in Cities"; Leslie Kanes Weisman, *Discrimination By Design: A Feminist Critique of the Man-Made Environment* (Urbana, IL: University of Illinois Press, 1992); Estelle Freedman, "The New Woman: Changing Views of Women in the 1920s," *Journal of American History*, Volume 61, Number 2, September 1974, pp. 372–93; Karen Tucker Anderson, "Last Hired, First Fired: Black Women Workers During World War II," *Journal of American History*, Volume 69, Number 1, June 1982, pp. 82–97; Margaret Marsh, "From Separation to Togetherness: The Social Construction of Domestic Space in American Suburbs, 1840–1915," *Journal of American History*, Volume 76, Number 2, September 1989, pp. 506–27; Julia Kirk, "Women in the Work Force: Atlanta, New Orleans, and San Antonio, 1930–1940," *Journal of Urban History*, Volume 5, Number 3, May 1979, pp. 279–307.

48   Contemporary women do more "neighboring" than men. They also belong to smaller, more "expressive" groups whose membership is more likely to be consist of other women. Men, by comparison, belong to more "instrumental" groups involved in business activities or politics. Their associations are more likely to be made up of men and women or only men. These differences are portrayed in language that is intended to remind us of the segregation endured by minority citizens. It implies that women are somehow being discriminated against or held away from more important cultural work. This view is wrong on several counts. First, it ignores the fact that women were forming associations of "business women" before the end of the nineteenth century in many towns and cities. Second, it demeans the vital contribution that "non-instrumental" groups like churches and lodges make to the smooth and effective operation of our civic culture. Third, it

ignores what has been identified here as the important preparatory stage which participation in so-called "expressive" groups played in women's eventual rise into more parts of the mainstream economy of American towns and cities. See: J. Miller McPherson and Lynn Smith-Lovin, "Women and Weak Ties: Differences by Sex in the Size of Voluntary Organizations," *American Journal of Sociology*, Volume 87, Number 4, 1982, pp. 883–904; J. Miller McPherson and Lynn Smith-Lovin, "Sex Segregation in Voluntary Associations," *American Sociological Review*, Volume 51, February 1986, pp. 61–79; Karen Campbell and Barrett A. Lee, "Gender Differences in Urban Neighboring," *Sociological Quarterly*, Volume 31, Number 4, 1990, pp. 495–512.

49 *San Diego Union*, September 8, 1905 and October 15, 1915.

50 *Valdosta Daily Times*, October 17 and December 12, 1914.

51 *Boston Globe*, February 18, March 27, and December 21, 1920.

52 *Cleveland Plain Dealer*, February 2 and March 6, 1943.

53 *Pittsburgh Post Gazette*, March 6, 1945.

54 Ibid., September 27, 1945.

55 *Omaha World Herald*, January 18, 1960.

56 It was not until 1950 that the US Census displayed the types of jobs held by men and women. Nevertheless, the movement of women into the workforce after World War II has been nothing short of amazing. Reviewing changes in the cities studied for this book, women made great advances in getting all types of jobs. The corresponding drop in men's share of those same jobs was equally stark. Similar changes occurred in the percentage of women who acquired a college education between 1950 and 1990. Surprisingly, perhaps, by 1950 the percentage of young women who had a high school degree already was greater than that of young men. Women only improved upon their performance on that criterion over the next 40 years. Whatever hard work generations of women had undertaken in behalf of their towns and cities before 1950 obviously prepared them well for the opportunities that were afforded them after World War II. See note 48.

57 *Germantown News*, January 11, 1979.

58 Ibid., January 18, 1979.

8

Doing Well by Doing Good

In one sense, it has always been about money. No one who read the *Boston Gazette* in 1810 could have missed all the announcements pertaining to business being conducted in the city. Insurance companies were mentioned in part, perhaps, because Boston was a major port and a great many persons who owned ships wanted to protect themselves against the catastrophic loss of their goods during ocean voyages. The comings and goings of merchant vessels were prominently displayed every day in the newspaper. Many other corporations also had their activities reported over the course of the year. Their meetings and elections of boards of directors were summarized in terse declarations that appeared alongside the shipping schedules and lists of goods that were being loaded or unloaded on Boston's docks.

Other ventures, even more speculative than the transatlantic voyages at this point, were featured in the newspaper that year as well. Proprietors of the West-Boston Bridge, for instance, met and decided to sell off part or all of the land they owned on the south side of the bridge to any interested party. They also discussed how much money they should set aside to construct new roads or to repair the old ones abutting their properties. Another group of businessmen began selling shares to the Rowes Wharf which they had constructed. Later in the year, merchants and persons who owned ships were invited to bid on space at Lewis's Wharf which only recently had been built out into the channel.[1]

Some years later in Burlington, Vermont the editors of the *Daily Free Press* praised the local savings bank. They declared it an altogether "excellent institution" whose "success thus far has been quite up to the expectations of its projectors." Operated by 20 local men who would "carry out the ... judicious designs of its founders," the editors were certain that "no institution could possess a higher guaranty of usefulness, integrity and business ability in the reputation ... of its Managers, than this."[2]

Although the bankers clearly came from the higher reaches of Burlington society, the same could not be said of the depositors. The bank was supposed to bring much "solid advantage to people of moderate means" and be a "friend of the poor man, who aims by industry and frugality 'to provide against a wet day.'" Thus far, at least, it appeared that the plan was working. There were, the editors noted, "large numbers of sagacious and prudent people, among the class whose *savings* are necessarily small, but nevertheless of material consequence to *them*, who only waited for the secure and beneficial facilities thus presented to them, to make investments." However modest their contributions may have been, these deposits enabled the bank's managers to promote new business ventures in Burlington and make the long-term prospects of working persons at least a little better.

Railroads were much on the minds of town and city builders in the nineteenth century, and business people from Spartanburg, South Carolina were no exception. Stockholders in the Spartanburg & Union Railroad met in the years before the Civil War to consider what progress their company was making. Though generally pleased with the response to their effort to attract investors, they complained in 1856 about the way other railroads had glutted the bond market. They also took strong exception to the failure of the state to send anyone to represent the interest of the citizens of South Carolina whose money had been invested in the Spartanburg railroad company.

The Spartanburg Agricultural Society also was busy in August of 1856. Its executive committee selected several persons to judge animals at the upcoming agricultural exhibition and beseeched other members to pay their dues. The first Annual Exhibition of that society took place the next month at Palmetto Hall.[3]

A meeting of gentlemen from Boston who were interested in establishing an Institute of Technology took place at the Board of Trade on October 10, 1860. The *Boston Daily Advertiser* reported that a committee composed of some of the "first scientists, merchants, and gentlemen of the city" was assigned the task of finding a suitable spot for the school on "the Back Bay lands." It was a good spot.

Today, the stately brownstones and businesses found atop the landfill that is Back Bay are among the most expensive in the city. Unfortunately, a center dedicated to the study of technology is not to be found among them. The Massachusetts Institute of Technology was built, of course. As local wags dryly observe, however, you can find it "on the other side of the river" in Cambridge.

Gentlemen of Omaha, Nebraska decided in 1866 that they wanted to establish a commercial college in their city. The curriculum was to consist of bookkeeping, railroading, steamboating, and banking. Disabled soldiers were expected to receive discounts on their tuition.

Just before Christmas that same year, a number of "monied men" from Omaha decided they would build a second large "block" or set of business buildings on Douglas Street. They pledged to make it every bit as good as the Republican Block which already had been erected.[4] Proprietors of the Central Block declared their intention to lay down "a splendid sidewalk" in front of their stores two years later.[5]

Much more news was being made that year, however, by the construction of different railroad lines gradually making their way to Omaha from the east, west, and south. Completion of the St Louis, Chilicothe, and Omaha Railroad had to be delayed until more money could be raised by its backers. On the other hand, the iron railroad bridge that would span the Missouri River and "lift their city to prosperity" was almost finished.[6]

Members of San Diego's Chamber of Commerce met in July of 1874 and decided to support the creation of a daily mail route between their city and Mesilla. Three years later an assembly was held in the city in order to elect 100 persons to a Citizens' Railroad Committee. Its duties were to protect the rights of citizens and aid the Board of City Trustees in securing the construction of the Texas & Pacific Railroad between their city and Yuma. Trade with the outside world increased so much as a result of these and similar ventures that by 1883 an executive committee was completing plans for a fruit grower's convention for all of San Diego County.[7]

Railroads also were big news in Sioux Falls during 1886. With the construction of a line between one or another town in the Dakotas and Duluth to the east in the works, editors of the *Daily Argus* on May 17 all but pleaded with their readers to support their city's bid to get the railroad. "In this at least let us be unanimous," they urged. Should Sioux Falls become the hub for rail traffic into the Dakotas, they went on to argue, it would dispel "all chance for doubt that here is to be the metropolis of Dakota."

There was no guarantee that local backers could be found for this new venture. New businesses were opening, to be sure. These included a Chicago wholesale clothing firm that rented one whole floor of a building. Several other businesses had gone bankrupt, however, and supporting the construction of a railroad was an expensive proposition. The town's Board of Trade had been unable to generate even $10,000 to establish a stock company for this project and to hire a secretary.[8]

At the same time, there were other signs that persons living in Sioux Falls might be enticed into supporting campaigns that promised to bring new enterprises and greater economic stability to their community. A branch lodge of the national AOUW had opened there one year earlier, and the workingmen who joined it secured a $2,000 life insurance policy and medical care for themselves. Membership among Sioux Falls workers was increasing rapidly.[9] There also was a lot of talk about Sioux Falls joining a baseball league from which Milwaukee had just withdrawn. Supporters formed a committee whose goal was to solicit funds from interested parties that would enable their team to join the Northwestern league. The sum of $500 would "give our citizens," the *Daily Argus* declared on July 24, "a chance to see some very fine games and ... will reflect great honor on the baseball enterprise of the Queen City."

Sioux Falls was a busy place. So much so, in fact, that citizens almost ignored the burning and loss of Jackson Smith's packing house. Something really had to be done to help Mr Smith and his employees. "The feeling everywhere is that the plant must be rebuilt and the men left idle by the fire put to work again," the newspaper reported on November 2, 1886. "A subscription list will be started in a few days ... for ... the immediate rebuilding of the packing house."

True to their word, a public meeting two days later marked the commencement of such a drive. Local residents organized a stock company worth $25,000, and within one week all but $5,000 of the shares had been sold. The plant was open for business before Christmas of that year.[10]

Sioux Falls got its railroad and fulfilled the expectations of its backers. The city became an agricultural and commercial center, and sponsored the annual state fair which drew in farmers and visitors from a wide area around Sioux Falls. By 1891, the fair needed a more permanent location. A committee that ran the event met in the Commercial Club to discuss the matter on February 5, 1891. The *Argus Leader* reported that the only bid to provide such a site had come from the South Dakota Rapid Transit and Railway Company.

Amid all the other business news reported on the pages on the *St Cloud Daily Times* on January 10, 1889 was an announcement that town leaders were considering whether to raise money that would be used to bring more manufacturing to their Minnesota community. Later that same year the merchant's protective association was revived when local businessmen decided to present a united front against wholesale companies that were charging them to transport goods from their warehouses to the depot.[11]

The fair that opened in Muskegon, Michigan on September 17, 1895 was the first one held for the county in 17 years. According to Tressa LaFayette, an avid local historian and long-time staff writer for the city's newspaper, the event took place on land donated decades earlier by several prominent families. Many local companies displayed their wares in a grandstand adjacent to the fair grounds and race track. This building was decorated with flowers provided by Wasserman's Flower Shop. Among the businesses that put up "fancy booths" were the local hardware and clothing stores, Beerman's Music House, and the Brundage Drug Store. "In addition to the merchants' displays, cattle, horses and farm products were in abundance," and a large space was set aside to show off embroidered items and many other pieces of handiwork made by local women. The final day of the fair was declared "Muskegon Day," LaFayette reported, and "all city and county offices and the post office closed at noon just so that everyone from the town who wanted to attend the event could do so.[12]

The Chamber of Commerce in San Diego was still hard at work trying to build up that city in 1895. Celebrating its 25th anniversary, that group of business people and civic boosters held a party at its headquarters on January 30th of that year. It was noteworthy because several of the organization's past presidents, who were quite old by then, rose to address those in attendance with inspiring speeches and recollections about the early days of San Diego. One was greeted by much applause when he declared that some young people in the audience would live to see the day when San Diego had 250,000 residents. He quickly added that "if I spoke my real sentiments, I would say 500,000." President-elect Philip Morse was invited at that point to close the proceedings. He complimented his predecessors handsomely and stated that all of them had been "sturdy, upright men and an honor to San Diego."[13]

It was all very inspiring and not much exaggerated. Things really were looking up for San Diego. Out-of-town investors were buying the stocks of the local water company and seeking to purchase parts of businesses dedicated to farming and mining. New railroad lines were being proposed, and the Chamber of Commerce initiated a subscription campaign in support of the venture. It also opened a Floral Fair with the help of local flower lovers and donated a portion of all the proceeds to retire the debt of the Women's Exchange and the Day Nursery. Citizens who were "interested in agitating the development of manufacturing industries" met at Brooklyn Hall in an attempt to achieve that goal. Three different lumber companies reduced their prices in order to prompt more persons to build new structures and provide work to "mechanics and others." And the Mid-Summer Association of San Diego was making plans to promote a varied program of activities for the many tourists who would visit the city.[14]

Not everyone in the city, however, could be counted on to march in step with the leaders of the Chamber of Commerce. Many well-to-do residents did not subscribe to the railroad campaign. "None of the rich men have aided the project," declared the editors of the *San Diego Union* on July 27, 1895. "What help we have had is principally from business men and the poorer people." Leaders also found it difficult to develop a consensus around major economic and development initiatives for the city. This was particularly so for plans to bring more water and better railroad lines to the city. Though leading businessmen in San Diego eventually voted in favor of a plan to accomplish both these goals, it was not altogether clear that they would contribute much money to see it implemented.[15]

But It Was Never Just About Money

Yes, in one sense, what happened in American towns and cities has always been about money. Yet it was never just about the money, or about individuals wanting to become richer, or about some persons wanting to "lord it over" their neighbors. There was more to it than that.

American towns and cities were founded as commercial enterprises, to be sure. Their residents were committed to ventures that would make them prosperous. Yet these persons had more in common than a desire to exploit the continent's natural resources, trade with their homeland, and make a lot of money. They also had come to build a world.

Their new world was a grand social experiment that started as an expression of mercantile capitalism, but ended with something much bigger and better. In the hands of the persons who first came to America, colonial villages and towns were important cultural outposts where like-minded men and women found their way together. Not too much later, many other persons who were not so like-minded as the original settlers came to America as well. Some stayed on. Others moved to more distant places before settling down.

Out of the collection of more permanent residents emerged a "community of believers" whose values and steady habits made collaboration among them easier and economic success more likely but by no means ensured it.[16] Buffeted by an unforgiving environment and events occurring a great distance from where they had settled, townsfolk drew personal strength from their social unity. Their commitment to each other preceded their investments in different business ventures. It also was more important.

What grew out of this curious blend of entrepreneurial zeal and social commitment was a bourgeois civic culture which continues to shape our private lives and give meaning to the larger public world we share. Fueled by the promise of prosperity and a belief in order, colonists built their new world around a kind of *commercial communalism* that wedded the principle of corporate responsibility to the practice of sharing risks with one's fellow townsfolk. No one could hope to do well unless many persons helped out. Sometimes this meant that individuals invested in each other's schemes or stood ready to catch them, if they fell down. On other occasions it meant only that individuals were willing to buy whatever it was that a business person was selling. The effect in either case was the same. Some persons may have risked more than others, but everyone was taking a chance and helping out the other guy.

Benjamin Franklin's Union, Fellowship, and Hand-in-Hand voluntary fire companies in mid-eighteenth century Philadelphia offer a wonderful illustration of how this principle worked out in practice. It also was no accident, so to speak, that one of these organizations also was a forerunner of the modern insurance company. All three of his fire societies were founded before 1742, and Franklin had the good sense to transform them "into what amounted to a lodge" which stressed both "private advantage and civic service" to its members. Like many private benevolent societies of the eighteenth and nineteenth centuries, these offered a kind of social insurance which in this case protected the members from the devastating effects of fire.

The Union Fire Company took a step into the modern world by offering protection against the ravages of fire to local business people and home owners who were not members. Most of the 75 subscribers to this insurance plan were Quakers, and the group's directors were led by none other than the estimable Mr Franklin. Their business venture was predicated on trust and the faith that firefighters would be there when they were needed.[17]

The same idea had more direct and broad-based application in many business practices of the era. After all, it took a while for goods to be transported to America from England, and even an immediate sale of items would result in the original owner having to wait a long time to be paid. It was not uncommon for a transaction and repayment to take a full year before it was completed, and sometimes it did not happen even that quickly.[18] The whole system was built on credit and the belief that one's business associate on the other side of the Atlantic Ocean was an honest person who would meet obligations, whether by sending high-quality materials or by paying debts. No good would have come from anyone's hard work, if many other persons involved in these transactions along the way had been untrustworthy.

Everyone who came to America or subscribed to the view that this was a land of opportunity may have wanted to improve their situation, but there was no guarantee that any of them would succeed. Whole towns were known to fail, after all, and most never lived up to the inflated expectations of their founders. Furthermore, only a few persons left this world with much more than they had coming into it. A good number achieved a degree of economic security, but most everyone else struggled to keep up and made no big mark on the world. No matter how much or little they accomplished during the course of their lives, however, the important thing from our standpoint was that they had done it together.

Ultimately, their successes and failures were shared with many other persons, only a portion of whom they may have known intimately or in anything like a face-to-face way. Setbacks, no less than advances, were something that many persons and sometimes the whole town or city had a hand in. It was never just the individual who rose or sunk on the basis of his or her good or bad fortune and hard work or sloth.

It was unlikely, of course, that anyone was ever fully aware of all the ways he or she was bound to other persons. Nevertheless, whatever sense of well-being townsfolk and city dwellers enjoyed as self-seeking individuals rested upon commitments they made to each other that went far beyond matters of profit and loss. Many of the customs to which they subscribed or pushed themselves to follow in business were designed to reinforce the idea that they were bound by a broad social compact. They were morally obliged to act like honorable persons even before they signed a contract that would have had them provide a good or service to each other.[19] Customs built around ideas found in the voluntary subscription campaign provided for the reenactment of these moral obligations in every American town and city. It was not a coincidence that commercial leaders pioneered the use of these customs and provided other persons with opportunities to use them.

Colonists came to the Americas with a pretty good idea about what they wanted to do and how they were going to do it. New worlds being what they are, of course, the colonists' plans did not always work out. Just to survive, the settlers had to fall back on their family ties, religious congregations, articles of confederation, built-in trading partners, and a lifetime's worth of practice in solving problems or making a community. The customs and institutional routines they followed were predicated on well-established understandings, but none of these was etched in stone. Colonists had to adapt their traditional beliefs and ways of doing things before they could hope to thrive in this new world; but they clearly were guided by tried-and-true rules regarding how one should look at the world and work together.

The most intriguing element of their world view and approach to each other was that so much of who they were and what they did was played out in public. Townsfolk had personal lives and kept secrets just like they do today. The difference back then was that the sphere which defined the limits of one's personal life was smaller and had a lot more holes in it.

This idea is laid out nicely by historians like Nancy Cott and Mary P.

Ryan, whose studies of eighteenth- and nineteenth-century America show the many ways in which the private lives of women were informed by what was going on around them and, in turn, played back on that larger public world.[20] What one did or did not do in public seems to have been taken into account far more seriously in early American towns and cities than it is today. Keeping a big public ledger made it a lot easier to identify who had been granted admission into the community of believers and who had not. Nevertheless, everyone in the city was touched by the routine and special responsibilities that members of the community of believers accepted.

Commercial Communalism: Piety, Sharing, and Public Accountability

Businessmen and, somewhat later, businesswomen were the architects of a particular way of being in the world that I have called *commercial communalism*. They looked at the world in the same way they would a formal compact or corporation. Every person had a good idea about what their role was and the value they added to the final product. Some jobs may have been more critical than others, and the persons who did those jobs got more pay or status inside the organization, but everyone made a contribution. Work schedules and performance criteria were spelled out, and everyone knew to check in from time to time so that the quality of whatever was being produced could be assessed.

Businessmen and women tried to build communities in much the same way. They believed in following rules, even those rules which felt more like a moral obligation and probably could not be enforced by laws. They also made their employees stakeholders in the process and held persons responsible for fulfilling their obligations to the city's team. That is to say, they embraced *piety*, believed in *sharing*, and demanded *public accountability* when assessing everyone's contribution to the community.

There are many ways in which business leaders shaped a community's agenda or daily routines. What they produced or sold surely made a difference. So, too, did the manner in which they organized the workforce and how well they paid their employees. Yet none of these had anything to do with commercial communalism or the way that businessmen and women applied themselves to the task of making a bourgeois civic culture inside towns and cities.

Whenever business leaders wanted to support a good cause or underwrite an activity that they thought would help the community they mounted a "subscription campaign" or something very much like it. The essential feature of subscription campaigns was that persons volunteered their own labor or gave money to a project that was deemed good but probably would not have been initiated otherwise. The cash or assistance stood as a "donation" when there was no expectation that the contributor would profit from it. The money or help sometimes was viewed as an "investment" when contributors thought that a profit might be realized or they wanted to make the point that the cause being supported someday would yield a social or economic dividend for the whole community.

Donations and investments, as we all know, are crucial to the success of any profit-making or charitable undertaking. In no way, however, do they ensure that a product actually will make any money for its producer or that a person's life will improve markedly as a result of being touched by some charitable work. The offer is made simply because it is deemed to be the right or smart thing to do. Thus, subscription campaigns are expressions of a people's faith in themselves and for each other. They serve the same purpose as glue, bonding persons together whenever a speculative venture is launched in uncertain times. It is the expression of support more than the provision of money or assistance which holds the community together during trying moments and convinces local residents that they have made a difference by contributing to something bigger than themselves.

The ceremonial reenactment of this custom in trade fairs and "dollar day" celebrations put local business people at substantial risk if residents failed to take advantage of the discounted prices or left new stock on the shelves. Local expositions also attracted outsiders who spent additional money or found the place sufficiently appealing to make them want to relocate there. Sometimes the subscription campaign took the form of an investment in a brand new business. When that happened, town leaders literally "passed the hat" in order to get sufficient funds to undertake a new venture themselves. They also took up collections to help smooth out some of the early bumps that might discourage an outside investor before he figured out what a great place and people he was joining. On other occasions, business people might try to help out one of their own whose shop burned down or who needed a short-term loan. The point in each case was the same. A number of persons voluntarily put themselves at some small or large risk in order to help out another person or the whole community. This was what being a community leader was really all about.

Towns and cities are corporate entities, if only in a legal or jurisdictional sense. Imagining a city as a big corporation or a business venture is something quite different, but it is something that social scientists at the end of the twentieth century are accustomed to doing. The reason is that social scientists, much more than contemporary historians, have struggled to find a way to describe how cities during this period are coping with big changes in their populations and economies.[21]

Whether we look at the entire city as a corporate-like being or simply explore the various ways in which corporations in cities exercise a disproportionate amount of power over what goes on there, the effect is much the same. Cities are viewed as big economic engines. They are all about markets, buildings, speculation, debt, and making more money. Everybody inside cities does pretty much what business leaders want them to do.

Historians have been mindful of the part that rich persons and business leaders played in building or running cities in the eighteenth and nineteenth centuries. They also chronicled what appeared to be a gradual withdrawal of these parties from the public realm sometime during the middle of the nineteenth century. Their view of elites is at once more complex and generous than that proffered by social scientists. Ultimately, however, it feeds the idea that business leaders and the well-to-do probably did little else at the end of the twentieth century except look out for their own short-term economic interests.

There was a long time during the eighteenth and nineteenth centuries when urban elites and business leaders could rightly claim to be stewards of the city in which they lived and worked. The Chamber of Commerce may have been the most prominent representative of their interests and an avid proponent of civic boosterism, but it was not alone. Family and church ties, connections to local and national organizations, and political wheeling and dealing at the state level all contributed to the way city leaders did business and fulfilled their obligations to the city.[22]

Wealthy and prominent city leaders did not accomplish things all by themselves. We saw in our short survey of business-inspired subscription campaigns that there were times when members of this leadership class looked for help from investors who did not live in their city. On occasion they also reached out to persons in their own community who had decidedly less wealth or status. They did this in order to share some of the responsibility for making the community more prosperous, to increase the economic security if not the wealth of artisans and mechanics, and to work together on important tasks.[23]

Less well-placed groups and individuals learned these lessons well and mimicked the ways in which their better-bred peers made the world a bit safer and more profitable for themselves. The best illustration I have found of just how far down the community's social ladder the instigation of subscription campaigns could go came from San Diego in 1895.[24] In many cities, the boys who sold newspapers on street corners were little more than street urchins. They were not highly regarded. Nevertheless, the Newsboys' Association of San Diego initiated a fundraising effort in behalf of one of its members who had lost parts of both legs in an accident. They wanted to buy him a bike so that he might continue his work, and they asked for the public to support their effort. It was the first time in the six-year history of that organization that the newsboys had asked for any kind of assistance.

Subscription campaigns mounted in behalf of charitable causes were common in the eighteenth and nineteenth centuries. They also were a crucial part of prominent and wealthy city residents' stewardship in their hometown or city.[25] Whether prosperous citizens made life appreciably better for those who were lower on the economic and social ladder or simply helped themselves become better organized by participating in charity organizations has been much disputed. Clearly, all their good works did not make the distribution of wealth inside cities more equal. Nor did it protect most poor persons from the harsh realities of industrial life or from whatever bad habits and character flaws they might have displayed.

Some persons have argued that all of the institutions which more prosperous city dwellers created during the nineteenth century only masked their retreat from public life and a deep-seated contempt for less well-to-do city residents. Other writers have noted that an increasingly fragmented and outnumbered class of urban leaders helped cities adjust to a more modern world by laying the groundwork for large public bureaucracies and by making alliances with some groups that were considered "outsiders" at the time.[26]

What comes through clearest in all this work is that sometime during the middle of the nineteenth century the public culture of American cities was supposed to be in decline. The increasing size and cultural diversity of urban populations, a more egalitarian ethos, and the presumed erosion of social ties and traditional bonds of fealty all made for a combustible and chaotic mix inside cities.[27] Life in cities allegedly alienated persons and make it hard for them to collaborate "in the matter of most immediate and lasting concern to them all: the building of the city itself."[28] Whether these fears were realistic is not the point. It only mattered that many persons inside cities began acting as if they were. The result for the civic culture of cities was the same.

Standing at the center of this decline in civic rituals and culture was the supposed withdrawal of traditional leaders from their role as stewards of the city and their retreat to mere profit-making enterprises. It seemed that the personal and paternalistic quality of social affairs shrunk as the city and its problems grew larger. The authority of distant experts and managers working in "faceless" bureaucracies was substituted for the sense of intimacy that had once been created by a city's very public leaders.[29] The practice of citizenship declined because it had become tougher to act heroically.

The city and elite persons occupy a special spot in classical treatments of citizenship. The latter were the only parties in antiquity who were supposed to be able to enjoy the fruits of citizenship. All that changed in the modern world, of course, because a larger number and more varied array of persons acquired the chance to participate more fully in the life of the city. The city, for its part, was the one human creation and place where men and women could "live full lives in the warmth of shared common endeavor." The highest purpose to be served was the revitalization of the city itself.[30] After the middle of the nineteenth century, however, it seemed that fewer of the city's traditional elite were eager to pursue this prize. They looked to be more interested in making money and in putting a prettier lid on a fractious population and dirty urban landscape.[31] Still, we all know that appearances can be deceiving.

The Persistence of Elite Participation in Local Civic Affairs

Realtors of San Diego met at the Chamber of Commerce offices in 1905 and promptly formed a new union among themselves.[32] Their goals were simple enough. They wanted to promote good fellowship, improve the image of their city, and encourage more persons to move to San Diego.

Although properties along 4th Street in San Diego were selling well during the spring of 1905, business property owners wanted to improve the area by adding electric lights. Several of them had visited Los Angeles and been impressed with the way that Broadway was all lit up at night. They learned that the law which enabled Los Angeles city council to pass the expenses for installing and running the street lights along to property owners in the district receiving the service might be applicable in San Diego. A petition to establish a similar service and taxing district for themselves was expected to be circulated soon by the property owners along 4th Street.[33]

Members of Tulsa's Commercial Club met on August 29, 1906 and discussed plans to improve local roads and the city's water supply. According to the story in the *Tulsa Daily Democrat*, they might also consider having the city develop its own water supply.

The upcoming Merchant's Banquet was front-page news for the *Wausau Daily Record Herald* on January 29, 1908. Prominent railway officials of the city would be present at the second annual gathering, and they hoped to become better acquainted with their "patrons" during the festivities. A reception committee expected the affair to be one of the highlights of the current social season. All of the association's 75 members were likely to attend, and the gathering would be catered by the St Elizabeth's Aid Society of St Mary's Catholic Church.

Local merchants in Perth Amboy, New Jersey held a mass meeting on February 2, 1910, according to a report in the *Perth Amboy Evening News*. They demanded that express trolleys be set up between Perth Amboy and New Brunswick so that more shoppers would come to their city. They met again on February 19 at the Odd Fellows Hall. The city's Board of Trade took up the question of improved suburban trade at its own meeting on February 25 and again at meetings on March 9 and March 12. Part of an overall plan to increase suburban patronage included a proposal for local merchants to refund the costs of running the railway for out-of-towners and on weekends.

Business people from Fairbanks, Alaska were busily promoting new enterprises at the end of the decade as well. A baseball game between two local teams, the ABs and NCs, was announced in the June 6, 1908 edition of the *Fairbanks Daily News*. Gate receipts were to go to a fund that would pay the travel expenses of the nine best players. This team would then tour communities some distance from Fairbanks in an attempt to boost the image of their city and to promote its businesses. The Chamber of Commerce endorsed the project. Proceeds from a second baseball game between local lawyers and doctors just two days later went to the local hospital.

The Fairbanks Chamber of Commerce endorsed another plan to bring new enterprises to the city that same year. This campaign would have opened a new quartz processing mill in the valley. It was backed by local businesses, banks, and nine mine owners who were the major stockholders. The article in the December 28, 1908 edition of the *Fairbanks Daily News* quoted a representative as saying that they had entered into the arrangement as a cooperative venture. It was "not launched as a money-making proposition, nor a dividend-paying company, but ... for the good of the city ... and for furthering the interests of those who are making every effort to develop the splendid quartz prospects that ... are being found daily." The paper published a list of all the subscribers to this plan and the amount of money that each had invested.

Two years later, Fairbanks residents were being encouraged to start a local chapter of the "Boosters' Club of America" which at that point was supposed to have had over one million members and "camps" in every state and territory of the union.[34] Reports of "booster club" activities from towns and cities across the nation were summarized in the article. The editors of the newspaper thought that such a club "couldn't hurt much." Indeed, it actually "might help some, if everyone would boost instead of knocking" their city.

Part of their concern might have had something to do with the fact that the campaign to develop the quartz deposits in the area had not been going especially well. However much collaboration local miners engaged in as a result of their earlier actions clearly had not worked. They still were concentrating on their own mines too much, and it was proving too difficult for individual miners to make a go of it on their own. So, local supporters held a meeting and discussed how to broaden the effort to extract more quartz and attract more investors.[35] They established a development company worth $100,000. The first $20,000 in stock was purchased straight away, and the balance was to be raised by selling the remaining shares at $1 a piece. Each share would be worth a single vote in determining the company's policies and management team. This was being done to attract more small investors to the enterprise, and it meant that "laboring men, mining men, business men, professional men, all who have any interest in the camp's [i.e. Fairbanks's] prosperity" were now being courted openly.

A most promising businessman from Muncie, Indiana, a Mr Goodrich, was scheduled to address a large gathering at that city's Commercial Club on December 29, 1915. The topic of his discussion was expected to be "Good Fellowship in Business."[36] That same year in another part of the country, the Commercial Club of Florence, Alabama seemed to be having some difficulty attracting members to its meetings. This did not stop the organization from getting a new and permanent headquarters, however. It also might have contributed to the willingness of the *Florence Times* on January 29 to make a big declaration in behalf of civic pride and responsibility.

A collection of merchants and business people in New Mexico were similarly motivated when they created the Northwest Las Cruces Improvement Association in 1915. Their object was to promote development in their part of the city. The Businessmen's Association of Las Cruces also was busy between 1915 and 1920. It held a "smoker and lunch" on April 10, 1917 during which the members discussed ways to secure federal and state funds for the construction of roads throughout the county. Less than one month later a committee appointed by the Businessmen's League visited El Paso, Texas. The purpose of their visit was to convince federal officials to make Las Cruces the place where a proposed military camp would be located.[37]

The *Casper Daily Tribune* reported on April 17, 1919 that the next meeting of the Chamber of Commerce was expected to be quite large. It was the first time that women had been invited to attend one of the organization's gatherings. Given the growing involvement of women in all aspects of civic life during World War I, the invitation to some women from this Wyoming community to join the Chamber was not surprising. The women of Casper, however, were a full step ahead of the men. The objective of Chamber members for this particular meeting was to "stimulate interest in the work of the club" and to outline plans to push subscriptions for the Fifth Liberty Loan program. A number of women from the city already had met at the Henning Hotel in order to lay out their own plans for helping to raise part of the $575,000 needed to complete the nation's Liberty Loan drive. They were enthusiastic, and they fully expected to raise their share "with the same expediency which has characterized other drives in the county."

Businessmen and women also were promoting their community's development in larger cities. The ever-eager boosters of San Diego had been instrumental in pushing for the "Panama–California Exposition" after the Panama Canal opened in 1914. They remained active well into 1916, raising funds to keep the Exposition up and going in order to attract more visitors and business to their city. The Chamber of Commerce was poised to double its membership from 1,068 to over 2,500. Its leaders also pushed to reorganize the group and launched a campaign to portray themselves as a "community building organization." "The Chamber of Commerce membership is not a donation," readers of the October 31, 1915 edition of the *San Diego Union* were told. "It is a safe investment." Progress could be made only if citizens had faith in the organization and business people contributed not only their money but also their labor to the cause of promoting San Diego.

In the midst of all the excitement over the Exposition, 48 local business people mounted a "Nimble Dollar Day" sale that took place on October 7, 1915. In what was described as a "friendly rivalry" among the participating merchants, "nearly every store" was prepared "to dispose of new goods recently arrived from the East." The *San Diego Union* story went on to say that "unless all signs fail, something will be started today that will continue during the remainder of the year, and that something will be the beginning of prosperity." Every "loyal San Diegan" was called upon to do their part, because "on the success of Dollar Day depends the success of many days to come."

It made good patriotic and business sense in 1915 for officers of the Commonwealth Trust Company of Pittsburgh to offer a United States flag to any school child who opened an account of $10 or more. Having been drawn into the great war in Europe, bank officials noted that "America now, more than ever before, needs thrifty people."[38] Other activities unrelated to the war effort but equally beneficial to Pittsburgh's long-term development also were initiated at this time. The local Chamber of Commerce threw its support behind the "good roads movement" and pledged to cooperate with local and state officials during "Good Roads Day." According to the report in the May 23rd edition of the *Pittsburgh Post*, thousands of volunteers from the city and suburbs were expected to work on roads and bridges in less-traveled parts of the metropolitan area.

The other major event reported on in that issue of the newspaper was the conclusion of the "Prosperity Carnival, Made in USA" at the Motor Square Garden. "We have just fairly started in our work of doing something tangible for Pittsburgh and its business interests,' stated Commercial Club President F. J. Kress. "The business men need just such events to stimulate trade and advertise Pittsburgh."

Ten years later, various groups of business people were still hard at work. A new office building for physicians was opened. Forty doctors were paying rent to support the stock they owned in the $250,000 structure. The Sixth District Association of the Graduate Nurse's Association of Pennsylvania, in the meantime, pledged $33,600 for the construction of a club building for their organization. Plans for the building were spelled out at a banquet hosted by public and private leaders who said they would need $50,000 to complete the project. Owners of a drug company asked the City Council for a bit more time to move out of their current building. Although this would postpone plans to widen and repair the street on which the property was located, the Department of Public Works was inclined to grant the waiver. A much larger real estate deal was completed for the downtown area. It entailed the transfer of the former YMCA building and several other properties to a developer who planned to put a new store and office building on the site. The land was sold to the developer for $3,000,000.

The Pittsburgh Association of Credit Men announced that they had raised $41,000 for a fund to fight commercial fraud at a luncheon held at the University of Pittsburgh Faculty Club. At the same time, representatives of the Chamber of Commerce, calling themselves "The Trade Crusaders," continued their tour of Pennsylvania towns. They met with members of the local Chamber of Commerce at each stop and discussed commercial opportunities with them. The local meetings were sponsored by different Kiwanis and Rotary Clubs.[39]

Among the local groups meeting in New Orleans on March 24, 1925, according to the *New Orleans Times-Picayune*, was the Business and Professional Woman's Club. Also announced in that issue of the newspaper were plans for the "Clean-Up" campaign in the city. The Civic Bureau of the Association of Commerce had divided the city into five districts and was soliciting support for the forthcoming program. The New Orleans Federation of Clubs, which consisted of women's organizations, publicly endorsed the clean-up campaign. They also admonished the State Highway Commission for holding closed-door meetings about a bridge project, called upon the police department to enforce the law against crowding in movie theater aisles and be more attentive to the condition of traffic signals, and called upon the US Congress to make a study of water resources that were available for New Orleans.

The Young Men's Business Club of New Orleans and several committees of the Association of Commerce met during August and September
of 1925. The New Orleans Public Service Baseball League and the
Laundry Dry Cleaning Baseball League completed their respective
schedules for the season. The fifth annual "Community Dollar Days" sale
also was announced in the August 19, 1925 edition of the *New Orleans
Times-Picayune*. It was held each year at this time in order to stimulate
trade during "the summer slump" and featured large discounts on a wide
array of items.

"Civic Enterprise" after the Great Depression

The involvement of business leaders in civic affairs at the end of the 1920s
did not drop off perceptibly during the Great Depression. If anything,
they increased their activities and public appeals for cooperation.
What happened in Idaho Falls appeared to be representative of what was
happening across the country at that time.

The local Chamber of Commerce continued to promote new projects,
hold banquets, and even issued a report on traffic accidents in 1927. It
included a list of tips on how to be a good driver and ways to avoid
running into other cars or pedestrians. The construction of the new Hotel
Bonneville that year was heralded "as a monument to the zeal and devotion of enterprising citizens" in Idaho Falls.

Increasingly this meant women, too. Idaho Falls sent 80 local women
to a district convention of the Business and Professional Women's Club
in 1927. The Women's Association announced one year later that it
would sponsor a woolgrower's exhibition in Idaho Falls. "Lamb Week"
was endorsed by the Chamber of Commerce which had all shops in the
city decorate their windows in a "lamb motif." Local restaurants added
mutton and lamb to their menus.[40]

Already one year into the Great Depression, the Chamber of Commerce sent letters to over 100 citizens commending them for beautifying
their homes and property during the past year. This yearly campaign was
endorsed by the local newspaper and involved a competition and review
of candidates by a team of judges. Its committees continued to meet and
lay plans for promoting Idaho Falls businesses.

The Chamber investigated price gouging by certain gasoline dis-
tributors in 1931. Its members threatened to set up a "gasoline
cooperative" if prices were not lowered and the principle of receiving
"fair profits" was not returned to practice. They also made an effort to
acquire more highway construction funds from Washington, DC that
year and encouraged local business owners to number their buildings so

that mailmen and prospective clients could more easily locate their establishment.[41]

Their efforts that year were capped by the city's "first annual Hospitality celebration."[42] Crowds estimated at between seven and ten thousand persons attended the festivities. They came from all over the valley to participate in different contests, sample various performances and foods, watch motorboat and surf board exhibitions on the Snake River, enjoy precision flying by members of the Army Reserve Corps out of Salt Lake City, and take in a grand parade. No fewer than 30 organizations participated in the parade, and the array of floats, bands, and drill teams was said to have put on quite a show for all the spectators. The celebration's sponsors included "the co-operative creamery, the county granges, the chamber of commerce, and civic organizations." The two-day affair closed with a massive fireworks display on the evening of September 17.

Florence, Alabama's Chamber of Commerce made a big push to help persons obtain federal loans for housing in 1935. The members of the organization's housing committee took this unprecedented step because there was a serious shortage of housing in the city and local efforts to deal with the problem had thus far proven disappointing. The Chamber also launched a campaign in collaboration with the Tennessee Valley Authority to raise $6,000 for economic development and infrastructure work. Included among the proposed projects was work on wharves and an effort to limit soil erosion from local farmlands.[43]

The Masonic Temple in Burlington, Vermont opened its doors to the General Motors Acceptance Corporation in February of 1936. "This concern," the local newspaper reported, "renders financial aid to purchasers of General Motors products." Local boosters held a "Burlington Day" celebration on September 3 of that year. It drew approximately 15,000 persons. Those in attendance were treated to music, horse races, a contest to select the best cattle from the surrounding area, a pet show, and a parade. Just before Thanksgiving, however, the director of Burlington's Chamber of Commerce resigned from his position because he did not believe that other members would give a hearing to the proposed Hudson–Champlain Seaway.[44]

Members of the Junior Chamber of Commerce in Valdosta, Georgia felt reinvigorated in 1936. They had launched three different initiatives and made progress with all of them. There was the subscription drive for a local baseball franchise, a campaign to promote street lighting, and the formation of a committee whose only responsibility was to aid cotton growers and wholesalers. Local business leaders also pushed for a stronger Christmas-buying season that year.[45]

More than in times past, however, their energy was spent petitioning one or another state and federal agency with authority or money that could help them pull Valdosta out of the Depression. The Jaycee Shell Committee met in the offices of the *Valdosta Times* on December 1, 1936. Their object, according to an account in that newspaper, was to come to an agreement over the construction of a basketball facility at the local high school. The new building could host tournaments for teams coming from across southwest Georgia and serve as a convention site for up to 1,500 persons. They estimated that it would bring in $1,000 a year. That sum, when combined with federal assistance, would have enabled the city to liquidate its share of the debt within six years. It was considered a "civic enterprise."

Tobacco growers and "others interested in tobacco culture" met in Valdosta's courthouse on December 16 in order to consider proposals being submitted to the Georgia legislature. They coordinated their activities with persons from Virginia, North Carolina, and South Carolina. For their part, the Chamber of Commerce came out against a proposed increase in the state's tobacco tax early in February 1937. By mid-February, the Chamber also had initiated an effort to have the State College of Agriculture send "extension" workers to help revive the local cotton industry.

Despite all their hard work, local farmers were unable to deal with the problems they faced. Many expressed an interest in forming a "Progressive Club" which, like other groups of its kind, was dedicated to improving farm techniques. However, they also learned to turn to the federal government for help. A story in the February 18, 1937 edition of the *Valdosta Daily Times* indicated that farmers had begun submitting applications to the Farm Credit Administration of the federal government for emergency crop and feed loans. Looking to Washington for answers was something that many groups would end up doing for the remainder of the twentieth century.

The Great Depression of the 1930s and the gradual shift from a peacetime economy to a wartime economy at the close of that decade and into the early 1940s did nothing to discourage local business and civic groups from continuing their good civic works. The size and focus of those efforts, on the other hand, definitely changed. Voluntary associations became more specialized in the services they provided, and they tended to target smaller groups for whatever funds they doled out. Almsgiving became something that the federal government did.[46] It provided "handouts" to the poor in the form of food and rent allowances, job training, medical assistance, and outright grants in bigger lots, more consistent dosages, and, at least until recently, with fewer strings attached than many local charities ever did.

This was a big change, but it was not unprecedented. After all, the federal government had helped to subsidize industries like the railroads and make it possible for settlers to plant new towns across its territory for a long time. It first flexed its charitable muscles in behalf of widows and orphans during the Civil War. During and after World War II, however, the federal government would become more aggressive in planning and executing such activities. It became an important patron of many more "civic enterprises" and assumed risks in promoting development projects that had once been taken on by local business leaders.

In terms of its impact on the urban scene, the federal government spawned something political scientist John Mollenkopf has called a "progrowth coalition." This coalition consisted of public and private groups that had a vested interest in promoting the development of urban and suburban areas, and it was responsible for putting together the federal programs and subsidies which pushed this process along. Public agents in the progrowth coalition were "political entrepreneurs" in that they used federal regulations and resources to support highly speculative ventures.[47] There were institutional caretakers and officials at all levels of government who acted like entrepreneurs. At the local level, however, those who were the instigative guts of development plans and served as the backbone of progrowth coalitions were said to be part of a political "regime" that favored economic expansion and big rebuilding campaigns.[48]

Great arguments are waged today over just how much impact these "regimes" have on the outcome of redevelopment campaigns and whether they help anyone other than the patrons of construction and rehabilitation projects. It seems pretty clear that the schemes which are hatched or fueled by these political regimes in different cities do make a difference. Local politics matters, and hometown politicians influence the content and direction of building campaigns. Developers may be more or less pleased by the outcome of all the wheeling and dealing that they do with local political entrepreneurs, but they are obliged to play along and cut the best deals they can.

It is the view of most social scientists who have studied various regime-inspired or federal development projects that business people and investors cut very good deals indeed. In fact, they are believed to get all or most of the goodies that can be grabbed whenever a regime goes into action. The city as a whole and the poorest of its residents are seen getting few of the benefits and having to put up with a lot of the grief that comes with these projects. In short, business people and investors are interested in revitalizing cities, but only if it means they can make a lot of money and do not have to be hassled by the peasants who live around their castles.

This is a rather sour view of business leaders and wealthy persons and the part they play in civic affairs at the end of the twentieth century. Yet there is more than enough anecdotal evidence in the person of high-rolling developers and tax-dodging investors to put flesh on the cynical bones laid bare by academic writers and political activists. Tearing down worn out but otherwise viable neighborhoods in many inner cities after World War II made a number of persons wealthy or saved persons who already were wealthy some money on their taxes by investing in risky ventures. How it made cities a more congenial place in which to live or work is less clear. On the other hand, the expense and pain endured by persons who were pushed from one place to another in order to make room for the grand designs of would-be developers and their public partners were real enough.[49]

It has been hard to make a convincing case that some transcendent good was served by many of the redevelopment projects launched after World War II. Indeed, some persons who approve of these efforts or benefit materially from them all but dismiss the idea that rebuilding campaigns need to be defended on those grounds. They think it romantic, even silly perhaps, to speak of redevelopment serving a larger "public good." Expecting a new building to contribute to the commonweal may be necessary to promote the project, but it is a hope without much foundation. It is good enough that properties are recycled and cities are refitted to satisfy the demands of a more modern economy.[50]

We used to think differently about cities and attempts to make them bigger or grander. Persons acted as if they were contributing to a greater good, and there was no reason to think that they did not believe what they were saying. The groups they represented often made a very public show of their contribution and left the clear impression that they were risking a great deal in making it. Sometimes they even went out of their way to share some of the risks and rewards of leadership with less powerful or wealthy groups.

If private leaders after World War II have been unwilling to risk more themselves or to share the risks and rewards that come with building cities with more persons, then there must be some good reasons for it. Part of the problem may be that private leaders grew less attentive to the need to make bold gestures or to put themselves at much jeopardy. It was just too easy to run to the federal government for help and too much trouble to slog it out in the trenches with the plebs. Having behaved this way, they should have been less surprised by the skeptical looks and catcalls they got when they stepped before the public and proclaimed that their acts were good and their hearts pure.

Another part of the problem, however, may be that the picture of elite participation in civic affairs that we have been fed is woefully incomplete, maybe even intentionally so. After all, we have seen some evidence that local business leaders were involved in civic projects right through the Great Depression. This appeared to be the case in a variety of cities, and it was not confined to the South whose communities sometimes are portrayed as being more receptive to business leadership.[51]

The civic involvement of elite, professional, and business persons did not end after World War II. Furthermore, it persisted in areas that had nothing immediately to do with rebuilding the city or improving its economy. Much more of what mercantile and corporate leaders were doing during this period, though, was related to economic development activities. When seen supporting a worthwhile social activity, elite members of the community usually were wearing a tuxedo or signing a check. If they donated funds to small groups, it was done quietly so as not to encourage others to bother them. More of the money they donated openly went to larger service organizations like the United Way or to major cultural institutions like the city symphony.

Many good causes in Pittsburgh were aided on February 28, 1945. The head of the local chapter of the American Red Cross praised the Heinz Company and the Howard Heinz Endowment for contributing $130,000 toward its campaign to raise $3,600,000 at the end of the war. People's Natural Gas Company was to begin its pledge drive in behalf of the Red Cross that same day. A luncheon sponsored by the group entitled Children's Charity and Women's Work featured a "sew" for the benefit of the city's hospitals. Finally, the Pittsburgh Section of the National Council of Jewish Women was working hard to put European refugees in touch with their American relatives and friends.[52]

A big parade marked the start of yet another campaign in Pittsburgh to raise funds for War Bonds. Many downtown businesses cooperated with this effort just as they had in the past. One of the new marketing techniques they used this time was to set aside one full hour when their employees sold nothing but bonds in their establishment. Businesses were supporting more than the war effort, however. Corporate gifts to the United Negro College Fund Drive, for instance, were reported to have doubled this past year. Local sponsors announced that they almost had reached their goal of $75,000.[53]

Boston business leaders in 1946 were no less concerned than they are today about the availability of parking for city workers and would-be shoppers. A number of them met at the Hotel Statler one evening, according to a story in the *Boston Globe* on February 26th, and described the parking situation as "intolerable." They proposed to build a huge garage beneath the Boston Common to help alleviate some of the problem. Once constructed it would have been the world's largest garage. It may no longer hold that distinction, but it is still pretty big.

The Manchester Dental Society declared on the pages of the

Manchester Union Leader on November 14, 1951 that its members wanted the city to put fluoride in the water supply. They were said to be prepared to "fight" with the Manchester Water Works to see that it happened.

Managers of Boston's World Trade Center joined with members of the Greater Boston Chamber of Commerce in sponsoring a "trade and travel" mission to sell Boston's culture and business to European nations. The story in the April 4, 1958 edition of the *Boston Globe* indicated that the purpose of the trip was to promote New England as a business, tourist, and cultural center for people from abroad.

The Chamber of Commerce for Hackensack, New Jersey declared in 1960 that it was pleased with relations between it and the city council. It also voted to support the city's attempt to change the location of the proposed Bergen–Passaic Expressway traffic interchange. Members of the local Lion's Club discussed plans to realign the bus terminal for New York's Port Authority so that the influx of commuters might be handled more efficiently. Finally, the guest speaker at the luncheon of the Bergen County Christian Businessmen's Committee issued a challenge to all persons in business to accept Christ.[54]

The *San Francisco Chronicle* reported on January 25, 1959 that 56 pounds of dust had been kept out of the sky each day last week thanks to a huge "vacuum cleaner" recently installed on the chimneys of the Bethlehem Pacific Coast Steel Corporation. A little more than two weeks later, the Down Town Association complimented the Bay Area Pollution Control District for its diligent efforts to relieve "the smog evil" from the skies above San Francisco. In the meantime, a man surveying the city for possible sites to redevelop declared that national investors were unwilling to give much money to underwrite projects in San Francisco because citizens showed no great interest in supporting a big rebuilding campaign.[55]

Participants in a seminar sponsored by the Mortgage Bankers Association in St Louis were treated to a discussion about the advantages and disadvantages of large urban renewal projects in 1962. They decided that large-scale projects were to be preferred over smaller, piecemeal developments. A little more than one month later, 50 business and civic leaders formed a new St Louis "town club."[56] This group and other business persons from the city had good seats from which to view all of the large projects undertaken by the "political entrepreneurs" who ran the Land Clearance for Redevelopment Authority in the city right up into the early 1970s. By then, they reached a much different conclusion about the advisability of undertaking large renewal projects.[57]

Larry Otis asked business and civic leaders of Tupelo, Mississippi to support the new Tupelo Vocational and Industrial Training Center that was scheduled to open in October of 1963. It was to be part of Itawamba

Junior College. Mr Otis, who was going to be the facility's director, made his plea at a luncheon sponsored by the Civitan Club of that city. There were 650 unemployed persons in the surrounding county who could use such an institution, he declared. That did not include all the persons who were "not now realizing their full job potential" or "who may be displaced by automation" in the future. Local support would be crucial, because "there's no Santa Claus in Washington" for this kind of facility.[58]

Hundreds of applicants lined up for job interviews at the Freedom House in Roxbury, one of Boston's historic neighborhoods, in December of 1964.[59] They were responding to a unique job recruitment program begun by eight Boston businesses that wanted to hire qualified black residents. The prospective jobs ranged from porters and mail clerks to sales representatives and advertising managers.

The Second Reform Church in Hackensack, New Jersey added a noon-time service during Lent "for the convenience of the business communities" and others who could not attend evening services in 1969.[60] This happened nine years after the representative of the Bergen County Christian Businessmen's Committee had urged all his listeners to accept Christ.

On a slightly more patriotic note, the Akron Board of Trade Council launched a new civic project on January 25, 1970. Its members planned on distributing a copy of the Bill of Rights to every classroom in Summit County. Editors of the *Akron Beacon Journal* also saluted "Junior Achievement Week" during its sixth anniversary. The newspaper reported that 1,000 teenagers from around the area gathered each evening to operate their own small businesses.

The Pittsburgh area Community Chest announced that it had raised $500,000 from local contributors in 1973. Another $1,500,000 came in from the federal government to provide services for local residents.[61]

A federal commission in June of 1977 recommended that the city of Chicago "set up a citizens committee as a means of ending frustration and hopelessness, rage and violence" in the city's Puerto Rican community. Two months later the *Chicago Tribune* carried a story in which it was alleged that several stable neighborhoods in the city had been "sentenced to death" by area financial institutions. These neighborhoods were near places where minority persons lived, and bankers had "redlined" them so that no new mortgage applications would be approved for houses sold there.[62]

Tupelo, Mississippi "didn't have a four-lane highway linking it to the rest of the world" until 1994, but it had amassed an impressive array of large corporations with national and even international markets.[63] Credit for this belonged to the Community Development Foundation, "an industry-seeking organization created by local businesses." Companies that had brought offices and plants to Tupelo were uniformly upbeat about the city's prospects and respectful of the work done by the Community Development Foundation. One even commented upon Itawamba Junior College, which by this time was "considered one of the top two-year technical schools in the country." Sometimes investing in one's community really paid off.

Doing Good by Doing Well

Elite community members and local businesses never completely abandoned difficult civic enterprises. Near the end of the twentieth century they still were involved in campaigns to promote what some persons called "human capital investment." This was to distinguish these efforts from "brick and mortar" projects which entailed building something. In any case, many of the attempts to invest in humans were directed toward young persons and undertaken in collaboration with public agencies.[64]

Boston, like many other cities, has a program each year in which the city government and local businesses try to provide summer jobs for thousands of inner-city teenagers. The Massachusetts Pre-Engineering Program and Wentworth Institute of Technology run a program called "Urban Girls Excel in Math and Science" or "Urban GEMS" which is funded by Nynex and a grant from the US Department of Education. As its title suggests, their collaborative effort is designed to entice young women to study math and science. It has counterparts in other cities across the United States. The Urban League of Massachusetts operates a "state-of-the-art Technology Center" in a troubled neighborhood in Boston. Intended to help local residents acquire skills that will help them secure better jobs, the Center's work is underwritten by a large grant from Bell Atlantic and a smaller grant provided by the city.[65]

The Boston Red Sox initiated two programs during the late 1990s that were designed to help young persons and, by extension, the whole city. In the first program, the organization donated 1,250 tickets to the team's home games for youngsters who read lots of books over the course of the summer. The second program fell a lot closer to the team's mission: playing good baseball. The Red Sox sponsored something called the RBI League or "Reviving Baseball in Inner Cities." Along with a number of groups and adults from several of the city's more rundown neighborhoods, the corporately sponsored league helped to inspire other leagues to make a comeback. In 1998 alone, some 30 leagues in the city worked with 11,000 boys and girls between the ages of 13 and 18. Youngsters not only learned how to play a team sport and hold friendly competitions with other teenage athletes, they also came to know other youngsters from their neighborhoods much better than they had in the past and push troublemakers off of city parks and playgrounds.[66]

These were valuable programs, and their sponsors should have garnered more praise for their good works. The point is that business leaders and elite persons were seen doing much less of this kind of "human capital investment" at the end of the twentieth century, and they became involved in fewer risky civic enterprises than they had in the past. Local corporations appeared reluctant to assume the same obligations they had in earlier times, and they actively courted the federal government for money to help pay for the problematic ventures they still were willing to take on. More and more, they seemed dedicated only to clean and non-controversial campaigns in behalf of museums, orchestras, libraries, the Red Cross, and United Way.[67]

Corporate leaders and business people were observed paying much more attention to deals that held the promise of making or saving them a great deal of money. Included among these deals have been attempts by property owners to establish taxing districts which provided funds for services to keep an area safe or looking cleaner. Major retailing stores or even whole shopping complexes have returned to inner-city neighborhoods abandoned by similar businesses decades ago. The owners of existing businesses in the city have been seen taking over properties whose most recent tenants had engaged in illicit or unsavory ventures, and some large banks have created investment funds that are intended to help new businesses to take root in less well-to-do neighborhoods.[68] By the end of the twentieth century it had become acceptable practice for business leaders and wealthy persons to claim to be doing good simply by doing well.

However satisfied investors and business owners may have been with this line of reasoning, many city dwellers simply were not buying it. Nor were less wealthy or powerful groups inclined to embrace the utilitarian logic that filled other persons' pockets while leaving their own empty. City dwellers did not object to business people making a profit. They were less than thrilled by profits which were judged too big, came with little effort, or were not plowed back into useful community enterprises.[69] All of these fell into the category of "unfair profits" and were countered by serious legal challenges and grassroots resistance by local citizens.

Elected officials in many cities across the United States have worked hard in recent years to develop ways for some of these profits to be returned to the community as a whole. Or, they have tried to ensure that grassroots groups had a chance to influence the content of development projects. In taking such steps, public leaders simply were turning the clock back to a time when a community's most elite residents, merchants, and corporation owners had made such gestures part of their everyday business routines.

It is no coincidence that a number of these subsidized services or facilities were supposed to help poor persons. Nor is it an accident that "community development corporations," which are set up by groups in poor neighborhoods and are supposed to help rebuild those areas "from the ground up," are built upon the same logic that informed the entrepreneurial schemes of early American merchants.[70] Make an investment in one's company an investment in one's community. Share the risks. Make a fair profit. Spread around some of the wealth.

These also happen to be the same principles which have made commercial communalism work as well as it has. Community development corporations, for all their faults and practical limitations, extend that logic in a creative way and down the city's social ladder. Their mere existence is testimony to the fact that no great gulf separates capitalism and community building.[71] Persons who live in one or the other of these two worlds can learn to work together on important matters, despite differences in their rhetoric. Much to the dismay of academic writers who would prefer neighborhood residents to take more aggressive stands against redevelopment plans, capitalists and activists build their arguments around similar ideas.

This is good news, but it should not be much of a surprise at this point. Earlier in the book I alluded to the term *embourgeoisement* and described how historians use it to account for the way working-class persons learn how to behave by watching persons who are a bit higher on their community's social and economic ladder. I argued that the process of learning how to be part of a bourgeois civic culture is shared, albeit unevenly, by groups found at every level of a town or city's social hierarchy. Not all groups will collaborate or even like each other, but they do teach each other how to behave and monitor each other's progress. I referred to this process as "parallel play."

Parallel play is important, because it exposes us to rules that are supposed to guide the way we act. The ultimate accomplishment of parallel play, however, is to prepare us for the time when we will play together. Parallel play may be good, but team work is better.

In America, the groups whose rules first guided our play, either together or apart, were run by the mercantile and elite leaders of colonial towns. I referred to their game and way of getting along as *commercial communalism*. The groups most closely identified with this way of building communities defined what a bourgeois civic culture was and who played a part in making it. They also laid out rules for how the game was to be played and how to keep score so that everyone could figure out whether their team was winning or losing.

The traditional leaders of American towns and cities had their pre-ferred way of playing the civic culture game and building communities. It did not take long for them to figure out that other persons did not want to play the same way they did and might have other ways of keeping score. Much to their credit, these same traditional leaders found ways to incorporate different players, to accommodate themselves to alternative ways of conducting the game and building communities, and in keeping score.

We have not always played well together and often argue about whose versions of the rules and style of play are more effective or commendable. Still, we usually work out our differences by the end of the game. At least we seem to have so far.

It is a credit to early-American community leaders that we still play a game and build our civic culture in ways that they would recognize. To be sure, our game is faster and more complicated. Our equipment is more extensive, and our strategies for winning sometimes defy any kind of conventional logic. The parks we play in are different sizes, and many of the players no longer speak English. But the game still works. The reason it works as well as it does, and has done so for such a long time, is that commercial communalism provided a really good way to make a civic culture inside towns and cities.

By the early nineteenth century, America was already becoming a bigger and far more diverse country than the founding fathers had settled. Their preferred way to build communities did not work as well as it once had, or at least it needed to be supplemented with additional ways for groups to learn from each other and to collaborate on important matters. The subscription campaigns of colonial America had grown into much larger and more ambitious charity crusades, and joint stock companies now dealt with projects and products as varied as the groups which created or used them. Leadership was no longer something that only the rich and well-born could exercise. Representatives of other groups made strong and convincing claims for membership in the community of believers.

Happily, the newer players pretty much accepted the rules and prin-ciples behind community building which the founders of American towns and cities had embraced. Commercial communalism had firmly taken root. It was the model for all other types of community building that subsequent Americans and would-be Americans would use.

The connection between commercial leaders and ethnic groups is clear, but not always pretty. American labor history is replete with episodes in which the members of different racial or ethnic populations fought when they had to compete for the same jobs. It may have been the fault of employers who set workers of different nationalities against each other in order to keep wages down and their work forces docile. Nevertheless, they did fight.

A few observers have noted occasions when business leaders reached out to the members of different ethnic groups in a more positive way. The principal motivation for employers to act more congenially was undoubtedly economic. Laborers from the same ethnic group could communicate more easily with each other and might respond more favorably to supervisors who came from the same country. This made it easier to teach them good work habits and increased their loyalty to the company. Still, it also had the effect of integrating them more fully into the life of the larger community. At times, it even may have helped them develop better relations with workers whose nationality was different from their own.[72]

There were moments as well when business leaders and more well-to-do persons collaborated with persons from different ethnic groups on matters outside the workplace. This did not happen everywhere. Historian Helena Flam has written that a more democratic culture existed inside smaller cities which were founded by manufacturing entrepreneurs.[73] Class antagonisms between well-to-do or professional natives and the artisans or unskilled laborers who came from different ethnic groups were muted in these places. Part of the reason was that ethnic workers were paid comparatively well. A more important reason, at least in Flam's mind, was the fact that credit institutions established by the city's more prosperous residents made a point of loaning money to ethnic workers so that they could acquire their own homes. Rates of home ownership for artisans and professionals or business persons in Patterson, New Jersey during the late-nineteenth and early-twentieth centuries, for instance, were essentially equal. Each held approximately 40 percent of the mortgages handed out in the city. Unskilled workers held the remaining 21 percent of the mortgages.

Political alliances between traditional leaders in cities and up-and-coming ethnic groups also were known. Geoffrey Blodgett and Robert Kolesar, writing about ethnic politics in Boston and Worcester, Massachusetts, have noted that Protestant elites in both cities struck a series of political deals with working-class Irishmen during the latter half of the nineteenth century.[74] The specific issues at hand or the details of their arrangements were less important than the fact that their collaboration brought an air of moderation and civility to politics in those cities for several decades. It also enabled elite politicians to continue to make a credible connection between their private preferences and their service in behalf of a broader public interest.

Local elites in some cities continued the practice of reaching out to help newcomers who were the members of distinct ethnic groups throughout the twentieth century. Sometimes they were instrumental in having the immigrants come to their city in order to fill a big hole in the local workforce. On other occasions, they just tried to do the best they could with persons who were dumped in their laps. This was the case in Cleveland, Ohio near the end of World War II when families of Japanese Americans were shipped to that city and community leaders worked hard to help them settle into their new surroundings.[75]

The connection between the way commercial leaders preferred to build communities and the way consumers are organized as a communal force has been explored much less and is not understood well. Nevertheless, shoppers and investors really do shape larger communal routines and make the places we live better or worse for having been there. One of the more obvious ways in which this connection has been accomplished in towns and cities across America is through the purchase of houses. Home ownership has long been held to be a crucial expression of how less well-to-do persons can literally "buy into" the capitalist system, and Americans have done a comparatively good job of helping each other to purchase their own home.

Helena Flam's study of how business people and professionals in Patterson, New Jersey promoted home ownership among working-class ethnic residents through mortgage companies provides a lovely illustration of how this process can work. To the extent that commercial communalism was made credible by sharing risks and rewards, then "spreading the wealth" by making home ownership readily available to persons stacked on the lower rungs of the city's social ladder was a good way to accomplish both ends simultaneously.

Historian Terrence McDonald has said that "home ownership tied a broad cross-section of the American population to 'booster politics,' which mobilized support for the investments and services of the 'promotional' city" favored by the community's elite members. This was accomplished by arguing that everyone "would profit in the long run from economic development that increased population growth and thus property values."[76] Home buying and other types of shopping extend an important piece of the logic built into commercial communalism to individuals who might not otherwise have a chance to play bigger roles in the local civic culture.

It is not hard to demonstrate a connection between commercial leadership and local governance. Civic leaders stopped being public officials a long time ago, but both often have shared a common view of the world and collaborated on the best ways to bring their vision to life. Indeed, there have been many moments throughout the history of American cities when "the distinction between commerce and civic improvement became increasingly blurred."[77] It is not a coincidence that principles articulated in commercial communalism would still hold considerable sway in city governments today.

Historians like Jon Teaford pay homage to the moment when traditional urban leaders ceded control of public institutions to groups with less status. They certainly are right to note the importance of the Progressive Era and all the structural and procedural innovations which upper-class business people and middle-class professionals brought to city governments. Teaford in particular has done a great service by showing how the logic of sharing risks (and tax revenues) made it possible for public services to be spread to more private citizens than had heretofore been possible. The brief sketch of commercial involvement in civic affairs offered in the present chapter indicates that public institutions created by better-off persons probably are committed to keeping these services, even if their former patrons are not.

The involvement of business and civic leaders today may be limited to only a few issues beyond urban redevelopment, but they have not fallen off our civic radar screens. Even when their interests are confined largely to matters of rebuilding cities, however, some corporate and business leaders can do a better job of spreading the wealth around than most persons expect. That certainly appears to have been the case in St Louis during the 1970s and 1980s when several major companies collaborated with local officials and some community groups in order to rebuild the neighborhoods that surrounded their headquarters. They did not run to the suburbs, and the neighborhoods look much better today. Furthermore, they also have a more racially and economically mixed residential population than at any other time in their history.[78]

In many other cases, unfortunately, business leaders have reduced their public exposure and accountability. That was not a good thing to do, because it created the impression that they were anxious about their status inside cities.[79] They may have been less anxious about themselves and more eager to extend their bourgeois civic culture to new groups than observers appreciate, but the effect was bad nonetheless. The same rich and well-born persons who were responsible for showing everyone else how to make communities now appeared uninspired by their own creation. They looked more interested in making safe business deals and limiting their personal liability than in taking on risky civic enterprises.

It has always been harder to build a community than to throw up a building. These leaders forgot that in community building it is never *just* about the money.

NOTES

1 *Boston Gazette*, February 15, October 11, and October 19, 1810.
2 *Daily Free Press*, May 10, 1848.
3 *Carolina Spartan*, July 10, August 21, August 28, and September 25, 1856.
4 *Nebraska Republican*, June 2 and December 21, 1866.
5 *Omaha Republican Weekly*, April 8, 1868.
6 Ibid., February 12, February 19, and April 8, 1868.
7 *San Diego Union*, July 2, 1874; June 28, 1877; March 9, 1883.
8 *Daily Argus*, May 25, 1886.
9 Ibid., July 24, 1886.
10 Ibid., November 2, November 4, November 12, and December 13, 1886.
11 *St Cloud Daily Times*, August 2, 1889.
12 *Sunday Chronicle*, September 21, 1986.
13 *San Diego Union*, January 30, 1895.
14 Ibid., January 3, February 11, April 9, April 28, May 1, May 26, June 1, and July 27, 1895.
15 Ibid., August 4, 1895.
16 Richard Alcorn, "Leadership and Stability in Mid-19th-Century America: A Case Study of an Illinois Town," *Journal of American History*, Volume 61, Number 3, December 1974, pp. 685–704; John Ingham, "Rags to Riches Revisited: The Effect of City Size and Related Factors on the Recruitment of Business Leaders," *Journal of American History*, Volume 63, Number 3, December 1976, pp. 615–37.
17 Carl Bridenbaugh, *Cities in Revolt: Urban Life in America, 1743–1776* (London: Oxford University Press, 1971), pp. 102–3.
18 Ibid., p. 253.
19 Emile Durkheim, *The Division of Labor in Society* (New York: Free Press, 1969); Talcott Parsons, *The Structure of Social Action. Volume I: Marshall, Pareto, and Durkheim* (New York: Free Press, 1968), pp. 308–13.
20 Nancy F. Cott, "Eighteenth-Century Family and Social Life Revealed in Massachusetts Divorce Records," *Journal of Social History*, Volume 10, Number 1, Fall 1976, pp. 20–43; Nancy F. Cott, *The Bonds of Womanhood* (New Haven, CT: Yale University Press, 1997); Mary P. Ryan, *Women in Public: Between Banners and Ballots, 1825–1880* (Baltimore, MD: Johns Hopkins University Press, 1992).
21 Harvey Molotch, "The City as a Growth Machine: Toward a Political Economy of Place," *American Journal of Sociology*, Volume 82, 1976, pp. 309–33; Joe R. Feagin, *Free Enterprise City: Houston in Political and Economic Perspective* (New Brunswick, NJ: Rutgers University Press, 1988); Sharon Zukin, *The Culture of Cities* (Oxford: Blackwell Publishers, 1995); Peter Hall, *Cities of Tomorrow* (Oxford: Blackwell Publishers, 1996); John Rennie Short, *The Urban Order* (Oxford: Blackwell Publishers, 1996); Anton C. Zijderveld, *A Theory of Urbanity: The Economic and Civic Culture of Cities* (New Brunswick, NJ: Transaction Publishers, 1998).

22 Richard Brown, "The Emergence of Urban Society in Rural Massachusetts, 1760–1820," *Journal of American History*, Volume 61, Number 1, June 1974, pp. 29–51; Sally Griffin and Clyde Griffin, "Family and Business in a Small City: Poughkeepsie, New York, 1850–1880," *Journal of Urban History*, Volume 1, Number 3, May 1975, pp. 316–38; John Ingham, "The American Upper Class: Cosmopolitans or Locals?" *Journal of Urban History*, Volume 2, Number 1, November 1975, pp. 67–87; William Issel, "Business Power and Political Culture in San Francisco, 1900–1940," *Journal of Urban History*, Volume 16, Number 1, November 1989, pp. 52–77; Terrence McDonald, "Rediscovering the Active City," *Journal of Urban History*, Volume 16, Number 3, May 1990, pp. 304–11; Melanie Archer, "Small Capitalism and Middle-Class Formation in Industrializing Detroit, 1880–1900," *Journal of Urban History*, Volume 21, Number 2, January 1995, pp. 218–25.

23 McDonald, "Rediscovering the Active City"; Karen Sawislak, "Relief, Aid, and Order: Class, Gender, and the Definition of Community in the Aftermath of Chicago's Great Fire," *Journal of Urban History*, Volume 20, Number 1, November 1993, pp. 3–18.

24 *San Diego Union*, January 30, 1895.

25 Raymond Mohl, "Humanitarianism in the Preindustrial City: The New York Society for the Prevention of Pauperism, 1817–1823," *Journal of American History*, Volume 57, Number 3, December 1970, pp. 576–99; Mark Haller, "Urban Crime and Criminal Justice: The Chicago Case," *Journal of American History*, Volume 57, Number 3, December 1970, pp. 619–35; Lois Banner, "Religious Benevolence as Social Control: A Critique of an Interpretation," *Journal of American History*, Volume 60, Number 1, June 1973, pp. 23–41; Kenneth Kusmer, "The Functions of Organized Charity in the Progressive Era: Chicago as a Case Study," *Journal of American History*, Volume 60, Number 3, December 1973, pp. 657–78; Edward Pessen, *Riches, Class, and Power Before the Civil War* (Lexington, MA: DC Heath, 1973); Amy Drustanley, "'Beggars Can't Be Choosers': Compulsion and Contract in Postbellum America," *Journal of American History*, Volume 78, Number 4, March 1992, pp. 1,265–93; Paul Boyer, *Urban Masses and Moral Order in America, 1820–1920* (Cambridge, MA: Harvard University Press, 1978); Eugenie Ladner Birch and Deborah Gardner, "The Seven Percent Solution: A Review of Philanthropic Housing, 1870–1910," *Journal of Urban History*, Volume 7, Number 4, August 1981, pp. 403–38; Jane Pease and William Pease, "Social Structure and the Potential for Urban Change: Boston and Charleston in the 1830s," *Journal of Urban History*, Volume 8, Number 2, February 1982, pp. 171–96; Marian Morton, "Seduced and Abandoned in an American City: Cleveland and Its Fallen Women, 1869–1936, *Journal of Urban History*, Volume 11, Number 4, August 1985, pp. 443–70; Susan Ellis and Katherine Noyes, *By the People: A History of Americans as Volunteers* (San Francisco, CA: Jossey-Bass Publishers, 1990); Martin Daunton, "Middle-Class Voluntarism and the City in Britain and America," *Journal of Urban History*, Volume 22, Number 2, January 1996, pp. 253–63.

26   John Higham, "Hanging Together: Divergent Unities in American History," *Journal of American History*, Volume 61, Number 1, June 1974, pp. 5–28; Ralph Luker, "Religion and Social Control in the 19th-Century American City," *Journal of Urban History*, Volume 2, Number 3, May 1976, pp. 363–8; Zane Miller, "Scarcity, Abundance, and American Urban History," *Journal of Urban History*, Volume 4, Number 2, February 1978, pp. 131–55; David Hammack, "Problems of Power in the Historical Study of Cities, 1800–1960," *American Historical Review*, Volume 83, Number 2, April 1978, pp. 323–49; Neil Lebowitz, "'Above Party, Class, or Creed': Rent Control in the United States, 1940–1947," *Journal of Urban History*, Volume 7, Number 4, August 1981, pp. 439–70; David C. Hammack, *Power and Society: Greater New York at the Turn of the Century* (New York: Russell Sage Foundation, 1982); Geoffrey Blodgett, "Yankee Leadership in a Divided City: Boston, 1860–1910," *Journal of Urban History*, Volume 8, Number 4, August 1982, pp. 371–96; Robert Kolesar, "Worcester, Massachusetts in the Late 19th Century," *Journal of Urban History*, Volume 16, Number 1, November 1989, pp. 3–28.

27   Thomas Bender, "The Erosion of Public Culture: Cities, Discourses, and Professional Disciplines," in Thomas L. Haskell (ed.), *The Authority of Experts: Studies in History and Theory* (Bloomington, IN: Indiana University Press, 1984), pp. 84–106.

28   Daniel J. Monti, Jr., "Legend, Science, and Citizenship in the Rebuilding of Urban America," *Journal of Urban Affairs*, Volume 15, Number 4, 1993, p. 310.

29   Dorothy Ross, "American Social Science and the Idea of Progress," in Haskell, *The Authority of Experts*, pp. 157–75; David A. Hollinger, "Inquiry and Uplift: Late 19th-Century American Academics and the Moral Efficacy of Scientific Practice," in Haskell, *The Authority of Experts*, pp. 142–55.

30   Norton Long, "The Citizenships: Local, State, and National," *Urban Affairs Quarterly*, Volume 23, 1987, p. 7; Norton Long, "The Paradox of a Community of Transients," *Urban Affairs Quarterly*, Volume 27, 1991, p. 13.

31   William H. Wilson, *The City Beautiful Movement* (Baltimore, MD: Johns Hopkins University Press, 1989).

32   *San Diego Union*, January 17, 1905.

33   Ibid., April 21, 1905.

34   *Fairbanks Daily News Miner*, June 18, 1910.

35   *Fairbanks Daily News Miner*, December 20 and December 29, 1910.

36   *Muncie Evening Press*, December 29, 1915.

37   *Rio Grande Republic*, January 5, 1915; April 10 and May 25, 1917.

38   *Pittsburgh Post*, May 15, 1915.

39   Ibid., May 13, May 20, May 28, and June 14, 1925.

40   *Idaho Falls Post*, April 26, September 29, and November 21, 1927; September 20, November 16, and November 25, 1928.

41   Ibid., October 19, 1930; January 14 and March 3, 1931.

42   Ibid., September 16, 1931.

43 *Florence Times*, February 9 and February 11, 1935.

44 *Burlington Free Press and Times*, February 27, September 3, and November 11, 1936.

45 *Valdosta Daily Times*, December 7, 1936.

46 Ralph M. Kramer, *Voluntary Agencies in the Welfare State* (Berkeley, CA: University of California Press, 1981).

47 John H. Mollenkopf, *The Contested City* (Princeton, NJ: Princeton University Press, 1983).

48 Clarence N. Stone, *Regime Politics: Governing Atlanta, 1946–1988* (Lawrence, KS: University Press of Kansas, 1989); Christine Cook and Mickey Lauria, "Urban Regeneration and Public Housing in New Orleans," *Urban Affairs Review*, Volume 30, Number 4, March 1995, pp. 538–57; Paul Kantor, Hank Savitch, and Serena Vicari Haddock, "The Political Economy of Urban Regimes: A Comparative Perspective," *Urban Affairs Review*, Volume 32, Number 3, January 1997, pp. 291–318.

49 Social scientists have produced many studies detailing the disruptive effect which big-city rebuilding projects and federally assisted suburban developments have had on residential neighborhoods in cities and the persons who lived there. Among those who have laid out the clearest picture of the social consequences of these campaigns are the following: Herbert J. Gans, *The Urban Villagers: Group and Class in the Life of Italian-Americans* (New York: Free Press, 1962); Elijah Anderson, *StreetWise: Race, Class, and Change in an Urban Community* (Chicago: University of Chicago Press, 1990); Hillel Levine and Lawrence Harmon, *The Death of an American Jewish Community* (New York: Free Press, 1992); Scott Cummings, *Left Behind in Rosedale: Race Relations and the Collapse of Community Institutions* (Boulder, CO: Westview Press, 1998). Also see: J. Michael McGuire, "Is the St Louis Redevelopment Program Fiscally Beneficial?" *Journal of Urban Affairs*, Volume 12, Number 2, 1990, pp. 103–21; Margaret Collins, "Rejoinder to: Is the St Louis Redevelopment Program Fiscally Beneficial?" *Journal of Urban Affairs*, Volume 12, Number 2, 1990, pp. 121–9; Robyne Turner, "Growth Politics and Downtown Development: The Economic Imperative in Sunbelt Cities," *Urban Affairs Quarterly*, Volume 28, Number 1, September 1992, pp. 3–22; Stacy Warren, "Disneyfication of the Metropolis: Popular Resistance in Seattle," *Journal of Urban Affairs*, Volume 16, Number 2, 1994, pp. 89–108.

50 Michael Goodman, "Cities, Corporations, and the Culture of Redevelopment," unpublished doctoral dissertation, Department of Sociology, Boston University, 1999.

51 Don Doyle, "The Urbanization of Dixie," *Journal of Urban History*, Volume 7, Number 1, November 1980, pp. 83–92; Clyde Haulman, "Changes in Wealth Holding in Richmond, Virginia, 1860–1870," *Journal of Urban History*, Volume 13, Number 1, November 1986, pp. 54–71; Philip Funigiello, "The New Deal in the Urban South," *Journal of Urban History*, Volume 16, Number 1, November 1989, pp. 99–103.

52 *Pittsburgh Post-Gazette*, February 28, 1945.

53 Ibid., April 30 and August 6, 1945.

54   *Bergen Evening Record*, January 11, March 26, and April 30, 1960.

55   *San Francisco Chronicle*, February 10, 1959.

56   *St Louis Post-Dispatch*, February 21 and March 25, 1962.

57   Daniel J. Monti, *Race, Development, and the New Company Town* (Albany, NY: State University of New York Press, 1990), pp. 25–41.

58   *Tupelo Area Journal*, August 2, 1963

59   *Boston Globe*, December 16, 1964.

60   *Bergen Evening Record*, February 14, 1969. A story in the January 12, 1998 edition of the *Boston Globe* described a much bigger resurgence in religious discussion groups among modern workers. As reporter Diego Ribadeneira saw it, the business people and their employees were "driven by a search for meaning unsatisfied by bigger paychecks or lofty promotions, and a desire to reconnect with their faith." As a result, "white-collar workers are crowding breakfast prayer meetings and lunchtime Bible studies in conference rooms and university clubs." Sometimes the businesses themselves sponsored the meetings. This was occurring not only in Boston but across the country.

61   *Pittsburgh Post-Gazette*, February 14, 1973.

62   *Chicago Tribune*, June 21 and August 8, 1977.

63   *New Orleans Times-Picayune*, January 1, 1995.

64   Jay Jurie and Cynthia Jurie, "Youth and National Urban Policy: The Florida Experience," *Journal of Urban Affairs*, Volume 14, Number 2, 1992, pp. 109–24; Marion Orr, "Urban Regimes and Human Capital Policies: A Study of Baltimore," *Journal of Urban Affairs*, Volume 14, Number 2, 1992, pp. 173–88; Alice O'Connor, "Community Action, Urban Reform, and the Fight Against Poverty: The Ford Foundation's Gray Areas Program," *Journal of Urban History*, Volume 22, Number 5, July 1996, pp. 586–625; Stephan Samuel Smith, "Hugh Governs? Regime and Education Policy in Charlotte, North Carolina," *Journal of Urban Affairs*, Volume 19, Number 3, 1997, pp. 247–74.

65   *Boston Globe*, May 28, August 7, and November 25, 1997.

66   Ibid., August 11 and August 8, 1998.

67   *Boston Globe*, April 21, 1997. Julian Wolpert and Thomas Reiner, "The Not-for-Profit Sector in Stable and Growing Metropolitan Regions," *Urban Affairs Quarterly*, Volume 20, Number 4, June 1985, pp. 469–86. Older and larger not-for-profit organizations get only about one-third of their annual revenues from contributions or dues. Most of their funds come from the sale of services or reimbursements from the federal government for services rendered to clients. Many groups draw on large endowments to support ongoing or new programs. These funds usually were acquired early on in the life of the organization. Thus, well-to-do patrons are not required to put themselves out too much when supporting even these activities.

68   *Boston Globe*, April 3, April 6, and September 6, 1997; May 28, 1998. It can be difficult to pull off these kinds of reinvestment strategies. See: Caren Grown and Timothy Bates, "Commercial Bank Lending Practices and the Development of Black Owned Construction Companies," *Journal of Urban Affairs*, Volume 14, Number 1, 1992, pp. 25–42. Specialists in urban affairs

are fond of tracing the development of Business Improvement Districts or
BIDs to the 1970s. See: Zukin, *The Culture of Cities*, p. 33. However, the
principle of allowing property and business owners to set up a special taxing
district so that they can get additional city services has a much longer
history. The operation of several special assessment districts was alluded to
in the present chapter. Historian Jon C. Teaford, in *The Unheralded
Triumph: City Government in America, 1870–1900* (Baltimore, MD: Johns
Hopkins University Press, 1984), p. 297, has argued that every major city
with the exception of Boston "relied heavily on special assessments to help
finance street improvements" during the last two decades of the nineteenth
century.

69 Monti, "Legend, Science, and Citizenship."
70 Pierre Clavel, *The Progressive City* (New Brunswick, NJ: Rutgers University
Press, 1986); Steven Soifer, "The Burlington Community Land Trust: A
Socialist Approach to Affordable Housing?" *Journal of Urban Affairs*,
Volume 12, Number 3, 1990, pp. 237–52; Peter Dreier and W. Dennis
Keating, "The Limits of Localism: Progressive Housing Policies in Boston,
1984–1989," *Urban Affairs Quarterly*, Volume 26, Number 2, December
1990, pp. 191–216; Louise Jexierski, "Neighborhoods and Public–Private
Partnerships in Pittsburgh," *Urban Affairs Quarterly*, Volume 26, Number
2, December 1990, pp. 217–49; Teresa Herrero, "Housing Linkage: Will It
Play a Role in the 1990s?" *Journal of Urban Affairs*, Volume 13, Number
1, 1991, pp. 1–20; Richard DeLeon, "The Urban Antiregime: Progressive
Politics in San Francisco," *Urban Affairs Quarterly*, Volume 27, Number
4, June 1992, pp. 555–79; Tony Robinson, "Gentrification and Grassroots
Resistance in San Francisco's Tenderloin," *Urban Affairs Review*, Volume
30, Number 4, March 1995, pp. 483–513; Janice Tulloss, "Citizen
Participation in Boston's Development Policy: The Political Economy of
Participation," *Urban Affairs Review*, Volume 30, Number 4, March 1995,
pp. 514–37; Christine Cook and Mickey Lauria, "Urban Regeneration and
Public Housing in New Orleans," *Urban Affairs Review*, Volume 30,
Number 4, March 1995, pp. 538–57; Randy Stoecker, "The CDC Model
of Urban Redevelopment: A Critique and an Alternative," *Journal of Urban
Affairs*, Volume 19, Number 1, 1997, pp. 1–22; Rachel Bratt, "CDCs:
Contributions Outweigh Contradictions, a Reply to Randy Stoecker,"
Journal of Urban Affairs, Volume 19, Number 1, 1997, pp. 23–8; W.
Dennis Keating, "The CDC Model of Urban Redevelopment, a Reply to
Randy Stoecker," *Journal of Urban Affairs*, Volume 19, Number 1, 1997,
pp. 29–34.
71 The idea that a built-in contradiction exists between capitalism and community building is central to much contemporary thinking in the social
sciences. See: Joe Feagin and R. Parker, *Building American Cities: The
Urban Real Estate Game* (Englewood Cliffs, NJ: Prentice-Hall, 1990); Stella
Capek and John Gilderbloom, *Community Versus Commodity: Tenants
and the American City* (Albany, NY: State University of New York Press,
1992); Todd Swanstrom, "Beyond Economism: Urban Political Economy
and the Postmodern Challenge," *Journal of Urban Affairs*, Volume 15,

1993, pp. 55–78; Stephen McGovern, "Cultural Hegemony as an Impediment to Urban Protest Movements: Grassroots Activism and Downtown Development in Washington, DC," *Journal of Urban Affairs*, Volume 19, Number 4, 1997, pp. 419–44.

72   William Kornblum, *Blue Collar Community* (Chicago: University of Chicago Press, 1974); Tamara Hareven, "Family Time and Industrial Time: Family and Work in a Planned Corporation Town, 1900–1924," *Journal of Urban History*, Volume 1, Number 3, May 1975, pp. 365–89.

73   Helena Flam, "Democracy in Debt: Credit and Politics in Patterson, New Jersey, 1890–1930," *Journal of Social History*, Volume 18, Number 3, September 1985, pp. 439–62.

74   Blodgett, "Yankee Leadership in a Divided City"; Robert Kolesar, "Worcester, Massachusetts in the Late Nineteenth Century," *Journal of Urban History*, Volume 16, Number 1, February 1989, pp. 3–28.

75   N. J. Demerath and Rhys Williams, "Between 'Town' and 'City': Religion and Ethnicity in Political and Economic Development," *Journal of Urban History*, Volume 19, Number 4, August 1993, pp. 26–62; Thomas Linehan, "Japanese American Resettlement in Cleveland During and After World War II," *Journal of Urban History*, Volume 20, Number 1, November 1993, pp. 54–80.

76   Terrence McDonald, "Rediscovering the Active City," *Journal of Urban History*, Volume 16, Number 3, May 1990, p. 306.

77   Teaford, *The Unheralded Triumph*, p. 189.

78   Daniel J. Monti, *Race, Redevelopment, and the New Company Town* (Albany, NY: State University of New York Press, 1990).

79   Robert Buroker, "From Voluntary Association to Welfare State: The Illinois Immigrants' Protective League, 1908–1926," *Journal of American History*, Volume 58, Number 3, December 1971, pp. 643–60; Nicola Beisel, "Class, Culture, and Campaigns Against Vice in Three American Cities, 1872–1892," *American Sociological Review*, Volume 55, February 1990, pp. 44–62.

9

Some Sort of Americans

Boston can be warm and a little muggy in August, but that's not what had Raymond Saintangelo all steamed up in 1996. "The yuppies," he had to concede, "they're good people." Problem is "they can't keep their mouths shut. They complain about the noise, about everything."[1]

The "noise and everything" that riles the "young urban professionals" who began moving into the North End in the late 1970s centers on the six Italian "festas" which take place on successive weekends in August and early September every year. It must be conceded that these are big and noisy affairs. Music and dancing can last well past midnight. Parking on the street, which is always in short supply, is made even harder on these weekends. Firecrackers are set off, and the air is heavy with the smell of sausages, onions, and calamari.

Complaining to any of the ten private men's clubs that actually run the feasts would have accomplished nothing for the newcomers, so they mobilized the North End Waterfront Neighborhood Council to petition City Hall in a vain attempt to end the street festivals. That tactic only managed to anger the long-time residents.

Domenic Strazzullo, president of the Sant Agrippina Di Mineo Benefit Society, said that "when we go to these city meetings, we let them know it's not gonna die. Just like you don't screw around with Mother Nature, you don't screw around with tradition. This is about the love we have for the saint and the love for family." Mr Strazzullo's words were heart-felt. Unfortunately, all this feeling was lost on the yuppies who do not live with their families and apparently have no great need for saints. No harm actually came to the persons who complained about the feasts, but the idea that it might certainly occurred to them. After all, this is still a neighborhood where a black family that tried to take up residence a few years ago was harassed until it left. The owner of an objectionable business found his shop set on fire, and local troublemakers are still kept in line with the help of a little "street justice." Nothing like that has happened to any of the yuppies, who are more annoying than they are dangerous. The presence of these young men and women is tolerated as long as they keep quiet. The streets still belong to the Italians.

It is important that the Italians know how to manage the streets, and their ability becomes most evident during the local festas. St Anthony's feast, the largest and oldest of the North End affairs, can draw up to 100,000 visitors to the neighborhood. There have been some changes over the years, but older members of the St Anthony di Padia da Montefalcione Society are pleased to have turned the leadership of their 150-man fraternity over to some younger and energetic men in the neighborhood.[2]

The tourists who came in 1998 to see local residents carry a statue of their patron saint up and down the narrow streets of the city's oldest neighborhood were not disappointed. Band members dressed in white shirts and blouses and wearing matching hats led the way as they always do. That year, at least, the custom of having only men carry St Anthony around on their shoulders was amended so that one or two women also took a turn at lifting the statue and caring for the streamers covered with dollar bills as they paraded through the neighborhood for over four hours.

The marchers used to stop at many buildings, play a few tunes, get some refreshments, and push on to another location. Now they stop at fewer places, and sometimes the party turns into a more private affair. At one family compound on Michelangelo Street, the statue of St Anthony was set gently on the ground and a favorite priest offered a special blessing to the family that was their host. Drinks and food prepared by the women were offered to band members and their guests. The men of the family shot off fireworks from the roof of one building and dropped confetti from another. White doves were released as the band offered a musical tribute to its host. The statue was then reclaimed with a few more dollars pasted to it, and the procession continued its march back down the hill. The family and their guests stayed behind and were treated to even more special foods and wine in what turned out to be a grand family reunion, complete with family patriarchs receiving tributes from everyone in attendance and a bunch of children running around making a great deal of noise.

Tourists are not invited to the family parties, and they do not attend the masses that still are offered in Italian to honor these saints or the Madonna. They also do not know that the money stuck to the statues will be used to support the men's clubs that actually run the festas or to the local charities they endorse. They come only to watch the spectacle, enjoy the free concerts, and sample Italian foods that are dispensed from booths set up at certain spots in the neighborhood. The yuppies, for their part, either leave for the weekend or shut their windows.

To walk the streets of the North End on these weekends is to be transported back to a time and to a way of life that is cherished by those who have lived there for several generations. It also is valued by the members of Italian-American organizations like the Renaissance Lodge of the Order Sons of Italy who live throughout the greater Boston area but return for many events and meetings in the North End. Dr Dean Saluti, who is president of the lodge, is proud of the several hundred men and women who belong to his group. Most of them are accomplished professionals and business owners. Just like the neighborhood men's clubs, his organization also contributes to charities and cultural institutions that are based in the North End.

Pictures taken of the neighborhood before 1920 show an unending row of buildings four and five stories tall lining both sides of the narrow streets that wind their way through the neighborhood. Most of the structures had shops or restaurants on the first floor and apartments above them back then. They still do, and the neighborhood looks much the way it did during the early twentieth century. Yet life as the North Enders had come to know it has been changing for some time.

Only one-third of the area's population in 1990 was Italian American. Ten years earlier more than half of the neighborhood's population had been of Italian descent. Moreover, the Italian American people who stayed in the North End were not being replaced by large families with children. By 1990, over 16 percent of the neighborhood's 11,000 residents were more than 60 years old. No other neighborhood in Boston had so large a share of its population filled by elderly persons.[3]

The appeal of the area to younger professionals is unmistakable. It is close to the central business district, and it has many amenities that unmarried persons seem to like. The smaller apartments found in the area apparently do not cramp their style of life. Nor have the yuppies been discouraged by the higher rents which came with the end of rent control in 1996. Many Italian-American families with children prefer to have more living space today and can afford to pay for it. On the other hand, elderly Italian Americans are finding it increasingly hard to lay out rent money that is two and three times greater today than it was only a few years ago.

Italian Americans know that their grip on the neighborhood is slipping. They have seen this happen before, and they do not like it. At the same time, they also know that there is little they can do about this situation. The yuppie invasion, such as it is, is only expected to grow larger in the coming years. How well the outsiders get along with "the real

North Enders" remains to be seen. However, the neighborhood is likely to remain a good place to live as long as the Italians control the streets. It has been that way for more than 50 years.

We know this because during the late 1930s the North End was the site of a classic study about life in an ethnic "ghetto." William Foote Whyte did the research for *Street Corner Society* during the height of the Great Depression when he was a graduate student at Harvard. Until the book was published in 1943, most persons believed that inner-city neighborhoods like the North End were as disorganized as their residents were poor. Whyte discovered that the neighborhood actually had "a very strict social order built around churches, social and political clubs, and corner gangs." The working-class and poor Italian Americans who lived in the neighborhood built the groups that Whyte observed. Whatever these organizations were doing apparently worked out well. Although nearly 40 percent of adults in the North End were unemployed and the area had more than its share of shady enterprises and criminals, it "was one of the safest places in the city" to live.[4] That is one thing about the neighborhood which has not changed.

Old-timers still mourn the loss of another neighborhood located just a block or two away from the North End. It, too, was home to a great many Italian Americans. In fact, the West End was portrayed as an Italian-American enclave by sociologist Herbert Gans in his well-known book *The Urban Villagers*. Yet it also was home to a robust mix of Poles, Albanians, Jews, Ukrainians, Greeks, a few elderly Irish families, and a smattering of newcomers who were "bohemian" types, singles males, "broken families," squatters, and some persons who worked in nearby medical facilities.[5]

Until the early 1960s when it was bulldozed and "renewed" to make room for an expanding central business district and more up-scale tenants, the West End was the most socially diverse neighborhood in the city. It had been a good place to live.[6] All the different persons who were there had no difficulty accepting each other. Given Boston's subsequent reckoning with racial mixing in the public schools and influxes of Asian, Caribbean, and Hispanic immigrants, the "West Enders" could have provided some invaluable lessons in tolerance for everyone else in the city to mimic. They never got the chance.

The Italians are far from the only cultural group in Boston that is proud of its heritage and ready to teach other persons how to get along. The Greek Independence Day parade down Boylston Street in 1998 was promoted by 60 organizations and attracted nearly 50,000 spectators. The Puerto Rican Fest has enjoyed a successful 30-year run and attracts tens of thousands who "hail from all Latin American countries" to a vibrant four-day celebration. Hundreds of persons came to Faneuil Hall in 1997 to commemorate Holocaust Remembrance Day, and Israel's 50th anniversary drew thousands of Jewish residents from across the area to Boston Common in order to mark that occasion.[7]

Not to be outdone, members of Boston's black population have been trying to make the annual Kwanza celebration into a formidable display of their growing unity. Civil rights activists in 1998 honored their leaders and reminded the city of how far they have come and have yet to go. The Boston-based Aristo Club for women continued to inspire young persons to learn about the history of black vernacular culture and black leaders. Other black citizens promoted a public debate over the future of Malcolm X's house in Roxbury. At the same time, volunteers from several dozen groups and church congregations worked to renovate Freedom House in Roxbury which served as a headquarters for the city's "civil rights struggle and court-ordered school desegregation of the 1960s and 1970s."[8]

Boston has served as the geographic heart or symbolic focal point for a variety of Asian peoples as well, including Koreans, Thai, and Vietnamese. Chinatown, of course, has been the center for the area's Chinese-American population for some time. Its annual August Moon Festival and New Year's celebration draw thousands to the neighborhood.[9] Like their Italian counterparts, however, they are worried that the continued expansion of the central business district may someday gobble up their neighborhood.

Many of the 6,000 Filipino Americans in the greater Boston area, lacking a residential and institutional enclave of their own, celebrated the 100th anniversary of their homeland's independence from Spain at City Hall Plaza. One Filipino immigrant who attended the celebration noted that "we are much more nationalistic now than ... in the Philippines." The radiation oncologist added that "we were all subject to a brainwashing ... and it was only when I came to the US that I learned about my history."[10]

Among the earliest of the immigrants to reach Boston and develop a sense of themselves as a distinctive people, of course, were the Irish. Some 7,000 Irish Americans were on hand in 1998 for the unveiling of a memorial to the many Irish immigrants who came to the city or died on their way to America during the Great Hunger of the late 1840s. Like the Filipino celebration and Holocaust Memorial, this sculpture also was placed in downtown Boston. To further commemorate their arrival and accomplishments in this country, however, each year several hundred thousand Irish Americans and would-be sons and daughters of Erin assemble along the streets of South Boston for an annual parade on St Patrick's Day. The breakfast held before the parade, which was under the direction of former Massachusetts Senate President William M.

Bulger for more than two decades, became an occasion that elected officials from Massachusetts and aspiring national politicians could not ignore.[11] Pilgrims still walk past the family's modest home in "Southie" and have been treated to greetings and, at least on one occasion, to fresh lemonade and home-made cookies by Mrs Bulger herself.

The point, if it is not yet clear, is that ethnicity remains a vital force in the lives of many persons who reside in and around cities. Parades and feasts may be the occasions when we see the greatest evidence of ethnic persons' continuing commitment to each other and to a certain way of looking at the world. However, many groups work throughout the year to keep ideas and customs associated with their ancestral "people" from passing away. It may be that some of their thinking and practices have changed over the years, or that not so many of them assemble at traditional gatherings today as they once did. On the other hand, many persons have found new ways to express their continuing identification with old worlds long after they became successful in this country. Some immigrants apparently did not even understand what it meant to be the member of an ethnic group until after they arrived in America and discovered that they had a great deal more in common than they ever imagined.

Being ethnic in America is just another way of being American. Building a community around ethnic ideals, customs, and institutions is part of what makes American cities alive and vital. Persons who subscribe to beliefs or customs that have an ethnic origin do not reject the larger culture of which they are a part any more than they stop thinking and acting like an ethnic person simply because they no longer live next door to someone with the same ancestry.[12] Their customs and beliefs are not that shallow.

Being ethnic in America also does not mean that everyone in your group is just like you. They can come from different levels of society and still see themselves as part of the same ancestral people. Furthermore, they do not have to associate only with members of their own ethnic group. They can work and play with a variety of persons outside of their ancestral population and move in settings much different from those they encounter with their fellow ethnic-group members.

Ethnicity entails the open courting or favoring of other persons from one's ancestral "group" no matter what their social status may be. Fellow ethnics share some values that are different from those held by other ancestral populations, and they have a history of working together or attending to each other's interests. The identity of an ethnic group also is strengthened to the extent that persons give a name to their people, offer an account of their common ancestry, and connect themselves to a special place.[13]

This special place in America often turned out to be an "urban village" or enclave. The residents of these places certainly mattered a great deal. What made these neighborhoods good places to live, however, were the organizations and businesses that integrated the residents into a viable community.[14] After all, the persons who lived there frequently did not last as long as the groups and businesses which gave the community its strength and a bigger voice. These "civic associations" also provided individuals with the experiences and means to move into larger social and economic worlds.

It turns out that all of these features enter into attempts by an ethnic people to build a community and contribute to our larger civic culture. In acting the way they do, persons who claim an ethnic identity remain faithful to the principles of *belonging*, *privacy*, and *tolerance* for their view of the world. They emphasize the distinctiveness of who they are, what they believe in, and how a good person is supposed to act.

On Fitting In and Being Different at the Same Time

It is no small irony that Americans have been more uncomfortable with the idea of ethnicity than with its practice. A good way to explain this, I think, is to look at how we worked past our unease over having so many different religious groups in this country. Prior to the American Revolution, it will be recalled, many persons were upset with the moral temper of colonial town life. They bemoaned the decline in church attendance. They also fretted about the proliferation of religious bodies and the splitting of denominations over differences in scriptural interpretation.[15]

No group working by itself could have come up with a workable solution to this problem. A proposal to create a single church, for instance, would not have been taken seriously or kindly. What leaders ended up offering was not a religious accord under which different bodies agreed to look at the world in the same way or to embrace the same rituals. Rather, it was a religious accommodation in which room was made for a variety of beliefs and practices that did not inconvenience other churches or crowd out other theological points of view.

This certainly was a good start. Simply accepting the presence of groups different from one's own, however, did not make it easier for them to build a successful community. Religious leaders were mindful that they also had to learn how to work together. We know that they did this on many occasions. We also know that they softened the harder edges of their religious rhetoric and talked to each other using ideas like mutual respect, hard work, sound moral habits, and prosperity which made no one uncomfortable.

This still left plenty of room for them to advance a special view of how the world had come into being, how it might end, and who, in that event, would get the first and last seats on the ark. The difference is that most of the time they kept these ideas to themselves and did not try to impose them on other groups. Disagreements over theological matters were not trivial, of course, but they also were not allowed to interfere with the hard work of putting a community together. Religious leaders found a way to make peace with each other without sacrificing the integrity of their group.

I submit that ethnic groups in America have done something very much like this. If we were to appropriate the tortured rhetoric used by students of race relations in this country, we might say that ethnic groups managed to assimilate even as they practiced pluralism.[16] They discovered a way to fit in and be different at the same time.

Success came with a price. There have been many occasions when representatives of more established groups tried to encourage newcomers to think and act more like the old-timers or actively punished the newcomers for being different. To a great extent the newcomers actually did become a whole lot more like the persons who already were here. However, they also managed to retain some important ideas and practices that were connected to their native cultures or early experiences in a new land.

In much the same way as persons new to San Diego created organizations which drew former Iowans or New Yorkers together for mutual support, foreigners and their children built part of their new world around old customs, beliefs, and institutions.[17] Old-timers tried to lecture the newcomers about how to be Americans, and the newcomers turned it into a conversation. They might not have liked each other or thought that the other group was as good as their own, but they found a way to work out their differences without sacrificing the integrity of their people.

The good news is that ethnicity has been practiced this way in America before there even was an America.[18] The bad news is that we have yet to accept that fact. Activists and scholars who worry about the future of different minority persons and ethnic peoples in this country are boxed in by their own rhetoric. They are stuck on the idea that ethnicity is an evanescent phenomenon. It may take a long time to dissipate, but the hold of ethnic ideas, customs, and associations on our lives is thought to lessen over time. They believe that all ethnic groups and minority persons give up who they were in order to become something different and better, something more "American" than what they are today. They keep looking for these various groups and persons to reach some sort of accord, when an accommodation not unlike that fashioned by America's different religious bodies has served them so well up to this point.

A basic outline of the accommodation worked out between foreign persons and the rest of us was laid out shortly after they began arriving in large numbers after the first third of the nineteenth century. It did not take long for them to make their presence felt and, in some instances, for more established groups to push back. It was not always pretty, but they managed to deal with each other better than their harsh words and callous actions would have led one to believe.

Jews in Boston declared their intention to hold a meeting in 1840 on the "cruelties" their people had recently endured in Damascus.[19] The "colored citizens" of Pittsburgh held their own convention in 1843 and decided to petition the state legislature to grant them the right of suffrage. There also was a meeting of German Democrats in Pittsburgh that same year. While all good Democrats were invited to attend the rally, our "German friends" were especially welcomed because most of the speeches would be made in that language.[20]

A new organization called "The Union Association" was formed in St Louis in 1854. Its membership consisted of "negroes, slaves, and freemen" and their purpose was primarily philanthropic in nature.[21] The Swedenborgian Society of Portland, Maine might well have been collecting funds to build a new house for their organization at the same time. Two years later they started construction on the $16,000 building.[22]

The *Florence Gazette* published an account on January 4, 1860 of a fair sponsored by "the colored population" of that city. Many of those in attendance were women, and not many white persons showed up. On the other hand, the newspaper was pleased to report that the fair showed a net profit of approximately $246. In May of that year, the public was invited to a lecture on education that was delivered at the German Church of Wheeling, West Virginia. The event's sponsors hoped to begin raising funds that would go toward the establishment of a German–English Institute.[23]

Residents of Cleveland were alerted to the fact on October 10, 1865 that the Jewish celebration known as the "Feast of Tabernacles" had commenced nearly a week earlier and would end the next day. The October 30th edition of the *Cleveland Daily Plain Dealer* carried a story about the Scottish festival of All Hallow E'en which would be held on the following evening. In "the old country" the event was marked by "games and mischievous sports." Pranks, parlor games, ball-pulling, and fortune telling were among the activities expected to take place in their city.

Omaha seemed to be an even busier place for different cultural groups in 1866. German residents were reported to be preparing dresses and masquerades for a great ball sponsored by the German Turners Society. Later in the year the same organization announced that it would take over Gise's Hall in the Republican Block and rename it after their own society. The Scandinavians of the city formed their own association with 36 initial members. Their object was to offer support and "cultivate a spirit of harmony" among the membership. The "colored people" of the city celebrated the anniversary of England's abolition of slavery by forming a procession of carriages in front of the courthouse and holding a picnic on the outskirts of town later that same afternoon. Finally, the Hibernian Benevolent Society of Omaha was formed in order to support its members and to encourage Irish immigration to that city. The parent society of this organization was reported to be in New York City.[24]

An anniversary ball sponsored by the Ladies' Hebrew Benevolent Society of Pine Bluff, Arkansas was reviewed on February 10, 1870. The banquet and dance were said to have made a "brilliant affair" of the evening. It came as no surprise to the editors of the *Pine Bluff Weekly Press* who noted that Jewish residents for some time had made "magnificent contributions to matters of the public."

Picnics were popular social affairs in Pine Bluff after the Civil War, and a number of different groups sponsored picnics for their members. Local Jewish residents were among them in 1872.[25] Earlier that same year the local newspaper also carried a report about how "our colored band" had purchased instruments formerly owned by the "Silver Cornet Band." The newspaper's editors admired "the initiative of the band" and wished them "the best success in their laudable endeavors." Of course, the paper also had carried coded announcements about forthcoming meetings of the local "Q-Klux" Klan for the three weeks preceding the report about the "colored band."[26]

Throughout 1875 Cleveland's major newspaper regularly reported the number of immigrants entering the city and noted the countries from which they had come. It also recorded the number of births according to the homeland of the parents. In the midst of all this counting, the newspaper went to some length to describe what organizations representing persons from these same countries were doing. Local German residents, for instance, took up collections for newly arrived German immigrants. They also formed the German–English School Society which brought together Protestant and Catholic Germans who wanted to learn English. Classes for adults were held in the evening so that persons coming from work could take advantage of them. Classes for children were provided on weekends, in German. Parents asked for these lessons so that their children might "have a knowledge of the language of their fathers." In general, however, the society was intended to help "convert our German people into American citizens, and to assimilate the component parts into a homogeneous whole."[27]

A number of "Irish societies" met during the year. Some of them were connected to the local Roman Catholic diocese. Others were not. The Irish Literary and Benevolent Association, Emmet Guard, Hiberia Guard, and Society of United Irishmen were among the groups that were independent of the church.[28]

Bohemian citizens also were active in 1875. A meeting was held under the auspices of the Bohemian Political Club on January 20th. The Bohemian Democratic Central Committee and Bohemian Workingmen met later that year on August 16th in order to decide which party to support in the upcoming election. The Cleveland Bohemian Brass Band, which was composed of 15 men, held a concert for the public on April 15th. One person who wrote a review of the performance said that the band had made "sweet music." He was "forced to acknowledge that there was something good in Bohemia."[29]

The "colored people" of Wilmington, Delaware celebrated the 18th anniversary of President Lincoln's emancipation proclamation on January 3, 1881. Many attended a service at the African Union Methodist Protestant Church and listened to the joyous music provided by the choir. The *Wilmington Morning News* reported on May 28th of that year that the annual meetings of the church were well under way. Church business was mixed in with healthy doses of "sacred readings, songs, and prayers." Later in the decade, the Irish nationalists gave their eighth annual picnic at Schuetren Park, and the German Mutual Beneficial Association celebrated its tenth anniversary. A new "colored" school was opened in 1887, and like all the other schools for black children in the area it was reported to have a surplus of students.[30]

In the midst of all the church services, lodge meetings, picnics, and lectures held in Sioux Falls, South Dakota in the early 1890s, there still was room for several ethnic groups to make their mark on the community. A literary club was organized for young Scandinavians just before Christmas in 1890. The South Dakota Scandinavian–American Building and Loan Association changed its name to the Cooperative Saving and Loan Company after moving to the city in 1891. There also was a celebration on May 17th that year in recognition of the "Scandinavian Fourth of July."[31]

Editors of the *Argus Leader* pointed out with some pride on March 26, 1891 that the Japanese have "assumed European manners and customs, ... resigned the absolutism of his ancestors and established a representative parliament ... and a free press." They also were coming to South Dakota. Fortunately, these immigrants were not members "of the coolie class." They were merchants who proposed "to build up here an extensive trade in Japanese goods."

Black Americans who lived in the South during the latter part of the nineteenth century managed to build an independent life for themselves despite all the barriers thrown in their way. What is more surprising, though, was the willingness of local newspaper editors to report on their activities and successes. The *Carolina Spartan* described the good time that persons had at a picnic and parade sponsored by the Colored Odd Fellows of Spartanburg, South Carolina in 1891. Another picnic outing to Little Mountain for "the colored people" of the city was described in 1892.

The first report offered by the president of the new Colored Industrial Training School of Spartanburg was given extensive coverage by the local newspaper in 1892. Contributions to the school were described. So, too, was all the good work done with the funds it received. The account in the newspaper observed that the 168 pupils enrolled in the institution took "the usual literary course" as well as carpentry, bricklaying, sewing, housekeeping, and cooking. The editors noted that the school was "doing excellent work in our community."

Mass meetings of the city's black residents and celebrations in behalf of Emancipation Day also were acknowledged. Of the latter the newspaper wrote, "the colored people celebrated ... in a quiet, orderly manner. There was a large crowd in the streets. They went out to the encampment grounds where an address was made by a preacher from Greenville."[32]

Events in South Africa at the top of the new century made their influence felt in Boston. A meeting was held at the Tremont Temple in order to raise money for the British South African Fund in January of 1900. Money acquired for the fund went to widows, orphans, and families of soldiers fighting in behalf of England. German residents of the area also were collecting money for soldiers in this war at the same time. Of course, they were supporting the Boers. A little more than one month later, a letter of acknowledgment and thanks from backers of "the Transvaal cause" was read at a meeting held in Faneuil Hall.[33]

Also taking place that year at the Paul Revere house in the North End was the 23rd annual dance and debutante party sponsored by prominent Jewish families. Like earlier affairs of this sort, the event that year was deemed a "financial and social success." Later that same year, the poor Jewish children of the city were thrown a big party by the federation of Jewish charities.[34]

During June of 1900, a reporter from the *Boston Globe* wrote a story about her excursions into another part of the North End. This section currently was occupied by Italians, about whom the reporter and residents of the city still knew comparatively little. She tried to capture something of the life that these persons led. Although she conveyed the fractured English of her informants in the process, she made an effort to portray her subjects in a favorable light. Part of the story is reproduced below.

> In the month of June, Little Italy bulges with festivals of the church and state. Little Italy seems to enjoy these "feste" exceedingly, although every Italian ... invariably declares, when he speaks of any celebration: "O, at home in Italy all is different; it is mooch better."
>
> When I went down to investigate, I found Guiseppe Ronca ... "Yes we keep Le festa dello Statuto," the Sicilian said ... "like your Fourth of July, only we fire no crackers."
>
> Then he told me of the festival which they were to celebrate on Sunday. It was in honor of "La Madona della Lettera," who is the patron saint of Messina.
>
> This festival is entirely local. It is kept only by those who come from Messina or its outlying suburbs ... Sig Ronca was very proud of this story and told me, in confidence, that the Sicilians were "the mooch nicest Italian people," then sighed for the Messina he had left, where the people decorate their houses with colored lanterns and squares shine at night like gaily colored flower beds.
>
> The Neapolitan padrone, Antonio Ciccone, was less regretful. He liked America. ... On June 22 comes the "Festa di San Pauline" ... but the 13th of June is Antonio Ciccone's great day, because it is the "festa" of St Antonio, his patron saint.
>
> At midnight ... his friends will come and serenade him with mandolin and guitar. On the 13th he will give away to the poor 200 kilograms of bread, he will pay the priest to celebrate masses for the ... dead, and dress three poor Italian children. He also will send a shout to his parents in Italy and to his friends here.
>
> "You coma here on my festa? I shout beer, I shout wine, I shout limonata. I give you ainythin."[35]

We never will know what Paul Revere might have thought about his home becoming the site of debutante balls or, somewhat later in the century, a place where tourists stop to hear a Ranger with the US Parks Service deliver a lecture about life in colonial America. More apparent to us is that many features of immigrant life and ethnic communities which have been studied by contemporary historians and social scientists were well in place by the end of the nineteenth century. Indeed, most of what we know about the immigrant experience and community building as ethnic peoples did it is taken from the history of the late-nineteenth and early-twentieth centuries.

We know that the process of immigration was anything but random, for instance, and that many newcomers were welcomed with unbridled ambivalence, if they were greeted at all. Persons tended to come from certain regions of their respective homelands, particularly those areas where manufactured goods replaced products made by local artisans and large-scale agriculture was not possible. They often came as families or sent for additional family members as soon as they were able. Individual emigrants may not have known each other, though sometimes they did come from the same village or from neighboring towns. In either case, they had at least a rudimentary understanding of each other's beliefs and customs, and they often were received by fellow family members and townsfolk upon their arrival in America. The experience of coming to America did not render immigrant customs and beliefs irrelevant. Indeed, these same foreign ideas and practices often made the transition of newcomers easier or were strengthened by the conditions that newcomers faced.[36]

Not all immigrants were poor or untrained. Some came quite well prepared to enter the commercial and industrial economies of nineteenth-century cities. Their numbers were not great and they may not have been "middle class" by conventional American standards. However, immigrant artisans and small shopkeepers who moved into the commercial world became the backbone of their respective populations and founded many of the organizations whose work was noted earlier.[37]

Business people and professionals eventually gained control of most of these groups, even when they did not create them. Many local lodges and fraternal groups became affiliated with national organizations and pursued the loftier cultural pursuits that often were reported on in the local newspaper. This showed that the up-and-coming ethnic leaders understood what it took to fit into the local cultural scene and were being recognized for their efforts by a larger audience.

There were many other members of minority and would-be ethnic populations who were not fitting in as well, of course. Unlike Neapolitan Antonio Ciccone, whose life as a "padrone" in the North End was good, not everyone who lived there was happy about it. They missed their homeland. They probably were not doing especially well financially or on the best of terms with everyone who lived around them.[38]

This most certainly would have included persons who had lived in America a lot longer than the immigrants had. Speaking in 1913 about the mass of Italian immigrants who recently had come to this country, one theologian was not sure that everything would turn out all right. "Within the next decade," he argued, "this army of strangers will be assimilated. They will be Americans of some sort." The only question was whether "our Protestantism" would "bear the test."[39]

They were not the only persons who worried about the prospects of these immigrants. Many of the newcomers themselves had their own doubts about how they would survive in this country. Churches and religious festivals, working-class lodges and clubs, one's family and friends all provided a modicum of relief and sociability for worn-out laborers. These groups and organizations were a great help and exercised much influence over the lives of community members. At the same time, they were not particularly influential in the city as a whole and could not help the newcomers improve their material standing in any significant way.

It did not help that "immigrant communities" were not necessarily "harmonious" or "united in purpose."[40] Differences in social status, wealth, and power among their residents were played out in America just as they had been in the "old country." There also were limits to the amount of assistance that better-off persons gave to their less well-to-do countrymen. The same was no doubt true of the formal training in running organizations that working and lower-class immigrants got from their more prosperous and mobile peers.

Immigrants certainly were familiar with institutions like the church or local societies that provided assistance to one's townsfolk and family members, and these customs were practiced in America. Independent business owners and self-employed persons or eager politicians may have built and supported many of these organizations in part to make their own future more secure. Nevertheless, ethnic entrepreneurs did help to mobilize some of the less articulate or prosperous individuals from among their countrymen and provided them with a modicum of financial assistance and opportunities to see how organizations were run. In this way, the leaders of ethnic communities introduced their fellow countrymen to the intricacies of an urban way of life in America.[41]

It was not just foreign immigrants who discovered how to adapt their customary ways of thinking and acting to the new world they found in American cities. Black persons, still an overwhelmingly rural and southern population at the end of the nineteenth century, worked hard to adapt their own vernacular culture to the city as they were becoming an urban people during the twentieth century. It is surprising in one sense, given the racist legacy with which they were contending, that black Americans were able to make these changes at all.[42] On the other hand, it is testimony to both the resilience of their everyday culture and the sacrifices their people made that they accomplished as much as they did. They were able to develop a viable middle class around business people and professionals, advanced in local politics, and made some stunning contributions in the arts. Some individuals went on to become wealthy even by American standards and, like their foreign-born counterparts, took on bigger roles in the cities where they lived.

There were moments when the leaders of black communities did a good job bridging the gap between themselves and the much larger number of black working-class and poor persons who lived around them. On many other occasions, however, black leaders either did not or could not reach enough of their peers to make themselves into a viable ethnic people.[43] The result has been to stall the development of an independent black ethnic group in America that is, at the same time, well-connected to the larger community surrounding it.

It seems to Harold McDougall that Baltimore's black leaders have been unable to make up their mind about which of two well-known approaches to improving the situation of black people they should follow.[44] There has been a strong contingent of professionals who want to push for more effective political participation and control over public agencies that serve their people. There also is a healthy tradition of developing vernacular institutions that look more toward their own community for assistance than to outside agencies and leaders. If there is a way to reconcile these two approaches, and clearly McDougall thinks there is, blacks in Baltimore had not yet found it by the 1990s.

McDougall's version of fitting in and being different at the same time for black Americans builds on ideas espoused by two of their own thinkers: Booker T. Washington and W. E. B. DuBois. McDougall has the following to say about their respective points of view:

> Washington was concerned with the role of mediating institutions, those social units of lesser scope and coercive power than the state which have a strong hand in shaping social life and which are deeply rooted in the vernacular community: family, church, university, small business, fraternal association, civic association, and the like. DuBois, younger and a radical, claimed that Washington's emphasis was misdirected and that social and political strategy should focus on confrontation with the racist state, on protest and agitation for reform.

The problem, McDougall suggests, is that these "two distinct lines of thought ... evolved separately." Washington's ideas have been "particularly attractive to the black working and lower classes" who remain tied to the vernacular tradition. DuBois's approach has been articulated most clearly by the National Association for the Advancement of Colored People, which he helped to organize. His greatest supporters have been found among the "upwardly mobile, middle-class, elite, the 'talented tenth' of the community, and particularly the northern black intellectuals, who later became more and more estranged from the vernacular community."[45] No one yet has figured out how to bring all of these persons together.

There is a difference between foreign immigrants who transformed themselves into viable ethnic groups and those populations which either failed to do so or still are struggling to become an ethnic people. It is that more successful groups develop these distinctive ways of building a community and reaching out to the larger society in tandem. They do not treat them as alternative strategies, but as complementary approaches to making a more secure place for their members in American society.

It is important for more accomplished individuals to emerge from an immigrant or minority population. Yet this is only the first step in a much longer and difficult process of transforming an inchoate mass of persons who might come from the same homeland into a viable ethnic people. Middle-class and elite individuals cannot build a community, much less a whole ethnic people, by themselves. They have to find ways to reach downward and bring their lesser-born or less successful countrymen along for more of the ride. The ability to do this on an everyday basis, historian Anthony D. Smith argues, is what distinguishes the modern ethnic group whose members are drawn from all social classes in the larger society.[46] More narrowly fashioned aristocratic ethnicities of ancient societies and some non-industrialized states pull off acts of democratic wizardry only during periods of war and other national calamities.

The development of a modern or more demotic form of ethnicity is built on the broad shoulders of a vernacular community. The organizations, customs, and unifying beliefs that are an integral part of these communities transcend one class and embrace all who would be counted as members. Sometimes the representatives of a would-be ethnic group, like black Americans, show signs that they can build a broad-based community and a collection of leaders that is able to work with their less-esteemed peers. Owing to some special feature in their culture or, for black Americans, their color and history in this country, however, they also may experience more problems in sustaining such a mix.[47]

Persons from a number of foreign countries were able to create this kind of ethnic people in America. The Irish were among the most successful. More accomplished members of this population hammered out a strong sense of themselves as Irish American in large measure because the Catholic church worked so hard to distinguish middle- and upper-class Irishmen from wealthy Protestants.[48] At the same time, however, poorer and working-class Irish Americans were not denied membership in that ethnic group and drew more than a little comfort from being associated with it.[49]

It is not hard to determine why the Irish, or any other ethnic people for that matter, were successful. Families and religious bodies were the bedrock institutions of every would-be ethnic people, and they certainly worked for the Irish. Important as these groups were, though, they could not create a community by themselves. Religious groups and families depended upon other organizations to do a lot of this work, and these associations were constructed on top of the foundation provided by families and the Roman Catholic Church.[50] Lodges, clubs, local businesses, neighborhood and professional associations, and friendship cliques gave structure and voice to the persons who belonged to them or who simply identified with them. The interlocking memberships, individual and collaborative projects they undertook, and values they espoused tied the various segments of the community together and served as a safety net for the persons who lived in their midst.

Creating these groups and institutions is a sign that an ethnic people is in the process of being made and, at the same time, is making a bid for membership in the local community of believers. It does not mean that the members of every ethnic organization will always agree with each other or be able to collaborate on matters of importance to their people. In fact, they often disagree and sometimes fight.[51] This happens even more regularly when the other groups in question belong to another ethnic people.[52] What matters is that their medium of exchange is corporate rather than personal. They act more or less in concert, just like the members of any group would.

Ethnic communalism, like its more mainstream counterpart commercial communalism, is a collective response to the problems and opportunities afforded by life in an urban setting. Indeed, these two ways of building communities and a larger civic culture perfectly complement each other. Proponents of each approach would give different answers to the question of how to build a good community, but the answers that one gave would be strong in precisely the spot where the other's answers were deficient. Common to both approaches, though, would be the idea that groups, not individuals, build the social world that is all around us and keep it in good order. Persons fit into the world and are known by the groups with which they are affiliated. They do not try to make it on their own. Nor do they expect the world to revolve around them.

Business leaders and ethnic groups certainly have distinctive styles and ways of looking at the world. Yet their paths cross on many occasions and their interests are not at all dissimilar. For instance, rotating credit associations and mutual trade associations which many immigrant populations use in order to magnify their economic clout are variations of the voluntary subscription campaigns used by commercial leaders to address their social concerns.[53] Furthermore, the traditional leaders of American cities wanted immigrants and newcomers to fit in, or at least behave as if they could, and the latter were desperate to make a new life for themselves. This helped both parties come to certain understandings about what they might do together and to appreciate what they could better do separately.

One thing that business leaders from different cities apparently have done for many years is to provide financial assistance to organizations which are closely identified with different ethnic groups or minority populations. When the National Urban League held its 88th annual convention in Philadelphia in 1998, for instance, it had a major corporate benefactor in Sears, Roebuck and Company. The theme of this meeting was "black capitalism" and it featured visits by the Vice President of the United States Al Gore, the Reverend Jesse Jackson, and retired astronaut Mae Jemison.[54]

Other well-known organizations such as the NAACP also have received a great deal of help over the years from some of the very business interests which have been the object of petitions and campaigns for better treatment of minority persons. Not all organizations associated with a particular minority population or ethnic people get this kind of support. This is particularly so, for instance, in the case of organizations like the Congress of Racial Equality which apparently never enjoyed the kind of corporate sponsorship that more moderate organizations like the NAACP received.[55]

This kind of assistance by business leaders has come and gone over the years. Companies in most cities during the industrial era tried to manage their own ethnic laborers by subsidizing the work of some organizations that were found in neighborhoods where their employees lived. There was no mystery in what business leaders were trying to accomplish. They wanted to keep their costs down, production up, and employees quiet. It often did not work out that way, and there were many instances when relations broke down and violence ensued.

On the other hand, there were occasions when factory owners worked with their foreign employees in a cooperative fashion and actually facilitated the growing ethnic awareness of the immigrants who worked for them. One notable example of how this union between business leaders and ethnic groups worked out on a daily basis was found in Manchester, New Hampshire. The Amoskeag Manufacturing Company of that city ran a large and successful cotton textile factory. Its owners and managers also constructed and allocated housing, organized work groups inside the plant, and set up after-work activities that reinforced their employees' ethnic identity. Laborers and their families took advantage of these opportunities and created churches and voluntary associations beyond those groups that were established by the company.[56] These organizations complemented ethnic family practices and helped to keep Manchester from experiencing much of the upheaval that other cities witnessed at the end of the nineteenth century.

It did not protect Manchester from labor unrest, of course, any more than similar efforts undertaken by business leaders in other cities stopped strikes or violence from occurring in those places. Persons commenting on the Pittsburgh steel strike of 1919, for instance, seemed surprised and a little embarrassed that their attempts to curry favor with immigrant laborers had not done them more good. In reports issued after the strike, observers described how some immigrant churches and newspapers or agencies which provided assistance to the immigrant community were themselves the beneficiaries of corporate largesse. Despite their disappointment at having failed to exercise greater influence over their employees, business leaders continued to subsidize ethnic organizations or agencies which serviced this population.[57] It probably helped to foster better relations between themselves and different ethnic and minority populations than they could appreciate at the time.

The proliferation of ethnic groups and styles of living in cities, then, was not an accident. Nor was it a coincidence that many organizations, customs, and ideas which one ethnic people claimed as its own mimicked those belonging to persons and groups that have been there a lot longer. More sharing and borrowing was taking place than many of the persons actually involved in the process of building their own ethnic group probably realized. This, too, was part of the experience of fitting in and being different at the same time.

Not Yet in the Twilight of Their Ethnicity

How intact an ethnic group's original values and customs remain after its members have been here for a while is a question that has concerned many persons. Some who have wondered about this believe that an ethnic people borrows so much from the host society that eventually its members come to think and act like everybody else. In short, they do so well at fitting in that they no longer have to be different. Other persons believe that an ethnic identity and ethnic habits are not given up or worn away that easily. They persist and continue to do a great deal of good for the persons who keep them.[58]

Persons who subscribe to the view that ethnicity eventually disappears think that newcomers made themselves into an ethnic people in part because they already had a great deal in common. They also worked their way into ethnicity as a way of adapting to an unfamiliar society. As more of them came to succeed in their new surroundings, however, they worked their way out of being ethnic. They no longer had to think of themselves as being part of a distinctive group in order to make it in America, because they had made it. It is almost as if their ethnicity had been shed like old skin as they pushed and scraped their way into the larger society.

A smaller but nonetheless sizable number of persons think that an ethnic people need not lose its beliefs and customs or give up associations which distinguish them from other groups. Once established, an ethnic way of acting and looking at the world can last a really long time. The collective accomplishment that is ethnicity may not be so easily ignored as many persons believe. It cannot be discarded as one would a pair of stockings with holes in the toes. It is rather more like the hem line on a skirt or coat, rising or falling in response to changes in style and seasons. Even among persons who take this position, though, there is recognition of the fact that ethnicity as it is practiced by immigrants does not last a long time, much less forever.

This much seems clear. One may be born into a population with certain ethnic habits. Yet what it means to think like an ethnic person or to practice customs peculiar to a particular group certainly will change. The types of organizations to which persons will belong during their lifetime may change as well. So, too, may their contacts with individuals both inside and outside their cultural group. Their position on the community's ladder of social classes also may rise or fall depending on how hard they work and how fortunate they are.

How much or little a person identifies with a particular ethnic group depends on a host of factors. It can vary over the course of a lifetime and with one's personal circumstances. It definitely is not confined to working-class persons, and more prosperous individuals do more with their ethnicity than to score style points and a good meal from time to time. The same can be said of the speed and ways in which the members of an ethnic group break into the larger society. They may no longer live in a family compound or speak the language of their forefathers, but they retain more of their cultural beliefs, habits, and associations than is commonly supposed.[59] The point is that ethnicity persists, even as members of an ethnic people find more spots inside the larger society to rest comfortably. It still is used by persons at the end of the twentieth century to make sense of the smaller and larger worlds they occupy.

George W. Gains, who was from Chicago and the presiding elder of the Methodist African Church at the time, met with members of one of their newest churches in 1905. The "colored" people of Sioux Falls, South Dakota had met with obstacles when setting up their church, but they had persevered. According to the account published in the January 25th edition of the *Sioux Falls Daily Press*, Mr Gains gave "an interesting sermon" to this new congregation.

Wausau, Wisconsin continued to recognize the several ethnic groups that lived there at the turn of the century. For instance, the Men's Club of the Norwegian Lutheran Church observed the passing of the old year and coming of the new year in 1908. They enjoyed a musical and literary program along with their evening meal at the church.[60] A story in the *Wausau Daily Record Herald* on March 14, 1908 heralded the start of the Irish-American League and noted the group's involvement in St Patrick's Day celebrations. On January 28th of the following year an Irish-American Club, which may have been the same organization, declared that its membership was composed "of all persons claiming Ireland as their birthplace or the birthplace of their ancestors, regardless of creed." It also announced plans for the next St Patrick's Day celebration and noted that part of the program this year would be held in Wausau's Grand Opera House.

The Beechview neighborhood in Pittsburgh was predominantly Italian in 1915. That year it had a business and residential fair to trumpet its accomplishments.[61] The area was decorated and there were many booths with items for sale. Apparently, the neighborhood also had its own Board of Trade in order to promote commerce with other parts of the city. On October 29th of that year, Pietro Vallone, an immigrant with no other family in the city, died while saving six girls from a spectacular fire at a local factory. His fellow Italians took it upon themselves to hold a public funeral suitable for a hero and to raise funds for a monument. The city council agreed that he had died heroically and paid for the costs of burying him in his adopted city. Even as the Italians of Pittsburgh were solidifying their place in that city, a smaller collection of Italians in Sparks, Nevada was opening their first "mission" with the help of a Father Simeoni from San Francisco.[62]

America's participation in what political scientist Edwin Fedder has called "the first half of the Second World War" prompted a great deal of soul searching on the part of immigrant peoples and natives alike. Their response with few exceptions was to support the United States and to declare their fidelity to an American people. For instance, the Irish Fellowship Club of Fargo, North Dakota endorsed "Loyalty Day" and passed resolutions commending President Wilson for his conduct. A bit later in the war black members of Casper, Wyoming's Second Baptist Church held a reception for their young men who were leaving for training camp. The community's several "colored churches" also formed Red Cross chapters with more than 100 members. President W. M. Dalley stated that their work "would be worthy of notice from citizens of Casper" and "as establishing the fact that there's no 'slackers'" among the town's black citizens.[63]

In the years immediately following the war, different nationality groups took steps to commemorate the contribution of their members in the conflict and to aid their fellow countrymen whose lands were ravaged by the carnage. The Friends of Poland in Boston raised funds for the Polish Relief Fund by staging a musical production and selling souvenir programs to those in attendance. The West End Young Men's Hebrew Association appointed a committee to raise money for a memorial to neighborhood Jews who served in the war.[64]

A mass meeting of "colored voters" was reported in Wilmington, Delaware on July 4, 1922. Those in attendance endorsed candidates for state offices. The chairman of the Colored Women's Republican City Committee also endorsed T. Coleman DuPont for Senator during a large meeting on November 11th at which Mayor Harvey was the principal speaker. Black leaders in Wilmington had things other than politics on their minds in 1922. On October 5th they urged fellow blacks to purchase homes. "A move is on foot," the *Wilmington Morning News* reported, "to educate the colored folk to a point where they will recognize the value, financial, economic, and moral, of owning their own domicile."

A number of cultural groups conducted business in New Orleans during 1925. The German Society held its 78th meeting in January. The purpose of that group was to "assist immigrants in finding employment and aid them to become useful citizens." German persons living in New Orleans also attended a concert and dance at the Labor Temple in February. In March, a group of black citizens announced that they had formed the Eagle Life Insurance Company which they hoped "would add to the material growth of the race in Louisiana." Members of the Young Men's Hebrew Association organized a baseball team, and Italians observed St Joseph's Day. Mexican Independence Day was celebrated in March. Altars found in many homes were decorated for the occasion. The American Church Institute for Negroes met in October. Its objective was to encourage their people "to help themselves." Finally, there was a mass meeting sponsored by the Italian Political Association in November. Those in attendance wanted to recognize efforts to "Americanize" the Latin people of New Orleans.[65]

An "old-time colored camp meeting" was held in Danville, Illinois on June 16, 1925, according to a report in the *Danville Commercial News*. It was organized by three preachers from the African Methodist Episcopalian Church. On September 19th of that year, a Negro Business League was formed in Danville. Its plans at that time were reported to be unclear.

The Parent Teachers Association of Lawrence, Kansas in 1926 announced that it would hold an all-Indian program in cooperation with Haskell Indian College. That college held its annual commencement one week before the University of Kansas conducted its own in June of that year. It also sent 45 representatives that month to the annual Quapau Indian Picnic. The college put out a call in October for persons to volunteer 50 automobiles that could take Indian students to a "Pow-Wow" being held in other Kansas cities. Sufficient transportation apparently was found to carry the young persons to the meetings.[66]

The Pittsburgh Polish Women's Alliance joined 67 other groups in Chicago for an annual convention in 1927. The story of this meeting published in the September 8th edition of the *Pittsburgh Post-Gazette* stated that the larger union had 50,000 women members nationwide. With nearly 7,500 members of its own, the Pittsburgh chapter was the largest in the country. It also sponsored 42 "junior leagues" for younger Polish-American women in Pittsburgh. These groups had just over 2,100 members.

The years between the Depression and the end of World War II were especially difficult for the members of various minority and ethnic populations in larger American cities. Lingering animosities over the control of certain neighborhoods, access to jobs and political clout, and nationalistic sentiments often came to a head on city streets and inside corporate boardrooms or council chambers. Anti-semitic violence grew particularly troublesome in Boston and eventually provoked public and private efforts to combat it.[67] Fights between Irish and Italian gangs were commonplace in that city as well, and the growing presence of black Americans was particularly troubling to Italian Americans in several of the neighborhoods where they had grown accustomed to being in charge.

International tensions stoked fires and fights over ethnic identity in this country well past the end of World War II. They also made groups aware that some of their more parochial concerns and self-imposed isolation would have to be tempered. At least for some of the older ethnic groups, life began to settle down. Near the end of World War II, the *Boston Globe* reported that an assembly of almost 4,000 Greeks was held in Boston's Symphony Hall. They came together to mark the 124th anniversary of Greece's independence from the Ottoman Empire and the liberation of their homeland from the Nazis in 1944. Local Greek leaders were joined by elected officials from both Massachusetts and Rhode Island. Later in the evening of March 26, 1945 the Greek Minister of Information addressed more than 800 persons in the ballroom of the Copley-Plaza Hotel.

It had been reported on September 23 that Lithuanian and Jewish groups also were sponsoring activities in Boston at the end of the war. The newspaper published a story on February 18, 1946 that four Holy Name Societies of North End churches had joined together for the first time. Their goal was to raise $500,000 so that a Christopher Columbus Catholic Center could be built in the neighborhood. Later in the decade, Archbishop Cushing supported the formation of the St Christopher Guild of Greater Boston Taxi Operators. Word of this new organization was issued in the January 7, 1949 edition of the *Boston Globe*. The group was to hold quarterly meetings, have an annual communion mass, and carry out charitable works in the Archdiocese.

In the two decades immediately following the end of World War II, the most impressive transformation of a minority population in the nation's cities of course belonged to black Americans. It also provoked a great deal of animosity on the part of more established ethnic groups whose members sometimes were displaced from neighborhoods they had come to view as their own.[68] In some cases, particularly in the western part of the country, this process also involved persons from Mexico, Central America, and South America. There, too, newcomers worked hard to make a place for themselves in the larger community even as they struggled to define themselves as a distinctive people.[69]

Their struggles to find secure places for themselves have been alluded to before, and I will not add much to the story here. I would be remiss if I did not note, however, that most attempts by black and Latino-American organizations to influence federal officials and courts during the postwar years were undertaken only after local initiatives failed. The St Louis chapter of the NAACP, for instance, threatened to seek a court injunction that would tie up construction projects across the metropolitan area in 1962 only if other efforts to secure skilled jobs for blacks did not succeed.[70] More often than not, minority activists in the 1960s and afterward came to rely on federal agencies or officials to take care of problems that ought to have been handled at the local level.

But for the fact that these black campaigns were designed to move a national audience to action, they would resemble attempts made by earlier minority populations to break into the local economic and political scene. Among these earlier petitioners, none is more prominent than the Irish. Historian John Bodnar observes that their ascension in local politics and their role in creating "political machines" during the nineteenth century had nothing to do with luck. It was hard work mixed with a lot of good sense.

> With occupational mobility limited ... aggressive individuals ... often found it possible to enhance the welfare of their families ... by extending small immigrant-based business ventures into centers of political activity. Thus, much political activity centered around local saloons where information could be exchanged and newcomers could acquire contacts for jobs and even a free lunch. To a remarkable extent both these ventures and political organizations emerged out of the combined efforts of relatives and friends.[71]

Thus it was that political machines were born and the Irish were able to capitalize a number of businesses on the back of government contracts paid for by local tax revenues and "booty" provided by companies whose profits depended upon a special kind of public relief.

Black Americans did not have the luxury of working out local solutions to their problems in this way. Nor, as I noted earlier, were they unified enough to make their petitions effective. Divisions among black leaders and between members of the several social classes represented in city populations made it all but impossible to replicate the successes of Irish Americans.

Despite all of the projects and protests initiated by civil rights groups in Cleveland during the 1960s, for instance, the city's black population was unable to pull itself together. Nearly 2,000 participants in a "national summit conference of Negro leaders" held in Cleveland in July 1968 issued what amounted to little more than an empty threat to the national Republican Party. They demanded that Nelson Rockefeller be its presidential nominee or be prepared for blacks to abandon it for candidates from the Democrat Party.

Less than one week later a gunfight between black nationalists and policemen left three white officers and seven other persons dead. Residents feared a repetition of the rioting that had engulfed part of the city two years earlier; and they turned out to be right. Mayor Carl Stokes, the city's first black chief administrator, went to the neighborhood several days later and met with black and white residents and shop owners. Families and businesses burned out of their buildings as a result of this most recent outburst could only express their frustration with what had happened to them.

The response to this incident was as fragmented in Cleveland as it was everywhere else that had riots during the 1960s. The Antioch Baptist Church initiated what in effect turned out to be its own rotating credit association by loaning money to needy neighborhood residents and serving as a kind of financial counseling center. From another level of the black community one found Thomas Westrepp being named Citizen of the Year by the Omega Psi Phi fraternity. In his acceptance speech, Mr Westrepp said that there was "a need for former slum dwellers to be motivated to preserve and upgrade their new neighborhoods." He appealed to middle-class blacks in Cleveland to assist their fellow brothers and sisters still living in ghettos in this endeavor.

At the same time this was going on, some persons in more established civil rights groups were expressing concern over the rise of the radical Black Panther Party. The extremism of that group and the violence on the part of police which fueled it made them more than a little uneasy. Other commentators were less sure that the Black Panthers were a danger to the black community. Indeed, they viewed the organization as a positive force in promoting a better sense of identity for black Americans.

A threatened split inside the national office of the NAACP was having little apparent effect on the operations of its Cleveland branch. If anything, the opinion that local blacks held of the organization was improving in 1968. Only Cleveland's churches were thought to be doing more to promote better conditions for the city's black residents.[72] It was, as I said, a very confusing picture of a divided political landscape.

Moving Forward by Looking Backward

In one sense, that is the whole point of ethnicity. It is supposed to be confusing. It frustrates every attempt to bring order to the city by throwing novel ideas and ways for persons to associate with each other into a combustible mix of human beings who do not know each other well and might not like each other if they did. By its very nature, however, the practice of ethnicity also throws light on some of the most crucial questions that a people must ask itself if its members are ever to be united.

If the city is properly understood as a place with many voices, then we will better understand the contrapuntal logic of its melodies only once we appreciate the different songs its people sing. Plato understood this very well.[73] That is why he viewed music, particularly choral singing, as a means by which persons reaffirmed their ties to each other. Yet he also saw that music could be used to introduce new, and at times even vulgar, ideas to a community whose members had grown too comfortable with themselves.

Keeping the pot stirred and melodies coming certainly was in the minds of minority activists in Boston during the mid-1980s when they declared their intention to secede from the city. Their plan was to take several neighborhoods and create a brand-new place called Mandela, Massachusetts.[74] It also figured into the decision of a group of gay Irish Americans in 1992 to sue the organizers of the annual St Patrick's Day parade in South Boston after being denied admission to the parade line.[75]

It probably was not what City Councilor Albert "Dapper" O'Neil had in mind when, during a parade through the Dorchester neighborhood, he shared his views about the Vietnamese stores that had opened in his district. "I thought I was in Saigon, for Chrissakes," O'Neil blurted out within earshot of someone making a videotape of the parade for a local television station. "I told them I'd come back tomorrow with the checks."[76] The not-so-veiled reference to welfare checks incensed members of the local Vietnamese community and some of his colleagues at City Hall, some of whose family members had themselves been immigrants not too long ago.

On the other hand, creating noise was exactly what Dr Nancy Caruso and a group of North End citizens and business people had in mind in 1995 when they took on officials managing the "Big Dig" construction project that was making their neighborhood unlivable. Caruso, who was called a "citizen soldier" by the *Boston Globe*, and the group worked tirelessly to ensure that their neighborhood was not buried along with the Central Artery highway which separates their part of the city from downtown Boston.[77]

These activists will likely be disappointed. Ethnic leaders often lose the bigger fights they pick with institutions that have more clout than they do. History also teaches us, however, that ethnic groups do not back down from a good fight, even when they know that the prospects of winning it are small. This is part of what makes them special and important to the city.

Individuals may accomplish a great deal as members of an ethnic people, or they might not. Independent of their personal triumphs and defeats, however, the corporate phenomenon I have called ethnic communalism makes two important contributions to our urban way of life. First, it adds a bit of constructive confusion to larger communal routines. Our lives are enriched and enlivened whenever persons struggle to create a meaningful corporate identity for themselves and to make their view of the world known to groups with no other compelling reason to take them seriously. Second, an ethnic people's claim to a place in the community of believers is made more credible by these good fights, even when they lose. Taken as a package, these two accomplishments make it possible for an ethnic people to be different from other groups and to find a comfortable spot among them at the same time. It also helps to explain how something wound so tightly around traditional practices and ancestral loyalties manages to thrive in a world with an insatiable appetite for everything new and a knee-jerk reaction against anything old.

Our modern society actually makes more space available for the practice of ethnicity than we imagine. Individual persons – whether they are acting as citizens, shoppers, or investors – are rewarded and punished for having an ethnic identity. This, in turn, affects how much or little they will be able to act in concert and help to shape our larger civic culture.

What public officials did to encourage private developers to rebuild inner-city neighborhoods after World War II, for example, had a profound effect on where members of certain minority populations and ethnic groups lived. Once an area was designated as a site for some kind of government-subsidized program and the middle-class and professional leaders of its current residents left, it did not take long for a community to melt around the ankles of the persons who were left behind.[78] Granted, the end of one enclave made it possible for new ones belonging to an entirely different people to take root. Nevertheless, this was not a pleasant experience either for the persons who were pushed out or the individuals who, quite literally, took their place.

One of the great sorrows visited upon those who took over these old ethnic enclaves is that their own people in some cases have yet to create the civic infrastructure which would make these good places to live again. The displaced groups have likewise been done a great disservice. Individuals certainly lost their homes. Even worse, however, they lost many organizations and businesses that kept them connected to each other even after they had moved away. The continuing pull of their old church, "hangout," or park, and the few buildings or institutions left in one's former neighborhood is testimony to the power that a place has on our lives. These are crucial reminders of what made us "us."

No small part of the hole left in us by the loss of such places and the disassociation of one's people has come to be filled by tribal shopping and internet ethnicity. I am not speaking of the kinds of economic "self-help" which involve a number of persons from the same cultural group in a coordinated effort to buy and sell to their own people. Businessmen and women of Vietnamese and Cambodian descent in the Boston area, for example, received some well-earned notoriety during the 1990s for their attempts to create ethnic marketplaces and newspapers.[79] Nor am I referring to leaders and followers who make a political organization and self-conscious voting bloc. Mexican Americans have tried to renew this custom across the southwest.[80]

I am referring instead to niche marketers whose only contact with their clients comes through phone, magazine, and internet solicitations and by fashioning "wedge" issues which drag out long-held fantasies and fears in the privacy of a voting booth. The commitment of salesperson and customer stretches no further than the length of an extension cord and probably is not as strong. It requires human engagement of the thinnest sort and conveys no more passion than the blinking cursor on a computer screen.[81]

Reduced to an empty shell, the ethnic person is filled with whatever deformities and moral failings the casual observer or huckster attributes to him. He becomes a cartoon character ready to be smacked in the head or run off a cliff. No matter how else he is portrayed, it will never be as a fully civilized man or woman.

It was the Roman author Pliny the Elder who first described beings of this sort. The monstrous races he catalogued found their way into much medieval art and thought. Printed on the margins of maps of the known world to signify their distance from the family of man, for example, these beings had shapes and habits which distinguished them from civilized humans. Eventually, historian John Block Friedman tells us, members of the monstrous races became better known to the civilized people who discovered them. They were portrayed a bit less monstrously and pictured on pieces of the earth that were closer to Europe.

No matter how much closer they may have come to regular human beings, however, there was still a persistent and irreducible gap between them and cultured Europeans. Aliens could lose a head and grow a second foot, but "everyday cultural differences in ... diet, speech, clothes, weapons, customs, and social organization" continued to set them apart.[82] They remained untrustworthy and, in what was no small co-incidence, ineligible for citizenship in cities.

We should be surprised if we did not find monstrous races among us today. They are here. Oddly enough, though, they are not drawn from the usual list of suspects. Fortunately for all of us, black persons, assorted Asians, and brown-skinned Latino-types, whose number once included Italian Americans but apparently no longer does, are viewed today as full-fledged members in the family of humanity. Their ascension has taken much too long, but much of the progress they enjoyed came after they moved into cities and became more familiar with our urban way of life during the second half of the twentieth century.

The hole they left in the long line of monstrous races in America has been filled by a people that has been here for a while and, as it happens, is known for its distinctly uncivilized behavior toward blacks, assorted Asians, and brown-skinned Latino-types. This would be the infamous race called "white people." I assure you that this is not a cheap or mean-spirited attempt to insult aggrieved minority persons. Nor is it intended to be a too-clever device that elevates beleaguered white persons back to their rightful spot in the human food chain.

While by no means reviled by all Americans, including themselves, white persons apparently were sinking at the end of the twentieth century as quickly as "colored" peoples in America were rising in esteem. At least that was the view of persons who considered themselves practitioners and scholars in "White studies" near the end of the century. These men and women were not well known outside the "community of antiracist activists and academics in the Boston–Cambridge area" in the late 1990s. Yet that did not make their message any less powerful. White-studies experts believed that white persons became "passive listeners in racial conversations, seldom venting their real feelings" when difficult questions regarding race were brought up and that this was not a good thing. White persons needed to talk through what it meant to be white, as if it were an infection, so that they could get over being white.

Not everyone in the academic and helping-out professions around Boston agreed with this approach. They did not think that making a bigger deal about being white just so that persons felt freer to talk about being part of some hegemonic racist conspiracy in America was a good idea. 'I think that to concede any validity to whiteness as a category is to perpetuate injustice,' said Noel Ignatiev, an author and fellow at Harvard University's W. E. B. DuBois Institute. He was not alone.

Advocates of "White studies" were not deterred by this kind of criticism. Were it not for progressive individuals like themselves, one practitioner suggested, the only role models that young persons had for being white would come out of the white supremacist movement. This was not an attractive option. "We need people who are conscious of being white and we need to give them the room to be white," he argued. "This is the way to create true multiracialists."[83]

It may not be the fault of persons in government or the marketplace that we entertain such ideas at the end of the twentieth century. These notions are more likely to pop up, however, when the practice of ethnicity is reduced to a never-ending search for alternative personal identities that can be put on and taken off like some frock or rendered meaningful by a government census taker. Fortunately, the accomplishment of ethnicity in the United States has been far more substantial than this and cannot be so easily erased.

The transformation of unwashed immigrants into something like a by-god American was made real by their immersion in a community whose members understood and appreciated their unique qualities even as they were trying to become more like everybody else. Their ethnic identity arose and stayed intact only as long as they associated with other like-minded persons. It required the labor of human beings who have much more in common than a credit rating or a grudge.

If there are persons who still claim to be ethnics today, then they mean it. Their involvement with other persons who share their ancestry, important values, and a distinctive way of looking at the world is something they take seriously. Crucial to their continued development and success is the growth of organizations which straddle all of the social classes represented in a community or which take the work of their more and less-esteemed peers into account. Far from being in the twilight of their ethnicity, they are just coming into their own. That is good news for all of us.

Whatever good can come of initiatives mounted by existing or would-be ethnic peoples on their own would be augmented greatly by collaborative ventures among them. Unfortunately, that kind of co-operation has not been a common theme in their corporate histories. Even in the political arena where such contacts are part of the routine way in which electoral business is conducted in this country, different ethnic groups and sets of minority citizens are more often competitors for the same array of positions and funds. Their collaboration is of a limited sort and not wed to the daily lives of their constituents.

Ethnic groups and minority persons in the United States have not yet found a comfortable vocabulary and way of looking at the world that would draw them together rather than keep them separated. They have not yet taken to heart, much less mastered, the lesson learned a long time ago by different religious denominations which had to find principles that they all could embrace. This did not diminish the vitality of their separate religious traditions or churches, mosques, and synagogues. It just made it easier for them to work together.

A much more effective way of binding different ethnic peoples together, I suggest, may be to renew their commitment to bourgeois principles of order and prosperity by way of joint projects that will make each of them richer. Inasmuch as both *commercial* and *ethnic communalism* are corporate approaches to making the world work better for those who live in it, there is no reason why their complementary skills and contacts could not play off each other well. There certainly are examples in the history of American cities when persons tried to broker this kind of marriage. That it did not happen often enough or take a more democratic turn in the past is no reason to ignore the potential good that can come of such a relationship in the future. Surely, the growing confidence and economic clout of many ethnic groups today suggests that they may now approach their social and economic betters on a more equal footing. Their union might not be neat or always pretty, but we know that few things in the history of city building are.

NOTES

1   *Boston Sunday Herald*, August 4, 1996.
2   *Boston Globe*, August 26, 1995.
3   Ibid., October 16, 1997.
4   Ibid., July 26, 1993.
5   Herbert J. Gans, *The Urban Villagers: Group and Class in the Life of Italian-Americans* (New York: Free Press, 1982), pp. 8–10.
6   Feelings still run high among the dwindling number of West Enders who today are scattered throughout the Boston metropolitan area. Some 40 years after the neighborhood was leveled, a new housing complex with 153 apartments was built on the periphery of their old neighborhood. They did not learn until the project was well under way that only 55 percent of the units were reserved for former West Enders. This only rekindled their sense of loss and betrayal. See: *Boston Globe*, January 10 and November 25, 1997.
7   *Boston Globe*, March 30, July 31, July 28, May 5, April 27, and August 11, 1998.

8 Ibid., December 27, 1993; November 9, 1997; February 8, March 10, and March 30, 1998.

9 Ibid., August 21, 1995; February 26, 1996; February 6 and February 17, 1997.

10 Ibid., June 6, 1998.

11 Ibid., June 29, March 16, and March 18, 1998.

12 Lawrence Glasco, "The Life Cycles and Household Structure of American Ethnic Groups: Irish, German, and Native-American Whites in Buffalo, New York, 1855," *Journal of Urban History*, Volume 1, Number 3, May 1975, pp. 339–64; Oliver Zunz, "The Organization of the American City in the Late nineteenth Century: Ethnic Structure and Spatial Arrangement in Detroit," *Journal of Urban History*, Volume 3, Number 4, August 1977, pp. 443–66; Timothy Smith, "Religion and Ethnicity in America," *American Historical Review*, Volume 83, Number 5, December 1978, pp. 1,155–87; Timothy Kelly, "Suburbanization and the Decline of Catholic Public Rituals in Pittsburgh," *Journal of Social History*, Volume 28, Number 2, Winter 1994, pp. 311–30.

13 Anthony D. Smith, *The Ethnic Origins of Nations* (Oxford: Blackwell Publishers, 1986); Edmund S. Morgan, *Inventing the People: The Rise of Popular Sovereignty in England and the United States* (New York: W.W. Norton, 1988).

14 Edward Kopf, "Untarnishing the Dream: Mobility, Opportunity, and Order in Modern America," *Journal of Social History*, Volume 11, Number 2, Winter 1977, pp. 206–27; John Bodnar, Michael Weber, and Roger Simon, "Migration, Kinship, and Urban Adjustment: Blacks and Poles in Pittsburgh, 1900–1930," *Journal of American History*, Volume 66, Number 3, December 1979, pp. 548–65; Kathleen Neils, "Immigrants, Immigrant Neighborhoods, and Ethnic Identity: Historical Issues," *Journal of American History*, Volume 66, Number 3, December 1979, pp. 603–15.

15 Carl Bridenbaugh, *Cities in Revolt: Urban Life in America, 1743–1776* (London: Oxford University Press, 1971), pp. 150–6, 352–8.

16 For a good treatment of this particular view, see J. Milton Yinger, *Ethnicity: Source of Strength? Source of Conflict?* (Albany, NY: State University of New York Press, 1994), p. 41.

17 *San Diego Union*, July 28, 1915.

18 Yinger, *Ethnicity*, pp. 323, 421.

19 *Boston Daily Evening Transcript*, August 20, 1840.

20 *Pittsburgh Post*, August 24 and September 23, 1843.

21 *Daily Missouri Democrat*, August 26, 1854.

22 *Eastern Argus*, February 19, 1856.

23 *Daily Intelligencer*, May 3, 1860.

24 *Nebraska Republican*, February 9, December 14, July 20, and August 3, 1866; January 26, 1867.

25 *Pine Bluff Press*, June 16, 1872.

26 Ibid., June 16, January 25, January 4, January 11, and January 18, 1872.

27 *Cleveland Daily Plain Dealer*, January 2, May 3, May 19, and November 24, 1875.

28   Ibid., January 12, March 1, and March 18, 1875.

29   Ibid., January 20, August 16, and April 15, 1875.

30   *Wilmington Morning News*, April 28 and May 6, 1885; September 22, 1887.

31   *Argus Leader*, December 23, 1890; May 18 and May 16, 1891.

32   *Carolina Spartan*, July 8, 1891; April 27, June 1, and July 27, 1892; January 4, 1893.

33   *Boston Globe*, January 3 and February 20, 1900.

34   Ibid., January 17 and July 12, 1900.

35   Ibid., June 20, 1900.

36   John Bodnar, *The Transplanted: A History of Immigrants in Urban America* (Bloomington, IN: University of Indiana Press, 1985), pp. 54–6, 83–4; John McClymer, "The Study of Community and the 'New' Social History," *Journal of Urban History*, Volume 7, Number 1, November 1980, pp. 103–18; Daniel Walkowitz, "Working-Class Women in the Gilded Age: Factory and Family Life Among Cohes, New York Cotton Workers," *Journal of Social History*, Volume 5, Number 4, Summer 1972, pp. 464–90; Virginia Yans-McLaughlin, "A Flexible Tradition: South Italian Immigrants Confronting a New Work Experience," *Journal of Social History*, Volume 7, Number 4, Summer 1974, pp. 429–45; Rowland Berthoff, "Peasants and Artisans, Puritans and Republicans: Personal Liberty and Communal Equality in American History," *Journal of American History*, Volume 69, Number 3, December 1982, pp. 579–98.

37   John Bodnar, "The Immigrant and the City," *Journal of Urban History*, Volume 3, Number 2, February 1977, pp. 241–50.

38   Stephan Thernstrom offered a classic study of occupational mobility among natives and newcomers in the Boston area during the industrial era. He showed that as late as 1950 the children of some immigrant populations, notably the Irish and Italians but others as well, lagged well behind the offspring of more established groups in terms of their movement into more skilled jobs and white-collar professions. See his book *The Other Bostonians: Poverty and Progress in the American Metropolis, 1880–1970* (Cambridge, MA: Harvard University Press, 1973), pp. 111–44.

39   Silvano Tomasi, "The Ethnic Church and the Integration of Italian Immigrants in the United States," in Silvano Tomasi and Madeline Engel (eds), *The Italian Experience in the United States* (Staten Island, NY: Center for Migration Studies, 1970), p. 170.

40   Bodnar, *The Transplanted*, p. 117. Also see pp. 118–43.

41   David Montgomery, "The Shuttle and the Cross: Weavers and Artisans in the Kensington Riots of 1844," *Journal of Social History*, Volume 5, Number 4, Summer 1972, pp. 411–46; James Barrett, "Unity and Fragmentation: Class, Race, and Ethnicity on Chicago's South Side, 1900–1922," *Journal of Social History*, Volume 18, Number 1, Fall 1984, pp. 37–56; Helena Flam, "Democracy in Debt: Credit and Politics in Patterson, New Jersey, 1890–1930," *Journal of Social History*, Volume 18, Number 3, Spring 1985, pp. 439–62; Timothy Meager, "'Irish All the Time': Ethnic Consciousness Among the Irish of Worcester, Massachusetts,

1880–1905," *Journal of Social History*, Volume 19, Number 2, Winter 1985, pp. 277–304; Joseph Rodriguez, "Mexicans in US Cities: New Perspectives," *Journal of Urban History*, Volume 20, Number 4, August 1994, pp. 554–63; Dong Ok Lee, "Commodification of Ethnicity: The Sociospatial Reproduction of Immigrant Entrepreneurs," *Urban Affairs Quarterly*, Volume 28, Number 2, December 1992, pp. 258–75; Tomasz Inglot and John Pelissero, "Ethnic Political Power in a Machine City: Chicago's Poles at Rainbow's End," *Urban Affairs Quarterly*, Volume 28, Number 4, June 1993, pp. 526–43; Patrick Joyce, "A Reversal of Fortunes: Black Empowerment, Political Machines, and City Jobs in New York City and Chicago," *Urban Affairs Review*, Volume 32, Number 3, January 1997, pp. 291–318. Working with one's fellow immigrants sometimes did not increase their occupational opportunities, even if it helped to keep their enclave whole. See: Suzanne Model, "The Effects of Ethnicity in the Workplace on Blacks, Italians, and Jews in 1910 New York," *Journal of Urban History*, Volume 16, Number 1, November 1989, pp. 29–51; Suzanne Model, "The Ethnic Economy: Cubans and Chinese Reconsidered," *Sociological Quarterly*, Volume 33, Number 1, 1992, pp. 63–82; Stephen Greenberg, "Neighborhood Change, Racial Transition, and Work Location: A Case Study of an Industrial City, Philadelphia, 1880–1930," *Journal of Urban History*, Volume 7, Number 3, May 1981, pp. 267–314; Dominic Pacyga, "The Russell Square Community Committee: An Ethnic Response to Urban Problems," *Journal of Urban History*, Volume 15, Number 2, February 1989, pp. 159–84.

42 A number of researchers have emphasized the continuing barriers faced by black Americans as the reason why they were unable to develop strong ties among themselves or with persons from other cultural groups. See: Harvard Sitkoff, "Racial Militancy and Interracial Violence in the Second World War," *Journal of American History*, Volume 58, Number 3, December 1971, pp. 661–81; Arnold Hirsch, "On the Waterfront: Race, Class, and Politics in Post-Reconstruction New Orleans," *Journal of Urban History*, Volume 21, Number 4, May 1995, pp. 511–17; Howard Rabinowitz, "From Reconstruction to Redemption in the United States," *Journal of Urban History*, Volume 2, Number 2, February 1976, pp. 169–94; Eugene Watts, "Black and Blue: African-American Police Officers in 20th-Century St Louis," *Journal of Urban History*, Volume 7, Number 2, February 1981, pp. 131–68; James Grossman, "Migration, Race, and Class," *Journal of Urban History*, Volume 15, Number 2, February 1989, pp. 224–32; Earl Lewis, "Connecting Memory, Self, and the Power of Place in African American Urban History," *Journal of Urban History*, Volume 21, Number 3, March 1995, pp. 347–71; Elsa Barkley Brown and Gregory Kimball, "Mapping the Terrain of Black Richmond," *Journal of Urban History*, Volume 21, Number 3, March 1995, pp. 296–346; Joe Trotter, "African Americans in the City: The Industrial Era, 1900–1950," *Journal of Urban History*, Volume 21, Number 4, May 1995, pp. 438–57; Kenneth Kusmer, "African Americans in the City Since World War II: From the Industrial to the Post-Industrial Era," *Journal of Urban History*, Volume 21, Number 4,

May 1995, pp. 458–504. Much of the social scientific research done since the early 1960s has taken the position that the life chances of black Americans have been limited by their continuing separation from whites in particular and mainstream American society generally. See: Andrew Hacker, *Two Nations: Black, White, Separate, Hostile, Unequal* (New York: Charles Scribner's Sons, 1992); Douglas Massey and Nancy Denton, *American Apartheid: Segregation and the Making of the Underclass* (Cambridge, MA: Harvard University Press, 1993); Elijah Anderson, *StreetWise: Race, Class, and Change in an Urban Community* (Chicago: University of Chicago Press, 1990).

43 St Clair Drake and Horace R. Cayton, *Black Metropolis: A Study of Negro Life in a Northern City* (New York: Harper & Row, 1962); Gilbert Osofsky, *Harlem: The Making of a Ghetto* (New York: Harper & Row, 1966); Arnold R. Hirsch, *Making the Second Ghetto: Race and Housing in Chicago, 1940–1960* (Cambridge: Cambridge University Press, 1985); Leonard Curry, "Philadelphia's Free Blacks: Two Views," *Journal of Urban History*, Volume 16, Number 3, May 1990, pp. 319–25; Christopher Linsin, "Points of Conflict: Twentieth-Century Black Migration and Urbanization," *Journal of Urban History*, Volume 21, Number 4, May 1995, pp. 527–35; Norman Fainstein and Susan Nesbitt, "Did the Black Ghetto Have a Golden Age? Class Structure and Class Segregation in New York City, 1949–1970," *Journal of Urban History*, Volume 23, Number 1, November 1996, pp. 3–28; Andor Skotnes, "'Buying Where You Can Work': Boycotting for Jobs in African-American Baltimore, 1933–1934," *Journal of Social History*, Volume 27, Number 4, Summer 1994, pp. 735–62.

44 Harold A. McDougall, *Black Baltimore: A New Theory of Community* (Philadelphia: Temple University Press, 1993).

45 Ibid., pp. 12–13.

46 Smith, *The Ethnic Origins of Nations*; Edward Kantowicz, "Cardinal Mundelein of Chicago and the Shaping of 20th-Century American Catholicism," *Journal of American History*, Volume 68, Number 1, June 1981, pp. 52–68; Kerby Miller, "Urban Immigrants: The Irish in the Cities," *Journal of Urban History*, Volume 16, Number 4, August 1990, pp. 428–41; Janice Reiff Webster, "Domestication and Americanization: Scandinavian Women in Seattle, 1888–1900," *Journal of Urban History*, Volume 4, Number 3, May 1978, pp. 275–90; Dennis Rousey, "Hibernian Leatherheads': Irish Cops in New Orleans, 1830–1880," *Journal of Urban History*, Volume 10, Number 1, November 1983, pp. 61–84.

47 Ivan Light, *Ethnic Enterprise in America* (Berkeley, CA: University of California Press, 1972); Ivan Light, *Race, Ethnicity and Entrepreneurship in Urban America* (New York: Alden deGruyter, 1995); Scott Cummings (ed.), *Self-Help in Urban America* (Port Washington, NY: Kennikat Press, 1980); Edna Bonacich and John Modell, *The Economic Basis of Ethnic Solidarity: Small Business in the Japanese Community* (Berkeley, CA: University of California Press, 1980); Robin Ward and Richard Jenkins (eds), *Ethnic Communities in Business: Strategies for Economic Survival*

(Cambridge: Cambridge University Press, 1984); John Sibley Butler, *Entrepreneurship and Self-Help Among Black Americans: A Reconsideration of Race and Economics* (Albany, NY: State University of New York Press, 1991); Laura Foner, "The Free People of Color in Louisiana and Saint Dominique," *Journal of Social History*, Volume 3, Number 4, Summer 1970, pp. 406–30; Theodore Hershberg, "Free Blacks in Antebellum Philadelphia: A Study of Ex-Slaves, Freeborn, and Socio-economic Decline," *Journal of Social History*, Volume 5, Number 2, Winter 1971, pp. 183–209; John Blassingame, "Before the Ghetto: The Making of the Black Community in Savannah, Georgia, 1865–1880," *Journal of Social History*, Volume 6, Number 4, Summer 1973, pp. 463–88; David Levering Lewis, "Parallels and Divergencies: Assimilationist Strategies of African-American and Jewish Elites from 1910 to the Early 1930s," *Journal of American History*, Volume 71, Number 3, December 1984, pp. 543–64; David Goldfield, "The Black Ghetto: 'A Tragic Sameness'," *Journal of Urban History*, Volume 3, Number 3, May 1977, pp. 361–70; Andrew Wiese, "Places of Our Own: Suburban Black Towns Before 1960," *Journal of Urban History*, Volume 19, Number 3, May 1993, pp. 30–54; Kenneth Goings and Gerald Smith, "'Unhidden' Transcripts: Memphis and African American Agency, 1862–1920," *Journal of Urban History*, Volume 21, Number 3, March 1995, pp. 372–94.

48　Paula Kane, *Separatism and Subculture: Boston Catholicism, 1900–1920* (Chapel Hill, NC: University of North Carolina Press, 1994).

49　Thomas H. O'Connor, *South Boston My Home Town: The History of an Ethnic Neighborhood* (Boston: Northeastern University Press, 1994).

50　Bodnar, *The Transplanted*, pp. 83–4, 166–8; Tamara Hareven, "Family Time and Industrial Time: Family and Work in a Planned Corporation Town, 1900–1924," *Journal of Urban History*, Volume 1, Number 3, May 1975, pp. 365–89; Carol Groneman, "Working-Class Immigrant Women in Mid-19th Century New York: The Irish Woman's Experience," *Journal of Urban History*, Volume 4, Number 3, May 1978, pp. 255–74; Corinne Azen Krause, "Urbanization Without Breakdown: Italian, Jewish, and Slavic Immigrant Women in Pittsburgh, 1900–1945," *Journal of Urban History*, Volume 4, Number 3, May 1978, pp. 291–306; Samuel Baily, "The Italian Immigrant Experience: Understanding Continuity and Change," *Journal of Urban History*, Volume 11, Number 4, August 1985, pp. 503–13; Lizabeth Cohen, *Making a New Deal: Industrial Workers in Chicago, 1919–1939* (Cambridge: Cambridge University Press, 1990); Ewa Moraswka, *Insecure Prosperity: Small-Town Jews in Industrial America, 1890–1940* (Princeton, NJ: Princeton University Press, 1996).

51　Rudolph Vecoli, "Prelates and Peasants: Italian Immigrants and the Catholic Church," *Journal of Social History*, Volume 2, Number 3, Spring 1969, pp. 217–68; Ewa Morawskce, "The Internal Status Hierarchy in the Eastern European Communities in Johnstown, Pennsylvania 1890–1930s," *Journal of Social History*, Volume 16, Number 1, Fall 1982, pp. 75–108; Jon Gjerde, "Conflict and Community: A Case Study of the Immigrant Church in the United States," *Journal of Social History*, Volume 19,

Number 4, Summer 1986, pp. 681–98; James Borchert, "Urban Neighborhood Life and Community: Informal Group Life, 1850–1970," *Journal of Interdisciplinary History*, Volume 11, Number 4, Spring 1981, pp. 607–31; Howard Chudacoff, "A New Look at Ethnic Neighborhoods: Residential Dispersion and the Concept of Visibility in a Medium-Sized City," *Journal of American History*, Volume 60, Number 1, June 1973, pp. 76–93; David Gerber, "Cutting Out Shylock: Elite Anti-Semitism and the Quest for Moral Order in the Mid-Nineteenth-Century American Market Place," *Journal of American History*, Volume 69, Number 3, December 1982, pp. 615–37; John Bodnar, "Symbols and Servants: Immigrant Americans and the Limits of Public History," *Journal of American History*, Volume 73, Number 1, June 1986, pp. 137–51; April Schultz, "'The Pride of the Race Had Been Touched': The 1925 Norse-American Immigration Centennial and Ethnic Identity," *Journal of American History*, Volume 77, Number 4, March 1991, pp. 1,265–95; James Barrett, "Americanization From the Bottom Up: Immigration and the Remaking of the Working Class in the United States, 1880–1930," *Journal of American History*, Volume 79, Number 3, December 1992, pp. 996–1,020.

52 Humbert Nelli, "John Powers and the Italians: Politics in a Chicago Ward, 1896–1921," *Journal of American History*, Volume 57, Number 1, June 1970, pp. 67–84; Jonathan Sarna, "The American Jewish Response to 19th-Century Christian Missions," *Journal of American History*, Volume 68, Number 1, June 1981, pp. 35–51; Gilbert Osofsky, "Abolitionists, Irish Immigrants, and the Dilemmas of Romantic Nationalism," *American Historical Review*, Volume 80, Number 4, October 1975, pp. 889–912; John Jentz, "Class and Politics in an Emerging Industrial City: Chicago in the 1860s and 1870s," *Journal of Urban History*, Volume 17, Number 3, May 1991, pp. 227–63; Jeffrey Mirel, "Urban Schools as Contested Terrain," *Journal of Urban History*, Volume 19, Number 1, November 1992, pp. 111–26; Philip Bean, "The Irish, the Italians, and Machine Politics, a Case Study: Utica, New York (1870–1960)," *Journal of Urban History*, Volume 20, Number 2, February 1994, pp. 205–39; David Beito, "The 'Lodge Practice Evil' Reconsidered: Medical Care Through Fraternal Societies, 1900–1930," *Journal of Urban History*, Volume 23, Number 5, July 1997, pp. 569–600.

53 Light, *Race*; Cummings, *Self-Help in Urban America* ; Butler, *Entrepreneurship and Self-Help*; Bonacich and Modell, *The Economic Basis of Ethnic Solidarity*; Ward and Jenkins, *Ethnic Communities in Business*.

54 *Boston Globe*, August 2, 1998.

55 August Meier and Elliott Rudwick, *CORE: A Study in the Civil Rights Movement, 1942–1968* (New York: Oxford University Press, 1973).

56 Tamara Hareven, *Family Time and Industrial Time: The Relationship between the Family and Work in a New England Industrial Community* (Cambridge: Cambridge University Press, 1982); Ewa Morawska, *For Bread With Butter: The Life-worlds of East Central Europeans in Johnstown, Pennsylvania, 1890–1940* (Cambridge: Cambridge University

Press, 1985), p. 87. A number of manufacturing companies in England during the Victorian era also supported the work of churches and voluntary associations belonging to their employees. There, too, the idea was to draw employees into a collaborative and deferential arrangement with their bosses. See: Patrick Joyce, *Work, Society and Politics: The Culture of the Factors in Later Victorian England* (New Brunswick, NJ: Rutgers University Press, 1980).

57 David J. Saposs, "The Immigrant Community and the Steel Strike of 1919," in Roy Lubove (ed.), *Pittsburgh* (New York: New Viewpoints, 1976), pp. 127–39; Philip Klein, "The Ethnic Community," in Lubove, pp. 139–58.

58 As with other arguments and references presented in this book, there is no way that I can do justice to all of the subtle points that authors make. Nor can I offer an elaborate discussion of their findings. This is particularly frustrating in the present case, where passions and rhetorical broadsides are as overheated as they are commonplace. For a good overview of the arguments that stand behind our debates about race and ethnic relations in this country, however, I suggest the reader consult the following works: Max Weber, *Economy and Society* (New York: Bedminster Press, 1968), pp. 385–98; Milton Gordon, *Assimilation in American Life: The Role of Race, Religion, and National Origins* (New York: Oxford University Press, 1964); Milton Gordon, *Human Nature, Class, and Ethnicity* (New York: Oxford University Press, 1978); Jeffrey Reitz, *The Survival of Ethnic Groups* (Toronto: McGraw-Hill Ryerson, 1980); Ronald Bayor, "Ethnicity in America," *Journal of Urban History*, Volume 7, Number 4, August 1981, pp. 499–506; R. Fred Wacker, *Ethnicity, Pluralism, and Race: Race Relations Theory in America Before Myrdal* (Westport, CT: Greenwood Press, 1983); Stow Persons, *Ethnic Studies at Chicago: 1905–1945* (Urbana, IL: University of Illinois Press, 1987); Andrea Tuttle Kornbluh, "From Culture to Cuisine: 20th-Century Views of Race and Ethnicity in the City," in Howard Gillette and Zane Miller (eds), *American Urbanism: A Historiographical Review* (Westport, CT: Greenwood Press, 1987), pp. 49–71; Werner Sollors, "Introduction: The Invention of Ethnicity," in Werner Sollors (ed.), *The Invention of Ethnicity* (New York: Oxford University Press, 1989), pp. ix–xx; Lawrence Fuchs, *The American Kaleidoscope: Race, Ethnicity, and the Civic Culture* (Hanover: University Press of New England, 1990); Barbara Ballis Lal, *The Romance of Culture in an Urban Civilization* (London: Routledge, 1990); Andrew Greeley, "The Ethnic Miracle," in Norman Yetman (ed.), *Majority and Minority* (Boston: Allyn and Bacon, 1991), pp. 275–85; Richard Alba, "The Twilight of Ethnicity Among American Catholics of European Ancestry," in Yetman, *Majority and Minority*, pp. 420–9; Herbert Gans, "Symbolic Ethnicity: The Future of Ethnic Groups and Cultures in America," in Yetman, *Majority and Minority*, pp. 430–43; J. Milton Yinger, *Ethnicity*; Russell Kazal, "Revisiting Assimilation: The Rise, Fall, and Reappraisal of a Concept in American Ethnic History," *American Historical Review*, Volume 100, Number 2, April 1995, pp. 437–71; Elliot Barkan, "Race, Religion and Nationality in American Society: A Model of Ethnicity – From Contact to

Assimilation," *Journal of American Ethnic History*, Volume 14, Number 2, Winter 1995, pp. 38–75.

59 Joane Nagel, "Constructing Ethnicity: Creating and Recreating Ethnic Identity and Culture," *Social Problems*, Volume 41, Number 1, February 1994, pp. 152–76; Stephen Fugita and David O'Brien, *Japanese American Ethnicity: The Persistence of Community* (Seattle: University of Washington Press, 1991).

60 *Wausau Record-Herald*, January 2, 1908.

61 *Pittsburgh Post*, January 11, 1915.

62 *Sparks Tribune*, May 7, 1915.

63 *Fargo Forum and Daily Republican*, April 13, 1917; *Casper Daily Tribune*, March 12 and July 31, 1918.

64 *Boston Globe*, May 8 and January 1, 1920.

65 *New Orleans Times-Picayune*, January 25, February 19, March 11, March 20, September 15, October 14, and November 27, 1925.

66 *Lawrence Daily Journal-World*, June 1, 1 June 17, and October 19, 1926.

67 John F. Stack, *International Conflict in an American City: Boston's Irish, Italians, and Jews, 1935–1944* (Westport, CT: Greenwood Press, 1979).

68 Jonathan Rieder, *Canarsie: The Jews and Italians of Brooklyn Against Liberalism* (Cambridge, MA: Harvard University Press, 1985).

69 Peter Skerry, *Mexican Americans: The Ambivalent Minority* (New York: Free Press, 1993).

70 *St Louis Post-Dispatch*, April 2, 1962.

71 Bodnar, *The Transplanted*, p. 203; Meager, "'Irish All the Time.'"

72 *Cleveland Plain Dealer*, July 19, July 27, November 9, November 17, and November 25, 1968.

73 Glenn R. Morrow, *Plato's Cretan City: A Historical Interpretation of the Laws* (Princeton, NJ: Princeton University Press, 1993), pp. 302–18, 356–74.

74 *Boston Globe*, August 10, 1986.

75 Ibid., March 10, 1992.

76 Ibid., June 11, 1992.

77 Ibid., January 10, 1995 and June 19, 1997.

78 Hillel Levine and Lawrence Harmon, *The Death of an American Jewish Community* (New York: Free Press, 1992).

79 *Boston Globe*, September 14, 1991; June 18, 1992; February 5, 1995.

80 Skerry, *Mexican Americans*.

81 *Boston Globe*, April 27, 1998; Gans, "Symbolic Ethnicity."

82 John Block Friedman, *The Monstrous Races in Medieval Art and Thought* (Cambridge, MA: Harvard University Press, 1981), p. 26.

83 *Boston Globe*, December 21, 1997.

10

Articles of Faith: Personal Adornment as a Communal Accomplishment

We live in an affluent society. The full measure of our wealth, the size and mix of our economy, the complex ways in which persons relate to each other as producers, investors, and consumers, and the ideas we have about all of these things are too big for us to describe clearly much less hold in our head. To say that we have or use more stuff than persons who live in other societies does not do justice to all the big and little ways that affluence shapes our daily routines and larger social worlds.

It means, at a minimum, that tens of millions of men and women rise each day and go to jobs that enable them to house, clothe, and feed themselves. The work may not be glamorous or touch many persons in big ways, but it does allow them to buy things they need or want. Most adults can support themselves and family members, and they are able to save something for the future. In many cases, of course, persons who live in an affluent society do considerably better than that. The most important point to take from all of this, and perhaps the best thing that one can say about living in an affluent society, is that a great many individuals are able to lead productive lives. There are many countries where the vast majority of persons cannot make this claim.

There is a darker side to all this affluence, unfortunately. It is driven by staggering amounts of debt. The money is borrowed by individuals, corporations, and governments to get something today which they want but cannot pay for out of their own cash reserves.

More than half of the 100 million or more households in the
United States at the end of the twentieth century carried an average
of $7,000 worth of debt on their credit cards. By one estimate, household
credit-card debt more than doubled during the late 1990s, and fewer than
one-third of all the American households which had credit cards actually
paid their monthly balance in full.[1] This meant that they paid no interest
on the money they borrowed from credit card firms.

Everyone else who used credit cards was paying a stiff price for their
affluence. The average household with credit-card debt paid more then
$1,000 each year in interest penalties alone. For persons who declared
bankruptcy, their credit-card debt was equal to about 90 percent of their
yearly income. To make matters worse, more persons were taking this
route out of indebtedness. A record 1,350,000 persons declared personal
bankruptcy in 1997, and this figure was many times greater than the
number of persons who went bankrupt during the Great Depression of
the 1930s.

What is interesting about all of this from the standpoint of someone
who is supposed to make sense of how human beings make the world
work is that so much of labor and spending feels unscripted or unforced.
It does not surprise or upset us. It just sort of happens.

The reason it looks and feels this way is that much of the world we see
and most of the world we never see firsthand but still touches us is well
organized. It is set to a regular schedule, and the rules which guide it
generally are understood and accepted by the persons who have to live
with them. Furthermore, most of our daily life unfolds in settings
we know or in places we are comfortable. These predictable routines
and familiar locales are an integral part of the social spaces we call
"communities."

Buying, selling, investing, and everything we associate with a modern
"consumer culture" are integral parts of our communities. They help to
shape what we do every day. They also help us define who we are to other
persons as well as to ourselves.

If the figures dealing with personal debt are anywhere close to accurate, then a much bigger part of our world today is wrapped up in buying
goods and services than it used to be and most of the damage is being
done by individual persons. It is not done by groups. This, too, represents
a big change from the way life used to be organized.

In the past, much of the labor that went into making communities was
accomplished by groups tied to commercial and ethnic interests. Ideas
espoused by business leaders and ethnic peoples may not have been liked
by everyone. Nonetheless, what persons did in the name of those ideas
or in behalf of the groups which expressed them was crucial in organizing
the world inside towns and cities. Principles embraced by businessmen

and women or ethnic groups were more flexible than we imagine, but the hard lines they laid down made it possible for the rest of us to find a spot inside these places where we could fit.

Human beings recommit themselves to certain beliefs and practices every day, usually without thinking much about it. It is a good thing, however, that they do not have to re-invent these principles and routines every day. Otherwise, nothing much ever would be accomplished and even less would last.

Commercial leaders and ethnic groups made it possible for us to understand that our hard work was dedicated to something bigger than the individuals who actually carried it out. The standards they set and the routines they followed allowed the rest of us to get on with our lives without having to ask and answer big questions about the meaning of our actions every time we took a breath. The staying power of their group-based approach to making communities came from the way they organized the world for everyone else. It was not because great numbers of persons ever claimed to be business persons or openly adopted the parochial views of the ethnic groups that happened to live there at the time.

Inasmuch as business people and ethnic leaders never commanded the loyalty of more than a small portion of their city's population, other ways had to be discovered to draw in the majority of persons who lived and worked in cities every day. Appeals to broader collections of persons in American towns and cities usually were made through the marketplace. Local governments reached out to a more inclusive set of individuals called "citizens."

It is to these broader and more inclusive assemblages of human beings and the part they play in making a community of believers that our attention now turns. In this chapter we will consider how city dwellers used ideas and habits fashioned in the marketplace to tie them to a much larger world and make their communities better. In the next chapter, we will explore how men and women used local governments to draw a clean line around their community even as political entities they could not control did their best to erase it.

What we talk about here is not so much the economy of cities as how persons have tried to make a bigger deal out of buying something for oneself or investing in someone else's hard work. Shopping and investing of the sort we associate with a modern "consumer culture" and market economy actually helps make communities better. Both are updated expressions of voluntary subscription campaigns in which individuals give up part of their wealth so that they might improve their own situation or the lives of other persons they know only slightly or maybe not at all. It is a strategy that works equally well in profit-making ventures, philanthropy, and in the solicitation of funds for government-sponsored projects.

How much individual benefactors "profit" from their contributions cannot be known. Indeed, what distinguishes these voluntary subscriptions from things like wages, an allowance, or a gift is that persons may have little knowledge or control over their eventual destination and use. Each purchase and donation is an act of faith by the contributor toward the company or individuals to whom money has been given. When we shop for an item or invest in some enterprise the payoff for our faith is represented in the article we purchased or the parchment which declares that we own a small piece of something we may never have occasion to use or even see. We may wear them like a banner or take them as a sign not so much of a preordained state of grace but of our fidelity to the standards and practices embraced by members of the community of believers.

Personal adornment is thus transformed into a communal accomplishment, and not just because we rely on strangers to put everything we buy in front of us or sometimes shop with our friends. It is because the marketplace routinely draws more persons from different backgrounds into something approximating a community of equals far better than either commercial leaders and ethnic groups ever have. Furthermore, unlike government-backed public goods, shoppers and investors actually take something home that they can show off to their friends after being relieved of their money.

It matters, of course, that the community of equals frequented by investors and shoppers does not last long and often unites them in behalf of prizes no grander than a hula hoop or a manufacturer's logo. Even when men and women are showing off their investments and purchases, however, they are engaged in something more important than conspicuous display. They are living out a particular kind of faith.

An economy works well and only so long as a people believes in it and is willing to extend credit to the persons who run it. An economy will not last, produce much that is worth buying, or get persons to support it with their labor and money, when a people no longer believes. Shatter their faith, cut off credit to persons or groups, and an economy will falter, and the larger community of believers locking arms beneath it will come apart and maybe never come back together.

In a large urban world like that found in cities, men and women have to work exceptionally hard to make beliefs they all can share and customs they can follow. They take equally exceptional risks whenever they keep the faith and extend credit to each other. After all, they may know a manufacturer, merchant, shopper, or investor only by reputation, and sometimes not even that well. It is for this reason that the customs and codes built up around investing, buying goods, and using services are among the most widely shared, most intricately prescribed, and carefully managed that we have.

Consumer communalism is a shorthanded way of talking about all those conventions and rules. When we speak of fashioning better communities through the discipline afforded by the marketplace, therefore, we embrace *piety*, *sharing*, and *private-regardfulness* as principles of right conduct. Fidelity to these principles does not guarantee that a person understands or holds dear all of the values implied therein. Nevertheless, it is one of the surest ways we can show that we are "buying into the system" laid out by our ancestors more than three centuries ago and remaining faithful to each other.

The miracle of our "consumer culture" is not found in all the goods we can buy or all the services to which we avail ourselves, the quality of the work that went into producing them, or the taste we reveal in using all these items. Rather, it is apparent every day in the discipline which most persons exercise as they plunge headlong into all the yummy stuff laid out before them and in the promise that it will be someone else's turn to grab some tomorrow. We could scarcely have contrived a more efficient and credible set of customs and beliefs to keep us more or less in line when we are encouraged every day to let our appetites run wild. Thus, something bigger at stake and more important than any one of us takes place whenever we go shopping. It is the order and propriety enforced under consumer communalism that keeps our civic culture in mind even when we are losing ours at the boutique or outlet mall.

Of course, as the large amount of debt being carried by individual Americans and households demonstrates, sometimes the magic works better than others.

The Origins of a Modern "Consumer Culture" in America

Many elements of our modern consumer culture already were well in place by the middle of the eighteenth century. Included on this list were not only items to buy but also many customs and rules intended to guide the purchases which persons made and to limit public expressions of private extravagance.[2] The bottom line, so to speak, was this. Anyone with a little extra money was able to buy a variety of finished goods and foods imported from Europe and the Caribbean as well as specialty items produced in the colonies. Not all colonial Americans had enough money to purchase these things, of course, but the number of those persons who could was increasing even before the Revolution.

It did not take long for some colonists to acquire substantial wealth and to find ways to spend it. Many persons constructed expensive country and town houses and furnished their residences lavishly. They also held cultural events and social gatherings which gave them an opportunity to display themselves before other prominent families. These events may not have been as grand as those found in many European cities of the day, but they were every bit as socially ambitious.

Other members of colonial society became more economically secure during these years. Among them were artisans – carpenters, bricklayers, masons, paperhangers, upholsterers, tinsmiths, silversmiths, pewterers, and the like – who built the grand houses and served up the expensive goods that more prominent families used. These people were unable to match the displays of wealth presented by colonial town leaders, but they aped the styles of the gentry and took on such airs as their smaller pocketbooks would allow. If wealthy persons bought wheeled carriages to transport them from one place to another, for instance, members of a nascent "middle class" like Benjamin Franklin might rent them instead.[3] Their houses were smaller and not furnished as extravagantly as those of the gentry, but they were far better off than the laborers who had to work hard just to keep a roof over their heads and food on their plates.

Amidst displays of plenty, then, one could find many signs that some persons were better off than others and that they behaved differently. Men and women often shopped with persons who were more like themselves and there were times when they did not associate with their lesser- or better-born neighbors. Theatrical performances that appealed to audiences composed of the gentry in Philadelphia, for instance, were criticized as "an unnecessary expense and 'Encouraging to Idleness'" by middle-class Quakers.[4]

On the other hand, there were occasions when persons from different social ranks tried to be sensitive to each other's feelings. The leaders of eighteenth-century Portland, Maine took it upon themselves, for example, to remove the signs of their elevated status during official public gatherings like court hearings and council meetings just so they would not offend their less-esteemed neighbors. This courtesy did not extend to their private lives and in their daily contacts where distinctions based on class still were accepted.[5] There also were moments during the day that persons from different social ranks came together. Thus, colonial men came together within the comfortable walls of "public houses" or inns to eat, sleep, and be entertained. The social line between the classes taking comfort there apparently "was often blurred."[6]

Favorites with all classes were a variety of tavern entertainments somewhat resembling circus sideshows of our day. An African leopard was on view in Boston, New York, and Philadelphia in 1743–4; Charlestonians were paying to see another kind of an African, "A White Negro girl," having gray eyes and white woolly hair. David Lockwood's Musical Clock and Camera Obscura, a microscope, a set of perspective views of leading European cities, Punch and Judy show, waxworks, and the celebrated Philosophical–Optical Machine all toured Northern cities before 1750.[7]

Taverns also were sites where associations of men from the upper and middle ranks of local society often met in order to discuss politics and business.[8] Some of the taverns and associations catered to a less exclusive clientele whose taste ran more to horse racing, cockfights, billiards, and bowling.[9] Nevertheless, these establishments were universally admired and treated as important gathering spots by city residents.

All the different persons who were Americans did not mix all the time, but they did live in a world shot through with oddly arranged combinations of men and women drawn from the several classes found in their local society. Many urban dwellers lived out a marginal existence before and after the American Revolution; but the economies of colonial towns and early-American cities quickly pushed beyond the level of subsistence in the late-eighteenth century and many persons lived very well indeed. The incongruities and disparities in wealth and consumption revealed inside towns and cities meant that persons had to find ways to identify with the growth of the local economy and each other, even though most persons did not share equally in that prosperity. The moments they shared made it easier for them to devise ways for this to happen.

We have seen that persons from a town's several social classes could come together in celebration of their community's prosperity. We also have learned something of how they tried to mute differences that were apparent in their wealth and styles of living. Such assistance as was offered to those in need came through alms giving and programs administered by local churches. Less often it came as public charity. Even more public displays of religious fervor that were frowned upon by regular church attendees as wild and suspicious events had the unexpected effect of making men and women fit more comfortably into a conventional but ever more modern world.[10]

Charitable giving mimicked potlatch rituals in more traditional or "primitive" societies. In these rituals prosperous persons gave away food they did not need or made "presents" of money and goods to individuals who had much less. Colonial Americans, it appears, were less drawn to the conspicuous destruction of goods that also took place in those societies. On the other hand, anthropologists looking back on our own habits someday may say that we achieved the same effect with modern casinos and lotteries. They might also draw their readers' attention to junkyards, re-sell-it and consignment shops, and those acres of unsightly storage bins where we stash things we no longer use or have room to display.

The most effective strategy to soften the obvious inequalities built into our economic system, however, was created by the persons who profited most from it. Their solution was elegant in its simplicity. Furthermore, it worked. Businessmen and women set out to increase the number of persons who could consume more of what was being made. More men, women, and children would have a chance to acquire the trappings of prosperity and show their fidelity to the community of believers, though they probably had no real interest in joining it. This was done by making it possible for them to adorn themselves and their homes with items like those more prosperous individuals might have purchased.[11] By drawing more modest persons into the kind of shopping rituals generally reserved for wealthier folks in less affluent societies, the marketplace was "democratized" more than any other part of American society. Less well-to-do persons could shop more like more well-to-do persons did, even if they would never possess much wealth or own big businesses.

The preferred tool for trumpeting the spread of conspicuous spending and display was the local newspaper. The array of goods and services advertised on its pages during the eighteenth, nineteenth, and twentieth centuries was too long for anyone to catalogue, but such a list would have included many inventive and amusing entries. Clothing and foodstuffs were always popular, as were ads for many household appliances and gadgets. There were tutors for every social grace a person might want to master and schools for every skill one needed to make a success of himself or herself. Invitations could be found to join one bright economic venture or another, and newspapers carried many notices of local meetings for stockholders in these various companies.

My favorite ads are for food supplements, medicines, and clinics that were intended to cure everything from alcoholism and baldness to "self abuse" and chronic gas. I suppose we can take some comfort from the promise of perfection conveyed in these ads, at least in the sense that there is not much new in our own quest to look, smile, and smell better than our neighbors. Most everything we know today about being self-absorbed and the art of tucking, scraping, and drugging ourselves into a toy-like state of bliss was practiced first by the inhabitants of nineteenth-century American cities.

Men certainly played in all the games to transform the solitary person into an object of veneration, but women were subjected to much more of this and seemed to play harder at it. As early as 1820, for instance, the *Boston Chronicle Gazette* announced the start of a new weekly publication for women in the city. The new magazine was called *Ladies Portfolio*, and it was to focus on literature and fine arts that would appeal to women.[12] Later in the century daily newspapers all over the country would dedicate whole pages to "women's stories" and columns offering advice on topics involving personal grooming and health, friendship and courting, cooking, household items, and jobs. Some newspapers eventually added pages dedicated to children as well. Though largely bereft of advertising, much of the material echoed ideas about self-improvement, sound values, and hard work that were found in articles written for women.

All the columns, manuals, and books published during the nineteenth century that told persons how to present themselves to others did much more than make men and women feel or look better. They tried to prepare men and women for a world where they were more in charge of their own destiny than they had been in the past. It was possible for men and women to make themselves into someone other than who they had been.

Adults had not been cut loose from society and left to drift with the tide in the company of strangers. Nor were they cheated and conned at every turn by individuals who were not what they appeared to be.[13] It was more that they had to create new points of reference for what made a person worthy of trust and a credit to whatever people he or she claimed allegiance. However difficult a chore men and women would find this in ordinary times and less busy places was made tougher by having so many jobs, goods, and services that they could use to show that they had a solid bourgeois identity. No longer satisfied with the identities allowed under commercial and ethnic communalism, men and women could turn to a marketplace where being a made-man or woman could be reduced to wearing the most up-to-date styles, eating in the proper restaurants, and reading the right books.

Fortunately for all of us, the old ways of making oneself into a worthy person were not abandoned and the new ways of becoming a credible man or woman could be made compatible with standards and habits well-understood inside the community of believers.

The owners of Palmetto Hall in Spartanburg, South Carolina had to be happy in 1856, for instance, because several local organizations used the facility for functions that raised money for worthwhile causes and to launch a new private dancing academy. Furthermore, when the circus came to Spartanburg in the spring of 1856, just as it did to many towns and cities across the south, persons did not lose themselves in the moment. To be sure, there would be ponies performing tricks and wild animals to see. Yet calmer and more experienced persons openly declared their hope that the clowns would not be too profane or throw out double entendres which offended the ladies and children.[14]

Shopping, the most refined and cherished ritual practiced under

consumer communalism, was to serve more noble ends and local prejudices. At the start of the Civil War, for instance, the editors of the
Florence Gazette declared that local residents should patronize only
hometown businesses. After all, "if we expect to be independent," they
said, "we must not pass shops of neighbors and give patronage to our
enemies." The good people of Spartanburg had a slightly different
problem before them as the war was beginning to wind down. They held
a concert to raise money for the war effort and were pleased with the
$720 that they took in as a result of Professor E. Falk's splendid
command of his orchestra.[15]

Hackensack businessman Samuel Feder asked his customers to be
patient with him in the spring of 1864. He made the following declaration in the April 15, 1864 edition of the *Bergen County Democrat*. "I
have been robbed, but I hope that my friends and customers, knowing
my reliable nature, will give me credit for the time being. I'm still in business – selling clothing at the best prices anywhere." Trust and faith in the
consumer world still counted for something.

In fact, it counted for a lot. Many newspapers during the nineteenth
century published the names of persons who went bankrupt or who were
delinquent in paying their tax bills. Editors of the *Louisville Daily
Democrat*, for their part, carried such lists on a routine basis. They
observed in the June 4, 1868 issue of their paper, however, that bankruptcy petitions had taken a noticeable dip. They attributed the decrease
to a new law requiring persons to pay 50 cents to process such a
declaration.

Local customs still mattered. Publishers of the *Pine Bluff Press*, for
instance, expressed their displeasure with a new skating rink that recently
had opened.[16] "It seems to be a 'Yankee' concern to have been established
principally or rather entirely for the purpose of making money," they
wrote. Having to pay admission to enter the roller rink succeeded only
in turning "neighbors into a circus show benefiting the managers of the
rink." On the other hand, it was reported in the same issue of the newspaper that a fair to benefit a new synagogue had been held at a local hotel.
It was described as one of the most "successful affairs that ever came off
in this city or any city."

Civility could still be prized as well. This was apparent in the spring of
1875 when the Chicago White Stockings visited St Louis for a few games
against the local baseball team. According to a report in the May 6, 1875
edition of the *St Louis Dispatch*, this was a big occasion and would
inspire a great deal of betting on the outcome of the contests.
Notwithstanding all that was at stake, so to speak, the newspaper's
editors admonished their readers to behave properly toward the visiting
ball players. Good taste was not limited to the ballpark. Two weeks later

it was announced that the Women's Christian Temperance Union in St Louis was prepared to open a "Friendly Inn" or "Temperance Lunch and Free Reading Room" in order to show the practical advantages of temperance.[17]

Good taste, civility, and support for local customs found their finest expression at special times of the year. Social clubs, the German-American school, Masonic Temple, and even the mayor of Wilmington, Delaware were holding special dinners and parties prior to Christmas in 1885, for instance. Four churches opened fairs in the hope of raising funds for organizations whose work they supported, and even more churches announced their upcoming Christmas programs. Yet shop owners in the city were despondent in the days before this special holiday, for although "the streets have never been more crowded ... the purchases as a rule have not been expensive ... [or] as varied as last year."[18] Shopping had taken its rightful place among the other great truths practiced during celebrations of the Christian savior's birth.

At the other end of the communal food chain, one found Boxer John L. Sullivan bringing his road show to Sioux Falls, South Dakota early in 1887. Even here, however, there was room for propriety and a keen mind. According to a report in the *Sioux Falls Daily Argus* on January 8, 1887, the troupe entertained about 600 men and boys at Germania Hall. "The crowd was a jolly and enthusiastic one, and was not made up by any means of what is technically known as the 'sporting element.'" The event was somehow made more acceptable by the faces of so many "lawyers, bankers and prominent men in other businesses" in the audience. It was a comfort to know that they had come "not to see Sullivan spar, but merely in the interest of physical science."

The relationship between prosperity and loyalty to one's city could be expressed in a variety of ways. Directors of the People's Building and Loan Association in Spartanburg did it in 1891 by offering an 8 percent return on all deposits. They encouraged patrons to buy shares in the bank with the money that was earned in these accounts. Another call to invest in the Association was made at its annual meeting that year. It was reported at the meeting that the organization had loaned out $40,600 during the first two years of operation and thus far had earned $2.49 on each share for its stockholders. Buying shares of stock and depositing money in interest-bearing accounts was viewed as a good way to invest in the city's future.[19]

Loyalty also was made apparent when residents declared who could do business in their city and who was not welcomed. This was one of the reasons why Spartanburg business people expressed great concern over the growing presence of businesses originating from North Carolina. "How long before a 'North Carolina society' is established in

Spartanburg?" asked the publishers of the *Carolina Spartan* on October 14, 1891. They named eight firms in the city that were owned or run by North Carolinians and suggested that other unnamed enterprises had the same pedigree. The "Tarheels" were declared "an aggressive people," and the residents of Spartanburg were warned that they would have "to 'hump' themselves to keep up with them."

Outsiders of another sort were a perpetual concern for the residents of San Diego in 1895. Hobos were so numerous that one hardware store owner was inspired to place a tongue-in-cheek advertisement in the December 14, 1895 edition of the *San Diego Union*. In this ad he invited members of an Anti-Hobo Society to round up vagrants and make them sit in front of his powerful oil heaters until they begged to be taken away on the chain gang.

The ever-growing number and array of persons with a putative claim to membership in the community of believers inside San Diego did not include transients. In that city and elsewhere it probably would have excluded the poor, more recent immigrants, children, and most black persons as well. Their time would come eventually, and when it did they would follow paths laid down by real and aspiring middle-class men and women who had found work and more secure lives inside nineteenth-century American cities.

For most persons, these paths did not lead to higher levels of partici-pation in time-honored forms of civic engagement. Men and women remained well-connected to their friends and neighborhood groups.[20] However, persons who had to work hard and for long hours just to sustain themselves and their families did not invest in new economic ventures sponsored by the city's elite. They were more likely to be the beneficiaries of charity than contributors to it. Their church attendance probably could have been better. Subscription campaigns were directed at more prosperous individuals, and working-class persons did not work especially hard to elect candidates to posts inside city governments. Investments outside the neighborhood and work site for laborers and working-class families were confined largely to the marketplace. Their connection to a broader community of equals through the market, though oft repeated and substantial, was predicated more on what they could get than what they could give.

It could hardly have been otherwise. Notwithstanding the higher salaries they drew and improvements they saw at the workplace and by the spread of public services, most Americans were not rich. Nor did they have any realistic chance of acquiring a much bigger piece of the pie, no matter how much wealth was created in the economy as a whole. The best they probably could hope to do was to become more socially and economically secure, act and look a bit more like their betters, have greater freedom in choosing a career and place of residence, and hope that the economy would continue to grow.

Much to their good fortune and credit, that was precisely what happened to them during the better part of the nineteenth century and what they did with the opportunities which came their way.[21] Still, their numbers were so large and the impact of their buying power was so immense that some commentators have picked out shopping and commercial entertainment as the defining features of urban culture during the latter part of the nineteenth century.[22] Given what we have learned about the civic culture of American cities thus far, the attention paid to shopping and personal adornment clearly is overblown. It is nonetheless true that America's consumer culture came of age during the waning years of the nineteenth century.

Few parts of that culture grew faster and bigger than professional sports and so-called "commercial holidays." Baseball, to take one prominent example, was admired for its blending of pastoral settings, leisurely play, teamwork, and the mechanical certainty of box scores and profit margins. It became the perfect bridge between modern corporate America and millions of fans with more time and a little cash to spend. The lesson that paid work could be fun, or at least not drudgery, became an important idea for persons whose jobs were in service industries which were destined to become even bigger in the twentieth century. The ability of baseball and other professional sports to bring persons from markedly different backgrounds and social classes together both as players and spectators anticipated changes that would later push their way into the larger society and economy as well.[23]

Changes to holidays in America also were tied to a world inhabited by shoppers who had spare time and more cash. When America was less affluent, its holidays had been occasions when persons gathered in public and marked the day with a spectacle of some sort. Such private moments of reflection and celebration as may have accompanied these ceremonies were far less important than the short time that men and women spent together in church or on the streets. Leisure of the sort associated with rich persons came only after affluence became more widespread inside America. Only after that happened were more ordinary men and women released from collective obligations and left free to cater to their own whims.[24]

The problem in America was that the big ideas and lofty purposes built into its holidays were sometimes lost in all the noise and rowdy behavior which accompanied public celebrations. City leaders worked hard to curb the wilder excesses associated with some of these holidays and, whenever possible, they tried to transform the events into private or family affairs. Or, men and women also invented brand-new holidays like Mother's Day and Father's Day which were explicitly designed to be quiet and home-bound affairs. By and large, these efforts succeeded. Holidays became occasions for exchanging presents rather than punches and treats rather than ill-timed tricks.[25] High purposes and consumerism were joined at the pocketbook, if not at the hip, and as much in celebration of our growing prosperity and security as for the moral lessons we were supposed to remember on a special day. All one had to do to make the magic work was believe.

Corporate Princes, Not-For-Profit Makers, and the Ever-Hungry Hippo

It was no less true in the twentieth century, but sometimes harder to pull off.

That century certainly started innocently enough. Managers of the Armory Hall in Idaho Falls declared in 1901 that whistling and screeching during stage performances had to stop or else they would be compelled to close down the theater.[26] There were limits that persons dare not test even when entertaining the masses, as everyone who attends a sports event where alcohol is served knows.

Someone had to watch out for us, because we were ill-equipped to keep up with – much less beat – all the faceless business people who hid behind their products. Vigilance came in many forms. For instance, the Anti-Cigarette League of Danville, Illinois held a picnic for the president of the organization on July 21, 1905. One week later the Secretary of the National Anti-Cigarette League visited Danville's jail and spoke about the ills of drinking and smoking to his captive audience.[27]

The same week that cigarettes were being decried in Danville, members of the Women's Christian Temperance Union in San Diego spoke out against adulterated beverages and ice cream as well as the "deleterious effects" brought on by drinking coffee and tea. During that same meeting at the Methodist Episcopal Church, "another member of the union brought up the subject of cola," whose active ingredients were taken from a shrub much used by natives in South America and known to include cocaine. Earlier in the month the same church had sponsored a meeting of the Epworth Young Persons League whose members held a discussion about "Doing Good" and the "Christian Businessman." In August the WCTU met again at the ME Church and stated its opposition to the addition of opiates to chewing gum and intoxicants to candy.[28] By the end of the century, there would be a variety of groups serving as "watch dogs" for consumers and several agencies of the federal government dedicated to keeping the products we use safe and the environment clean.

Residents of Sparks, Nevada were warned of a different kind of threat to their community's economic health in 1911. A story contained in the March 3rd edition of the *Sparks Tribune* described the danger posed to both local merchants and their customers by an infestation of businessmen who were not worthy of trust or much inclined to give credit to hometown folks. Parts of the newspaper story are reproduced below.

BE FAIR TO SELF AND MERCHANT

A few weeks ago a couple of "gripmen" made a house canvas of Sparks. At first sight one might have taken either one of them to be an old-fashioned itinerant quack doctor ... and his methods were as dangerous and menacing to the city, as were the methods of the old time "quack" to the body.

The "doctor" might simply kill a person here or there, while the other individual's workings would have a tendency to kill and destroy the vitality, progress and prosperity of the whole community.

The individuals in question were taking orders for groceries for a house in Salt Lake City. They made pretenses of cutting under prices charged by local business houses. Perhaps they did, in a small degree. [And] some of the people in Sparks fell for this.

Yesterday a dray load of these goods arrived ... and the agents waxed very wroth when ... informed that they would have to pay a license ... [of] $5.

THEY WERE UNWILLING TO PUT UP EVEN THIS INSIGNIFICANT AMOUNT TOWARDS THE MAINTENANCE OF THE CITY.

This shows just how much they care for Sparks, its prosperity or its people, aside from the dollars they can filch ... and take away to other states.

Of course these people advance no credit. You might trade with them for years and then starve to death when you got into hard luck.

But you wouldn't starve to death for the real public spirited home merchant would have the mercy to extend you credit until you got on your feet again, many times to his financial sorrow.

THE "AGENT" DON'T GIVE A TINKER'S DAMN FOR YOU OR THE WELFARE OF YOUR CITY.

He don't care if there is a school.

He don't care whether you have churches, or whether your ... social and church functions are successful or not.

He don't care if any encouragement is given to any progressive movement in your community.

He don't care if any of the people ... are employed.

All this is left up to the home concerns. They rent local buildings and the money is circulated in local channels.

They employ local men.

They pay local taxes and licenses.

> And thus the school subsists and is held at a high standard; the churches
> subsist and the moral standard of the town is raised; instead of wading
> through bog holes, you are able to walk on well kept thoroughfares.

The message could not have been clearer. Business people and shoppers were tied to each other in ways that reached well beyond the articles
they sold and bought. This was the case in Sparks, just as it had been in
Spartanburg 20 years earlier. Both parties would do well in the long run,
if they had faith in each other and worked together. Furthermore, it was
the only way that they could ensure the continued well-being of the place
they both called home.

But for their collaboration on important tasks, they might well end up
viewing *The Last Days of Pompeii* in 1915 as something more than an
amusing way to pass an evening, which is what patrons of the Orpheum
Theater in Fairbanks, Alaska did in February of that year. Reserve seats
cost 75 cents and all other seats cost 50 cents. The $1.50 admission to
the first anniversary dance of the Moose Lodge of Fairbanks held in May
of 1915 was waived for women. It was only going to cost 25 cents, on
the other hand, for fans to watch the first of several baseball games
between the Fairbanks nine and the team from Fort Gibbon on June 9th.
Local merchants donated many prizes and pledged to shut down their
stores for the initial game. All the money taken at the gate was to be dedicated to improving the diamond and grounds surrounding the playing
field.[29]

The Miles Theater in Pittsburgh staged two interesting plays during
the month of September of 1915. The first was entitled *The Melting Pot*.
It was a big hit back then, and today we consider it a good example of
the early twentieth-century campaign to make all foreign persons more
like Americans. The second play was called *An Alien*.[30] It, too, dealt with
problems faced by immigrants in America.

Patriotism and display of a different sort was on the minds of local
merchants in Las Cruces, New Mexico in 1916. They decided to decorate the windows of their stores in blue and white in honor of Baby Week
that year.[31] This event was celebrated in 43 states and lasted a full week
in Las Cruces and furthered the effort to treat our children as objects of
adornment second only to ourselves.

There still was room for propriety and piety, of course. Parishioners
of the First Presbyterian Church in Fargo, for instance, held their annual
meeting in January of 1917. They passed a resolution objecting to "Open
Sunday" laws. Members of the congregation did not want commercial
amusements such as baseball, pool halls, movies, and stage shows to be
open on the Sabbath.[32]

On the other hand, persons who took advantage of mass entertainment could do their community some good at the same time. That certainly was the case in Fairbanks, Alaska in June of 1919 when receipts from matinee shows at Thorne's Theater were donated to a fund that would be used to pay for the construction of a new gymnasium at Fairbanks High School. The new facility was to be a monument to young men from the city who died while on duty in World War I.[33]

Good business practices, however, were not monuments to themselves. They had to be enforced. That is why Congressmen attending the annual dinner of the New Orleans Credit Men's Association in November of 1925 pledged to support efforts to prosecute fraudulent debtors.[34] Business people in New Orleans and elsewhere surely would have more than a few bad debtors to worry about within a few years. In the meantime, though, persons were much more likely to embrace both the ritual of shopping and the display of goods paraded past them in stores and consumer fairs.

The traveling consumer road show which stopped in Charlotte, North Carolina in March of 1928 coincided with one of the city's two semi-annual "Dollar Day" sales. Discounts offered by local merchants were set against the 38 exhibits of new food products and big-ticket items like automobiles. A second exhibition of consumer goods heralded under the banner of "Own Your Own Home" in June of that year featured more items for the modern household.[35] These special sales and shows drew in potential shoppers from towns surrounding Charlotte and connected the city to the practice of consumptive display for persons other than the local elite.

Business people continued to hold such fairs and sales throughout the Great Depression. Under the drumbeat of progress and prosperity, shop owners in Idaho Falls mounted a big publicity campaign in behalf of their Annual Spring Opening in February and March of 1931. Contests were to be run for the store with the best window decorations and for writing the best ads for a local business. Band concerts, street dances, displays of new automobiles, and other activities were planned for the affair.[36]

Even during the height of the Great Depression, bankers in Burlington, Vermont were pleased to announce that depositors had saved $800,000 in their Christmas Savings Accounts. All of the money that individual depositors had squirreled away in 1934 would have been spent on presents and food for the holiday season. Local merchants held a successful Dollar Day Sale later in 1935.[37]

The slowdown in consumer spending that had come with the Great Depression was lengthened but easier to accept during World War II, because everybody finally had a good way to explain why they were doing without things they wanted or needed. Cleveland's merchants and shoppers both suffered under rules laid down by federal agencies, but then so too did business people and customers in every American town and city. In May and June of 1943, for instance, the Office of Defense Transportation stopped the delivery of 15 different luxury items to towns and cities in the eastern part of the country. The War Production Board banned the manufacture of certain women's and children's garments in order to ensure that material could be saved; at the same time it lifted the prohibition against putting cuffs on men's pants. Cleveland merchants were singled out on at least one occasion, however. They had their right to sell rationed footwear suspended for one week because a shoe salesman sold a single pair of children's sandals without requiring a Number 17 ration stamp in exchange.[38]

Notwithstanding all the rules and enforcement officials thrown at consumers and merchants during World War II, there still was a healthy black market in hoarded or stolen goods that stayed in operation throughout the war years. In cities like Pittsburgh it was run quite openly. Indeed, it was not until the end of the war that officials in that city finally mounted a challenge to "black marketers" and began dragging them into court.[39] By then, of course, the point of the whole exercise was moot.

The situation was much different two decades later during the war in Vietnam. The unofficial government position at that time was to promote both "guns and butter." By this Americans meant that they could make war and splurge on themselves at the same time. Part of the reason officials pursued such an imprudent policy was that they did not want to further anger citizens about the conduct of a war that few persons openly endorsed. There also were pressing domestic problems related to race relations, and the federal government had set aside a great deal of money to work on these matters as well.

Local residents and merchants were deeply involved in many efforts to address these domestic concerns. In the case of Cleveland during the late 1960s, for example, some citizens who were interested in stabilizing their East Side neighborhood started a housing information center and hoped to encourage whites to move into the area. Merchants from the same neighborhood initiated a campaign to fight local criminals and even went so far as to hire off-duty policemen to patrol the area.[40]

Persons who lived in smaller cities also created devices to help them promote their community through the power of the marketplace. To take but one example, residents of Columbia, Maryland were urged in 1970 to purchase a coupon book which provided discounts for different products and services offered by local merchants. Its backers hoped that the book would increase traffic and business in these shops and eventually boost their profits. Later in the year a local car dealer sponsored a city-wide contest to see which village could do the best job of painting a vehicle manufactured by the company whose cars he sold. Two weeks after the contest was launched the village of Harper's Choice was declared the winner of the prize.[41]

Several years later, a bank in Germantown, Tennessee sponsored a contest in which persons were invited to come up with a name for its new ATM machine. A number of persons submitted the same name: "The Apple Tree." A liquor store employee who offered that name was selected to receive the $500 US Savings Bond which had been set aside for the winning entry. Other "winners" each received a $25 bond.[42]

Thanks to the efforts of a civic-minded resident named Leo Levi, starting in the early 1990s persons from all over Newton, Massachusetts had a chance to donate money to their hometown every time they shopped. The Visa card issued to any credit-worthy adult living in that city brought much-needed revenue to five groups whose work in behalf of residents was deemed beneficial. These included the Parent–Teacher Organization, the city's Senior Center, support for child care, a Foundation for Racial, Religious, and Ethnic Harmony, and a committee known as Newton Pride which was responsible for doing good works across the city. The 900 cards in use as of 1998 generated about $16,000 each year, and that sum was divided evenly among the five groups.[43]

Whole neighborhoods played an even more prominent part in the commercial restructuring of larger American cities during the second half of the twentieth century. Business districts expanded because professional and service industries finally needed at least as much space downtown as the middle-class shoppers who had redefined these areas for "higher" purposes in the late-nineteenth century. Older residential areas were transformed into havens for upscale families in anticipation of the arrival of even more white-collar laborers like those, one supposes, who had attended nineteenth-century baseball games wearing suits and dresses.

A part of Pittsburgh known as the "Golden Triangle" drew particular attention from city leaders in the early 1970s because of its proximity to the downtown area and potential appeal to upscale residents and visitors. This former industrial zone became one of the "hottest" spots to be in the city once it was redeveloped as an entertainment and residential district in 1973.[44] Adding further evidence of the downtown area's revival, a jazz festival held at Three Rivers Stadium on two consecutive evenings in July of that year drew some 16,000 music lovers to this part of Pittsburgh.[45]

The problem with so many attempts to rebuild downtown areas around businesses dedicated to investments, services, and shopping of one sort or another was that the benefit to persons who lived elsewhere in the city was not readily apparent. Attempts by city leaders to paint these campaigns as being beneficial to the whole city, we learned earlier, were viewed skeptically by persons who did not work or shop downtown. No clear connection was made between their well-being and all the candy being poured into the pockets of persons they did not know. This collection of businessmen and women surely would have included corporate princes who likened tall buildings to crowns. There also were the not-for-profit makers who ran medical complexes and other "cultural" institutions in the updated city. Among the most annoying members of this gallery, however, were the ever-hungry hippos who owned sports franchises and threatened to move the "home team" if they did not get a brand-new stadium with expensive seats that many working-class persons could not afford to fill.

Inner-city neighborhoods away from the central business district were overlooked as potential investment sites and centers of commerce for the better part of the late-twentieth century. Banks and retail chains began to move into some of these neighborhoods during the 1990s, but only cautiously and with mixed results. In Boston, for instance, bank managers made slow progress in backing loans for home buyers in predominantly black neighborhoods, and large retailing stores still balked at the chance to move into these areas.[46] Business owners and public leaders were warming up slowly to the idea that there were human beings outside of the downtown area who wanted to buy houses and shop under the same terms applied to persons who lived in more obviously prosperous settings. Until that realization sank in deeper and was acted on more often, the social and economic hole between downtown areas and residential neighborhoods would remain unfilled.

The really unfortunate thing about all the bad feelings and sour behavior which continue to seep into the hole today is that we really do know how to fill it better. A great many of the congenial and profitable ways in which this could be accomplished are embedded in the kind of community building we associate with consumer communalism. It has brought an understanding of what it means to be part of a community to countless millions of Americans by helping them fall into habits and ways of viewing the world that once were reserved for wealthier persons. No matter how modest their individual contributions may have been, the continuous engagement of persons in commonplace rituals tied to commodities put them in league with men and women who made the community of believers inside their city.

Most individuals with limited capital and spare time have no realistic chance of becoming full-blown members in that community. Nor do they show much interest and willingness to assume the burdens that historically had come to individuals who did. On the other hand, they can be engaged by beliefs and practices that animate the larger bourgeois civic culture, and the part of that culture dedicated to our consumerism provides an excellent way for them to learn these lessons.

In the past, men and women of limited means may have hoped that their children would "do better" than they had or at least be more economically secure. Even though they may have had good reason to believe this, life never has been easy for persons who work hard just to keep themselves fed, clothed, and housed. Getting more is a lot harder to do.

To increase the chance that they or their children might improve their chances for a better life, adults often made big sacrifices and worked extraordinarily hard during their lifetimes. The biggest article of faith they invested in usually was a house; but even becoming the owner of a house did not propel families into a higher social class. It only enabled them to solidify their current status and blurred the differences between themselves and persons who were financially better off. That may not seem like a big accomplishment, but it certainly opened up places and possibilities for members of the working and barely-middle classes that had heretofore been closed to them and their families.[47]

More well-to-do persons also bought housing and participated in the same ritual of shopping and investing, of course. Their purpose was somewhat different. They tried and often succeeded in walling themselves off from less prosperous individuals when they purchased homes.[48]

Many of the social contacts and group affiliations available to wealthier and less well-to-do Americans were narrowed because they often lived among persons who were not all that different from themselves. In other parts of the consumer culture, however, individuals from different backgrounds and social classes still had many opportunities to observe and interact with each other. The best chances for this kind of contact came while browsing and making purchases at department stores and more specialized retail shops or by attending "public" events staged in and around these establishments.

The forerunner of this custom, of course, was the medieval fair which provided persons living inside and outside the castle walls the chance to sample goods they rarely saw and to witness spectacles staged for their amusement. Fairs of this sort came to the residents of nineteenth- and twentieth-century towns and cities in the form of "Dollar Day" sales and traveling trade shows. Persons in bigger cities had the chance to participate in shopping rituals and amusements reminiscent of these affairs every day in the new "department stores" that were built during the second half of the nineteenth century. Many more women than men also took advantage of the employment opportunities afforded them in these emporiums. This tradition was further updated during the second half of the twentieth century with the proliferation of suburban shopping malls and the creation of mall-like environments inside the central city.[49]

Despite the incredible growth of the postwar consumer culture in America, it bears repeating that relations with family members and friends and affiliations with groups dedicated to helping their members and doing good works did not diminish substantially. All the meetings and chances to observe other persons that we have talked about in the context of the consumer culture supplemented these more traditional contacts.[50] Indeed, the world occupied by store owners and shoppers often made these more intimate and long-term relations easier to find and carry on. The supermarket juice bar became a meeting place for young men and women who did not drink liquor; and the broad concourses of enclosed shopping centers were transformed into places for friends to mingle and sites where retired persons took safe and vigorous walks.[51]

Credit Without Worth, Consumption Without Status

Daily newspapers in older and larger cities chronicled the flowering of a consumer culture in the United States beginning in the early 1800s. The reason for its arrival and spread was clear enough. All kinds of Americans began to have more money, and all manner of business people did their best to offer men and women more things to buy and use. Luxury items were featured in many of the advertisements carried by local newspapers, but mass-produced objects and everyday goods received more attention and attracted more purchasers as the century unfolded.

The question was not whether men and women bought and used more stuff than they had in the past. Clearly they did. The troubling question they left us to resolve is what they hoped to accomplish with all their shopping and showing off.

The conventional view of conspicuous consumption is that individuals shop and adorn themselves in order to gain prestige in the eyes of their peers and with persons outside of their social circle.[52] Whether they had earned the privilege of showing off in that way is quite beside the point. Many men and women buy lots of items for selfish purposes and display them prominently as a way of making themselves look bigger than they really are. At least that is what many observers say has been going on since the mid-nineteenth century.[53]

Our answer to this question is a little different. Men and women who live and work in cities sometimes purchase goods with no bigger idea in mind than to appear more important than they are. This plan, such as it is, may even work for a while. More often than not, however, shopping and display only serve to affirm one's position in the communal pecking order. They cannot change it.

The larger social achievement of consumer communalism is seen in the way it ties persons of distinctly unequal means together. They hold the same values, practice the same habits, and embrace ceremonies which reinforce the legitimacy of inequality even as they scurry home with their arms full of shiny packages and bags stuffed with food. Conspicuous consumption does not increase social inequality or make the differences between us more stark. It promotes a sense of equality among distinctly unequal persons by letting them buy similar objects in places they like while practicing customs they accept as good and fair. The fact that these rituals often occur in the company of persons we know and like or result in purchases that will draw us closer to them just makes it better.

No matter how valid and important the connection between shopping and social solidarity may be, it is almost too easy to lampoon large parts of our consumer culture as wasteful or mindless and hard to see how it makes communities better. This is particularly so when we compare the way we display our affluence today against the way we handled riches and prestige in an earlier time. It was once the case that only persons who made a contribution to their community were accorded much respect and that one had to be respectful before one was invited to make a bigger contribution to the community. Today the time-honored practice of equating personal responsibility and accomplishment with material well-being and display does not seem to hold us as strongly as it once did.

Narcissism has taken up part of this space. Whether seen through the personal revelations we make to strangers or by all the flitting about we do for new experiences and partners, so many of us have never seemed quite so gloriously and painfully fond of ourselves as we are today. There is so much of it that we cannot turn away without seeing more extravagance or another example of conspicuous display either on our person or of ourselves. It is difficult to escape the conclusion that too much credit may have been given to men and women who are not worthy of it and getting more things no longer has anything to do with being an accomplished person.

Without denying the validity of these observations, we have seen that there is another way to look at all the investing and shopping which men and women, and to some extent even children, of modest means have been doing since the end of the nineteenth century. It is to see shopping and personal adornment as expressions of values and habits that are vital to the well-being of the whole community. The items we buy are much more than trinkets that make it easier for us to show off or to identify persons we would like to meet or become. They are articles of the faith we have in each other and particularly in the way we manage the ticklish business of accepting each other as equals in some settings and not in others.

Persons who lived in Sparks, Nevada in 1911 saw very clearly that business people and their customers had a great deal in common. Their relation did not begin or end with the mere exchange of money for goods. They were tied to each other and supported each other in a variety of ways. That one probably had more money than the other was at once irrelevant and an important part of the cultural puzzle that they had assembled inside their city. They needed each other. More important to the story I have been trying to tell, they had found a way to get along and contribute to each other's well-being despite what might have been some obvious differences in their background and wealth. Values and habits of the sort we associate with consumer communalism are key to understanding how they reached such accommodations and were able to collaborate with each other.

Most of us can distinguish cheaper cars from more expensive models and know that mansions are more substantial dwellings than bungalows. It just seems harder today to figure out whether the person driving the expensive automobile or living in the fancier house really can afford such items or has the social esteem of someone who in the past could have done so. If historians are correct, sometime in the middle of the nineteenth century it became easier to be fooled by persons with little wealth and to be taken in by individuals who appeared more trustworthy than they really were.[54]

If we ignore persons who have made a career out of being a fake or a fraud, we have to return to the vast majority of men and women who affirm their status with the items they buy and the way they show off. The only way these persons are likely to change their position in the community's pecking order, probably for the worse, is by abusing the customs and codes associated with consumer communalism. After all, it is hard to sustain the fiction that one is better off than one really is. Buying expensive articles and adorning oneself lavishly does not alter the fact that some of us still will be wealthy after the bills are paid while others will have nothing left.

Better evidence could not be found of too much credit going to unworthy persons and of excessive consumer spending than the spike in personal bankruptcy that occurred in the last years of the twentieth century. Newspapers and news magazines chronicled the slide of so many persons into gross indebtedness under titles like "Big lenders bring debt to the masses," "Another fatal American addiction: The Plastic," "Deadbeat Nation," and "We want what we cannot afford."[55] Many men and women simply bought much more than they could afford, and they paid a really stiff price for indulging themselves.

To the extent that they drove themselves into bankruptcy by trying to look more important than they really were, they learned that conspicuous consumption did not improve one's social standing.[56] Their public undressing made them valuable object lessons in what happens when consumption no longer bears any relation to one's social status. It did nothing, however, to make them credible candidates for membership in the community of believers.

The debt incurred by individuals and households during the last two decades of the twentieth century did not vanish. Nor was it forgiven by lenders in most cases. Indeed, companies which issued credit cards were pushing lawmakers in 1997 to make it harder for persons to have their debts forgiven once they declared bankruptcy.

To the extent that individuals had to pay back borrowed money out of their future earnings, they certainly would solidify their low status in the community's economic pecking order. They also would reduce the chances that they would acquire much wealth during their lifetime. There was good news, too, however. For in the process of paying off their debt they would have to recommit themselves to the discipline and good bourgeois values which make prosperity possible in the first place.

Many late-nineteenth century critics of modern consumer culture feared that conspicuous spending by persons who really could not afford all the items they purchased would corrupt these individuals.[57] While the ridiculous spending habits and debt accumulated by many persons do boggle the mind at times, in the long run it probably turns out all right. Instead of being corrupted, men and women who buy too much stuff and slide into great debt eventually are compelled to learn the very kinds of self-control and work habits which only more bourgeois or prosperous individuals are supposed to know.

Far from driving us apart and showing bad faith, shopping, even when done to excess, ends up enforcing a kind of social solidarity and faithfulness in most of us that is not experienced or felt in other parts of our everyday lives. I am reminded of a conversation between two married couples a few years back that bears on this very point. Alerted to the fact that their friends were celebrating a notable anniversary, the first couple congratulated them on their accomplishment. The celebrated bride took great satisfaction from this and, smiling at her husband, asked him what he thought the foundation of their long and stable marriage had been. Her husband, grinning a bit more than he probably should have, replied without hesitation. "Shared debt."

We can take comfort in knowing that this works better in society at large than it apparently does in many marriages.

NOTES

1 Andrew Tobias, "Take Control Of Your Credit Cards," *Boston Sunday Globe Parade Magazine,* November 1, 1998.

2 Roger S. Mason, *Conspicuous Consumption: A Study of Exceptional Consumer Behavior* (New York: St Martin's Press, 1981); Carole Shammas, "How Self-Sufficient Was Early America?" *Journal of Interdisciplinary History,* Volume 13, Number 2, Autumn 1982, pp. 247–72; Colin Campbell, *The Romantic Ethic and the Spirit of Modern Consumerism* (Oxford: Blackwell Publishers, 1987); Paul Lewis, "In Buying We Trust," *New York Times,* May 30, 1998.

3 Carl Bridenbaugh, *Cities in Revolt: Urban Life in America, 1743–1776* (Oxford: Oxford University Press, 1971), p. 146.

4 Ibid., p. 168.

5 William Willis, *History of Portland, From 1632 to 1864* (Press of Brown Thurston, 1865), p. 776.

6 Bridenbaugh, *Cities in Revolt,* p. 159.

7 Ibid., p. 167.

8 Ibid., p. 363.

9 Ibid., p. 169.

10 Richard Carwardine, "The Second Great Awakening in the Urban Centers: An Examination of Methodism and the New Measures," *Journal of American History,* Volume 58, Number 2, September 1972, pp. 327–40; James Moorhead, "Between Progress and Apocalypse: A Reassessment of Millennialism in American Religious Thought, 1800–1880," *Journal of American History,* Volume 71, Number 3, December 1984, pp. 524–42.

11 Mason, *Conspicuous Consumption,* pp. 50–5.

12 *Boston Chronicle Gazette,* January 10, 1820.

13 Karen Halttunen, *Confidence Men and Painted Women: A Study of Middle-class Culture in America, 1830–1870* (New Haven, CT: Yale University Press, 1982), pp. 13, 20, 51, 193.

14 *Carolina Spartan,* March 27, May 22, and August 21, 1856.

15 *Florence Gazette,* February 20, 1861 and July 4, 1864.

16 *Pine Bluff Press,* February 1, 1872.

17 *St Louis Dispatch,* May 21, 1875.

18 *Wilmington Morning News,* December 25, 1885.

19 *Carolina Spartan,* October 7 and November 18, 1891.

20 Mark Goldman, "Buffalo's Black Rock: A Neighborhood and the City," *Journal of Urban History,* Volume 5, Number 4, August 1979, pp. 447–68.

21 Carolyn Tyirin Kirk and Gordon Kirk, "The Impact of the City on Home Ownership: A Comparison of Immigrants and Native Whites at the Turn of the Century," *Journal of Urban History,* Volume 7, Number 4, August 1981, pp. 471–98; Mary Lou Locke, "Out of the Shadows and into the Western Sun: Working Women of the Late Nineteenth-Century Urban Far West," *Journal of Urban History,* Volume 16, Number 2, February 1990,

pp. 175–204; Terrence McDonald, "Rediscovering The Active City," *Journal of Urban History*, Volume 16, Number 3, May 1990, pp. 304–11; Dominic Pacyga, "The Making of Working-Class Chicago," *Journal of Urban History*, Volume 18, Number 4, August 1992, pp. 498–503; Samuel P. Hays, "From the History of the City to the History of the Urbanized Society," *Journal of Urban History*, Volume 19, Number 4, August 1993, pp. 3–25; Elaine Tyler May, "The Pressure to Provide: Class, Consumption, and Divorce in Urban America, 1820–1920," *Journal of Social History*, Volume 12, Number 2, Winter 1978, pp. 180–93; E. Anthony Rotundo, "Body and Soul: Changing Ideals of Middle-Class Manhood, 1790–1920," *Journal of Social History*, Volume 16, Number 4, Spring 1983, pp. 23–38; Janice Weiss, "Educating for Clerical Work: The 19th-Century Private Commercial School," *Journal of Social History*, Volume 14, Number 3, Spring 1981, pp. 407–24; Donald Scott, "The Popular Lecture and the Creation of a Public in Mid-Nineteenth-Century America," *Journal of American History*, Volume 66, Number 4, March 1980, pp. 791–809.

22 Gunther Barth, *City People: The Rise of Modern City Culture in Nineteenth-Century America* (New York: Oxford University Press, 1980); Daniel Horowitz, "Consumption and its Discontents: Simon N. Patten, Thorstein Veblin, and George Gunton," *Journal of American History*, Volume 67, Number 2, September 1980, pp. 301–17; Gregory Bush, "'Genial Evasion' in the Big Time: Changing Norms of Respectability Within an Expansive Urban Culture," *Journal of Urban History*, Volume 19, Number 3, May 1993, pp. 121–38; Joan Shelly Rubin, "Self, Culture, and Self-Culture in Modern America: The Early History of the Book-of-the-Month Club," *Journal of American History*, Volume 71, Number 4, March 1985, pp. 782–806.

23 Steven Riess, "Sport and the American Dream," *Journal of Social History*, Volume 14, Number 2, Winter 1980, pp. 295–304; Jeffrey Mirel, "From Student Control to Institutional Control of High School Athletics: Three Michigan Cities, 1883–1905," *Journal of Social History*, Volume 16, Number 2, Winter 1982, pp. 83–100; Steven Gelber, "Working at Play: The Culture of the Workplace and the Rise of Baseball," *Journal of Social History*, Volume 16, Number 4, Spring 1983, pp. 3–22; Melvin Adelman, "Baseball, Business, and the Work Place: Gelber's Thesis Revisited," *Journal of Social History*, Volume 23, Number 2, Winter 1989, pp. 285–302; Steven Pope, "Negotiating the 'Folk Highway' of the Nation: Sport, Public Culture, and American Identity, 1870–1940," *Journal of Social History*, Volume 27, Number 2, Winter 1993, pp. 327–40; Timothy Kelly, "Suburbanization and the Decline of Catholic Public Rituals in Pittsburgh," *Journal of Social History*, Volume 28, Number 2, Winter 1994, pp. 311–30; James Olson, "Sports as Cultural Currency in Modern America," *Journal of Urban History*, Volume 19, Number 1, November 1992, pp. 127–30.

24 Stanley Parker, *The Sociology of Leisure* (New York: International Publications Services, 1976), pp. 20–3.

25 Leigh Eric Schmidt, "The Commercialization of the Calendar: American

Holidays and the Culture of Consumption, 1870–1930," *Journal of American History*, Volume 78, Number 3, December 1991, pp. 887–916; Michael Kazin and Steven Ross, "America's Labor Day: The Dilemma of a Workers' Celebration," *Journal of American History*, Volume 78, Number 4, March 1992, pp. 1,294–1,323; Leigh Eric Schmidt, *Consumer Rites: The Buying and Selling of American Holidays* (Princeton, NJ: Princeton University Press, 1995); Stephen Nissenbaum, *The Battle for Christmas* (New York: Alfred A. Knopf, 1996); Lesley Pratt Bannatyne, *Halloween: An American Holiday, An American History* (New York: Facts On File, 1990); Jack Santino, *Halloween and Other Festivals of Death and Life* (Knoxville, TN: University of Tennessee Press, 1994); Sylvia Ann Grider, "Conservatism and Dynamism in the Contemporary Celebration of Halloween: Institutionalization, Commercialization, Gentrification," *Southern Folklore*, Volume 53, Number 1, 1996, pp. 3–15.

26 *Idaho Register*, April 12, 1901.
27 *Commercial News*, July 13 and July 21, 1905.
28 *San Diego Union*, July 27, July 8, and August 3, 1905.
29 *Fairbanks Daily News-Miner*, February 8, May 8, and June 9, 1915.
30 *Pittsburgh Gazette*, September 16 and September 25, 1915.
31 *Rio Grande Republic*, April 14, 1916.
32 *Fargo Forum and Daily Republican*, January 19, 1917.
33 *The Fairbanks Daily News-Miner*, June 21, 1919.
34 *New Orleans Times-Picayune*, November 18, 1925.
35 *Charlotte Observer*, March 15 and June 28, 1928.
36 *Idaho Falls Post*, February 15, 1931.
37 *Burlington Free Press*, January 1 and August 9, 1935.
38 *Cleveland Plain Dealer*, May 18, June 2, and June 10, 1943.
39 *Pittsburgh Post-Gazette*, April 13 and April 14, 1945.
40 *Cleveland Plain Dealer*, February 10 and February 18, 1968.
41 *Columbia Flier*, April 24, August 12, and August 29, 1970.
42 *Germantown News*, November 23, 1978.
43 I am grateful to Linda Plaut, who works tirelessly in behalf of her city as its director of cultural affairs, for this report.
44 *Pittsburgh Post-Gazette*, March 21and July 4, 1973.
45 Ibid., July 17, 1973.
46 *Boston Globe*, December 16, 1996; March 10 and June 12, 1998.
47 Robert Barrows, "Beyond the Tenement: Patterns of American Urban Housing, 1870–1930," *Journal of Urban History*, Volume 9, Number 4, August 1983, pp. 395–420; Carol O'Connor, "The Rise and Fall of Suburbia," *Journal of Urban History*, Volume 13, Number 3, May 1987, pp. 354–61; Mary Cobin Sies, "The City Transformed: Nature, Technology, and the Suburban Ideal, 1877–1917," *Journal of Urban History*, Volume 14, Number 1, November 1987, pp. 88–111; Richard Harris, "American Suburbs: A Sketch of a New Interpretation," *Journal of Urban History*, Volume 15, Number 1, November 1988, pp. 98–103; Richard Harris, "Working-Class Home Ownership in the American Metropolis," *Journal of Urban History*, Volume 17, Number 1, November

1990, pp. 46–69; Ronald Tobey, Charles Wetherell, and Jay Brigham, "Moving Out and Settling In: Residential Mobility, Home Owning, and the Public Framing of Citizenship, 1921–1950," *American Historical Review*, Volume 95, Number 5, December 1990, pp. 1,395–422; David Schuyler, "The Peripheral View From Sever Hall," *Journal of Urban History*, Volume 17, Number 3, May 1991, pp. 303–8; Steven Hoffman, "'A Plan of Quality': The Development of Mt Lebanon, a 1920s Automobile Suburb," *Journal of Urban History*, Volume 18, Number 2, February 1992, pp. 141–81; Alexander Von Hoffman, "Weaving the Urban Fabric: Nineteenth-Century Patterns of Residential Real Estate Development in Outer Boston," *Journal of Urban History*, Volume 22, Number 2, January 1996, pp. 191–230; James Borchert, "Residential City Suburbs: The Emergence of a New Suburban Type, 1880–1930," *Journal of Urban History*, Volume 22, Number 3, March 1996, pp. 283–307.

48   John Archer, "Ideology and Aspiration: Individualism, the Middle Class, and the Genesis of the Anglo-American Suburb," *Journal of Urban History*, Volume 14, Number 2, February 1988, pp. 214–53; Patricia Burgess Stach, "Deed Restrictions and Subdivision Development in Columbus, Ohio, 1900–1970," *Journal of Urban History*, Volume 15, Number 1, November 1988, pp. 42–68; David Beito and Bruce Smith, "The Formation of Urban Infrastructure Through Nongovernmental Planning: The Private Places of St Louis, 1869–1920," *Journal of Urban History*, Volume 16, Number 3, May 1990, pp. 263–303.

49   William Leach, "Transformations in a Culture of Consumption: Women and Department Stores, 1890–1925," *Journal of American History*, Volume 71, Number 2, September 1984, pp. 319–42; Lizabeth Cohen, "From Town Center to Shopping Center: The Reconfiguration of Community Marketplaces in Postwar America," *American Historical Review*, Volume 101, Number 4, October 1996, pp. 1,050–81; Kenneth Jackson, "All the World's a Mall: Reflections on the Social and Economic Consequences of the American Shopping Center," *American Historical Review*, Volume 101, Number 4, October 1996, pp. 1,111–21.

50   Claude Fischer, "Changes in Leisure Activities, 1890–1940," *Journal of Social History*, Volume 27, Number 3, Spring 1994, pp. 453–76.

51   *Boston Globe*, October 15, 1995 and May 3, 1998.

52   Mason, *Conspicuous Consumption*, pp. 9–17.

53   Thorstein Veblen, *The Theory of the Leisure Class* (New York: Macmillan, 1899).

54   Halttunen, *Confidence Men and Painted Women*.

55   *Boston Globe*, March 2, 1997; *Newsweek*, April 14, 1997; *Boston Globe*, May 17, 1998.

56   Mason, *Conspicuous Consumption*, p. 119.

57   Daniel Horowitz, *The Morality of Spending:Attitudes toward the Consumer Society in America, 1875–1940* (Baltimore, MD: Johns Hopkins University Press, 1985).

11

Private Entitlements as a Public Good

American cities are large unfinished pieces of civic sculpture. Over the years they have been whacked at, chiseled, cut, and polished by a great number of persons with markedly different tastes and talents. That is why no two of them look exactly alike. At the same time, there is something hauntingly familiar about all of these pieces that can be seen in any one of them. They may not have been worked on by the same hands, but most of the underlying ideas or themes emerging from these sculptures and many of the techniques used to shape each piece have been borrowed from other places and artists.

More socially esteemed and wealthy persons were among the earliest and most important artists to leave their mark on the civic culture of American cities. These *commercial communalists* looked at the world in a special way. They understood that human beings might lead very different lives. Yet it was important for them always to have a broader public good in mind whenever they undertook a new venture. They also were supposed to approach the world in the right way, making sure that they followed the rules and behaved in a pious manner in their dealings with others. To the extent that they were successful they had an obligation to share some portion of what they had with their fellow townsfolk. Finally, persons did not accomplish anything worthwhile by themselves. Their best work in behalf of the community would be done in collaboration with like-minded persons. It was a group project.

Another collection of persons who approached their civic sculpture as a group project were the *ethnic communalists*. They lacked the expensive tools and refined technique of their better-off peers. Like any good student, however, they also had a different but complementary vision of what a good community should look like. They were more introspective and, in a sense, selfish. Their foremost concern was with those persons who belonged to their group, and they were more likely to work in behalf of that group's private interests rather than some abstract or broadly applied notion of the public good. They also played by more tolerant rules, if only because the beliefs and practices they embraced often were quite different from those of most other persons living in the city.

Both of these corporate approaches to the world continue to shape the civic culture of American cities. Indeed, some of their more important work probably remains unfinished. Notwithstanding the vital contributions made by commercial and ethnic communalism since the eighteenth century, these approaches to fashioning an orderly and prosperous world no longer seem to dominate the civic culture of American cities as they once did. That honor goes to the market and the state and to the types of artists who work inside these arenas.

Consumer communalists and *government communalists* approach the task of sculpting a civic culture in ways that are qualitatively different from those associated with business leaders and ethnic groups. They make a community of believers out of a large and sometimes fractious mass of individuals through the logic and grueling mechanics of addition: one person at a time.

This feat is accomplished in the marketplace by spreading the risks and potential rewards of membership to more workers and consumers. Petitioners must be pious and play by rules that establish them as worthy or creditable persons. Their worthiness may reach no farther than the length of their credit cards placed end to end, but it is a kind of acceptance or certification that many persons can recognize and share at the same time.

A market-oriented approach to community building extends to humble persons some of the same privileges attached to privacy and opportunities for self-indulgence that were once enjoyed only by wealthier persons. It does so, however, without undermining the authority of the men and women who actually run the economy or without cutting into their wealth very much. If less well-to-do persons do not play by the rules and lose their credit worthiness, all the perks and prerogatives of acting like a more prosperous person go away. They may regain the privileges of acting like a more prosperous individual some day. It is unlikely, however, that they will ever feel the obligation and sense of responsibility for making the world a better place which is supposed to be expressed in the life of every accomplished and blessed person.

The trick of turning a bunch of seemingly unrelated individuals into a community of believers is achieved differently by the state. Instead of allowing anyone who can pay the price of a ticket into the community, and sometimes letting someone in even when he or she cannot afford it, the state tries to make its club more exclusive. It does this by building a big wall around persons called "citizens" and distinguishing them from aliens, foreign devils, infidels, or any outsider who could not possibly qualify for membership.

The state is obliged to reject other ways of attributing worth to persons or ranking them. Such novel assignments are better managed in the shifting sensibilities of the marketplace where, at least in theory, everyone can have his or her own niche. The only status with formal standing under government communalism is that of "citizen." The only ranking that matters is centered on the question of who is a citizen or can become one.

Great importance is attributed to the role of citizen in modern republics, at least as a matter of principle. The practice of citizenship at the end of the twentieth century and the start of the twenty-first century, on the other hand, seems much reduced or at least not as highly regarded as it was in the past. There probably are a host of good reasons for why this might be the case. Certainly, the rituals and ceremonies attached to government communalism are more elaborate and exciting than those witnessed in the marketplace, but one does not have to use them as often and there are no shiny packages to open once one has finished shopping for a candidate, helped to pass a law, or paid one's taxes. From the perspective afforded by American urban history, then, the most likely explanation is that the club to which citizens belong is easy to join, really hard to be bounced from, and not especially demanding or much fun.

Sloth is more easily accepted in citizens than is heresy. We do not often punish lazy citizens. One does not have to vote or even pay attention to the larger issues of the day. Acting like a heretic, on the other hand, can put one in a really tough spot. That is why persons are banished for a long time or forfeit their lives when they openly repudiate ideas which "real citizens" hold dear or willfully challenge standards citizens depend upon to keep their world whole.

It sometimes happens that such persons are returned to us. Even when they regain the privilege of walking among other free men and women, however, they still may not be able to practice other customs associated with being a good citizen. We may no longer brand heretics or carry out public executions, but we do keep lists with the names of persons who are liable to be hounded by agents of the state or shunned by their neighbors.

Most of us do not end up that way, of course. Yet it is not clear that we take much comfort from being members in the community of equals composed of "citizens." Though too important to give up and perhaps too easily awarded, citizenship does not confer the same privileges upon all of us or make us all count in the same way most of the time. Nor does it appear that we really expect such blessings to be conferred upon us by virtue of being a citizen in good standing.

The rituals and codes tied to government and politics are able to soften the effects of inequality, at least for some of us. They also are good for reducing some of the risks associated with living in an uncertain and sometimes unkind world. Again, not everyone is treated this way; but they do not have to be for it to work out all right most of the time. The marketplace draws us in and keeps us quiet by spreading some of these same risks around to a much larger collection of persons. It also lets us act in ways that make the differences between us look a whole lot smaller than they really are.

Neither the marketplace nor the state, however, can eliminate differences or end inequality. State-sponsored routines and rhetoric may play down differences in status or rank. However, advantages gained by talent, luck, and legacy are likely to be legitimated or ratified by what governments do. Politicians appeal to specific blocs of voters such as "minorities" or "conservatives" by making rules that favor such classes of citizens and wrapping these presents in noise about "leveling playing fields" or "undoing the harm" visited upon innocent or helpless persons. The reality, of course, is that only a portion of those persons with well-founded grievances usually receive help, and whatever they get usually is not enough to improve their long-term prospects or social standing in a big way.[1]

Men and women who turn to politics or the government in order to make the lives of other persons better do accomplish something. What they do, however, does not eliminate hardship or wash away the ill will that we sometimes feel toward persons who are not like us. Their achievement is at once more modest and far-reaching than that. They reduce the risks which citizens face every day by regulating many of the contacts they have with each other, by moderating the effects of ideas and objects hurled at them from the outside world, and, frankly, by doing favors for them.

The problem is that our sense of entitlement often outstrips our obligation to watch out for each other's well-being. The support we give other persons is thin, enforced only by institutions to which we all subscribe by paying taxes. We may all take something from the customs, codes, and ceremonies wrapped up as government communalism, but persons are not equally comforted by them. New government services usually go to well-off persons or better areas first. Assistance to less well-to-do individuals and places comes later or last.

Many academic writers, activists, policy experts, legislators, and regular everyday folk who worry about the way things are done in cities, are discouraged by this state of affairs. They take particular exception to it when attempts to smooth out some of the city's bigger bumps for its less able or accomplished residents are at stake. They see too much exclusion, inequality, and meanness being practiced in cities and far too little equity, sharing, and good will. They would gladly trade some of the city's wealth and power for a more humane existence. In their view, local governments should take a much bigger role in making this happen and pay much less attention to ensuring that business people and wealthy persons make out like bandits.[2]

These men and women offer impassioned critiques about what governments do, or do not do, to help less successful persons. They also point out all the injustices that continue to be visited upon such persons. Given what we know about the way persons often treat each other in cities, one would be hard pressed to say that injustices do not occur, the hardships they talk about are a fiction, or that governments always make things better.

Scratch them even a little and I think you find a bourgeois critic. That is someone who really dislikes the fact that bad things keep happening to the same persons but who is not especially keen on giving up his own wealth or privileges to stop it or insists that somebody else should pay to make the bad stuff go away. They are upset that Americans value orderliness and prosperity over coarse democratic pretensions and equality. They also find it hard to accept the idea that an urban way of life not only is built upon differences in talent, wealth, and accomplishment but also celebrates our sorry attempts to reduce, get around, get over, and, yes, even ignore these differences. We should not be surprised, therefore, when thoughtful persons take no solace from governments that do a little good for some persons and a whole lot more for others.

There certainly was a time when town or city governments did comparatively little in the way of providing services to their less well-off citizens and local politics was an avocation practiced by men of substance and standing in the community. Such men could see quite clearly how projects undertaken with the blessing of the public bodies they ran and the regulations governing commerce that they passed might improve their personal standing and wealth. It was not always easy to raise capital for a new economic venture or piece of publicly backed hardware like a wharf or road, but the several paths that lay between them and their town's prosperity were not hard to describe.

Connecting the dots between themselves and those citizens whose consultation was deemed appropriate or necessary to the future of the city posed no great challenge, and not only because they owned most of the pencils. It was that there were comparatively few of them, and their daily contact with each other in business deals or on purely social occasions made collaboration on public matters a pretty straightforward affair. Their lesser peers would follow and their fortunes also would rise, albeit with a less remarkable trajectory, as long as social and economic relations inside the city were well regulated. It fell to local governments to do a lot of the formal ordering and overseeing which put the town on a fast track to prosperity.[3]

Then there was a time when city governments did a great deal for their constituents generally and tried to do at least a little more to help less well-to-do persons. Local politics during this more recent period was overseen by professional caretakers and elected office holders whose sight was firmly fixed on another public job or simply keeping the one they already had. Men and women of substance found other ways to make a difference and keep their legacy alive.

Life in cities generally became more complex and confusing in part because more persons made bids to become a major player in the city's development. There also were more paths to economic wealth and privileged positions for them to reach that goal, and these paths criss-crossed in new and unexpected ways. An individual's improved standing in the community still was tied to the fate of the larger city. It simply was not as easy as it once had been to see how the city's prosperity and the well-being of everyone who lived there were tied to a particular project or one person's accomplishments.

It was not a coincidence that a more expansive style of local governance was introduced to cities around the middle of the nineteenth century. The number and size of cities had swollen. So, too, had the variety of problems with which government officers had to deal and the cost of the remedies they prescribed. There was too much to do and not enough money or hands to accomplish what needed to be done to keep the city running well.

The formal obligation to mind the city's business at one time had been shouldered by a small number of the city's more permanent residents. It was now too much a load for them to carry alone. A larger pool of subscribers and office holders had to be brought into the political arena. The burden or privilege of paying for good public works was passed along to more persons in the form of involuntary subscriptions called "taxes." The office holders were found among the growing number of petty bourgeois business persons, lesser professionals, and persons trained for careers in government or "public service" who lived and worked in cities. Emerging as important contenders for a place inside the community of believers, these men and women had more technical skills than wealth or social prominence.

The big men of manufacturing and commerce also found more congenial distractions. They tended to economic affairs and helped to create a whole new class of institutions to do the hard work of overseeing and improving life in the city. Lodges and churches had taken on some of these chores in the past. Now it fell to bigger and more permanent organizations working with full-time staffs to deal with the problems faced by urban residents. Never as intrusive or powerful as their detractors suggested, these institutions succeeded in reducing at least some of the risks that came with living in a big city and did help a great many persons, if only one at a time.

Short of printing their own money and waging war, there was little that cities did which bigger governments also did not try to do at a later date. Nevertheless, cities remained creatures of the state. Their legal status was dependent on the good will of governors and legislators who did not live in cities or much like them but could be bullied and bribed into cooperating with big-city legislators. For all the grief that cities took from state legislatures and the tax dollars they returned to state and federal coffers, it did not stop city residents from teaching the rest of America how to run a big government or to play politics as if it really mattered.

Many men and women may have had a thin sense of obligation to their fellow residents and only been posing as good citizens. They managed nonetheless to take what was in their own self-interest and turn it into everyone else's business. In the process of making their case, they also figured out how to portray the favors and entitlements they got as serving a greater public good.

Important as their accomplishments may have been back then, business leaders today are routinely criticized for getting favors from government officials. Critics of these arrangements might not see a connection between such deals and the demands for compensation or special treatment that are made by citizens of all stripes and smaller sizes today, but it is there. These favors are no less offensive for being modest, but not only because the cumulative effect of their nibbling is great. Rather, it is because many of the petitioners are biting into a pie whose recipe they do not know, are not doing much to prepare, and seem willing to take credit for baking only after the pie is out of the oven.

Baking a good pie is a lot like making a good community. Knowing what it should look like and having a sense of what should go into the mix is good, even necessary. It is more important, however, to get the help of persons who know how to put the ingredients together, are not afraid to make a bit of a mess as they prepare their masterpiece, and are happy to help you clean up afterward.

City governments are all about the business of finding that kind of help, not being bashful about making a mess, and tidying up the kitchen before we all sit down to enjoy dessert. Sometimes this plan works. Sometimes it does not. On those occasions when it has not, we would be well-advised to recall the words of Kermit the Frog who warned both children and their parents some time ago that "some kinds of help are the kinds of help we all can do without."

Blatherskites of Small Caliber, the Usual Strikers, and Quite a Number of Hacks

George Washington died in the closing days of 1799, and Americans could not have conceived of a sadder or more auspicious way to end a century of revolutionary change than with the death of their most prominent hero. His passing was chronicled right down to the bloodletting, injections, and vinegar administered to him in the faint hope that his life might be prolonged. It must have seemed that all Americans had a hand in his funeral arrangements and burial.

In Boston, whole pages of *Russell's Gazette* were dedicated to speeches about Washington and plans to mark his death.[4] Ladies wore mourning badges and local mechanics assembled to pay their respects. The youth and militia of Roxbury held a march in his honor, and letters were published about his life and the lessons that Americans might take from his death. Among them was a note expressing admiration for the mechanics' behavior during the public procession and offering the observation that apprentices needed to be taught well, if they were to make a lasting contribution to their country.

Precisely 35 years later ward delegates in Pittsburgh met at the Washington Hall Coffee House to elect their officers and to choose nominees for mayor as well as the Select and Common Councils. Some 200 persons attended a formal dinner to celebrate these appointments and nominations, and they were treated to 70 different speeches delivered from the floor. Another 17 formal toasts were made by party leaders for every public leader from Washington to Andrew Jackson and for every American institution from West Point to womanhood.

The re-election of current Mayor Pettigrew in February prompted charges of corruption from his opponent. Editors of the *Pittsburgh Mercury* declared the mayor's response to be "a triumphant refutation of vile insinuations." Later in the month another group of citizens met for dinner and to make toasts in honor of George Washington's birthday.[5]

The residents of Boston had much to celebrate themselves by the early months of 1845. The city was so successful that local officials struggled just to keep up with everything that businesses and persons in the city needed to make the city habitable. They did not always succeed.

Elections were planned for the end of February of that year, but at least for a little while the city's business was conducted without having a mayor. The chairman of the Board of Aldermen temporarily took the job before the election was held. Members of the Massachusetts legislature felt compelled to ensure that such a breach would not open again.

Life in the capital seemed to proceed pretty much as it had in the recent past, despite all the confusion occasioned by the mayoral election. Ships entering the port still had to be inspected and new sewer systems built. A new law imposing a fine of one dollar on property owners who did not sweep snow from their sidewalks had to be enforced. City legislators also had to consider more permanent solutions to the problem of removing dirt and offal from Boston's streets.[6]

The residents of Florence, Alabama and surrounding townships had more than human and animal waste on their mind when they met in August of 1860 to consider the "great issues" of the upcoming presidential election. "Thousands of free and true patriotic citizens" came from all around Florence and stood at the city courthouse to hear "distinguished fellow citizens of this state" discuss their present and future role in a United States of America. There was music, and many banners fluttered and waved over the assemblage.

Several months later, and only shortly after Lincoln was elected president, members of the "Lauderdale Dragoons" Cavalry Company and "Florence Guards" were meeting and practicing on the same courthouse grounds. This time they were anticipating the conflict which would engage the whole nation before too long. An informational meeting was held at the courthouse in December of 1860 for the purpose of appointing representatives to attend a state convention where the issue of secession would be considered.[7]

A notice to all "Millers and Manufacturers" was published in the March 10, 1864 edition of the *Carolina Spartan*. It reminded them to make a "sizable contribution" to the Soldiers' Board of Relief by the end of the month. Business persons who did not comply would be forced to pay twice what they were accustomed to being dunned for in their taxes.

Publishers of the *Bergen County Democrat* that year had different concerns. They were happy to report in the July 16th edition of their newspaper that "there was no demonstration" in Hackensack, New Jersey on July 4 except for "a pathetic little one organized by two or three loyal abolitionists." They added that "because the protest was largely controlled by the local Negro party, it's no surprise that no one paid attention to it." The County Democratic Club, on the other hand, received a big write-up for its annual picnic and soiree in the August 8th edition of the newspaper. The party was scheduled for August 10 and would be held at Washington Grove. Tickets for the event cost one dollar.

A big dispute between leaders of Omaha, Nebraska and Council Bluffs, Iowa for rights to the new railroad bridge seemed to be settled, if a report in the April 29, 1868 edition of the *Omaha Republican Weekly* was to be believed. Persons from Council Bluffs apparently thought they had won, even though the bridge was to be located within Omaha's city limits and the Iowa town was more than three miles away from the river and the proposed site for the bridge. Not to be out done by Council Bluffs, Omaha's leaders made a determined push to get the bridge and finally declared themselves victorious on May 6, 1868. It also happened to be the same day that representatives of the Omaha Baseball Club held their annual meeting in the mayor's office and the local newspaper reported the creation of an association for detectives in the city.

The late summer and fall of 1868 were filled with partisan politics as both Democrats and Republicans mobilized their forces for the upcoming election. The "colored" electors of Omaha held a public meeting with a host of fired torches, brass band, and large American flag in August. They shouted in concert as they marched through the city, declaring "thanks to Lincoln for his mighty work" and "liberty and union, one and inseparable." "We are happy to be free." "We are all Republicans." Not all black persons supported the Republican ticket, and they even provided local Democrats with several hundred torches for a march in late August.

What was striking about these efforts was that they ran near but never with meetings, picnics, and street-corner rallies being held by white Democrats and Republicans. The former hoped to push black voters to work outside of the city, and the latter tried to woo blacks into supporting city candidates. True to its name, the *Omaha Republican Weekly* complimented black Republicans and demeaned black Democrats. One Democratic rally was described as having consisted of 77 "stragglers and little boys," while their black supporters had twice that many marchers in their procession. "The poor Democrats of Omaha," the paper declared, "can't even make even half so good a show as the despised niggers."[8]

In the middle of April in 1869, Governor Clayton of Arkansas made some changes to the city government in Pine Bluff. He replaced the current mayor and council. Several of the new office holders were "American citizens of African descent." For his efforts, the governor was referred to as "his Excellency" on the pages of the April 15th edition of the *Pine Bluff Weekly Press*.

Partly in response to the takeover of local governments by state officials who supported Reconstruction in the South, citizens in Pine Bluff were encouraged to reassert themselves and exercise their right to be heard. The *Pine Bluff Weekly Press* declared on August 18, 1870 that political parties should redouble their efforts by forming clubs and holding town meetings. "Victory will follow organization," the editors asserted, "as certainly as night follows day."

It was a lesson that many town and city leaders were trying to push on their residents, some of whom had never been active in politics before the Civil War. The Workingmen's Union of Burlington, Vermont, otherwise known as the Democratic Party, held a meeting in February of 1869 for the purpose of nominating persons to run for city offices. Only one dozen men showed up, however, and local boosters had to schedule additional meetings just to scare up enough candidates to run.

Apparently enough candidates were found to run for office, because a new mayor, four aldermen, and three members of the Common Council were elected in late March of 1869. It was not apparent from the local newspaper that they had much to do. They did manage to oversee the replacement of J. R. Hickok as city clerk with William H. Root, however. Mr Root was expected to be "very skillful and perform his duties well due to his handsome penmanship."[9]

There was plenty of work to do for persons who wanted to run city governments in the years after the Civil War. Some contributors, as we have seen, were more welcomed than others. While good penmanship was not often mentioned as a prerequisite for holding a government job or volunteering in a political campaign, other personal features were. Notable among these were the color and gender of the would-be job holders and volunteers.

When the Republicans of San Diego met at the city's only skating rink in late August of 1877, they were treated to songs performed by the Glee Club and heard speeches from the men nominated to be the new superintendent of schools and district attorney. It was an especially large gathering, according to one newspaper account. It also was noteworthy because of "the large number of ladies" in attendance.[10] Their presence was put in a positive light.

Sam Carey was embraced much less warmly by neighbors in Danville, Illinois for his attempt to influence federal policy in 1877. It seemed that he and several "other blatherskites of small caliber" had taken to writing the president and telling him how to run the federal government. Mr Carey and his confederates might well have worked themselves into a lather over their frustration that no one seemed to care about electing a new circuit judge for Danville.

Fewer than 800 voters in the city cast a ballot for either Mr Wilkin, whose friends "were quiet and made little exertion" in his behalf, and Mr Nelson, whose friends "worked hard" to elect their man. Although "the usual strikers were around the polls all day, and quite a number of hacks were brought into requisition, very little interest was manifested in the election."[11] In the end, Mr Nelson's hacks and strikers carried the day and he became the area's new circuit judge.

This did not mean that the citizens of Danville were kept in the dark about their town's business. The local newspaper published a summary of the mayor and council's deliberations and votes on a host of matters, most of which were pretty mundane or small. Included among the items described in the September 25, 1877 edition of the *Danville Daily News* was an accounting of city bills that were paid, a petition to change the name of a street, word of some delinquent tax payers, and an appropriation to cover the expense of laying a stone curb around the courthouse. Politics also was discussed. Local Republicans were encouraged to mobilize their forces for the upcoming county elections. As if they needed any more inspiration, the imminent publication of a "new Democratic weekly" was announced in the October 10th edition of the newspaper. "Its politics, while being Democratic, will be of the western zebra character, having several stripes of decided color," the local Republican paper advised.

Larger cities like New Orleans had a whole lot more going on in the closing years of the nineteenth century and more persons worked up over whatever problems were being brought before elected officials. Washington Artillery Hall was the site of a large public meeting in early June of 1895 where many persons gathered to consider a question much on the mind of New Orleans's citizens at that moment. Part of what was reported in the June 4, 1895 edition of the *Daily Picayune* is reproduced below.

LAW MUST AND SHALL PREVAIL
The rich man and the poor man, the laborer, and the great middle class of citizens gathered side by side to give the weight of their presence and the approbation of their voices, to ... the majesty of the law and the law's enforcement. There was never a more diverse assemblage. ... No religious or political faith was without representation ... both those who do not believe the Sunday law is a wise one, and those ... who are of the firm opinion that there was never a better law enacted.

But there was one sentiment that bubbled forth in free expression. "It is the law, and while it stands on the statute books it must and shall be enforced."

Men cannot be made good by law. ... The law does not keep men from getting drunk.

In every country and under all religions there is a day of rest to which man is entitled ... and it was proclaimed by God Almighty. But there is a broader question ... because the men arrayed against the law were saloonkeepers ... [and] it was time for orderly, decent, and respectable men to put down and control this element.

"You know who the bosses are ... the masters in every city were the saloonkeepers and their bosses were the men who robbed and plundered the public treasury."

It is pretty clear that there were persons in New Orleans who did not like swaggering ward heelers and beer-swilling saloonkeepers. Otherwise, it is hard to believe that the violation of a divinely inspired edict could somehow be less bad than anything that political bosses and their cronies ever imagined doing on their worst day. What tweaked all the good persons who turned out for this meeting is not that some poor schnook might tie one on after church, if he waited that long. Indeed, like most other nineteenth-century moralists, these persons firmly believed that laws did not make weak persons strong or good persons out of bad ones. What apparently bothered them was that saloonkeepers and political bosses were breaking faith with the public by stealing its money and repudiating values that were as good as God.

The assault upon "unprincipled politicians" did not end with the battle over Sunday laws. It popped up again the next month in a Ballot Reform Convention and the question of instituting a poll tax to keep undesirable persons from voting. As far as the good citizens of New Orleans were concerned, it was "impossible to get rid of all the rascals." What they could do, however, was "get rid of the voting power of the ignorant, the depraved, and the shiftless classes" who sold their votes to rascals and debased the practice of citizenship.[12]

These were serious matters to many persons in New Orleans who did not view politics as a trivial pursuit or citizenship as a birthright. What is most interesting about their campaigns to clean up politics in the city, however, is that they held themselves responsible for the apparent decay in civic rituals. The ignorant and shiftless could not help themselves, and there always would be unprincipled persons ready to take advantage of such poor souls. The city was in a tough spot not because of these folks, but because "the better element" was not vigilant. The city of God could be built in the city of man, but only if citizens did their duty.[13]

The other feature of government in New Orleans worth noting during these disputes was that it did not stop. Committees met and considered measures related to the disposal of garbage. Citizens offered petitions to have certain roads worked on or not. The Board of Health took steps to protect the city from persons who might have smallpox and to ensure that the water supply was clean. Post offices were opened. Street lights were checked. Fire Commissioners asked for more equipment, and the courts fined a local newspaper editor $100 for libeling a local official.[14]

Local residents could ill afford to stop their government from conducting its everyday business just because troublemakers seemed bent on corrupting its good work. The streets still needed to be repaired, garbage disposed of, and clean water had to be provided. Even when good persons did all they could to make these things happen, however, sometimes it just was not enough. They needed help.

Not infrequently, this help came from persons and governments outside of the city in the form of loans and investments. The municipality promised to pay back this money with interest. They did so with the expectation that improvements to their town would make land more valuable and draw more tax-paying residents and businesses to settle there.

Thus, when the leaders of Flagstaff thought they needed more water in 1897, they decided to sell bonds to outside investors in order to raise the funds to build a "waterworks" or plant where water was purified. This was easier to propose than carry out, unfortunately. A municipal or county government at the time could not issue bonds without the permission of Congress, if the value of those bonds exceeded 4 percent of the assessed value of property within its boundaries. The $65,000 that Flagstaff leaders needed to secure from bonds exceeded that 4 percent figure, so they went to Congress for permission to sell the more expensive bonds.

Word that the town's application had been approved was announced in the January 14, 1897 edition of the *Flagstaff Sun-Democrat*. It was received enthusiastically by the editors who claimed that the waterworks would bring hundreds of new jobs to the town, "manufactories ... and the hum of industry." "Workingmen," they declared, "will come here with their families and establish homes and add to our population and wealth. All branches of business have already taken on a new lease of life and our merchants ... are hopeful once more."

There still was the matter of local voters approving the proposal to sell these bonds to outside investors, of course, but everyone was pretty sure which way the vote would go. They were right. A special election was held in February, and the vote was decidedly lopsided in favor of issuing the bonds. When all the votes were tallied, only five persons had objected to the idea while 168 approved of it.

The cost of the project grew a bit over the next two years. So, by the time that the West End Taxpayers' Improvement Association met to select a route for the pipes going to the new West End Waterworks, the city had already invested $105,000 on the facility. This group met every Monday and was supposed to protect the interests of taxpayers and beautify the area. Notwithstanding the sum of money involved, they were certain that sales of the remaining bonds would more than cover the increased cost of the project.[15]

In the next century, the sums of money that had to be raised in order to promote municipal growth would become much larger, and convincing enough citizens to invest in their own future became much harder. Voting oneself into debt, after all, was nothing more or less than an act of faith on the part of citizens that everything would turn out all right in the end. Spreading the risks entailed in such big projects to outside investors, including federal taxpayers, made it easier for local voters and subscribers to the community of believers to keep their faith intact.

The Rise of the Dependent City and Other Pieces of Political Fiction

We begin with the simple observation that most Americans in nineteenth-century towns and cities liked George Washington. Beyond that it seems pretty clear that some men and women worked hard at politics and paid a lot of attention to what their local government did. Many others, perhaps most of them, did not, or they treated politics and the city government merely as a way to get something. Despite the confusion and conflict sometimes inspired by all this attending, ignoring, and using, local politics and government actually made quite a difference in the lives of many urban residents.

Men and women who had no earthly reason to take each other seriously were compelled to do so in politics or through the work of their local government. They were both citizens and strangers. Nevertheless, government provided them with an arena where they could meet, and politics gave them an effective medium of exchange as well as a reason to mind each other's business. Other parts of the urban world were not as open to the kinds of routine and ceremonial contacts made available by government or politics. Granted, these citizen–strangers may have been drawn together only occasionally or by nothing more than the taxes they paid. Yet the persons who were elected, appointed, or hired to represent them tackled chores that no other group in the city was willing or able to address satisfactorily.

The most important accomplishments of citizens and their representatives during the nineteenth century fit on a tidy three-item list. Simply keeping up with the physical expansion, economic growth, and population increases that cities experienced probably would be at the top. Until recently, of course, observers had not thought much of the advances that politicians and government officials made in this area. Indeed, as late as 1984 historian Jon C. Teaford was referring to all the services and work done to create the city's infrastructure as "the unheralded triumph" of urban governance and politics in the late-nineteenth century.[16] By any reasonable measure, American cities of that era had better public facilities and services than their European counter-parts. Government officials did not invent the technological wonders that made daily living in a large city possible; but they did push for the new technologies to be used. They did not educate children, put out fires, or actually check the quality of the food that persons bought; but they created institutions whose caretakers provided those and many other services. They no longer paid for such improvements and services themselves; but they did figure out ways of get the money from their fellow residents or outsiders.

Men and women who worked in politics and for local governments certainly helped to make cities habitable. Yet they accomplished much more than that. They actually succeeded in reducing some of the bigger problems and risks attendant to living in a modern urban world. In so doing, they made it possible for more of their fellow residents and laborers to enjoy life and to develop their own interests.[17]

A second achievement of local politicians and government officers in the nineteenth century was more social in nature. It was that they maintained good working relations with their counterparts outside of the city. This would not have looked as important as tall buildings, paved streets, mass transportation, and sewer lines. Without the cooperation of persons who worked for state and federal governments, however, local officials would have been hard pressed to meet the needs of their constituents or build a bigger city.

Observers of politics and government at the local level have maintained for a long time that cities were at a singular disadvantage when dealing with state officials. In more recent decades, the attention of government watchers and political pundits has shifted. Now we worry about all the money that cities get from federal coffers and how the national government sets down conditions which local officials must satisfy in order to get most any kind of help. Important as this assistance has been, federal intervention in cities did not begin with the Great Depression or with urban renewal programs after World War II. The national government actually has been involved in efforts to help new towns and would-be cities ever since the early 1800s.

It is apparent even from the brief walk we took through nineteenth-century urban political and governmental history that local governments never have been left to their own devices or had exclusive control over their political destiny. State and federal officials have always been deeply involved in what local municipalities did, and their calendars often determined when cities were able to launch a new initiative or respond to a pressing local problem. Higher levels of government also had a great deal to say about where towns would be planted and whether they might someday grow into a great city.

When we think about the ways in which cities relate to state governments, it is common to contrast the wealth of cities and their big populations to the political and legal control that state governments hold over them. While the legal dependence of cities upon state governments is real enough and urban legislators still have to petition state officials for the power and money to do many things inside their own borders, states and cities usually find a way of working out their disagreements.

The animosity that existed between rural and urban state legislators during the nineteenth century was both real and rhetorical. Partisan differences were every bit as important as sectional differences in bottling up legislation that urban representatives wanted to pass. Arguments between amateur legislators from cities and local officials or would-be reformers from the same place, however, also played a part in conflicts over laws and programs destined for urban population centers.

Big-city representatives may have been less than patrician in their sensibilities, hopelessly ethnic, and at times even corrupt, though no more so than legislators from rural areas. Yet they also were successful. They managed to work with legislators who were not from cities and got a great deal of what they wanted in the way of administrative control over daily governance and service delivery, taxing privileges, and programs to meet the needs of their constituents.[18]

Relations between local and federal officials have been every bit as long-standing and productive. During the first half of the nineteenth century, historian Eric Monkkonen observes, "the federal government aided cities in conscious, crucial, and varied ways."[19] Some of the bigger pieces of assistance included granting the land on which towns were planted and across which railroad tracks were laid. It also included dredging harbors and rivers to make them more navigable and ready for commerce. There were times, of course, when cities requested aid from the national government and did not get it. This happened in the early 1820s, for instance, when both St Louis and Lexington, Kentucky asked for help to combat the effects of an economic depression and were turned away.[20]

Despite such predictable setbacks, local officials worked hard to stay on good terms with state and local governments. Much of the aid they acquired went to the physical and economic development of their cities. Some of it came from unexpected and decidedly modern-looking sources. There was stiff competition to become the home campus for a state university or some other state-sponsored institution, for instance, and residents from the winning town or city saw new buildings and state jobs as a good hedge against bad economic times.

It certainly was important to deliver services and be on good terms with state and federal officials. Neither of these accomplishments would have mattered in the long run, however, had local leaders not used ideas and practices rooted in their bourgeois civic culture as the building blocks for government routines and political discourse. Even more vital to their legacy was their ability to pass these same bourgeois impulses and habits on to newer groups and would-be contenders for political influence. Sometimes they did this happily. On many occasions they probably did it grudgingly. The effect, in either case, was the same.

Of the three major accomplishments that can be attributed to big-city politicians and governments in the nineteenth century, this is probably the least well understood. It is not hard to see why. Historians who try to make sense of urban politics in contemporary times focus on the years between the Civil War and Great Depression when a more modern form of urban government was being created. This is understandable, because we are familiar with governments that do more and are run by persons whose ancestry, while certainly respectable in many cases, is better represented by a bush than a tree and, even under the kindest reading, has more berries than trust funds hanging from it.

On the other hand, this approach took us back to an especially tumultuous time when patricians no longer ruled the roost and tried mightily to keep as much influence as they could in cities where their kind of person was increasingly outnumbered by "other" kinds of persons. Urban politics came to be seen as a struggle between individuals who wanted to help the whole city and persons who were more interested in taking care of themselves and their pals. Native-born business persons who favored strong mayors and bureaucracies run by experts were matched against "bosses" and their working-class minions who lived in colonies of immigrants and preferred presents over principles.[21]

Their disagreements and fights were genuine and often exciting, but rarely definitive. Representatives from these two camps took turns running local governments, failing to solidify a political base that could last for more than a few years, losing elections, and, when they were not in office, doing what they could to make life miserable for their office-holding adversaries.[22] Despite all the pyrotechnics and sniping, they managed to create a way to govern themselves which enabled cities to grow and citizens to get more and better services.

The principles they invoked, the institutions they created, and the programs they implemented were all invented or first championed by the very persons who saw their formal power ebbing in the closing years of the nineteenth century. That would be solid, often uninspiring, but always confident and hard-working patricians and their bourgeois minions. Institutions and policies favored by higher-status residents, though often portrayed as a last-ditch effort to hold back a rising tide of immigrant and working-class impertinence, proved surprisingly robust.

The good works of wealthy and well-placed persons never stopped. In fact, many of their programs eventually became part of what local governments did. Even when that was not the case, however, the ideas and organizations which these persons added to the mix had the effect of moderating local politics rather than sharpening the lines between themselves and the less well-to-do city residents.[23] This would not have been possible had persons from different classes and backgrounds not agreed at least some of the time about what problems they faced or been unable to cooperate with each other, if only by finding different ways to pledge money to local subscription campaigns.[24]

The often noisy retreat of more well-to-do persons from the increasingly messy business of government at the end of the nineteenth century pushed their best and most enduring success story into the background. The political legacy of the community of believers was passed on successfully, just like its admiration for commercial leadership, grumpy tolerance of ethnic diversity and immoral practices (especially drinking liquor, illicit sex, and not paying one's taxes), and the organized frenzy of the consumer marketplace.[25] Those parts of the bourgeois civic culture dedicated to local politics and governance stretched and bent enough to take in many new ideas and would-be rulers but they never broke, not even when city governments went into debt or ran out of money.[26]

"There's Nothing ... Wrong with Cleveland that $160,543,674 Wouldn't Cure"

Tulsa, Oklahoma was a busy place in the spring of 1905. The city's local newspapers, like those of virtually all American towns and cities, described a variety of ordinances which were up for consideration or had been approved or voted down by local officials. Democrats and Republicans met in order to choose candidates for the upcoming city elections. Only 100 more persons were registered as Democrats than Republicans for the whole city, pretty much guaranteeing that these contests would be heated. This turned out to be case. Large rallies held by each party in behalf of its would-be office holders near the end of the campaign were noisy affairs, noteworthy, as one reporter noted, for their "brilliant verbal fireworks."[27]

The new town council in Fairbanks, Alaska took steps to mobilize the local health, fire, and police departments in April of 1909 to remove refuse from back yards, front yards, and whole buildings, if necessary, once the spring thaw arrived. Their object was to keep the community sanitary and "sweet smelling," and they promised a "crusade ... that will make the work of the New York Purity Party look like willful neglect."

The local post master also threatened to close up shop, if Washington did not send a replacement for him. At that point, he had been waiting ten months for someone to take his job. Washington also had not gotten around to sending a new federal judge for the area as well.

It was decided that once the ice broke later in the month an effort would be made to dismantle and repair the wooden bridge at Turner Street. Once ice on the river finally broke and the bridge was taken down, a little fight erupted between men who wanted to run a ferry service across the river. A citizens' committee was set up to run the ferry for a time. The current operator would be compensated for his time, and all excess revenues from running the ferry would be spent on repairing or replacing the current bridge. Complaints by citizens also were directed against several property owners who were not clearing their sidewalks of snow and persons who were dumping junk into the Sixth Avenue slough and making it impossible to drain excess water from surrounding streets. The City Council also initiated actions that members hoped would end the erosion of First Avenue along the river. This was particularly important, because that was Fairbanks's main business street in 1909.[28]

In what was described as a "rousing meeting" on March 3, 1911, no fewer than 200 business people and taxpayers from Sparks, Nevada voted down all the proposed amendments to the city charter that had been hurriedly introduced to the state senate by "a small coterie of men" with mischief on their mind. Senator Ascher from Carson arrived by train and was elected to serve as the meeting's chairman. He had introduced the bill to the legislature only after being told that it had received a thorough hearing by the City Council. It quickly became apparent that popular sentiment was against each and every proposed amendment. The community had barely avoided being damaged by a few willful persons. The good news, however, was that "the stable citizenship of this city showed conclusively that when they were aroused it did not take them very long to get active and look out for the best interests of the town."[29]

In March of 1915, Pittsburgh's Department of Public Safety sponsored its third "walk-rite" parade in as many weeks to remind pedestrians to keep to the right, cross streets only at designated spots, and always move in the direction that traffic was flowing. As residents of that city were learning how to deal with automobile traffic, the citizens of Fargo, North Dakota were preparing to make driving a little easier for its car owners by paving more of its roads. It apparently had such good credit in 1915 that investors were coming from great distances just to buy $140,000 worth of city-backed bonds for the proposed street-paving project.[30]

Later that year, the San Diego City Council took up the matter of regulating bus companies. An ordinance was passed requiring "jitney owners" to hold to fixed routes and schedules. The city law was challenged by these companies but eventually upheld by the State Appellate Court.[31]

The Board of Health launched an attack on mosquitoes. Dr Banks, the director of that agency, also initiated a clean-up effort that was directed at unsanitary conditions in the city's Chinatown district. As in many campaigns of this sort, officials made a connection between the dirt and filth which could be washed away and the social corruption which lay just beneath the surface in such unclean places. "Unsanitation in the Celestial Realm Must Go," declared the good Dr Banks in the September 19, 1915 edition of the *San Diego Union*. "Many of these buildings are ... hiding places for hoboes and crooks and the underworld element," he said. "They are an eyesore to the city and in their present condition intolerable on account of the risk from a health standpoint. Since housing is considered to have a great influence on the health of a community," he concluded, "such conditions ... must be abolished."

Communities across the United States mobilized themselves to support the nation during World War I. Not surprisingly, local governments were at the forefront of these efforts. One of the casualties of the war effort was the German language, which was cut from the curriculum of the high school serving Casper, Wyoming and many other towns and cities. The Governor of Wyoming issued a proclamation which set aside May 12 as Mother's Day. His purpose was to use the day to pray for success in war and the deliverance of young men back to their mothers, wives, sisters, and sweethearts. The state's bankers promoted a plan for workers to invest their spare cash in Liberty Loans and War Saving Certificates. Young children in Casper, not to be outdone by their parents, gathered junk that they could sell and then invest their money in saving stamps whose proceeds also went to the war effort.[32]

The attention of many city leaders after 1920 returned to a problem that had bothered their predecessors for decades: the apparent shortage of decent housing for persons of modest means. Members of a state commission in Massachusetts declared in 1920 that "large organizations" should take up the problem of building housing for working-class families. Recommended in the report "Necessary for Life" was the idea that such organizations could promote simpler ways of financing housing for such persons by working with existing savings and loan institutions.[33] Several years later business people and the League of Women Voters in Pittsburgh urged the City Council to provide for a new zoning designation which would set aside areas for single-family residences only. Apartment buildings would not be allowed.[34]

City governments failed to discover a good solution to the housing problem inside their own borders, and this issue would continue to plague local officials right to the end of the twentieth century and into the twenty-first. This was not the only problem facing city office holders, of course. They faced a bewildering array of challenges in the years leading up to the Great Depression.

Democrats in Wilmington, Delaware in 1922 wrestled with the question of how much representation women should have within their party, and officials faced heated protests from the Methodist and Episcopal Preacher's Association about the prospect of persons manufacturing light wines and beer. The City Council discussed whether the gongs and bells used by volunteer fire fighters were obsolete now that the city had a full-time department of fire fighters manned by paid professionals.

Cleanliness was also much on the minds of Wilmington's residents that year. April brought "clean-up week" in the city. Prizes were awarded to the most improved districts, and a permanent body was organized to carry on the good work that started as a result of this event. Apparently it was needed, because Wilmington seemed to have a problem with keeping itself clean. The Street and Sewer Department made controversial decisions regarding parking, requiring a trolley company to pave streets on which their tracks were laid, stopping a proposed bus route between Wilmington and Dover, and how to stop a typhoid epidemic in light of a sewer line break in one part of the city. The Board of Health received complaints from 50 residents and property owners regarding horrible smells in another neighborhood. It was determined that an "ancient, defective sewer line" was the source of the odors. Citizens and businesses from across the city complained about a demand by the City Council that they wrap their garbage as long as the city incinerator was shut down.[35]

Keeping cities clean seemed to be a perennial problem in most parts of the country. Officials in Idaho Falls coordinated its clean-up campaign in 1931. The Chamber of Commerce, civic organizations, city departments, neighborhood groups, households, and even the Boy Scouts played a part in the week-long initiative that started in early April. They all would wage an attack "on dirt, rubbish in the streets and in alleys and yards." After all, "the appearance, cleanliness and health of a city are very important," the campaign's sponsors declared. Conditions in the country were hard in 1931, but that did not stop local residents from keeping their community looking good and everyone from working together on projects that mattered to all of them.

The Chamber of Commerce in Idaho Falls announced later in the year that Congressmen from their state and across the country would be visiting their community and the surrounding area in order to decide whether a flood control program was advisable. The appropriation of six million dollars would bring money and jobs to the area. That was enough money to inspire a delegation of "irrigation company officials, Chambers of Commerce representatives, prominent farmers and civic leaders" from the city and state to meet with the visitors from Washington, DC in August.[36]

Local municipalities of all sizes lacked money to make necessary repairs to many of their roads, bridges, sewers, and water supplies during the Great Depression. The prospect of bringing a bold, new initiative and economic resources to a community, therefore, was understandably exciting. The federal government, which had begun to use its considerable resources and reach to help shape the destinies of towns and cities well before the end of the nineteenth century, now turned open all the spigots with a variety of programs and a great deal of money.

The cumulative effect of these initiatives, particularly in the West and South, was staggering. Areas that heretofore had lacked much economic clout now were being visited by companies and enjoying the benefits of large public works projects. Within a few decades, places that had been small towns ballooned into large cities spread over pieces of territory the likes of which older Eastern and Midwestern cities had long ago been denied by their suburban neighbors.[37] The social impact of these changes was not always good. This was especially true for lower-income persons and minorities who found their housing choices confined to certain areas, their job opportunities limited, and the self-help tradition inspired by their vernacular culture undermined by big welfare programs.[38]

Although much of the money that had gone to such projects was siphoned off for the war effort during World War II, the expectation that renewed growth and development would come with the end of fighting was hard to discourage. Mayor Frank J. Lausche of Cleveland and other speakers expressed their hope for "extensive postwar developments in better housing by both public and private financing" at a public housing complex celebrating its sixth anniversary. American Legion commanders dedicated the service to the 103 soldiers, sailors, and marines currently serving their country overseas whose families lived in the complex.[39]

Local officials had big plans for Cleveland, and everyone could help bring these plans to life. All it would cost them was eight cents per day. At least that was what the city planning commissioner thought would do it. If every citizen of Cleveland contributed that much for the next six years, he guessed there would be enough money to take care of all the "existing deficiencies in public services" which Ohio's largest city had in 1943. Airport improvements could be made. More playgrounds could be built. Street lights would be repaired. And all it was going to cost was $160,543,674.[40]

Granted, $160 million went a lot further back then than it does today. Yet in 1943, with the United States right in the middle of a war in Asia and Europe, that was a lot of money to be talking about spending on bridges, parks, and roadways. It was also a remarkable display of confidence in the national government's capacity to wage war even as local officials planned for a day when the biggest problem Cleveland's residents would face was where to take their children to play.

Federally inspired and funded programs to rebuild American cities after the war were far-reaching and expensive. The social consequences of these efforts often led persons to question the necessity for all the tearing up and displacement that was visited upon areas reclaimed under "urban renewal" projects, but that did not stop the work from going forward. Citizen involvement in these projects was limited in most cases; and persons who lived in affected areas usually had to satisfy themselves by mounting noisy but rarely successful campaigns against plans that were supposed to make the city a better place to live and work.

In the midst of all this activity, local officials still made time for annual clean-up campaigns and ribbon-cutting ceremonies. So, officials from Sioux City in 1960 could welcome the prospect of federal projects to cut a better channel to the Floyd River and replace an old industrial site with brand-new public housing one month. Then, the next month, the mayor could issue a proclamation in honor of National Beauty Salon Week and commend local citizens to "recognize the hairdressers and cosmetologists for their high sense of civic responsibility."[41]

The Boston Parks Department staged more than 100 Halloween parties in October of 1960. Church, civic, and other community organizations offered different programs to supplement the city's efforts to prevent vandalism on the evening of the 31st. To that end, the city contributed 50,000 apples, 70,000 dishes of ice cream, and 18,000 doughnuts.[42]

Boston city officials had bigger social problems to deal with before that decade was over. Particularly troubling were challenges to the Boston School Committee by black parents and civil-rights groups. These parties criticized the schools for being ineffective in every regard except their ability to keep minority children segregated. Protests, fights, expulsions, and little educating became the hallmarks of public schooling in Boston and elsewhere throughout the 1960s and 1970s. City officials and education leaders did their best to manage these disputes and do something that might calm the situation they faced. More often than not, they succeeded. Despite all their fancy stepping and special programs, however, the quality of public education did not seem much improved.[43]

Local officials during the 1970s also found themselves embroiled in a series of increasingly nasty public confrontations over the conduct of the war in Vietnam. The Democratic Club of Columbia, Maryland sought new members, regardless of their political affiliation. Its primary goal was to "reject all candidates who support the war in Asia and perpetuate racism at home – either by their actions or by their inactions." In bigger cities, like Pittsburgh, hundreds and sometimes thousands of persons could be found mounting street protests against the war, arguing with their elected officials in public fora, and sending volunteers off to Washington, DC for even larger marches and demonstrations.[44]

Cities continued to be places where loud and often divisive debates over the big moral questions of the day were lined up against some of the smallest and most mundane problems with which men, women, and children had to deal just to make it through every day. In general, local officials did a much better job handling "free-roaming dogs," garbage pick-ups, inadequate drainage, traffic flow, and limited office space or public parks than they did with questions of public morality, justice, and even bad taste. On many occasions, however, it was difficult to see where one type of problem stopped and the other one began.[45]

This, more than anything else, helps to explain why political leaders and government agencies sometimes succeed in making communities better and sometimes fall flat on their faces when trying. Simply put, they succeed when they are able to make a big deal out of doing small favors for persons. Officials and agencies fail when citizens stop believing that the favors also help them or believe that they are always at the end of the line when the presents are being handed out.

The good news is that when trust in public officials and local government is at its lowest point, a city's commercial leaders often are turned to for help. The bad news, at least for the resurrected leaders, is that they usually give it. When that happens, they run the risk of being swallowed by the very beast they were sent in to slay.

One had only to look to the sorry state of local government in Miami at the end of the twentieth century for evidence bearing on this point. Blatherskites of the lowest caliber had gained control of the city government with the assistance of assorted strikers and hacks. The only thing more corrupt than the electoral process apparently was the system for awarding contracts for city services. Driven to despair by a national media portrayal of their city as a "Third World banana republic" and a seemingly endless queue of scandals, citizens and business leaders from the Miami-Dade County area declared they had seen enough and vowed to clean up politics and restore faith in the local government.[46]

There was a good reason why business leaders left the everyday business of government to other persons some time ago and turned their attention to making more money and giving it away to institutions they knew better and causes they liked more. The connection between doing good and doing well was easier to see, and no one was going to point a suspicious finger at business people who used their own money to do favors for persons who really needed help.

Well-intentioned businessmen and woman probably will not come away looking this good in Miami once they start turning over rocks in the city government and find that most of the persons for whom favors have been done look an awful lot like themselves.

NOTES

1   Daniel J. Monti, *A Semblance of Justice: St Louis School Desegregation and Order in Urban America* (Columbia, MO: University of Missouri Press, 1985); Daniel J. Monti, "Ethnic Economies, Affirmative Action, and Mining Cultural Capital," *American Sociologist*, Winter 1997, pp. 101–12.

2   In earlier chapters, I cited a number of authors working in one or another of the social sciences who take this position. By far and away the most articulate defender for this point of view, however, is historian Sam Bass Warner. His take on these matters is spelled out most clearly in his book entitled *The Private City: Philadelphia in Three Periods of its Growth* (Philadelphia, PA: University of Pennsylvania Press, 1987).

3   Eric H. Monkkonen, *America Becomes Urban: The Development of US Cities and Towns, 1780–1980* (Berkeley, CA: University of California Press, 1988), pp. 89–110. Monkkonen's book, though technically a text containing a general survey of American urban history, is best appreciated for its fine introduction to urban politics and governance. Particularly helpful, I think, is his distinction between "regulated cities" and "service cities" which I build on here.

4   *Russell's Gazette*, January 2 and January 13, 1800.

5   *Pittsburgh Mercury*, January 8, February 5, and February 26, 1835.

6   *Daily Evening Transcript*, February 3, February 11, February 19, March 24, April 1, April 17, and May 28, 1845.

7   *Florence Gazette*, August 8, November 21, November 28, and December 5, 1860.

8   *Omaha Republican Weekly*, August 19, August 26, September 9, and October 7, 1868.

9   *Burlington Free Press*, March 1, March 25, and April 29, 1869.

10 *San Diego Union*, August 31, 1877.

11 *Danville Daily News*, August 7, 1877.

12 *Daily Picayune*, July 20, 1895.

13 Ibid., November 25, 1895.

14 Ibid., July 20, August 23, September 13, September 20, and September 29, 1895.

15 *Coconino Sun*, February 4, 1899.

16 Jon C. Teaford, *The Unheralded Triumph: City Government in America, 1870–1900* (Baltimore, MD: Johns Hopkins University Press, 1984), pp. 217–306; Monkkonen, *America Becomes Urban*, pp. 89–110, 131–81.

17 Clay McShane, "Transforming the Use of Urban Space: A Look at the Revolution in Street Pavements, 1880–1924," *Journal of Urban History*,

Volume 5, Number 3, May 1979, pp. 297–307; Joel Tarr, "The Separate vs Combined Sewer Problem: A Case Study in Urban Technology Design Choice," *Journal of Urban History*, Volume 5, Number 3, May 1979, pp. 308–39; Mark Rose and John Clark, "Light, Heat, and Power: Energy Choices in Kansas City, Wichita, and Denver, 1900–1940," *Journal of Urban History*, Volume 5, Number 3, May 1979, pp. 340–64; Mark Foster, "City Planners and Urban Transportation: The American Response, 1900–1940," *Journal of Urban History*, Volume 5, Number 3, May 1979, pp. 365–96; Alan Marcus, "The Strange Career of Municipal Health Initiatives: Cincinnati and City Government in the Early Nineteenth Century," *Journal of Urban History*, Volume 7, Number 1, November 1980, pp. 3–30; Clayton Koppes and William Norris, "Ethnicity, Class, and Mortality in the Industrial City: A Case Study of Typhoid Fever in Pittsburgh, 1890–1910," *Journal of Urban History*, Volume 11, Number 3, May 1985, pp. 259–79; Eugenie Ladner Birch and Deborah Gardner, "The Seven Percent Solution: A Review of Philanthropic Housing, 1870–1947," *Journal of Urban History*, Volume 7, Number 4, August 1981, pp. 439–70; Christine Meisner Rosen, "Infrastructural Improvements in Nineteenth-Century Cities: A Conceptual Framework and Cases," *Journal of Urban History*, Volume 12, Number 3, May 1986, pp. 211–56; Philip Bean, "The Irish, the Italians, and Machine Politics, a Case Study: Utica, New York (1870–1960)," *Journal of Urban History*, Volume 20, Number 2, February 1994, pp. 205–39.

18 Teaford, *The Unheralded Triumph*, pp. 83–131.
19 Monkkonen, *America Becomes Urban*, p. 129.
20 Richard C. Wade, *The Urban Frontier: Pioneer Life in Early Pittsburgh, Cincinnati, Lexington, Louisville, and St Louis* (Chicago: University of Chicago Press, 1976, pp. 176, 185, and 199.
21 Alexander Callow, *The Tweed Ring* (New York: Oxford University Press, 1966); Zane Miller, *Boss Cox's Cincinnati: Urban Politics in the Progressive Era* (New York: Oxford University Press, 1968); Melvin G. Holli, *Reform in Detroit: Hazen S. Pingree and Urban Politics* (New York: Oxford University Press, 1969); Jon C. Teaford, "New Life for an Old Subject: Investigating the Structure of Urban Rule," in Howard Gillette and Zane Miller (eds), *American Urbanism: A Historiographical Review* (New York: Greenwood Press, 1987), pp. 91–104.
22 Humbert Nelli, "John Powers and the Italians: Politics in a Chicago Ward, 1896–1921," *Journal of American History*, Volume 57, Number 1, June 1970, pp. 67–84; Samuel Hays, "The Changing Political Structure of the City in Industrial America," *Journal of Urban History*, Volume 1, Number 1, November 1974, pp. 6–38; Eugene Watts, "Property and Politics in Atlanta: 1865–1903," *Journal of Urban History*, Volume 3, Number 3, May 1977, pp. 295–322; Joseph Arnold, "The Neighborhood and City Hall: The Origin of Neighborhood Associations in Baltimore, 1880–1911," *Journal of Urban History*, Volume 6, Number 1, November 1979, pp. 3–30; M. Craig Brown and Charles M. Halaby, "Machine Politics in America: 1870–1945," *Journal of Interdisciplinary History*, Volume 17, Number 3,

Winter 1987, pp. 587–612; Alan DiGaetano, "Urban Political Reform: Did It Kill the Machine?" *Journal of Urban History*, Volume 18, Number 1, November 1991, pp. 36–67; Dale Baum and Worth Robert Miller, "Ethnic Conflict and Machine Politics in San Antonio, 1892–1899," *Journal of Urban History*, Volume 19, Number 4, August 1993, pp. 63–84.

23 Teaford, *The Unheralded Triumph*, pp. 68–82, 132–73, 174–214; Monkkonen, *America Becomes Urban*, pp. 206–22. Also see Harvey Boulay and Alan DiGaetano, "Why Did Political Machines Disappear?" *Journal of Urban History*, Volume 12, Number 1, November 1985, pp. 25–50.

24 Teaford, *The Unheralded Triumph*, pp. 293–306. Wealthy persons paid taxes, though certainly not all that they should have. In some ways, their more important contribution came through the purchase of stocks for companies that provided jobs and tax revenues. They also purchased bonds that helped to subsidize many economic development projects including those which improved the infrastructure of cities. Persons of more modest means bought a spot at the table with their taxes and housing purchases. All would-be players paid, one way or another.

25 Robert Buroker, "From Voluntary Association to Welfare State: The Illinois Immigrants Protective League, 1908–1926," *Journal of American History*, Volume 58, Number 3, December 1971, pp. 643–60; Gary Nash, "The Transformation of Urban Politics, 1700–1765," *Journal of American History*, Volume 60, Number 3, December 1973, pp. 657–78; Howard Rabinowitz, "From Exclusion to Segregation: Southern Race Relations, 1865–1890," *Journal of American History*, Volume 63, Number 2, September 1976, pp. 325–50; Boulay and DiGaetano, "Why Did Political Machines Disappear?"; Douglas Booth, "Municipal Socialism and City Government Reform: The Milwaukee Experience, 1910–1940," *Journal of Urban History*, Volume 12, Number 1, November 1985, pp. 51–74; Maureen Flanagan, "Charter Reform in Chicago: Political Culture and Urban Progressive Reform," *Journal of Urban History*, Volume 12, Number 2, February 1986, pp. 109–30; Timothy Kinsella, "Traditional Manufacturing Cities in Transition to Human-Centered Cities," *Journal of Urban History*, Volume 13, Number 1, November 1986, pp. 31–53; David Plank, "Educational Reform and Organizational Change: Atlanta in the Progressive Era," *Journal of Urban History*, Volume 15, Number 1, November 1988, pp. 22–41.

26 Monkkonen, *America Becomes Urban*, pp. 125, 131–57; Teaford, *The Unheralded Triumph*, pp. 65, 283–306.

27 *Tulsa Daily Democrat*, March 10, March 18, March 27, and April 4, 1905.

28 *Fairbanks Daily News-Miner*, April 12, April 20, and May 21, 1909.

29 *Sparks Tribune*, March 3, 1911.

30 *Pittsburgh Post*, March 27, 1915; *Fargo Forum & Daily Republican*, March 30, 1915.

31 *San Diego Union*, September 19, September 28, and November 6, 1915.

32 *Casper Daily Tribune*, January 16, April 16, April 24, and August 10, 1918.

33 *Boston Globe*, February 18, 1920.

34 *Gazette Times*, April 9, 1925.

35 *Wilmington Morning News*, January 20, February 25, March 28, April 8, April 13, July 4, July 20, and September 11, 1922.

36 *Idaho Falls Post*, April 5, August 10, and August 12, 1931.

37 Roger Lotchin, "The City and the Sword: San Francisco and the Rise of the Metropolitan–Military Complex, 1919–1941," *Journal of American History*, Volume 65, Number 4, March 1979, pp. 996–1,020; Roger Biles, "Cities in the South," *Journal of Urban History*, Volume 17, Number 3, May 1991, pp. 309–15; Bradford Luckingham, "The Urban Sunbelt: Images and Realities," *Journal of Urban History*, Volume 17, Number 3, May 1991, pp. 316–23; John H. Mollenkopf, *The Contested City* (Princeton, NJ: Princeton University Press, 1983). Mollenkopf's tracing of the transformation of towns into cities in the southern and western parts of the United States is particularly helpful. The role of the federal government in subsidizing new industrial development in these regions and, by extension, the growth of their cities is laid out in a convincing and careful manner. Also see: Peter Wiley and Robert Gottlieb, *Empires in the Sun: The Rise of the New American West* (Tuscon, AZ: University of Arizona Press, 1982); Bradford Luckingham, *Phoenix: The History of a Southwestern Metropolis* (Tuscon, AZ: University of Arizona Press, 1989).

38 Rita Werner Gordon, "The Change in the Political Alignment of Chicago's Negroes During the New Deal," *Journal of American History*, Volume 56, Number 3, December 1969, pp. 584–603; Christopher Wye, "The New Deal and the Negro Community: Toward a Broader Conceptualization," *Journal of American History*, Volume 59, Number 3, December 1972, pp. 621–39; Kenneth Jackson, "Race, Ethnicity, and Real Estate Appraisal: The Home Owners Loan Corporation and the Federal Housing Administration," *Journal of Urban History*, Volume 6, Number 4, August 1980, pp. 419–52; Ann Durkin Keating, "The Federal Government and US Cities," *Journal of Urban History*, Volume 12, Number 3, May 1986, pp. 318–24; Ronald Tobey, Charles Wetherell, and Jay Brigham, "Moving Out and Settling In: Residential Mobility, Home Owning, and the Public Framing of Citizenship, 1921–1950," *American Historical Review*, Volume 95, Number 5, December 1990, pp. 1,395–422; John Bauman, Norman Hummon, and Edward Muller, "Public Housing, Isolation, and the Urban Underclass: Philadelphia's Richard Allen Homes, 1941–1965," *Journal of Urban History*, Volume 17, Number 3, May 1991, pp. 264–92; Thomas Hinehan, "Japanese American Resettlement in Cleveland During and After World War II," *Journal of Urban History*, Volume 20, Number 1, November 1993, pp. 54–80; Linda Gordon, "Black and White Visions of Welfare: Women's Welfare Activism, 1890–1945," *Journal of American History*, Volume 78, Number 2, September 1991, pp. 559–90; Sandra O'Donnell, "The Care of Dependent African-American Children in Chicago: The Struggle Between Black Self-Help and Professionalism," *Journal of Social History*, Volume 27, Number 4, Summer 1994, pp. 763–76; Arnold Hirsch, "Massive Resistance in the Urban North: Trunbull Park, Chicago, 1953–1966," *Journal of American History*, Volume 82, Number 2, September 1995, pp. 522–50. One need look no

further than the failure of tenant-managed public housing sites for a good illustration of how recent federal attempts to encourage minority persons to build better communities for themselves can come unglued. In the late 1990s the public housing authorities of St Louis and Boston revoked the contracts of two of the best-known and well-established tenant management corporations in the country. Tenant leaders in St Louis became too enmeshed in mayoral politics for their own good, and Boston's tenant leaders apparently had a nasty habit of letting young men sell drugs from apartments on the site. In both cases, however, tenant leaders had grown far too comfortable with their status as national celebrities. They also spent far too little time keeping an eye on what was going on in their developments and bringing the next generation of residents into the management of their developments. *Boston Globe*, December 20, 1998.

39 *Cleveland Plain Dealer*, November 11, 1943.
40 Ibid., November 17, 1943.
41 *Sioux City Journal*, January 17 and February 9, 1960.
42 *Boston Globe*, October 31, 1960.
43 Monti, *A Semblance of Justice*; Ronald P. Formisano, *Boston Against Busing: Race, Class, and Ethnicity in the 1960s and 1970s* (Chapel Hill, NC: University of North Carolina Press, 1991).
44 *Columbia Flier*, June 15, 1970; *Pittsburgh Post-Gazette*, January 17, and February 22, 1973.
45 *Germantown News*, September 27, 1974; January 10, 1975; October 10, 1977; January 18, 1990.
46 *Boston Globe*, November 1, 1998.

12

Some Concluding Observations About the "Good Old Days"

Life was better in the "good old days," especially inside cities but maybe elsewhere, too.

A variety of social philosophers and scientists have found contemporary American cities to be sinkholes of civic indifference or, at times, even of depravity. Whatever cultural or moral vision once animated the residents of cities and was shared with a larger, uncivilized, and distinctly un-urban world no longer seems to work especially well or has been lost altogether in the rush to claim a spot in a new world order dominated by "global cities." We are not a whole people today, it is said, not in terms of how we relate to each other or in the values we embrace. It may even be the case that we never were as "together" as we thought or some politicians and big thinkers told us. In any case, we hold out little hope that the city's different inhabitants will find ways to address what have always been their most immediate and lasting concerns: building the city and creating a meaningful way of life inside the city they constructed.

I have a different view of American cities and the kind of civic life that everyday men, women, and children make for themselves in these places. I find that cities have not lost the capacity to inspire a certain kind of public spirit or civic mindedness among their people. Nor have Americans forgotten how to make viable and vital communities within the borders of the cities where they live.

Meaningful human action and discourse, as I have argued elsewhere, are rooted in a specific place and make one a contributor to history.[1] The practice of citizenship, broadly construed here as the first responsibility of a community of believers, is the most important human enterprise insofar as it requires both collaboration and an explicit attention to serving high purposes. The accomplishment of such high purposes, in this case the creation of a bourgeois civic culture dedicated to prosperity and order, is the means by which a people discovers itself. It also transforms the places where the discovery is made into a living memorial where services never end and a laboratory in which experimentation is a birthright. This happens more in cities than in any other place I know.

The "good city" is not necessarily a fair city or a just city, and it is most certainly not an equal city. It is instead where a people creates a viable civic culture that makes sense to them and works. The civic culture of American cities is revealed to us as an interesting and even a paradoxical mix of conservative and liberal ways of "doing community." It works well, or at least a great deal better than we have been led to believe. The good news is that the rest of us share in the civic and cultural bounty of cities anyway. The bad news is that we do not see the urban way of life made in cities as part of our cultural inheritance, and we do not appreciate the contribution it has made to our lives.

I have offered this way of looking at our urban way of life as a working hypothesis, rather than as a complete picture or polished theory about how the world works inside cities. Yet if I managed to shake up our comfortable way of looking at the world only a little bit, I would be sorely disappointed. I aimed to pick a much bigger fight.

Time will tell whether I succeeded.

I can only hope that any debate over the ideas presented in this book will come close to inspiring the kind of honorable exchange that Professor Evans had with Professor McElroy in Laurens County, South Carolina back in 1891. Their meeting was prompted by the strong reaction which Professor McElroy had to an invitation made by Professor Evans, who was principal of the Laurens Male Academy at the time, to a Mr Haskell in the hope that Mr Haskell would address the school body. Professor McElroy, apparently a well-known fellow in the area, wrote an article in the *Laurensville Herald* "severely criticizing Professor Evans and making statements which that gentleman considered untrue and injurious."

What follows is a report of the exchange between Professors Evans and McElroy, published in the *Carolina Spartan* on May 27, 1891, on the occasion of their meeting afterward.

"You'll have to retract them," quietly said Professor Evans.

"You are not going to attack me?" queried Professor McElroy.

"I mean what I say," spoke Professor Evans. "You'll have to retract those statements."

Professor McElroy said that he was unarmed, whereupon Professor

Evans told him to go and arm himself and he would wait for him where he was standing.

Professor McElroy went away and did not return. Professor Evans searched for him and found him at J. T. Roland's hardware store. "Have you armed yourself?" Professor Evans asked.

"No."

It is said that Professor McElroy then drew a knife. Professor Evans raised a walking cane and sternly commanded Professor McElroy to put the weapon back in his pocket. This was done, and Professor McElroy again said he was unarmed.

Professor Evans told him to get a pistol from Mr Roland and if he would not, he would not buy it for him. Professor McElroy refused to get a weapon and Professor Evans brought the matter to a crisis by ordering a paper, pen, and ink and having it put before Professor McElroy.

"Now write and retract the false statements you have made," said Professor Evans, and Professor McElroy obeyed. The retraction was written to suit Professor Evans, signed properly, and then the two men separated. Professor Evans taking the retraction to the *Herald* office for publication.

Well, maybe they really were the good old days.

NOTE

1   Daniel J. Monti, "Legend, Science, and Citizenship in the Rebuilding of Urban America," *Journal of Urban Affairs*, Volume 15, Number 4, 1993, p. 31.

Further Reading

Anyone who makes an effort to read the endnotes for each chapter will see that I have noted certain books and articles that I found especially helpful in my work. This is especially true of the social science literature on the subject of cities, which is really quite large and too varied to cite here in any detail.

All authors with scholarly pretensions, however, have particular books to which they find themselves returning for good insights and the occasional perfect quote. Inasmuch as the author of this book is full of such pretensions, and perhaps several other things as well, he, too, has favorite authors and pieces to which he returns time and again. Here, in no particular order, is his own partial list of books that any aspiring social scientist and historian should read, if he or she is interested in cities.

There has been an outpouring of literature on the subject of communitarianism, particularly by social scientists and philosophers. Certainly the reader should consult most anything written by Robert Wuthnow or Amitai Etzioni for treatments of this debate. You will find no better summary of basic "liberal" and "conservative" approaches to this subject, however, than in the following two books. Glenn R. Morrow's book *Plato's Cretan City* (Princeton: Princeton University Press, 1993) is a nice treatment of what is arguably the first urban planning text, Plato's *Discourse on The Laws*. I also like Philip Selznick's book *The Moral Commonwealth* (Berkeley: University of California Press, 1992) for its more modern, and decidedly liberal take on these matters.

If you are going to claim to know something about cities, whether in the United States or Europe, you had better read Lewis Mumford's books entitled *The Culture of Cities* (1938) and *The City in History* (1961). Both were published in New York by Harcourt, Brace. Capping off a long and luminous career, Sir Peter Hall's recent book entitled *Cities In Civilization* (New York: Pantheon Books, 1998) is sure to become a modern classic. While Mumford's treatment of culture is more thorough, I like Hall's book more, if only because he actually loves cities. Mumford did not admire modern cities or urban life generally. Hall is not ignorant of their shortcomings, but is genuinely enthused by what cities hold and why we should take them seriously.

Social scientists, particularly those who fancy themselves Marxists, neo-Marxists, political economists, postmodernist whatevers, or most anything other than human ecologists, do not have much use for the work of Amos Hawley and others who write in that tradition. But Hawley's book *Urban Society* (New York: Roland Press, 1971) remains a classic in the field. I never was comfortable with Amos's failure to treat the subject of culture as something other than a by-product of larger structural, economic, and technological forces, but it provides one with a fine overview of the human ecological tradition and how his critics stood on his shoulders.

What I know about American urban history I owe to Roger Lotchin, who put books in my lap and ideas in my head. Read his book entitled *The Martial Metropolis* (New York: Praeger, 1984) for a really nice treatment of the modern urban world ushered in by America's military build-up starting in the late nineteenth century. For a general treatment and introduction to American urban history, the reader would be well-advised to absorb both volumes of Carl Bridenbaugh's work on early American cities. *Cities in the Wilderness* (1938, 1966) and *Cities in Revolt* (1955) are wonderful and rich works. Robert Wade's book *The Urban Frontier* (Chicago: University of Chicago Press, 1964) is a modern classic; and the reader can never go wrong by reading anything by Sam Bass Warner, whose *Streetcar Suburbs* (Cambridge, MA: Harvard University Press/MIT Press, 1962) is equally and rightly venerated. Two of Stephan Thernsrom's books, *Poverty and Progress* (1964) and *The Other Bostonians* (1973), were both published by Harvard University Press and must be read by anyone interested in social mobility and ethnic relations in American cities. They, too, are fine pieces of work.

Three other works dealing with important late-nineteenth and twentieth-century themes in American city building should not be ignored. John Bodnar's book *The Transplanted* (Bloomington: University of Indiana Press, 1985) is a nice survey of immigrant and ethnic relations. Harold McDougall's book *Black Baltimore* (Philadelphia: Temple University Press, 1993) provides some fine insights into the "failure" of black Americans to make themselves into a self-conscious ethnic group. Paul Boyer's book *Urban Masses and Moral Order in America* (Cambridge, MA: Harvard University Press, 1978) is a first-rate piece of social history and a great introduction to the development of moral reform campaigns in the United States.

For a general treatment of how we have come to view cities and urban life the way we do, the reader's first, and maybe last, stop should be Andrew Lees's book *Cities Perceived: Urban Society in European and American Thought, 1820–1940* (New York: Columbia University Press, 1993).

I know there are other works and authors that deserve to be mentioned in this little essay, but I have only two pages available to tell you everything you should read.

Daniel Monti
Associate Professor of Sociology and Urban Studies
Boston University

Index